I can't go on, I'll go on

Samuel Beckett

I can't go on, I'll go on

A Selection from Samuel Beckett's Work
Edited and Introduced by Richard W. Seaver

Grove Press
New York

Library of Congress Cataloging-in-Publication Data

Beckett, Samuel, 1906–
    I can't go on, I'll go on: a selection from Samuel Beckett's work/
Samuel Beckett; edited and introduced by Richard W. Seaver.
        p.   cm.
    Includes bibliographical references (p.   )
    ISBN 0-8021-3287-1
    1. Seaver, Richard.   II. Title.
[PR6003.E282A6   1991]
848'.91409—dc20   91-21178
                                                                CIP

Grove Press
841 Broadway
New York, NY 10003

99 00 01 02   10 9 8 7 6

Nothing is more real than nothing.   —Democritus*

Where you are worth nothing, there you should
want nothing.   —Geulincx*

---

* Beckett noted, on several occasions, that were he a critic commenting on Beckett's work—assuming that unfortunate situation ever arose—he would begin the work with the above two quotes.

The danger is in the neatness of identification.
—*Dante . . . Bruno. Vico . . Joyce* (1929)

The expression that there is nothing to express, nothing with which to express, no power to express, no desire to express, together with the obligation to express.
—*Three Dialogues with George Duthuit* (1946)

ESTRAGON: I can't go on like this.
VLADIMIR: That's what you think.
—*Waiting for Godot* (1948)

only dust and not a sound only what was it it said come and gone was that it something like that come and gone come and gone no one come and gone in no time gone in no time.
—*That Time* (1975)

Contents

Introduction

Samuel Beckett is, in my opinion, one of the two or three most important writers of the twentieth century. Further, he will, I am convinced, ultimately be ranked as one of the giants not only of contemporary but of all literature. If that assessment strikes one as rather weighty and forbidding, let me hasten to add that he is also—despite various efforts to bury him beneath an intolerable burden of analysis and erudition—one of the most accessible writers of the age. And one of the funniest. How many writers have you ever read who make you laugh out loud even as they edify? True, the laughter often dies aborning, and tears can mingle before you know it, but laughter there is, in great Irish abundance. For like Chaplin—a tiny, vulnerable figure in a scarcely fathomable landscape—Beckett's characters, however dimly or acutely aware of the Void and all its terrors, are also clowns.

If my stated prejudice seems excessive, at least it has the merit of durability. In 1952, when I was a Sorbonne student, I wrote a piece in the Paris-based English-language quarterly *Merlin*, entitled "Samuel Beckett: An Introduction," which began:

> Samuel Beckett, an Irish writer long established in France, has recently published two novels which, although they defy all commentary, merit the attention of anyone interested in this century's literature. . . .

The two novels in question were *Molloy* and *Malone meurt*, which had just been published, in French, by Les Editions de Minuit. If one excepts the phrase "although they defy all commentary,"* that opening sentence is one I still stand by.

---

* For the simple reason that, in the succeeding two and a half decades, those novels, as well as Beckett's later works, have probably been more commented on than any other works of the twentieth century, with the possible exception of those of Beckett's compatriot and fellow exile, James Joyce.

Geography

Fortuitous contiguity. Or do we make our own geography? Be that as it may, the early fifties found me in Paris, fresh out of college, in search of I'm not sure what gods or ghosts but convinced they could be discovered only in that magic city. I had found quarters, if that term can be applied to an abandoned warehouse, on the rue du Sabot, a tiny street directly behind St.-Germain-des-Prés. The owner was a Swiss dealer in primitive art. In return for my tending the shop a few hours a week, he gave me free lodging in an empty ground-floor warehouse at the end of the courtyard. I mention the geography because this *dépôt*—which, my Swiss landlord proudly informed me, had once been a banana-drying shed—was destined to become the headquarters of the magazine and book-publishing enterprise known to history as *Merlin* and also because it was a scant fifty yards from the offices of the most daring and perceptive French publisher of the time, Les Editions de Minuit.

There were two routes from my warehouse-home to the bright cafés of St.-Germain-des-Prés, one by the rue du Dragon, the other by the rue Bernard-Palissy, and since I took at least two trips to St.-Germain every day, and always tried to avoid taking the same route twice in a row, it happened, almost inevitably, that I passed Number 7 of the latter street at least once a day. Number 7, a bordel until the puritanical wrath of a famous female Gallic zealot of the period. Marthe Robert, caused these dens of iniquity to close in 1948, now housed Les Editions de Minuit. The grilled peephole was still on the thick wooden door. To the right of the door was a tiny display window set into the wall, which in times past had housed God knows what bawdy come-ons. Now, in the winter of 1951–2, it housed two works, whose blue titles stared out at me each day as I passed: *Molloy* and *Malone meurt*. Closer scrutiny revealed the name of the author: Samuel Beckett. I passed that window several times before I made the connection. I was then very deeply into Joyce, and remembered that it was

Beckett who, twenty-odd years before, had contributed the opening essay to that collection of twelve odes to the Master, *Our
Exagmination Round His Factification For Incamination Of Work
In Progress*. It was Beckett, too, I recalled, who had with French
writer Alfred Péron translated the "Anna Livia Plurabelle" episode of *Finnegans Wake* into French.* What was this Irishman,
whom I had also heard referred to as "Joyce's secretary," doing
writing in French? Or were the Minuit books translations from
novels Beckett had written in English? If so, I had never heard of
them.

Finally, curiosity won out over avarice: one morning, on my
trek to St.-Germain-des-Prés, I went into Number 7 and bought
both books. Later that day I opened *Molloy* and began to read: "Je
suis dans la chambre de ma mère. C'est moi qui y vis maintenant.
Je ne sais pas comment j'y suis arrivé. . . ." Before nightfall I had
finished *Molloy*. I will not say I understood all I had read, but if
there is such a thing as a shock of discovery, I experienced it that
day. The simplicity, the beauty, yes, and the terror of the words
shook me as little had before or has since. And the man's vision of
the world, his painfully honest portrayal thereof, his anti-
illusionist stance. And the humor; God the humor. . . . I waited a
day or two, then reread *Molloy*, tempted to plunge into *Malone*
but resisting the temptation, as one resists the seductive sweet.
The second reading was more exciting than the first. I went on to
Malone. Full worthy of the first. Two stunning works. Miracles.

The following morning I walked over again to Number 7, and
asked an employee if Minuit had published any more works by
Beckett. "Who?" was the answer. "Samuel Beckett," I said. "The
man who wrote *Molloy* and *Malone Dies*." I motioned to the back

---

* When the translation finally appeared, in the May, 1931, issue of *La nouvelle
revue française*, credit for the translation went to a "committee" composed of
Beckett, Alfred Péron, Ivan Goll, Eugene Jolas, Paul-L. Leon, Adrienne Monnier,
and Philippe Soupault, in collaboration with the author. The truth of the matter
seems to be that Beckett did most of it, that Alfred Péron went over Beckett's draft.
But Joyce, who enjoyed the devotion, submitted their text to the scrutiny of the
"committee," which argued over it endlessly and did, finally, make numerous
changes.

of the display case in which the two masterpieces were still standing. The man shrugged and gestured me upstairs.

In a second-floor office I repeated my question to a lady at a typewriter. "I don't think so," she said, "but let me check." She picked up an antiquated telephone and dialed. The person she called, I later learned, was Jérôme Lindon, owner and editor of Minuit, a man I would soon meet and come to admire beyond measure. "No," the secretary informed me, "although another work is in preparation.* But," she went on, "there *is* another Beckett novel available from another publisher, Bordas, which I believe is still in print. It is called *Murphy*." Murphy, Molloy, Malone. . . . Decidedly, Beckett had a thing about M's. I thanked her, went outside, and bicycled directly over to Bordas, a stone's throw away on the rue de Tournon. Not only was *Murphy* still in print (it had been published in French, in Beckett's own translation, five years before, in 1947), but by the look of the stock in the back of the shop (Bordas was primarily a bookseller who published occasional works himself), the original printing was all but intact. (According to A. Alvarez,† ninety-five copies had been sold by 1951.) I presume, from the delighted reaction of the clerk to my request, that my copy was ninety-six. I took my new treasure home and read it that same night. The comedy was fully as strong as in *Molloy* and *Malone*, the sense of the grotesque, the unfailing gift for dialogue, but the magic fusion of comedy and tragedy, of form and content, had not, I felt, yet wholly occurred. I would await *L'Innommable*.

While waiting, I was informed by a Parisian actress-friend that the French radio was scheduled to record part of an as yet unproduced Beckett play. I went to the taping. Rumor had it that Beckett would be present. In all, there were about a dozen of us in the studio, including the actors; like Godot, however, Beckett did not come. Instead he sent a note of apology which Roger Blin, who was not only to direct but to perform in the original stage production of *Waiting for Godot* the following year, read prior to the

---

* *L'Innommable*, published in 1953.

† *Samuel Beckett* (New York: The Viking Press, 1973), p. 1.

taping itself. I do not know whether that "note" still exists in any form, but I remember the gist of it clearly: after apologizing for his absence, Beckett went on to say that, since he knew little or nothing about the theater anyway, he could not see how his presence would add anything to the occasion. Blin, a remarkable actor, was plagued offstage with a pronounced stutter, and had considerable difficulty reading Beckett's note. Thus it was with a certain trepidation that the hardy handful of Beckett fans and friends gathered in the RTF studios watched as the actual taping began. For Blin was playing Lucky, and though I do not think any of us present had read the as yet unpublished play, we had heard that Lucky's part contained a tongue-twisting monologue that would tax the talent of the most accomplished actor. When Blin, for the first time anywhere in the world, at least publicly, launched into the French original of these lines:

> Given the existence as uttered forth in the public
> works of Puncher and Wattmann of a personal
> God quaquaquaqua with white beard
> quaquaquaqua outside time without extension . . .

there was incredible tension in the room. But on-mike, as on stage, Blin was a professional, and as such he delivered the monologue beautifully, without the least hitch.

Over the next month or so I uncovered two other Beckett pieces, both short stories, or, to be more exact, one complete story and a portion of another. The latter, called "Suite," had appeared in Sartre's *Les temps modernes* half a dozen years before, in 1946. Not unusual for France in those days, the offices of the magazine still had copies of the issue. I read it with the same pleasure with which I had consumed *Molloy*. And yet it seemed strangely incomplete. Still, with Beckett, I reasoned, his ideas of "complete" or "incomplete" doubtless had little to do with those with which I had been inculcated. It was only later that I learned, from Beckett himself, that my first reaction had not been all that wrong: "Suite" represented only the first part of the story "La Fin." In sending it to *Les temps modernes*, Beckett rightly or wrongly assumed that at some later date the magazine would publish the rest of the work.

But when he sent it on, Simone de Beauvoir returned it with a note indicating it was not the magazine's policy to publish sequels. She, or Sartre, had presumably thought that what Beckett had sent them first was the complete work. Or perhaps they thought Beckett was putting them on, testing their ability to tell a part from a whole. I'm not sure Beckett ever forgave the pair for their myopia. In any event, the story was not published in its entirety till the following year, in *Merlin*, in my translation. Well, sort of my translation. About which more later.

The second story, also extraordinary, was called "L'Expulsé," which had been published in *Fontaine*, an influential literary periodical of the time, in 1947.

Until *En attendant Godot* was published later in 1952, these comprised the Beckett *oeuvres complètes* on which I could lay my hands. While I talked, apparently obsessively, about it to all who would listen, I also decided that I would try to write a critical essay imparting my "discovery" to the world. A magazine called *Points*, published sporadically by Sinbad Vail, the son of Peggy Guggenheim, operated out of a top-floor sublet in the same building that housed Les Editions de Minuit. It was for this magazine, for want of a better outlet, that I decided to write the piece. But before I had finished it a new English-language magazine had sprung up, as literary mushrooms had been doing for decades in the fertile Paris soil: *Merlin*, run by an impressively serious, craggy-featured young Scotsman, Alexander Trocchi. I met Trocchi, liked him, and talked to him at length about Beckett. "Stop talking, Mon, and put it on paper!" he said at last. "There's a deadline next Thursday!" Within a week I had put my notes into shape and written the piece which appeared in the second issue of *Merlin*.

I sent a copy of the magazine to Mr. Beckett, whose address on the rue des Favorites I had managed to pilfer. Silence. But then one day Jérôme Lindon, to whom I had also sent the issue, let it slip that Beckett had in hiding a work, in English, written during the war and never published: *Watt*. By then I was an editor of *Merlin*, and wrote Beckett asking if we could see the work with a view toward publishing an extract in the magazine. More silence. But I had rather expected that.

We had all but given up when one rainy afternoon, at the rue du Sabot banana-drying *dépôt*, a knock came at the door and a tall, gaunt figure in a raincoat handed in a manuscript in a black imitation-leather binding, and left almost without a word. That night, half a dozen of us—Trocchi; Jane Lougee, *Merlin's* publisher; English poet Christopher Logue and South African Patrick Bowles; a Canadian writer, Charles Hatcher; and I—sat up half the night and read *Watt* aloud, taking turns till our voices gave out. If it took many more hours than it should have, it was because we kept pausing to wait for the laughter to subside.

We never had a real editorial discussion about which section we would use in the issue: Beckett had seen to that. He had specified which section we could use: Mr. Knott's inventory of the possibilities of his attire ("As for his feet, sometimes he wore on each a sock, or on the one a sock and on the other a stocking, or a boot, or a shoe, or a slipper, or a sock and a boot, or a sock and a shoe, or a sock and a slipper, or nothing at all. . . .") and the possible stations of the furniture in his room ("Thus it was not rare to find, on the Sunday, the tallboy on its feet by the fire, and the dressing-table on its head by the bed, and the night-stool on its face by the door, and the washhand-stand on its back by the window; and, on the Monday, the tallboy on its head by the bed . . . ," etc.). I suspect Beckett was testing the artistic fiber of *Merlin* in so specifying, for, taken out of context, that passage might well have been considered boring or pedantic, waggish or wearily experimental-for-experimental's-sake, by any literary review less dedicated to berating and attacking the Philistines without mercy. When, years later, I confronted Beckett with this accusation, he responded with a broad, bad-boy grin.

At any rate, we published the designated extract of *Watt* in our next issue. I will not say the reaction was world-wide, but we received several angry letters, and cancellation of five percent of our subscribers (i.e., five cancellations). Avant-garde, all right, the letters said, but let's keep some sense of proportion, let's draw the line somewhere! We knew we were on the right track. Thereafter, virtually every issue of *Merlin* contained something by Beckett. And when, in the autumn of 1953, having lost relatively little money on the magazine, we determined we would expand and see if we could lose more money more quickly by publishing books, the first book we chose to publish was, of course, *Watt*.

In July, 1953, Beckett wrote to his old friend and former literary agent, George Reavey, who since the war had been living in New York, to bring him up to date on his literary activities. After detailing those works which by then were out in French, he went on:

> . . . Also, (tiens-toi bien) our old misery, *Watt*, with the *Merlin* juveniles here in Paris who are beginning a publishing business.

Earlier that year an agreement—I do not recall whether there was ever an actual formal contract—was reached with Mr. Beckett,* an advance of 50,000 francs ($100) duly paid, and we were ready to go into production. As is always the case with Beckett manuscripts, *Watt* was in impeccable condition. Although we proofread it, we found virtually nothing even to query, much less change. Two months later, Beckett would write again to Reavey noting that "Watt is just out in an awful magenta cover from the Merlin Press." A full-page ad for the book appeared on the back cover of the spring-summer, 1953, issue of *Merlin*, although I suspect the book had not then appeared. The fall issue ran a further ad, detailing the printing:

> *Watt* (a novel) by SAMUEL BECKETT
> Ordinary Edition (*1100 numbered copies*)   850 fr.
> Special Edition (*25 signed copies of a de luxe paper*)   2,500 fr.

As to the awful color of the cover paper, I can only assume there was a special on magenta. The book was typeset and printed at the Imprimerie Richard in Paris, and despite all the author's care in typescript, the "Printer Richard," who was touted to us

---

* For years after we first met, we "*Merlin* juveniles," who were mostly in our early or middle twenties, always called him "Mr. Beckett." It was not merely the age difference that accounted for it: there was a certain formality about the man, an awesome presence that overwhelmed even his own constant self-derogation, that prevented the first-name intimacy. Nor was it peculiar to us: in the reverse situation twenty years earlier, when Beckett-the-younger-man was involved with Joyce, both men apparently referred to each other inevitably as "Mr. Joyce" and "Mr. Beckett."

as especially good because of his knowledge of English, managed to infiltrate so many typos that no matter how carefully we tried, we could never eliminate them all. If Beckett despaired of the garish color of the cover, I can only guess at the depths of his depression as he perused page after page of his printed work, replete with misspellings such as "scatch" for "scratch" (p. 50),* "nenomena" for "phenomena" (p. 79), and several dozen more. Not to mention a dropped word here and there, and a line set half a paragraph beyond where it appeared in manuscript.† His only consolation, perhaps, was the memory that Joyce, too, had suffered the same indignity at the hands of French printers with *Ulysses*, and survived.

Up to this point, despite a brief glimpse in the misty Paris dusk, none of us had ever met Beckett. We had tried to trap him into a meeting through the ploy of needing his presence to sign the tip sheets of the twenty-five-copy limited edition of *Watt* during the summer, but he had eluded that one by having the sheets sent over to him via Les Editions de Minuit. If, from all this, anyone is under the impression that Beckett was being coy, let me reassure that insofar as that term can imply false shyness, nothing could be further from the truth. Beckett was a very private person, shy to a fault, and at least in those days uncomfortable with strangers. And since despite our efforts in his behalf we were still "strangers," Beckett preferred to deal with us from afar.

Our pro-Beckett stance soon contributed to *Merlin*'s growing list of practical problems. For more than a year, we had been waging a battle with the French postal authorities—pleading, wheedling, cajoling—to obtain magazine-rate postal privileges. The cost of mailing the magazine was slowly strangling us, and

---

* Page numbers in parentheses refer to original *Merlin* edition.
† When Grove Press, which became Beckett's American publisher a short while later, printed the American edition of *Watt* in 1959, it decided, as young, struggling publishers often do, to offset the Paris edition rather than reset from "scatch." Though Beckett and Grove combined managed to eliminate most of the original misprints, a few still crept through. But at least the magenta cover was not perpetuated.

further prevented us from even attempting to enlarge our meager subscription list. We had submitted each of the issues of the magazine to the postal authorities as it had appeared, and slowly, agonizingly, inched our way up the bureaucratic ladder, each Gauloises-smoking rung passing the buck and sending us on to some vague superior. Our application was rejected variously on the grounds that the magazine appeared much too infrequently (true), that we could not demonstrate that we were a legitimate business, which required that we have a French *gérant*, or manager (which we did not), that we had failed to fill out certain basic forms (we had indeed failed to), etc. Since we considered the postal matter essential to survival, we one by one corrected these deficiencies until finally, one brisk day in late March, 1953, we were referred to a highly placed functionary, grizzled but not unkindly, whose office in the shadow of the Arc de Triomphe looked as though it had not been cleaned since Napoleon left town. He leafed through the folder on his desk, which like W. C. Fields he had, with almost no warm up, magically located in the top third of a meter-high pile of similar files, and listened impassively as Trocchi and I repeated our impassioned plea in the name of Art, of France as the beacon of Freedom, not to mention Fraternity and Equality. He heard us out, then said: "Messieurs, I am not without sympathy with your arguments. But I regret to inform you that the department has turned down your request. You see, mailing privileges do not apply to organs of propaganda."

Trocchi and I looked at each other, stunned. We pressed for clarification, muttering that while we were propagandists for the Furtherance of Literature, that is all we could legitimately be accused of. The man held up one of the issues of *Merlin* containing a full-page ad for *Watt*. Then another announcing the forthcoming publication, in English, of *Molloy*. "Messieurs, *who* is Samuel Beckett?" he asked evenly. A writer, we chorused. A very fine writer. We have published several of his works in our magazine. "Indeed," he went on. "Several. More, I might add, than of any other writer, far more. . . . This Mr. Beckett . . . does he not finance your magazine?" Most assuredly not. "Hmmmm." Silence. "Because it is the studied opinion of our examiners that your magazine exists primarily as an organ of propaganda dedicated to furthering the name and fortunes of Mr. Beckett. I'm afraid the case is closed."

While we were shocked at the time by the allegation, and depressed at the bureaucrats' short-sighted assessment, looking back I realize they were not all that far from the mark: without doubt *Merlin*'s major contribution to posterity lay in its attempt to further the fame and fortune of Samuel Beckett. Fortune? Well, fame anyway.

Biography-cum-Bibliography

Who was this man, this ghost-in-the-night we had still never met?

At that time Beckett, who had been living in France for a decade and a half, was in his mid-forties. Born at Foxrock, near Dublin, on April 13—a Friday to be sure—1906, Samuel was the second son of William and Mary Beckett. A quantity surveyor, whose job was to act as a middleman between architect and contractor in estimating the costs for a projected building, William was successful in his profession, a loving father who enjoyed nothing more than a weekend of hiking with his two young sons, a sports-oriented man who especially enjoyed golf.* Mary Roe Beckett, who before her marriage had been a nurse in a Dublin hospital, was a strong-willed woman. To critic Lawrence Harvey Beckett described her as "a pillar of strength and security." And, of his childhood: "You might say I had a happy childhood. . . . My parents did everything they could to make a child happy." But he was quick to add: ". . . although I had little talent for happiness."

---

* Beckett's French publisher, Jérôme Lindon, once told how he had invited Beckett to the country with him for the weekend. Almost apologetically, Lindon excused himself at one point, saying he was going out to play a round of golf. Beckett asked to join him and, although apparently he had not played in many years, stroked the ball with surprising skill. When pressed, he admitted that he had a certain acquaintance with the sport, aeons and aeons ago, as he put it. Lindon maintains that his "acquaintance" was sufficient to record the lowest score of the day.

It is clear that those looking for a facile link between the lonely despair in Beckett's work and his formative years will have to look elsewhere.

As so often happens with siblings, Samuel and his brother Frank were studies in contrast. Frank was an excellent athlete but only a good student. Samuel, a notch or two below in athletics, was a superb student. When they went to Portora Royal School, a preparatory school in Northern Ireland, Samuel was a member of the cricket team, of which his elder brother was captain. But young Beckett was also a member of the Portora swimming team, and excelled as well not only in rugby but in boxing. When, later, he went on to Trinity College, Dublin, his interest in sports continued unabated, and although he deprecated his performance, he was a bona-fide member of the Trinity cricket team.* Beckett also credited Portora with inculcating in him a profound interest in French and France, an interest he was to pursue at Trinity, under the tutelage of Dr. A. A. Luce, one of the period's leading authorities on Berkeley, and Professor Thomas Rudmose-Brown, an eclectic and influential teacher whose assistant lecturer Beckett later became. Alec Reid, in an interview with Beckett, also reported that during those Trinity years "going to the cinema" ranked high among his extracurricular pursuits. Not surprisingly, the comic geniuses of the silent era were among his favorites: Buster Keaton (who three and a half decades later would star in Beckett's only cinematic venture, which Grove Press produced in 1964, *Film*); Chaplin; Laurel and Hardy; and The Marx Brothers. Some of the business in *Waiting for Godot*, and notably the hat maneuvers, owes more than a nodding debt to the shenanigans of the above buffoons.

By tradition, l'Ecole Normale Supérieure in Paris has on its staff each year two *lecteurs d'anglais*, one appointed from Oxford, the other from Trinity College, Dublin. By tradition, too, the

---

* "When I was at Trinity," Beckett once told English drama critic Harold Hobson, "there were only fifteen people in the place who knew how the game was played. . . . It was therefore easier to get on the team than keep off it." (*The London Sunday Times*, June 18, 1961.)

appointees are chosen from among the most brilliant recent graduates. In 1928, Trinity scholar Samuel Beckett was awarded the much-coveted post, and at the ripe old age of twenty-two set off for Paris. He held the post for two years. ("Post" is perhaps too formal a term, for the job entailed no teaching as such but, rather, making oneself generally available to students of English who had problems or questions they wanted to discuss with the *lecteur*. Thus Beckett had plenty of time to explore the nonacademic aspects of Paris.)

His predecessor at l'Ecole Normale was a man named Thomas MacGreevy, a pleasant, gregarious young man who was already a friend of James Joyce. Through MacGreevy, Beckett met not only Joyce but George Reavey, a poet who would later publish Beckett's book of poems, *Echo's Bones*, as well as act as his literary agent in a vain effort to get other works published. Through these initial contacts Beckett soon met other literary figures of the time, among them Eugene Jolas, the publisher of *transition*; Paul Valéry; Adrienne Monnier; Léon-Paul Fargue, and Nancy Cunard.

Much has been written about the relationship between Joyce and Beckett, and about the influence of the former on the latter. I remember clearly, shortly after discovering Beckett, hearing a French friend to whom I was extolling the virtues of *Molloy* respond: "Ah, oui, oui. Beckett, c'est l'ancien secrétaire de Joyce." ("Oh, yes, Beckett. He's the one who used to be Joyce's secretary.") It's a tag I have since heard dozens of times, though Ellmann and others have tended to clarify the misunderstanding. Beckett was never Joyce's secretary, or otherwise in his employ. That he, as a young Irishman in Paris, with literary aspirations, was drawn to his elder compatriot and the growing circle of admiring figures around him is only natural. That he performed numerous services for Joyce, including reading aloud to the near-blind poet and carrying out "free, gratis, and for nothing" a number of other helpful, and often scholarly, tasks, there can be no doubt. In an interview with *New York Times* writer Israel Shenker in the mid-fifties, Beckett himself gave this assessment, which also dispelled the story that he had actually handled some of the Master's correspondence:

I was never Joyce's secretary, but like all his friends I helped him. He was greatly handicapped because of his eyes. I did odd jobs for him, marking passages for him or reading to him, but I never wrote any of his letters.

As for the "influence" itself, Beckett has given what is no doubt the best and fairest assessment of what he owes to Joyce, and how their goals are diametrically different:

> Joyce was a superb manipulator of material—perhaps the greatest. He was making words do the absolute maximum of work. There isn't a syllable that is superfluous. The kind of work I do is one in which I'm not the master of my own material. The more Joyce knew the more he could. He's tending toward omniscience and omnipotence as an artist. I'm working with impotence, ignorance. . . . My little exploration is the whole zone of being that has always been set aside by artists as something unusable— as something by definition incompatible with art.*

To me, Beckett said simply: "Joyce taught me what it meant to be a real artist." By which he meant the dedication, the single-mindedness necessary to realize, against all odds, one's artistic potential. It is noteworthy too, and quite typical, that Beckett described his extraordinary undertaking as "my little exploration." Even late in his life, when his fame was world-wide, he had trouble taking himself, or his work, seriously—or, more properly, judging it fairly. Anyone who spent more than a little time with Beckett knows this to be true. It was a self-doubt, and a self-questioning, so deeply anchored in his soul that all the world's fame or recognition never uprooted it.

In the mid-fifties, when I was working with Beckett over a translation—from French to English—of his short story "La Fin," I noted his inreasing despair not only at our seeming inability to transpose the story from one language to another but at what seemed to Beckett to be the painful inadequacy of the original. Beckett had once told me how hard it was for him to translate his own work, and how much time it took him. In my youthful

---

* Israel Shenker, *The New York Times*, May 6, 1956.

exuberance—and ignorance—I suggested that, if it would give him more time to devote to creative work, I would attempt to translate something, essentially to save him time. *Molloy* seemed the most likely candidate, for hard on our publication of *Watt* we next wanted to bring out *Molloy*. I began work on a draft but had not progressed far when the financial pressures on *Merlin* became such that I landed a job that paid me enough not only to live on but to finance a couple of issues of the magazine. The hitch was that it took me out of Paris for six months, so I passed the task on to Patrick Bowles. Later, however, when I was back in Paris, Beckett suggested I try my hand at "The End." For weeks I labored over the text, which when I had read it in the French had struck me as beautifully simple. But the more I worked the more I realized how deceptive that initial impression had been. When I had finally completed the translation I informed Beckett, who suggested that we meet to go over it. We met at Le Dôme at Montparnasse, ensconced ourselves at an isolated table near the back, and began to work. Or rather: Beckett began to read. After a few minutes of perusing first my translation, then the original, his wire-framed glasses pushed up into the thick shock of hair above—the better to see, no doubt—he shook his head. My heart sank. Clearly, the translation was inadequate. "You can't translate that," he said, fingering the original with utter disdain. "It makes no sense." Again he squinted at the two texts. Several more minutes of ruminations and cross-checking produced a more optimistic report. "That's good," he murmured. "Those first three sentences read very nicely indeed." The opening passage to which he referred went, in my translation:

> They dressed me and gave me money. I knew what the money was to be used for, it was for my travelling expenses. When it was gone, they said, I would have to get some more, if I wanted to go on travelling.

"What do you think of the word 'clothed'," Beckett said, "instead of 'dressed'? 'They *clothed* me and gave me money.' Do you like the ring of it better?"

Yes, clearly: "clothed" was the better word.

"In the next sentence," he said, "you're literally right. In French I spelled it out, said 'travelling expenses' all right. But maybe we can make it a bit tighter here, just say something like, 'it was to get me going' or 'it was to get me started.' Do you like either of them at all? . . ."

On we went, phrase by phrase, Beckett praising my translation as prelude to shaping it to what he really wanted, reworking here a word, there a whole sentence, chipping away, tightening, shortening, always finding the better word if one existed, exchanging the ordinary for the poetic, until the work sang. Never, I am sure, to his satisfaction, but certainly to my ear. Under Beckett's tireless wand that opening passage soon became:

> They clothed me and gave me money. I knew what the
> money was for, it was to get me started. When it was gone
> I would have to get more, if I wanted to go on.

During those long but edifying sessions, there were low moments and high, but for Beckett, faced with going back over a text he had left behind some years before, from which he had progressed to other levels and other considerations, it was too often painful. Finally, in response to one particularly long moment of despair, I blurted, "But Mr. Beckett. You're crazy! Don't you realize who you are? Why . . . you're a thousand times more important than . . . than Albert Camus, for example!" Searching for superlatives, I had grasped at this French writer who, at least at the time, was world famous. Camus had not yet won the Nobel Prize, but he was clearly headed for it, and readers and critics alike clamored for each new work, a response in total contrast to the virtual silence that greeted, and had always greeted, each new Beckett publication.

At that youthfully enthusiastic but obviously outlandish declaration, Beckett gazed compassionately across the table, his gaunt, hawklike features mirroring a response midway between disbelief and pity. "You don't know what you're saying, Dick," he shook his head sadly. "No one's interested in this . . . this rubbish," and he gestured contemptuously toward the untidy pile of manuscript pages on the table beside him. "Camus!" He laughed. "Why, Camus is known even on the moon!"

I took that bit of hyperbole as a statement not necessarily of admiration but of simple fact. "Wait," I remember admonishing, "just wait." For if there was one conviction I had held unfailingly since my first encounter with Beckett's work, it was that, sooner or later, the world would catch up and give proper recognition to Samuel Beckett. As he shook his head slightly, doubtless thinking me but a step or two from Saint-Anne's, the local loony bin, I remember thinking: "It's true. He *doesn't* believe. He really is convinced he'll go on writing, completely unrecognized, till the end of his days."

And yet it was not as though Beckett's assessment was based solely on his own predilection for pessimism. After all, the man had been writing since he was twenty-two or -three, and here he was, pushing fifty, with no more than a handful of faithful friends and fanatics caring about his work. What, in fact, had he accomplished after more than twenty years of effort?

Following his 1929 contribution to *Our Exagmination . . .* , that laudatory harbinger of *Finnegans Wake*, and his co-translation into French of the "Anna Livia Plurabelle" section of that same work the following year, Beckett published, also in 1930, a long, original poem, *Whoroscope*, a ninety-eight-line work whose appended explanatory notes exceeded even those with which T. S. Eliot had, eight years before, adorned *The Waste Land*. A year later he published a monograph on Proust which, while brief and often youthfully iconoclastic, contains pages of brilliance and originality which, to me, revealed more about Proust, or at least certain facets of Proust, than did far longer and weightier tomes read years later. The 1932 harvest is relatively meager: a segment of the novel *Dream of Fair to Middling Women*—still unpublished—printed in *transition* No. 21, in March of that year; and, in December, a story, "Dante and the Lobster," printed in Edward Titus's *This Quarter*. In addition, some splendid translations of poems by André Breton, Paul Eluard, and René Crevel, also in *This Quarter*.

Before the end of 1932, Beckett had apparently finished *Dream of Fair to Middling Women*, and was looking for a publisher. But in vain. He resumed his efforts on that score in a letter to George Reavey in Paris—Beckett was back living in Dublin by then—dated October 8, 1932:

> The novel doesn't go. Shatton and Windup thought it was wonderful, but they couldn't, they simply could not. The Hogarth Private Lunatic Asylum rejected it the way Punch would. Cape was écoeuré in pipe and cardigan and his aberdeen terrier agreed with him. Grayson has lost it or cleaned himself with it. Kick his balls off. They are all over 66 Curzon St. W.1.
>
> I'll be here till I die, creeping along genteel roads on a stranger's bike.

One notes, with astonishment, that last, prophetic sentence, for though Beckett was soon to leave his native Ireland forever, he, like Joyce before him, in a very basic sense never left it; rather he took it with him. How many Beckett characters spend their novelistic lives "creeping along genteel roads," wandering over those "fields and hedges" outside Dublin that Beckett knew so well and that he had wandered so many times alone, and as a young man with his father? The prophecy is complete, in fact, even down to the recurrent "bike" with which so many Beckett heroes cope—riding is generally beyond their dimming strength—in work after work.

In such a letter, too, one sees, more clearly than in a good deal of the early fiction, that side of Beckett which, when it finds its ease, will produce those startling, totally original works of the forties and fifties: the mordant, earthy humor which, in the works of his youth, is often overwhelmed by considerations of Art and technical experimentation.

In 1933, following the sudden death of his father in early summer, Beckett moved to London, there to pursue, with the help of a very modest inheritance, his literary career. Chatto and Windus—the "Shatton and Windup" who had a year before

turned down *Dream of Fair to Middling Women*—partly re-
deemed themselves by contracting to publish Beckett's collection
of short stories, *More Pricks Than Kicks*. While publication did
not garner him instant recognition, there were several reviews,
and notably a very favorable notice in *The Bookman*, on the basis
of which the magazine commissioned him to write several reviews
for them, including critical assessments of Dante, Sean O'Casey,
and Ezra Pound. *The Bookman* also published, in their August,
1934, issue, a Beckett short story entitled "A Case in a Thousand."

Beckett lived in London until the end of 1935, and despite the
appearance of occasional poems and pieces, progress seemed
slow. It was, as Beckett remarked to John Fletcher, a bad time "in
every way, psychologically, financially. . . ." The sole light in the
darkness was the publication, in the autumn of 1935, of a volume
of poems, thanks again to the enterprise of his friend George
Reavey. At first Beckett contemplated calling the collection simply *Poems* (as, later, there would be a theatrical work called,
simply, *Play*), but later he decided the title was too pretentious! In
a letter to Reavey dated May 23, 1935, written from London,
Beckett notes: "Not *Poems*, after all, but *Echo's Bones and Other
Precipitates*. C'est plus modeste." Thirteen poems in all, of
greatly varying length, published in an edition of 200, in a plain
"putty-colored" wrapper.*

The next two years were *Wanderjahre* for Beckett, with the
points of rest between journeys London, Dublin, Hamburg, Berlin, Dresden. . . . He worked sometimes during that period on a
play about Samuel Johnson—his first known foray into the
theater—but could never get it right, or to his satisfaction, and he
jettisoned the manuscript. The other work was *Murphy*, the precise date of whose composition remains somewhat of a mystery:
some critics claim it was written between 1933 and 1935, others
say it was done in 1934; still others assert it was conceived in

---

* The announcement for the volume had been printed on a bright yellow stock,
and Beckett was worried the book might appear in a cover of the same color. He
wrote to Reavey and asked, if it were not too late, to "be an angel and change it to
putty." Putty-beige it was.

London but actually written between the end of 1935 and late 1936, in Dublin. In any case, the author was hoping that, through its publication, his stagnating literary career might be revived. Reavey began circulating the manuscript, on both sides of the Atlantic, and rejections flowed back with alarming regularity. Virtually every British publisher rejected it. In the United States, Simon & Schuster, which had written evincing interest in Beckett's work, had first crack, and were presumably baffled. An editor at Houghton Mifflin went so far as to suggest that, if the novel were radically cut and surgically mended in about a dozen places, there might be hope for it. Viking, perhaps through Joyce, who genuinely liked the work, considered it, and politely declined. (Beckett, sensitive to the possibility that Viking might be swayed by Joyce's recommendation, asked Reavey to make sure that Joyce "not move in." However badly he wanted the book published in America, he wanted it published on its own merits.) When in midsummer of 1937 Doubleday-Doran turned *Murphy* down, Beckett reacted in verse, in a letter to Reavey dated August 6:

> Oh Doubleday Doran
> Less Oxy than moron
> You've a mind like a whore on
> The Way to Bundoran.

Finally, however, through the help and recommendation of Herbert Read, the firm of Routledge & Son, Ltd., reversed the trend and decided to take on the novel. The author received an advance of £25 which, if it seems trifling by today's standards, was not all that small in the 1930s, for literary novels and works which the publishers judged—rightly or wrongly—as not "immediately remunerative."

The book finally appeared in 1938, and although one can say that Beckett was far more fortunate in the timing of its publication than were his compatriots James Joyce and Flann O'Brien, both of whom published novels the following year—Joyce's *Finnegans Wake* appeared in May, 1939, and Flann O'Brien's *At Swim Two Birds* on September 3, just as Germany was invading Poland—it was hardly to be expected that an abstruse albeit comic novel dealing with a number of basic philosophical problems would make much of an impact on the world. History was moving in inexorably, and a whole new problem was posed almost overnight: survival.

When war finally did break out, Beckett was back in Dublin visiting his mother. But rather than wait to see how events would turn, he hurried back to Paris—after years of nomadlike hotel living he had, in 1938, found a small apartment in the somewhat remote 15th arrondissement—apparently preferring, as he declared later to Israel Shenker, "Paris in war to Ireland in peace." If the remark seems glib, the fact is that Beckett, I would strongly suspect, had, after years of wandering, finally found a home.

In the early months of the war, Beckett spent much time with Joyce, who considered the holocaust a world-wide vendetta against him, or rather against the just-published *Finnegans Wake*. After the Joyces moved south in December, Beckett remained behind, with very limited funds and little possibility of earning any. He had, with the help of Alfred Péron, already begun to translate *Murphy* into French, and as he reported to Reavey in December, 1939:

> I . . . scarcely go out. I have been working hard at *Murphy* and only four chapters to translate. Another month should see it finished . . . and then I think it as a French roman at last.

Six months later, as the Germans routed the French and Belgian armies and moved steadily on Paris, Beckett joined the exodus south, stopping to see the Joyces at St.-Gerand-le-Puy. It was to be the last time he would ever see the author of *Ulysses*. Beckett made it to the southern coast of France, mostly by foot, from where, after a month or so, he made his way back to occupied Paris, doubtless for the same reasons that had prompted his return to Paris from Dublin the year before. Shortly thereafter, Beckett joined the Resistance. Although he evaded most questions about his wartime activities in the Underground, and tended to dismiss them as "boyscout stuff," he was in fact an active member of a group whose code name was GLORIA S.M.H., of whose eighty

agents only twenty—including Beckett—survived. During the
first year or two of the war, he also finished translating *Murphy*
into French, though the possibility of publication was obviously
almost nil.

Beckett's friend Alfred Péron, with whom he had collaborated
in translating the "Anna Livia Plurabelle" episode into French,
was also a member of the GLORIA group. On the morning of
August 16, 1942, Péron was arrested by the Gestapo and, as
Lawrence Harvey reports, Péron's wife sent Beckett a telegram
which, had it been detected by the proper authorities, in itself
could have done the author in: "Alfred arrested by the Gestapo.
Please take necessary steps to correct the error." Beckett, rightly,
took the telegram, which arrived at 11 A.M., as a warning. By mid-
afternoon he was on the move. For the balance of the month and
throughout September he moved from place to place in Paris
until, by mid-October, he and his friend Suzanne Dumesnil, who
would later become his wife, had procured false papers and
crossed over into the unoccupied zone. They settled in the town of
Roussillon in the Vaucluse—Sade country—and for the next three
years eked out a living by performing whatever odd jobs could
bring in a little food or money.

It was during this bleak time that Beckett also wrote *Watt*,
from 1942 to 1944. Richard Coe calls it "one of the most difficult
and at the same time brilliant novels that Beckett has written."
Beckett himself says that it was "only a game, a means of staying
sane, a way to keep my hand in." The apparent contradiction is
only superficial. For the author it doubtless was therapeutic, an
exercise to keep the mind trim and alert, as exercise would
an athlete deprived of his normal environment. There is, in
the endless permutations and mathematical explorations, a
gamelike quality. But there is also notable progress artistically
from *Murphy* to *Watt*. The language, less mannered though still
shot through with echoes of the academic—Beckett was too
much the scholar, albeit a defrocked one, to give it up entirely—
is closer to that which in the coming decades would become so
clearly and uniquely his own stark poetry, with the infallible
rhythms and feeling for language. Here too the construction is

much more complex and musical than in any of the earlier work. *Watt is* divided into four parts, but not in the order one might expect:

> As Watt told the beginning of his story, not first, but second, so not fourth, but third, now he told its end. Two, one, four, three, that was the order in which Watt told his story. Heroic quatrains are not otherwise elaborated.

It is a circular construction, with the protagonist departing on some unknown voyage or quest as the novel opens and, as it ends, buying a ticket for "the end of the line." Nothing is changed, all is changed. But in between, Watt's mind, which one critic has labeled the true hero of the novel, has undergone all manner of change, during his service on the ground floor of Mr. Knott's house, then on the floor above, and, finally, at the end of the line, where in an asylum the broken mind attempts to reconstruct the details of the voyage to a fellow inmate, Sam, who records the unclear events as best he can. Lacunae and uncertainties abound, as well they might, for

> it is so difficult, with a long story like the story that Watt told, even when one is most careful to note down all at the time, in one's little notebook, not to leave out some of the things that were told, and not to foist in other things that were never told, never told at all.

What is more, both Sam and Watt are inmates in a mental asylum, presumably for cause, at least by outside standards, which increases the chance of inaccuracy, either in the telling or the recording, by a factor each will have to judge for himself. Add to that the fact that Sam and Watt get together only on days when the weather is right for both, and as Sam likes the sun and Watt the wind, few and far between are the times they meet. Thus the narrative Sam assembles takes him several years.

The opening pages of *Watt*, some of the most humorous that Beckett wrote—and so visual they clearly presaged the theater yet to come—rival the best and most effective sections of *Murphy*. But soon, in among the general hilarity and mad antics, intimations of darkness and pain appear, with ever-increasing force. If till now in Beckett's work the mask of comedy has prevailed, with the pedant's pointer in hand, that of tragedy impinges from here on, by slow degrees. With *Watt*, there is a discernible change, both in tone and content, doubtless due, in whole or in part, to the painful events to which Beckett was witness.

If the setting of *Watt* is still recognizably real and Irish—trains and trams; benches and canals; ditches filled with long wild grass, foxgloves, and hyssop; porters with milk cans and stationmasters with keys—elements of mystery, imponderables, intrude into the everyday, rational world wherein, with bags in hand, Watt sets out on his journey. What begins as a straightforward, third-person account in the style of *Murphy* soon moves to other levels, other concerns. If what Murphy sought, and ultimately found, was the peace of nonbeing, from this point on Beckett's characters—in stories, novels, and plays—are all errant pilgrims, in search of a meaning which, like the ultimate center of the circle, constantly eludes them. Watt is the first in that unforgettable gallery of willful wanderers who, by their very impotence and lack of success, touch and move us as few figures in modern literature ever have.

At the end of *Watt*, it might be noted, Beckett has offered Addenda of "unincorporated" material which offer further insights and possibilities ("change all the names") and which could have prolonged the novel, if not indefinitely, at least well beyond its present length. Beckett's footnote—a sure sign of the unrepentant scholar—to the Addenda reads: "The following precious and illuminating material should be carefully studied. Only fatigue and disgust prevent its incorporation." The attitude is typical. Yet how else is one to deal with the cul-de-sac into which the word and world have driven us? Watt, notes Michael Robinson, is "the suffering Cartesian condemned to define the universe in rational terms. However, Watt's only aid in the task of rendering phenomena acceptable to the mind is language: *Watt* is the opening of Beckett's struggle to subdue language into revealing both the instantaneous and the verifiably true."

* * *

When the war ended Beckett was approaching forty. As soon as he was able, he went back to Ireland to visit his mother, stopping on his way to leave his only copy of *Watt* with Reavey, who was still acting as his agent. *Watt* began to make the rounds of the English publishers, much as *Murphy* had almost a decade before, and with similar results. If *Murphy* had been hardly the kind of reading the public wanted as war clouds gathered, so *Watt* seemed hardly the kind of novel publishers were interested in as the clouds lifted. After about three years of trying, Reavey gave up and, at Beckett's request, returned the manuscript to him in Paris. Given all the ground it had covered in its various submissions, and the fact that it was an only copy, the miracle is that the typescript survived until it was finally published in 1953, by us "Merlin juveniles."

Beckett returned to France in 1945 as soon as he could. After a short interlude working in a field hospital in Saint-Lô, he went back to his apartment in the 15th arrondissement, to his papers and his books. There, for the next five years, in a remarkable burst of sustained creativity which kept him virtually isolated from friends and acquaintances, Beckett wrote a dozen major works, including the masterpieces *Waiting for Godot* and the Trilogy. Taking them chronologically—and recognizing that dating Beckett has always been somewhat difficult because the author himself was not always sure of precise dates of composition—the period from 1945 to 1950 produced:

Mercier and Camier, a novel—1945
"The Expelled," "The Calmative," "The End," "First Love," stories—1945
Molloy, a novel—1947
Eleuthéria, a play—1947–48
Malone Dies, a novel—1948
Waiting for Godot, a play—1948–49
The Unnamable, a novel—1949
Three Dialogues with Georges Duthuit, criticism—1949
Texts for Nothing, short prose works—1950

Even more remarkable is the fact that all the above were written not in Beckett's native language, English, but in his adopted tongue, French. Many reasons have been advanced to explain why Beckett switched from English to French, and probably the truth will never be completely known. Perhaps a number of factors contributed: his despair at the continued indifference of the English publishers and public; his seemingly inalterable decision to make Paris his home; his translation of *Murphy* from English to French, which must have revealed to him both the possibilities of the new language and his ability to work within it; or, finally, the fact that with *Watt* Beckett had gone as far in one direction as he could, in English, and French offered new horizons, where style and content could truly become one. But one should listen to Beckett himself on the subject. To Niklaus Gessner, who in 1957 wrote the first thesis on Beckett's work, the author said he wrote in French *"parce qu'en français c'est plus facile d'écrire sans style,"** while to Israel Shenker he said he wrote in French because he "just felt like it. It was a different experience from writing in English. It was more exciting for me—writing in French."

Twenty years before, in *Our Exagmination . . .* , Beckett wrote, in reference to Joyce's *Work in Progress*: "Here form *is* content, content *is* form. . . . His writing is not *about* something; *it is that something itself."*† In his own quest, too, Beckett sought the fusion of form and content. It is a tenuous balance, and in English, I suspect, it was hard for the ex-Trinity scholar not to yield to the manifold temptations of that language. It was somehow easier in French to strip language bare; and, in truth, it is a more precise language, not a negligible factor in the Beckettian equation.

There was another factor, too, one suggested by Maria Jolas, that Beckett by now was quite aware that French critics, and readers too, were more sophisticated than their English counter-

---

* "Because in French it's easier to write without style." Quoted in Michael Robinson, *The Long Sonata of the Dead* (New York: Grove Press, 1969), p. 133.
† The italics are Beckett's.

parts, especially for the kind of thing he was up to. In any case, the change was propitious: the enormous output of those early post-war years was matched by a maturity, an acuity of vision, and a mastery of language unrivaled in contemporary literature.

Three of the works cited above did not, in Beckett's judgment, stand up—the play *Eleuthéria*, still unpublished and unperformed, though a few scholars have had a peek at it; *Mercier and Camier*, which he only reluctantly allowed into print twenty-four years after it was written; and "First Love," a story which he kept in his desk drawer almost as long. The others—nine works in all, including three short stories—appeared over a ten-year span from July, 1946, when *Les temps modernes* published part of "The End" under the title "La Suite," and 1955, when Les Editions de Minuit issued *Stories and Texts for Nothing* in a single volume.

The key year, however, is 1950. Two years before, in the summer of 1948, Suzanne Dumesnil had assumed the task vis-à-vis French publishers that George Reavey had been so heroically yet fruitlessly pursuing among the English and Americans, namely, that of circulating the growing backlog of unpublished Beckett manuscripts. For a while her efforts seemed doomed to the same results as Reavey's, as Beckett reports, with typical irony, to the latter in a letter dated July 8, 1948:

> I am now retyping for rejection by the publishers *Malone Meurt*. The last I hope of the series *Murphy, Watt, Mercier and Camier, Molloy*, not to mention four nouvelles and *Eleuthéria*. A young publisher here is interested. Editions K, I think, and I am preparing him for burial.

Actually, Beckett would have to wait another two years before finding a publisher for *Molloy* and *Malone Dies*. But it was worth the wait. A remarkable young Frenchman named Jérôme Lindon had recently taken over a small publishing house started as a clandestine press during the Occupation, Les Editions de Minuit. A man of taste and discernment, he saw immediately what the advisers and reading committees of the larger houses had failed to detect—six French publishers had already declined *Molloy*—that here was a new, exciting voice. Whether the world was ready to hear it mattered not; all Lindon knew was that *he* was ready for it. Far from "burying" his new publisher-to-be, Beckett was laying the cornerstone of what was to become the most innovative new publishing venture in France during the 1950s. In his contribution to the *Festschrift* published in celebration of Beckett's sixtieth birthday in 1966, Lindon relates how he had wanted originally to contract for *Molloy* alone, doubtless aware of the precarious commerciality of the entire trilogy and wanting to spread the risk, but Beckett insisted he take all three or none at all. Lindon acquiesced. On December 11, 1950, Beckett wrote once again to Reavey announcing the good news:

> I have signed a contract with the Editions de Minuit for all work. They contracted specifically for the three novels already written. The first, *Molloy*, should be out in January. Bordas, on the brink of bankruptcy (not *entirely* my fault), have released me.

It was the beginning of a new era for Samuel Beckett. *Molloy*, the first of the masterpieces, appeared, not in January but on March 15, 1951, in a first printing of 3000 copies. *Malone meurt* followed seven months later, also in a printing of 3000 copies. It was those two "first editions" that had haunted me from their niche in the window on the rue Bernard-Palissy several months later, on my daily treks to St.-Germain-des-Prés.

If 1950 has to be considered a crucial year for Beckett's "career" (he would cringe at the term), 1953 was the *"annus mirabilis,"* or, as he puts it, *"annix terribilis"*: on January 4, 1953, his second play—*Eleuthéria* being his first, if one excepts the Johnson experiment, as Beckett does—*En attendant Godot*, opened at the Théâtre de Babylone on the rue de Rennes, in Roger Blin's direction. Three days later the first review appeared, in *La Libération*, which said, in part: "Paris has just recognized in Samuel Beckett one of today's best playwrights." The critical acclaim may not have been unanimous, but within a short time *Godot* became the most discussed new play of Paris. Two leading French playwrights soon joined the chorus: "An author has appeared," wrote

Armand Salacrou, "who has taken us by the hand to lead us into his universe." And Jean Anouilh: "*Waiting for Godot* is Pascal's *Pensées* as played by the Fratellini clowns."

The original title of *Godot* had been, simply, *En attendant*—"waiting"—which was not only an apt title for the work itself but for so much of Beckett's life up to then. Even the production of this play, which seemed imminent in 1950, entailed a long, painful wait. Beckett finished the play—which he told Colin Duckworth he had written "as a relaxation, to get away from the awful prose I was writing at the time"—in 1949. Later that same year he saw Roger Blin's production of Strindberg's *Ghost Sonata at the* Gaieté-Montparnasse, liked what he saw, and decided that Blin was the man to direct *Godot*. But reluctant producers, recalcitrant theater owners, and Blin's other commitments kept *Godot* off the boards for another four years. Once it did appear, however, Beckett's life would never be quite the same. In its essence it would not change; no person, in my experience, has ever been more faithful to himself, and to his art. But the quarter-century of near-poverty and almost complete lack of recognition was at an end. Foreign productions followed in quick succession, and within a few years *Waiting for Godot* had been performed in dozens of countries around the world, with the sale of the play's text also in the ascendant. Perhaps he was not yet famous on the moon, as I had rashly predicted a year or two before, but he soon would be.

After the extraordinary burst of creative activity ending in 1950, Beckett spent several relatively frustrating years in which he felt it difficult if not impossible to work. Five months after *Godot* opened in Paris he wrote to Reavey that "since 1950 I have succeeded only in writing a dozen very short abortive texts in French, and there is nothing in sight." The "abortive texts" to which he refers were actually a baker's dozen,* the *Texts for Nothing*, some of which appeared in 1953 (numbers 3, 6, 10, and 11) and two others in 1955 (numbers 1 and 12) before being collected in book form later that year, together with the three

---

* Beckett's dozen seems to run to thirteen. *Echo's Bones* also consists of thirteen poems.

stories written ten years before, under the title *Nouvelles et textes pour rien*. Compared to the *Trilogy* these are indeed minor works—Beckett considered them "failures," but if they are it is only in terms of his impossible standards—ranging in length from 700 to 1700 words. They are, really, stunning prose poems, musical both in structure and in sound. (Fletcher says that Beckett got the title from *mesure pour rien*, a rest bar in music, though of course the sense of "minor" or "meaningless" is also implicit.) They are a clear continuation of the *Trilogy*, but here the disembodied voice, in search of its own identity or the knowledge that the Self truly exists, is even more tentative and disconnected, groping, stabbing, memory faint and all but gone. Here one notes the increasing dominance of the negative, the intruding "no's" that jab and constantly cut at the affirmative ("Ah, if no were content to cut yes's throat and never cut its own"), which undoubtedly reflects accurately Beckett's state of mind at the time. To Vladimir's almost hearty "We always find something, eh, Didi? . . ." is juxtaposed the *Texts'* "Suddenly, no, at last, long last, I couldn't any more. I couldn't go on. . . ."

But if during the balance of that "sterile" decade Beckett was finding it increasingly difficult to produce any prose that satisfied him, he found nonetheless an outlet in the theater. Late in 1955 he wrote to his American director, Alan Schneider, that he was holed up at his tiny country place in the "Marne mud . . . struggling with a play." Six months later he made a progress report, on June 21, 1956:

> Have at last written another, one act, longish, hour and a quarter I fancy. Rather difficult and elliptic, mostly depending on the power of the text to claw, more inhuman than *Godot*. My feeling, strong at the moment, is to leave it in French for a year at least. . . .

By mid-October he had begun to work on the play with Roger Blin and Jean Martin, both of whom had collaborated on the production of *Godot*, and he now described it in more detail:

> A very long one act, over an hour and a half I should think. . . . I am panting to see the realization and know if

I am on some kind of road and can stumble on, or in a swamp.

He was on a road all right: the play, of course, was *Fin de partie* (Endgame), which many critics feel is an achievement even superior to *Godot*. That same year, 1956, also produced two mimes, *Acte sans paroles I & II* (Act Without Words I & II), and a radio play, *All That Fall*, Beckett's first full work written directly in English since *Watt*.* Thereafter, he would alternate between French and English, his choice apparently depending on the circumstances of the original impulse or inspiration.

Another major play, *Krapp's Last Tape*, which Michael Robinson has called "the most remarkable monologue in the language," followed in 1958, this again written directly in English, with Beckett's translation of the work into French, under the title *La dernière bande*, coming a year later. The working title of this play had been *The Magee Monologue*, for the author got the idea for it after he had heard one of his favorite actors, Patrick Magee, reading a selection of his fiction on the radio. The double première of the British production of *Krapp* and *Endgame* took place—the latter play, being considered somewhat too short to stand by itself, had been made part of a double bill—at the Royal Court Theatre on October 28, 1958, with Patrick Magee as Krapp.

Actually, *Endgame* had had an earlier London première, also at the Royal Court, the year before, but in French. When Blin and company, who had begun rehearsing the play in October, 1956, found neither producer nor theater willing to back or book it, they finally moved it in desperation to London, where it opened on April 3, 1957. Given the language barrier, it was "rather grim," as Beckett describes it, "like playing to mahogany, or rather teak." French amour-propre was properly picqued, however, and the owner of the Studio des Champs-Elysées in Paris offered to put it on. It moved back across the channel and opened there on April

---

* Earlier Beckett had tried a new prose work in English, but had abandoned it. A surviving fragment, entitled *From an Abandoned Work*, was first read as a dramatic monologue on the BBC Third Programme, on January 13, 1957. It was later included in a collection of shorter Beckett works, but with no attempt to set it in the larger framework that the author had intended.

27, 1957, where the audience's reaction was much less teaklike. In Paris, Beckett wrote, "the hooks went in."*

Despite all this activity, admittedly mostly in the area of drama, Beckett still felt that the "stony ground" of his mind was growing ever less productive, or capable of producing. "I am finding it more and more difficult to write, but keep trying," he wrote to H. O. White at Trinity College early in 1959. "I never felt less literary in my life, which is saying a great deal. . . ." Such sentiments are fully understandable, given the nature of the enterprise. As far back as 1952, after reading only *Molloy* and *Malone Dies*, I remember wondering how Beckett could carry his experiment any further. "Is it possible," I wrote in *Merlin*, "for Mr. Beckett to progress further without succumbing to the complete incoherence of inarticulate sound, or to . . . silence?" Part of the answer, for more than a decade after the *Texts for Nothing*, was silence, at least in the realm of prose. The other part was drama, for in the theater, in its broadest sense—stage, radio, television, even film—language, that demon with which Beckett had been wrestling for thirty years, was not the only factor: mime, action, silence, setting all contribute to the communication, between actor and audience on the one hand, and among the actors themselves on the other. If Man-as-Clown is present in Beckett's prose in various forms, the stage is a logical extension, and performance an ideal way to give those clowns the physical presence they necessarily lack on the printed page, or within the confines of a single head.

Thus, through the 1960s, the Mallarméan effort gave birth to a series of plays, full-length and short, for stage, radio, and television, plus Beckett's only foray into the cinema, *Film*. On the cover of a notebook which contains an early draft of *Krapp's Last Tape* there is a notation, dated August 10, 1960, "Willie-Winnie notes." The play, later entitled *Happy Days*, was finished early the following year, and received its world première at the Cherry Lane

---

* Both quotes from a letter to the American director, Alan Schneider. The American première took place at the Cherry Lane Theater in New York, on January 28, 1958.

Theater on September 17, 1961, directed by Alan Schneider. The "old" plays, constantly being translated into foreign languages, were being performed throughout the world. And meanwhile, a fairly steady stream of new dramatic works was being written and presented:

—*Words and Music*: a radio play, with music by John Beckett, written in 1962, in English, and performed for the first time on the BBC Third Programme on November 13, 1962.

—*Play*: a short, three-character play for the stage, also written in 1962, in English. Its world première took place at the Ulmer Theater in Ulm-Donau, on June 13, 1963, in Elmer Tophoven's German version, entitled *Spiel*.

—*Cascando*: a radio play, written in French in 1963. It had its initial performance on French National Radio on October 13, 1963, with music by Marcel Mihalovici.

—*Film*: in 1963, Grove Press, Beckett's American publisher, encouraged him to write a film script, which it agreed to produce. The result, Beckett's only foray into the medium of film, was shot during the summer of 1964, in New York City. Beckett made his only trip to the United States to be present for the filming. The work was presented at the 1965 New York Film Festival, where it was sandwiched between two "standard" Buster Keaton films, and was roundly booed. It has since become a classic.

—*Come and Go*: a three-character stage playlet or, as Beckett termed it, "dramaticule," written in 1965 and first published in 1967.

—*Eh Joe*: a two-character television play (or, more accurately, a play for one female voice and one male body). Written in 1966, it was first televised in July of that year by the BBC.

—*Breath*: a thirty-second stage piece, written in 1966. He later sent it to Kenneth Tynan, who mis-staged it as part of *Oh! Calcutta!* in 1967.

—*Not I*: a stage play for two characters, written in 1972, *Not I* was given its world première at the Repertory Theater of Lincoln Center on December 7, 1972, with Alan Schneider directing.

—*That Time*: a stage play, written in 1975, directly in English. A haunting work for one character and three voices—all his—*That Time* is published here for the first time anywhere in the world.

Thus we can see that, although admittedly all these plays are relatively brief, there had nonetheless been a regular succession of dramatic works for over two decades. But what of fiction during that same period?

As noted, apart from an abandoned fragment written in 1956, six years after *Texts for Nothing*, Beckett had found it impossible to bring forth further fiction. By 1960, it was presumed by many that he had abandoned fiction. At one time, when asked about it, he replied, specifically in relation to the one fragment that had survived, *From an Abandoned Work*: "There was just no more to be said." He meant that he had had no more to say in that work, but the remark seemed equally to apply to his fiction in general. Then, in 1961 he confounded critics who had already come to the conclusion he would never write fiction again, or at most fragments—those "gasps" culled from the void—by publishing, in French, a major "novel," *Comment c'est*. Four years later, in his own English version— translation is hardly the proper term when Beckett renders his works from one language to another, for each is literally a recreation—the book appeared as *How It Is*.

If, as Jean Anouilh suggested, *Waiting for Godot* is Pascal's *Thoughts* as played by the Fratellini clowns, here the Beckettian clowns have been brought low. In a sense, its three parts are Beckett's sequel to the Trilogy. The protagonist is one Pim, toward whom, in Part I, the narrator is crawling; in Part II he is with Pim; Part III relates the journey away from Pim. Set in the primeval mud, *How It Is* ponders the eternal questions present in all Beckett works, but from the perspective of a nether world; pondering not only "how it is" but "how it was," once, in a "life said to have been mine above in the light before I fell."

After that, only fragments. In 1965 and 1966 four short works were written, all in French:

—*Imagination morte imaginez*
—*Assez*
—*Bing*
—*Le Depeupleur*

translated, respectively, as *Imagination Dead Imagine*, *Enough*, *Ping*, and *The Lost Ones*. It was three years before another short work—only twenty-four paragraphs in all, ranging in length from three to seven sentences each—appeared, also composed in French, *Sans*, which the author rendered in English as *Lessness*, rather than the more final, and more literal, *Without*.

In all probability, Beckett judged these later fictions harshly, and indeed, insofar as some of them were perhaps conceived as larger or more ambitious works, they represent "failures." But they can be so measured only in terms of the absolutes by which Samuel Beckett judged his own work.

Cosmography

Since Niklaus Gessner's 1957 doctoral dissertation on Beckett—the first full-length study of his work—there has been, during the intervening decades, a flood of criticism, probing not only the *real* meaning, but the sources, the influences, the symbols, the style, the method, ad infinitum, and—to Beckett no doubt—ad nauseum. If the present rate of exegesis continues—and there is no sign of its abating—it has been calculated that by the end of the century Beckett's *oeuvre* will have been the subject of more scholarly probes than that of any other writer in the history of the English language with the exception of Shakespeare. And even Will may soon have to move over. A forbidding prospect. And yet, in all fairness, not altogether incomprehensible, for in all Beckett's work there is a richness, an abundance of possibilities, a willful ambiguity which seems to cry for interpretation.

I have no intention of adding to the existing mass of exegetical material by voicing my own opinions about the works you are about to read. All of Beckett can be read without a Virgil at the elbow to guide and interpret. If a reader is familiar with Dante and Descartes, he will doubtless perceive resonances that one unfamiliar with those two authors will not. If one knows, for example, of Dante's Belacqua, that Florentine lute-maker who was so lazy when alive that he failed to repent and make peace with God until the very last moment, and was therefore condemned to spend the equivalent of his earthly lifetime languishing in the shadow of a rock in Antepurgatory, one may appreciate Beckett's Belacqua Shuah—a "sinfully ignorant" man "bogged in indolence, asking nothing better than to stay put"—all the more. But if one does not, the qualities of the latter-day Belacqua will still come through.

We could multiply such examples a hundredfold, for Samuel Beckett was both artist and artisan, a writer whose vision and inspiration, if one can use those weary terms, was matched by his craftsmanship. He was, too, a man of deep erudition, fluent in several languages, and the wealth of cross-linguistic references, the cognates and roots, the wordplays, the allusions—be they Biblical, historical, literary, or even internal (Molloy in the shadow of a rock, under which "I crouched like Belacqua, or Sordello, I forget which")—all weave themselves effortlessly into the immense and marvelous tapestry of the work, from the earliest stories to the latest plays and short fiction. And the more a reader can seize and understand the several levels that often exist, the greater the pleasure. Still, one should be careful not to mistake the means for the end, and I maintain that to read Beckett with no advance preparation, no prior perusal of those who warn of the difficulties ahead or the dangers of missing the deeper meaning, is still the best approach. At the end of the Addenda to *Watt* is written, small but clear:

no symbols where none intended

Let us take the man at his word. In one of his letters to Alan Schneider, Beckett writes:

I feel the only line is to refuse to be involved in exegesis of any kind. And to insist on the extreme simplicity of dramatic situation and issue. If that's not enough for them, and it obviously isn't, it's plenty for us, and we have no elucidations to offer of mysteries that are all of their own making. My work is a matter of fundamental sounds (no joke intended) made as fully as possible, and I accept responsibility for nothing else. If people have headaches among the overtones, let them. And provide their own aspirin. . . .

The point to remember is that, with or without exegesis, Beckett is great fun. The danger is that if we overinterpret we're liable to miss all the fun. For Beckett is one of the very few writers I have ever read who makes me laugh aloud, on almost every page, from work to work. That the laughter sometimes dies in the throat, that tears can well in close conjunction, is but further measure of his greatness.

Beckett's decision to work "with impotence, ignorance, that zone of being that has always been set aside by artists as something unusable—as something incompatible with art" may have seemed a defeat initially, an admission that the "omniscience" and "omnip-otence" which Joyce was striving toward were beyond his ken. And yet in the final analysis that terrain, hitherto ignored and unexplored, is precisely what gives his work its strength and universality. For in his dimming landscape, peopled with clowns and misfits, has-beens and ne'er-do-wells, the malformed and the deformed, those on the threshold of death or already on the other side ("I don't remember when I died"), he has created a stark world far different from our own, hardly recognizable, a nether world, a purgatory, or perhaps Antepurgatory, having nothing whatsoever to do with us.

Our world.

RICHARD SEAVER

Part I
Early Works
(1929–1946)

Fiction

Dante and the Lobster

Nineteen thirty-two was an important year for Samuel Beckett. At the end of the preceding year he had, after teaching four terms at Trinity College, resigned his post, having decided for whatever reasons—the reports are conflicting—that teaching was not for him. In the summer of 1932 he went back to Paris and re-immersed himself in the teeming literary life of the period.

He moved into the Trianon Hotel on the rue de Vaugirard, and for several months wrote both poetry and prose, as well as translating several of the surrealist poets—Breton, Eluard, and Crevel among them. His short story "Sedendo and Quiescendo" appeared in Eugene Jolas's *transition*; another short work of prose was published in *The New Review*; and, most important, "Dante and the Lobster" came out in Edward Titus's *This Quarter*.

Several critics have tended to dismiss all the early Beckett as too "schoolish" and "self-conscious," or quite simply too clearly under the inescapable influence of James Joyce. This story in itself suffices to refute that contention: while it is admittedly a harbinger of greater things to come, it stands by itself as a first-rate work of fiction. A. Alvarez, with whom I do not always agree on the subject of Beckett, is perfectly accurate in terming it "a minor masterpiece." Like so many later Beckett-heroes yet unborn, the protagonist of "Dante and the Lobster," Belacqua Shuah, named after Dante's Belacqua, is more than vaguely reminiscent of Goncharov's Oblomov. He is afflicted with many of the ills, mental and physical, that will attend virtually all of Beckett's subsequent heroes, from Watt to Molloy, from Mercier to Krapp, from Murphy to Malone. In its language "Dante" is simple and straightforward; in its attention to detail, exquisite; in the artist's willful intrusion into the work ("Let us call it

Winter, that dusk may fall now and a moon rise"), an anti-illusionist stance that will pervade all that follows; and in its concluding lines a vision of both the terrain and the method that Beckett has taken as his own.

Two years after "Dante and the Lobster" first appeared, Belacqua's adventures were further perpetuated in volume form with the appearance of *More Pricks Than Kicks* in 1934, a collection of ten stories of which "Dante and the Lobster" was the first.

I⊤ was morning and Belacqua was stuck in the first of the canti in the moon. He was so bogged that he could move neither backward nor forward. Blissful Beatrice was there, Dante also, and she explained the spots on the moon to him. She shewed him in the first place where he was at fault, then she put up her own explanation. She had it from God, therefore he could rely on its being accurate in every particular. All he had to do was to follow her step by step. Part one, the refutation, was plain sailing. She made her point clearly, she said what she had to say without fuss or loss of time. But part two, the demonstration, was so dense that Belacqua could not make head or tail of it. The disproof, the reproof, that was patent. But then came the proof, a rapid shorthand of the real facts, and Belacqua was bogged indeed. Bored also, impatient to get on to Piccarda. Still he pored over the enigma, he would not concede himself conquered, he would understand at least the meanings of the words, the order in which they were spoken and the nature of the satisfaction that they conferred on the misinformed poet, so that when they were ended he was refreshed and could raise his heavy head, intending to return thanks and make formal retraction of his old opinion.

He was still running his brain against this impenetrable passage when he heard midday strike. At once he switched

his mind off its task. He scooped his fingers under the book
and shovelled it back till it lay wholly on his palms. The
Divine Comedy face upward on the lectern of his palms.
Thus disposed he raised it under his nose and there he
slammed it shut. He held it aloft for a time, squinting at
it angrily, pressing the boards inwards with the heels of
his hands. Then he laid it aside.

He leaned back in his chair to feel his mind subside and
the itch of this mean quodlibet die down. Nothing could
be done until his mind got better and was still, which
gradually it did and was. Then he ventured to consider
what he had to do next. There was always something that
one had to do next. Three large obligations presented
themselves. First lunch, then the lobster, then the Italian
lesson. That would do to be going on with. After the
Italian lesson he had no very clear idea. No doubt some
niggling curriculum had been drawn up by someone for
the late afternoon and evening, but he did not know what.
In any case it did not matter. What did matter was: one,
lunch; two, the lobster; three, the Italian lesson. That was
more than enough to be going on with.

Lunch, to come off at all, was a very nice affair. If his
lunch was to be enjoyable, and it could be very enjoyable
indeed, he must be left in absolute tranquillity to prepare
it. But if he were disturbed now, if some brisk tattler were
to come bouncing in now big with a big idea or a petition,
he might just as well not eat at all, for the food would turn
to bitterness on his palate, or, worse again, taste of nothing. He must be left strictly alone, he must have complete
quiet and privacy, to prepare the food for his lunch.

The first thing to do was to lock the door. Now nobody
could come at him. He deployed an old *Herald* and
smoothed it out on the table. The rather handsome face
of McCabe the assassin stared up at him. Then he lit the

gas-ring and unhooked the square flat toaster, asbestos grill, from its nail and set it precisely on the flame. He found he had to lower the flame. Toast must not on any account be done too rapidly. For bread to be toasted as it ought, through and through, it must be done on a mild steady flame. Otherwise you only charred the outside and left the pith as sodden as before. If there was one thing he abominated more than another it was to feel his teeth meet in a bathos of pith and dough. And it was so easy to do the thing properly. So, he thought, having regulated the flow and adjusted the grill, by the time I have the bread cut that will be just right. Now the long barrel-loaf came out of its biscuit-tin and had its end evened off on the face of McCabe. Two inexorable drives with the bread-saw and a pair of neat rounds of raw bread, the main elements of his meal, lay before him, awaiting his pleasure. The stump of the loaf went back into prison, the crumbs, as though there were no such thing as a sparrow in the wide world, were swept in a fever away, and the slices snatched up and carried to the grill. All these preliminaries were very hasty and impersonal.

It was now that real skill began to be required, it was at this point that the average person began to make a hash of the entire proceedings. He laid his cheek against the soft of the bread, it was spongy and warm, alive. But he would very soon take that plush feel off it, by God but he would very quickly take that fat white look off its face. He lowered the gas a suspicion and plaqued one flabby slab plump down on the glowing fabric, but very pat and precise, so that the whole resembled the Japanese flag. Then on top, there not being room for the two to do evenly side by side, and if you did not do them evenly you might just as well save yourself the trouble of doing them at all, the other round was set to warm. When the first candidate

was done, which was only when it was black through and
through, it changed places with its comrade, so that now
it in its turn lay on top, done to a dead end, black and
smoking, waiting till as much could be said of the other.

For the tiller of the field the thing was simple, he had it
from his mother. The spots were Cain with his truss of
thorns, dispossessed, cursed from the earth, fugitive and
vagabond. The moon was that countenance fallen and
branded, seared with the first stigma of God's pity, that an
outcast might not die quickly. It was a mix-up in the mind
of the tiller, but that did not matter. It had been good
enough for his mother, it was good enough for him.

Belacqua on his knees before the flame, poring over the
grill, controlled every phase of the broiling. It took time,
but if a thing was worth doing at all it was worth doing
well, that was a true saying. Long before the end the room
was full of smoke and the reek of burning. He switched off
the gas, when all that human care and skill could do had
been done, and restored the toaster to its nail. This was an
act of dilapidation, for it seared a great weal in the paper.
This was hooliganism pure and simple. What the hell did
he care? Was it his wall? The same hopeless paper had
been there fifty years. It was livid with age. It could not
be disimproved.

Next a thick paste of Savora, salt and Cayenne on each
round, well worked in while the pores were still open with
the heat. No butter, God forbid, just a good foment of
mustard and salt and pepper on each round. Butter was a
blunder, it made the toast soggy. Buttered toast was all
right for Senior Fellows and Salvationists, for such as had
nothing but false teeth in their heads. It was no good at
all to a fairly strong young rose like Belacqua. This meal
that he was at such pains to make ready, he would devour
it with a sense of rapture and victory, it would be like

smiting the sledded Polacks on the ice. He would snap at
it with closed eyes, he would gnash it into a pulp, he
would vanquish it utterly with his fangs. Then the anguish
of pungency, the pang of the spices, as each mouthful died,
scorching his palate, bringing tears.

But he was not yet all set, there was yet much to be
done. He had burnt his offering, he had not fully dressed
it. Yes, he had put the horse behind the tumbrel.

He clapped the toasted rounds together, he brought
them smartly together like cymbals, they clave the one to
the other on the viscid salve of Savora. Then he wrapped
them up for the time being in any old sheet of paper. Then
he made himself ready for the road.

Now the great thing was to avoid being accosted.
To be stopped at this stage and have conversational nuisance committed all over him would be a disaster. His
whole being was straining forward towards the joy in
store. If he were accosted now he might just as well fling
his lunch into the gutter and walk straight back home.
Sometimes his hunger, more of mind, I need scarcely say,
than of body, for this meal amounted to such a frenzy that
he would not have hesitated to strike any man rash
enough to buttonhole and baulk him, he would have
shouldered him out of his path without ceremony. Woe
betide the meddler who crossed him when his mind was
really set on this meal.

He threaded his way rapidly, his head bowed, through
a familiar labyrinth of lanes and suddenly dived into a
little family grocery. In the shop they were not surprised.
Most days, about this hour, he shot in off the street in this
way.

The slab of cheese was prepared. Separated since morning from the piece, it was only waiting for Belacqua to call
and take it. Gorgonzola cheese. He knew a man who came

from Gorgonzola, his name was Angelo. He had been born
in Nice but all his youth had been spent in Gorgonzola.
He knew where to look for it. Every day it was there, in
the same corner, waiting to be called for. They were very
decent obliging people.

He looked sceptically at the cut of cheese. He turned
it over on its back to see was the other side any better.
The other side was worse. They had laid it better side up,
they had practised that little deception. Who shall blame
them? He rubbed it. It was sweating. That was something.
He stooped and smelt it. A faint fragrance of corruption.
What good was that? He didn't want fragrance, he wasn't
a bloody gourmet, he wanted a good stench. What he
wanted was a good green stenching rotten lump of Gorgonzola cheese, alive, and by God he would have it.

He looked fiercely at the grocer.

"What's that?" he demanded.

The grocer writhed.

"Well?" demanded Belacqua, he was without fear when
roused, "is that the best you can do?"

"In the length and breadth of Dublin" said the grocer
"you won't find a rottener bit this minute."

Belacqua was furious. The impudent dogsbody, for two
pins he would assault him.

"It won't do" he cried "do you hear me, it won't do at
all. I won't have it." He ground his teeth.

The grocer, instead of simply washing his hands like
Pilate, flung out his arms in a wild crucified gesture of
supplication. Sullenly Belacqua undid his packet and
slipped the cadaverous tablet of cheese between the hard
cold black boards of the toast. He stumped to the door
where he whirled round however.

"You heard me?" he cried.

"Sir" said the grocer. This was not a question, nor yet

an expression of acquiescence. The tone in which it was let fall made it quite impossible to know what was in the man's mind. It was a most ingenious riposte.

"I tell you" said Belacqua with great heat "this won't do at all. If you can't do better than this" he raised the hand that held the packet "I shall be obliged to go for my cheese elsewhere. Do you mark me?"

"Sir" said the grocer.

He came to the threshold of his store and watched the indignant customer hobble away. Belacqua had a spavined gait, his feet were in ruins, he suffered with them almost continuously. Even in the night they took no rest, or next to none. For then the cramps took over from the corns and hammer-toes, and carried on. So that he would press the fringes of his feet desperately against the end-rail of the bed or, better again, reach down with his hand and drag them up and back towards the instep. Skill and patience could disperse the pain, but there it was, complicating his night's rest.

The grocer, without closing his eyes or taking them off the receding figure, blew his nose in the skirt of his apron. Being a warm-hearted human man he felt sympathy and pity for this queer customer who always looked ill and dejected. But at the same time he was a small tradesman, don't forget that, with a small tradesman's sense of personal dignity and what was what. Thruppence, he cast it up, thruppence worth of cheese per day, one and a tanner per week. No, he would fawn on no man for that, no, not on the best in the land. He had his pride.

Stumbling along by devious ways towards the lowly public where he was expected, in the sense that the entry of his grotesque person would provoke no comment or laughter, Belacqua gradually got the upper hand of his choler. Now that lunch was as good as a *fait accompli*, be-

cause the incontinent bosthoons of his own class, itching
to pass on a big idea or inflict an appointment, were seldom at large in this shabby quarter of the city, he was free
to consider items two and three, the lobster and the lesson,
in closer detail.

At a quarter to three he was due at the school. Say five
to three. The public closed, the fishmonger reopened, at
half-past two. Assuming then that his lousy old bitch of
an aunt had given her order in good time that morning,
with strict injunctions that it should be ready and waiting
so that her blackguard boy should on no account be delayed when he called for it first thing in the afternoon, it
would be time enough if he left the public as it closed, he
could remain on till the last moment. Benissimo. He had
half-a-crown. That was two pints of draught anyway and
perhaps a bottle to wind up with. Their bottled stout was
particularly excellent and well up. And he would still be
left with enough coppers to buy a *Herald* and take a tram
if he felt tired or was pinched for time. Always assuming,
of course, that the lobster was all ready to be handed over.
God damn these tradesmen, he thought, you can never
rely on them. He had not done an exercise but that did not
matter. His Professoressa was so charming and remarkable. Signorina Adriana Ottolenghi! He did not believe it
possible for a woman to be more intelligent or better informed than the little Ottolenghi. So he had set her on a
pedestal in his mind, apart from other women. She had
said last day that they would read *Il Cinque Maggio* together. But she would not mind if he told her, as he proposed to, in Italian, he would frame a shining phrase on
his way from the public, that he would prefer to postpone
the *Cinque Maggio* to another occasion. Manzoni was an
old woman, Napoleon was another. *Napoleone di mezza
calzetta, fa l'amore a Giacominetta.* Why did he think of

Manzoni as an old woman? Why did he do him that in-
justice? Pellico was another. They were all old maids,
suffragettes. He must ask his Signorina where he could
have received that impression, that the 19th century in
Italy was full of old hens trying to cluck like Pindar. Car-
ducci was another. Also about the spots on the moon. If
she could not tell him there and then she would make it
up, only too gladly, against the next time. Everything was
all set now and in order. Bating, of course, the lobster,
which had to remain an incalculable factor. He must just
hope for the best. And expect the worst, he thought gaily,
diving into the public, as usual.

Belacqua drew near to the school, quite happy, for all
had gone swimmingly. The lunch had been a notable success, it would abide as a standard in his mind. Indeed he
could not imagine its ever being superseded. And such a
pale soapy piece of cheese to prove so strong! He must
only conclude that he had been abusing himself all these
years in relating the strength of cheese directly to its
greenness. We live and learn, that was a true saying. Also
his teeth and jaws had been in heaven, splinters of vanquished toast spraying forth at each gnash. It was like
eating glass. His mouth burned and ached with the ex-
ploit. Then the food had been further spiced by the intelligence, transmitted in a low tragic voice across the counter
by Oliver the improver, that the Malahide murderer's petition for mercy, signed by half the land, having been rejected, the man must swing at dawn in Mountjoy and nothing could save him. Ellis the hangman was even now
on his way. Belacqua, tearing at the sandwich and swill-
ing the precious stout, pondered on McCabe in his cell.

The lobster was ready after all, the man handed it over
instanter, and with such a pleasant smile. Really a little bit

of courtesy and goodwill went a long way in this world.
A smile and a cheerful word from a common working-man
and the face of the world was brightened. And it was so
easy, a mere question of muscular control.

"Lepping" he said cheerfully, handing it over.

"Lepping?" said Belacqua. What on earth was that?

"Lepping fresh, sir" said the man, "fresh in this morning."

Now Belacqua, on the analogy of mackerel and other fish
that he had heard described as lepping fresh when they
had been taken but an hour or two previously, supposed
the man to mean that the lobster had very recently been
killed.

Signorina Adriana Ottolenghi was waiting in the little
front room off the hall, which Belacqua was naturally inclined to think of rather as the vestibule. That was her
room, the Italian room. On the same side, but at the back,
was the French room. God knows where the German room
was. Who cared about the German room anyway?

He hung up his coat and hat, laid the long knobby
brown-paper parcel on the hall-table, and went prestly in
to the Ottolenghi.

After about half-an-hour of this and that obiter, she
complimented him on his grasp of the language.

"You make rapid progress" she said in her ruined voice.

There subsisted as much of the Ottolenghi as might be
expected to of the person of a lady of a certain age who
had found being young and beautiful and pure more of
a bore than anything else.

Belacqua, dissembling his great pleasure, laid open the
moon enigma.

"Yes" she said "I know the passage. It is a famous
teaser. Off-hand I cannot tell you, but I will look it up
when I get home."

The sweet creature! She would look it up in her big Dante when she got home. What a woman!

"It occurred to me" she said "apropos of I don't know what, that you might do worse than make up Dante's rare movements of compassion in Hell. That used to be" her past tenses were always sorrowful "a favourite question."

He assumed an expression of profundity.

"In that connexion" he said "I recall one superb pun anyway:

'*qui vive la pietà quando è ben morta . . .*'"

She said nothing.

"Is it not a great phrase?" he gushed.

She said nothing.

"Now" he said like a fool "I wonder how you could translate that?"

Still she said nothing. Then:

"Do you think" she murmured "it is absolutely necessary to translate it?"

Sounds as of conflict were borne in from the hall. Then silence. A knuckle tambourined on the door, it flew open and lo it was Mlle Glain, the French instructress, clutching her cat, her eyes out on stalks, in a state of the greatest agitation.

"Oh" she gasped "forgive me. I intrude, but what was in the bag?"

"The bag?" said the Ottolenghi.

Mlle Glain took a French step forward.

"The parcel" she buried her face in the cat "the parcel in the hall."

Belacqua spoke up composedly.

"Mine" he said, "a fish."

He did not know the French for lobster. Fish would do very well. Fish had been good enough for Jesus Christ,

Son of God, Saviour. It was good enough for Mlle Glain.

"Oh" said Mlle Glain, inexpressibly relieved, "I caught him in the nick of time." She administered a tap to the cat. "He would have tore it to flitters."

Belacqua began to feel a little anxious.

"Did he actually get at it?" he said.

"No no" said Mlle Glain "I caught him just in time. But I did not know" with a blue-stocking snigger "what it might be, so I thought I had better come and ask."

Base prying bitch.

The Ottolenghi was faintly amused.

"Puisqu'il n'y a pas de mal . . ." she said with great fatigue and elegance.

"Heureusement" it was clear at once that Mlle Glain was devout "heureusement."

Chastening the cat with little skelps she took herself off. The grey hairs of her maidenhead screamed at Belacqua. A devout, virginal blue-stocking, honing after a penny's worth of scandal.

"Where were we?" said Belacqua.

But Neapolitan patience has its limits.

"Where are we ever?" cried the Ottolenghi "where we were, as we were."

Belacqua drew near to the house of his aunt. Let us call it Winter, that dusk may fall now and a moon rise. At the corner of the street a horse was down and a man sat on its head. I know, thought Belacqua, that that is considered the right thing to do. But why? A lamplighter flew by on his bike, tilting with his pole at the standards, jousting a little yellow light into the evening. A poorly dressed couple stood in the bay of a pretentious gateway, she sagging against the railings, her head lowered, he standing facing her. He stood up close to her, his hands dangled by his sides. Where we were, thought Belacqua, as we were. He walked on gripping his parcel. Why not piety and pity both, even down below? Why not mercy and Godliness together? A little mercy in the stress of sacrifice, a little mercy to rejoice against judgment. He thought of Jonah and the gourd and the pity of a jealous God on Nineveh. And poor McCabe, he would get it in the neck at dawn. What was he doing now, how was he feeling? He would relish one more meal, one more night.

His aunt was in the garden, tending whatever flowers die at that time of year. She embraced him and together they went down into the bowels of the earth, into the kitchen in the basement. She took the parcel and undid it and abruptly the lobster was on the table, on the oil-cloth, discovered.

"They assured me it was fresh" said Belacqua.

Suddenly he saw the creature move, this neuter creature. Definitely it changed its position. His hand flew to his mouth.

"Christ!" he said "it's alive."

His aunt looked at the lobster. It moved again. It made a faint nervous act of life on the oilcloth. They stood above it, looking down on it, exposed cruciform on the oilcloth. It shuddered again. Belacqua felt he would be sick.

"My God" he whined "it's alive, what'll we do?"

The aunt simply had to laugh. She bustled off to the pantry to fetch her smart apron, leaving him goggling down at the lobster, and came back with it on and her sleeves rolled up, all business.

"Well" she said "it is to be hoped so, indeed."

"All this time" muttered Belacqua. Then, suddenly aware of her hideous equipment: "What are you going to do?" he cried.

"Boil the beast" she said, "what else?"

"But it's not dead" protested Belacqua "you can't boil it like that."

She looked at him in astonishment. Had he taken leave of his senses?

"Have sense" she said sharply, "lobsters are always boiled alive. They must be." She caught up the lobster and laid it on its back. It trembled. "They feel nothing" she said.

In the depths of the sea it had crept into the cruel pot. For hours, in the midst of its enemies, it had breathed secretly. It had survived the Frenchwoman's cat and his witless clutch. Now it was going alive into scalding water. It had to. Take into the air my quiet breath.

Belacqua looked at the old parchment of her face, grey in the dim kitchen.

"You make a fuss" she said angrily "and upset me and then lash into it for your dinner."

She lifted the lobster clear of the table. It had about thirty seconds to live.

Well, thought Belacqua, it's a quick death, God help us all.

It is not.

From Murphy

Beckett has tended to belittle his early prose, but in this first published novel,* there already is much of what makes Beckett unique.

Take the opening sentence: "The sun shone, having no alternative, on the nothing new." Or this, a paragraph into the work, putting our hero into perspective: "He sat naked in his rocking-chair of undressed teak, guaranteed not to crack, warp, shrink, corrode, or creak at night."

Beckett is a great humorist, and *Murphy* a wonderfully funny book. But *Murphy* has also been termed satire (it is), a novel of ideas (it is), and thickly veiled autobiography (maybe). As for the last, Murphy, like Beckett in the mid-thirties, was a young Irishman down on his luck, living in London. End of speculation.

E. M. Forster has commented that in the novel Murphy is the only round character; all the others are flat. But they are willfully flat, in that they are all extensions of Murphy's mind, which itself is controlled for us, for comic or other effect, by the omniscient narrator.

Unlike *More Pricks Than Kicks*, where the narrator existed in a tangible relationship with Belacqua, here the narrator is closer to the concept of the classic, omniscient narrator who controls and sometimes comments but rarely if ever intrudes. From his comments, which in themselves are often prodigiously funny, we learn the basics of Murphy's existence. A young man of considerable learning but much given to indolence, alone in the world except for a single uncle—"a well-to-do ne'er-do-well"—living in Holland from

---

* An earlier novel, *Dream of Fair to Middling Women*, was never published. It was written probably in 1932, or at least completed that year, for we know that in the autumn of 1932 it was making the rounds of the British publishers, none of whom thought it fit for their august lists.

whom he fraudulently extracts enough to keep himself barely
afloat, Murphy lives in London, West Brompton to be exact,
ostensibly there to find a home and amass sufficient fortune
to bring his intended, a Miss Counihan, to join him. But during Murphy's absence from Dublin, Neary, his ex-tutor, falls
in love with Miss Counihan, who refuses to requite until
proof of Murphy's demise is presented her. Thus Neary dis-
patches a clod named Cooper to find the wandering ex-scholar
and obtain the necessary proof. Meanwhile, however, our
hero, who wants only release and peace, to be "a mote in the
dark of absolute freedom," further complicates things by
encountering a girl named Celia Kelly, a streetwalker who
loves him and whom, strangely, he loves in turn. But for
Celia to cease her honored profession, Murphy must find
work—the very notion is anathema to him. Still, love finds a
way, and with the aid of astrological charts in which he
wholly believes, Murphy finds employ in a mental asylum,
the Magdalen Mental Mercyseat. There he yields to a happiness he has never known, discovering in the inmates "the
race of people he had long since despaired of finding."

Meanwhile, Cooper, Neary's envoy, finds Celia in London, and concluding (wrongly) that where she is Murphy
must not be far, informs Neary, Miss Counihan, and another
of Neary's students named Wylie (who has, at one point in
the narrative, replaced Neary in Miss Counihan's affections),
all of whom, after settling their numerous differences, move
in on Celia, to wait for Murphy. But they will have long to
wait. For Murphy leaves the asylum early one morning, in
the dark of foredawn, and returns to his garret where he ties
himself up in the chair, intending to have a short rock before
daylight and, yes, return to Celia. But such is not to be, for
the garret is heated by a gas fire, the tap for which is located
in the w.c. downstairs. And someone, inadvertently, turns
the tap instead of pulling the chain: exit Murphy, whose
charred remains are all that greet his pursuers when finally
they meet.

Murphy's last will and testament dictates that his ashes

shall be brought to the Abbey Theatre in Dublin, more precisely to "what the great and good Lord Chesterfield calls the necessary house," and there be flushed down the toilet, "if possible during the performance of a piece." But even in death Murphy's wishes are thwarted: Cooper, entrusted with the packet of ash, stops in a pub for a quick one (or two) and before the evening is over has thrown the packet "at a man who had given him great offence." Whereupon the mind and soul of Murphy are, by closing time, "freely distributed over the floor of the saloon; and before another dayspring greyened the earth had been swept away with the sand, the beer, the butts, the glass, the matches, the spits, the vomit."

A novel of circularity, from birthmark to deathmark, from rocker to rocker, Murphy is very much the forerunner of that remarkable series of works whose protagonists search endlessly for nonexistent answers, each embarked upon a journey that has no end.

Early in the novel, Neary says to Murphy: "Murphy, all life is figure and ground." To which Murphy replies: "But a wandering to find home."

It is a retort worthy of, and applicable to, all Beckett's long line of wandering heroes.

1

The sun shone, having no alternative, on the nothing new. Murphy sat out of it, as though he were free, in a mew in West Brompton. Here for what might have been six months he had eaten, drunk, slept, and put his clothes on and off, in a medium-sized cage of north-western aspect commanding an unbroken view of medium-sized cages of south-eastern aspect. Soon he would have to make other arrangements, for the mew had been condemned. Soon he would have to buckle to and start eating, drinking, sleeping, and putting his clothes on and off, in quite alien surroundings.

He sat naked in his rocking-chair of undressed teak, guaranteed not to crack, warp, shrink, corrode, or creak at night. It was his own, it never left him. The corner in which he sat was curtained off from the sun, the poor old sun in the Virgin again for the billionth time. Seven scarves held him in position. Two fastened his shins to the rockers, one his thighs to the seat, two his breast and belly to the back, one his wrists to the strut behind. Only the most local movements were possible. Sweat poured off him, tightened the thongs. The breath was not perceptible. The eyes, cold and unwavering as a gull's, stared up at an iridescence splashed over the cornice moulding, shrinking and fading. Somewhere a cuckoo-clock, having struck between twenty and thirty, became the echo of a street-cry, which now entering the mew gave *Quid pro quo! Quid pro quo!* directly.

These were sights and sounds that he did not like. They detained him in the world to which they belonged, but not he, as he fondly hoped. He wondered dimly what was breaking up his sunlight, what wares were being cried. Dimly, very dimly.

He sat in his chair in this way because it gave him pleasure! First it gave his body pleasure, it appeased his body. Then it set him free in his mind. For it was not until his body was appeased that he could come alive in his mind, as described in section six. And life in his mind gave him pleasure, such pleasure that pleasure was not the word.

Murphy had lately studied under a man in Cork called Neary. This man, at that time, could stop his heart more or less whenever he liked and keep it stopped, within reasonable limits, for as long as he liked. This rare faculty, acquired after years of application somewhere north of the Nerbudda, he exercised frugally, reserving it for situations irksome beyond endurance, as when he wanted a drink and could not get one, or fell among Gaels and could not escape, or felt the pangs of hopeless sexual inclination.

Murphy's purpose in going to sit at Neary's feet was not to develop the Neary heart, which he thought would quickly prove fatal to a man of his temper, but simply to invest his own with a little of what Neary, at that time a Pythagorean, called the Apmonia. For Murphy had such an irrational heart that no physician could get to the root of it. Inspected, palpated, auscultated, percussed, radiographed and cardiographed, it was all that a heart should be. Buttoned up and left to perform, it was like Petrouchka in his box. One moment in such labour that it seemed on the point of seizing, the next in such ebullition that it seemed on the point of bursting. It was the mediation between these extremes that Neary called the Apmonia. When he got tired of calling it the Apmonia he called it the Isonomy. When he got sick of the sound of Isonomy he called it the Attunement. But he might call it what he

liked, into Murphy's heart it would not enter. Neary
could not blend the opposites in Murphy's heart.

Their farewell was memorable. Neary came out of one
of his dead sleeps and said:

"Murphy, all life is figure and ground."

"But a wandering to find home," said Murphy.

"The face," said Neary, "or system of faces, against the
big blooming buzzing confusion. I think of Miss Dwyer."

Murphy could have thought of a Miss Counihan.
Neary clenched his fists and raised them before his face.

"To gain the affections of Miss Dwyer," he said, "even
for one short hour, would benefit me no end."

The knuckles stood out white under the skin in the
usual way—that was the position. The hands then opened
quite correctly to the utmost limit of their compass—that
was the negation. It now seemed to Murphy that there
were two equally legitimate ways in which the gesture
might be concluded, and the sublation effected. The hands
might be clapped to the head in a smart gesture of despair,
or let fall limply to the seams of the trousers, supposing
that to have been their point of departure. Judge then of
his annoyance when Neary clenched them again more
violently than before and dashed them against his breast-
bone.

"Half an hour," he said, "fifteen minutes."

"And then?" said Murphy. "Back to Teneriffe and the
apes?"

"You may sneer," said Neary, "and you may scoff, but
the fact remains that all is dross, for the moment at any
rate, that is not Miss Dwyer. The one closed figure in the
waste without form, and void! My tetrakyt!"

Of such was Neary's love for Miss Dwyer, who loved
a Flight-Lieutenant Elliman, who loved a Miss Farren of
Ringsakiddy, who loved a Father Fitt of Ballinclashet, who

in all sincerity was bound to acknowledge a certain voca-
tion for a Mrs. West of Passage, who loved Neary.

"Love requited," said Neary, "is a short circuit," a ball
that gave rise to a sparkling rally.

"The love that lifts up its eyes," said Neary, "being in
torments; that craves for the tip of her little finger, dipped
in lacquer, to cool its tongue—is foreign to you, Murphy,
I take it."

"Greek," said Murphy.

"Or put it another way," said Neary; "the single,
brilliant, organised, compact blotch in the tumult of
heterogeneous stimulation."

"Blotch is the word," said Murphy.

"Just so," said Neary. "Now pay attention to this. For
whatever reason you cannot love—But there is a Miss
Counihan, Murphy, is there not?"

There was indeed a Miss Counihan.

"Now say you were invited to define let us say your
commerce with this Miss Counihan, Murphy," said Neary.
"Come now, Murphy."

"Precordial," said Murphy, "rather than cordial. Tired.
Cork County. Depraved."

"Just so," said Neary. "Now then. For whatever reason
you cannot love in my way, and believe me there is no
other, for that same reason, whatever it may be, your heart
is as it is. And again for that same reason—"

"Whatever it may be," said Murphy.

"I can do nothing for you," said Neary.

"God bless my soul," said Murphy.

"Just so," said Neary. "I should say your conarium has
shrunk to nothing."

He worked up the chair to its maximum rock, then
relaxed. Slowly the world died down, the big world where

Quid pro quo was cried as wares and the light never waned the same way twice; in favour of the little, as described in section six, where he could love himself.

A foot from his ear the telephone burst into its rail. He had neglected to take down the receiver. If he did not answer it at once his landlady would come running to do so, or some other lodger. Then he would be discovered, for his door was not locked. There was no means of locking his door. It was a strange room, the door hanging off its hinges, and yet a telephone. But its last occupant had been a harlot, long past her best, which had been scarlet. The telephone that she had found useful in her prime, in her decline she found indispensable. For the only money she made was when a client from the old days rang her up. Then she was indemnified for having been put to unnecessary inconvenience.

Murphy could not free his hand. Every moment he expected to hear the urgent step of his landlady on the stairs, or of some other lodger. The loud calm crake of the telephone mocked him. At last he freed a hand and seized the receiver, which in his agitation he clapped to his head instead of dashing to the ground.

"God blast you," he said.

"He is doing so," she replied. Celia.

He laid the receiver hastily in his lap. The part of him that he hated craved for Celia, the part that he loved shrivelled up at the thought of her. The voice lamented faintly against his flesh. He bore it for a little, then took up the receiver and said:

"Are you never coming back?"

"I have it," she said.

"Don't I know," said Murphy.

"I don't mean that," she said, "I mean what you told me—"

"I know what you mean," said Murphy.

"Meet me at the usual at the usual," she said. "I'll have it with me."

"That is not possible," said Murphy. "I expect a friend."

"You have no friends," said Celia.

"Well," said Murphy, "not exactly a friend, a funny old chap I ran into."

"You can get rid of him before then," said Celia.

"That is not possible," said Murphy.

"Then I'll bring it round," said Celia.

"You mustn't do that," said Murphy.

"Why don't you want to see me?" said Celia.

"How often have I to tell you," said Murphy, "I—"

"Listen to me," said Celia. "I don't believe in your funny old chap. There isn't any such animal."

Murphy said nothing. The self that he tried to love was tired.

"I'll be with you at nine," said Celia, "and I'll have it with me. If you're not there—"

"Yes," said Murphy. "Suppose I have to go out?"

"Good-bye."

He listened for a little to the dead line, he dropped the receiver on the floor, he fastened his hand back to the strut, he worked up the chair. Slowly he felt better, astir in his mind, in the freedom of that light and dark that did not clash, nor alternate, nor fade nor lighten except to their communion, as described in section six. The rock got faster and faster, shorter and shorter, the iridescence was gone, the cry in the mew was gone, soon his body would be quiet. Most things under the moon got slower and slower and then stopped, a rock got faster and faster and then stopped. Soon his body would be quiet, soon he would be free.

2

Age.	Unimportant.
Head.	Small and round.
Eyes.	Green.
Complexion.	White.
Hair.	Yellow.
Features.	Mobile.
Neck.	13¾".
Upper arm.	11".
Forearm.	9½".
Wrist.	6".
Bust.	34".
Waist.	27".
Hips, etc.	35".
Thigh.	21¾".
Knee.	13¾".
Calf.	13".
Ankle.	8¼".
Instep.	Unimportant.
Height.	5′ 4".
Weight.	123 lbs.

She stormed away from the callbox, accompanied delightedly by her hips, etc. The fiery darts encompassing her about of the amorously disposed were quenched as tow. She entered the saloon bar of a Chef and Brewer and had a sandwich of prawn and tomato and a dock glass of white port off the zinc. She then made her way rapidly on foot, followed by four football pool collectors at four

shillings in the pound commission, to the apartment in
Tyburnia of her paternal grandfather, Mr. Willoughby
Kelly. She kept nothing from Mr. Kelly except what she
thought might give him pain, i.e. next to nothing.

She had left Ireland at the age of four.

Mr. Kelly's face was narrow and profoundly seamed
with a lifetime of dingy, stingy repose. Just as all hope
seemed lost it burst into a fine bulb of skull, unobscured
by hair. Yet a little while and his brain-body ratio would
have sunk to that of a small bird. He lay back in bed,
doing nothing, unless an occasional pluck at the counter-
pain be entered to his credit.

"You are all I have in the world," said Celia.

Mr. Kelly nestled.

"You," said Celia, "and possibly Murphy."

Mr. Kelly started up in the bed. His eyes could not
very well protrude, so deeply were they imbedded, but
they could open, and this they did.

"I have not spoken to you of Murphy," said Celia,
"because I thought it might give you pain."

"Pain my rump," said Mr. Kelly.

Mr. Kelly fell back in the bed, which closed his eyes,
as though he were a doll. He desired Celia to sit down,
but she preferred to pace to and fro, clasping and unclasp-
ing her hands, in the usual manner. The friendship of a
pair of hands.

Celia's account, expurgated, accelerated, improved
and reduced, of how she came to have to speak of Murphy, gives the following.

When her parents, Mr. and Mrs. Quentin Kelly died,
which they did clinging warmly to their respective part-
ners in the ill-fated *Morro Castle*, Celia, being an only
child, went on the street. While this was a step to which

Mr. Willoughby Kelly could not whole-heartedly sub-
scribe, yet he did not attempt to dissuade her. She was
a good girl, she would do well.

It was on the street, the previous midsummer's night,
the sun being then in the Crab, that she met Murphy. She
had turned out of Edith Grove into Cremorne Road,
intending to refresh herself with a smell of the Reach
and then return by Lot's Road, when chancing to glance
to her right she saw, motionless in the mouth of Stadium
Street, considering alternately the sky and a sheet of
paper, a man. Murphy.

"But I beseech you," said Mr. Kelly, "be less beastly
circumstantial. The junction for example of Edith Grove,
Cremorne Road and Stadium Street, is indifferent to me.
Get up to your man."

She halted—"Get away!" said Mr. Kelly—set herself
off in the line that his eyes must take on their next declension and waited. When his head moved at last, it was
to fall with such abandon on his breast that he caught and
lost sight of her simultaneously. He did not immediately
hoist it back to the level at which she could be assessed in
comfort, but occupied himself with his sheet. If on his
eyes' way back to the eternities she were still in position,
he would bid them stay and assess her.

"How do you know all this?" said Mr. Kelly.

"What?" said Celia.

"All these demented particulars," said Mr. Kelly.

"He tells me everything," said Celia.

"Lay off them," said Mr. Kelly. "Get up to your man."

When Murphy had found what he sought on the sheet
he despatched his head on its upward journey. Clearly the
effort was considerable. A little short of half way, grateful
for the breather, he arrested the movement and gazed at
Celia. For perhaps two minutes she suffered this gladly,

then with outstretched arms began slowly to rotate—
"Brava!" said Mr. Kelly—like the Roussel dummy in
Regent Street. When she came full circle she found, as
she had fully expected, the eyes of Murphy still open and
upon her. But almost at once they closed, as for a supreme
exertion, the jaws clenched, the chin jutted, the knees
sagged, the hypogastrium came forward, the mouth
opened, the head tilted slowly back. Murphy was returning to the brightness of the firmament.

Celia's course was clear: the water. The temptation
to enter it was strong, but she set it aside. There would be
time for that. She walked to a point about half-way between the Battersea and Albert Bridges and sat down on a
bench between a Chelsea pensioner and an Eldorado
hokey-pokey man, who had dismounted from his cruel
machine and was enjoying a short interlude in paradise.
Artists of every kind, writers, underwriters, devils, ghosts,
columnists, musicians, lyricists, organists, painters and
decorators, sculptors and statuaries, critics and reviewers,
major and minor, drunk and sober, laughing and crying,
in schools and singly, passed up and down. A flotilla of
barges, heaped high with waste paper of many colours,
riding at anchor or aground on the mud, waved to her
from across the water. A funnel vailed to Battersea Bridge.
A tug and barge, coupled abreast, foamed happily out of
the Reach. The Eldorado man slept in a heap, the Chelsea
pensioner tore at his scarlet tunic, exclaiming: "Hell roast
this weather, I shill niver fergit it." The clock of Chelsea
Old Church ground out grudgingly the hour of ten. Celia
rose and walked back the way she had come. But instead
of keeping straight on into Lot's Road, as she had hoped,
she found herself dragged to the right into Cremorne
Road. He was still in the mouth of Stadium Street, in a
modified attitude.

"Hell roast this story," said Mr. Kelly, "I shall never remember it."

Murphy had crossed his legs, pocketed his hands, dropped the sheet and was staring straight before him. Celia now accosted him in form—"Wretched girl!" said Mr. Kelly—whereupon they walked off happily arm-in-arm, leaving the star chart for June lying in the gutter.

"This is where we put on the light," said Mr. Kelly.

Celia put on the light and turned Mr. Kelly's pillows. From that time forward they were indispensable the one to the other.

"Hey!" exclaimed Mr. Kelly, "don't skip about like that, will you? You walked away happily arm-in-arm. What happened then?"

Celia loved Murphy, Murphy loved Celia, it was a striking case of love requited. It dated from that first long lingering look exchanged in the mouth of Stadium Street, not from their walking away arm-in-arm nor any subsequent accident. It was the condition of their walking away, etc., as Murphy had shown her many times in Barbara, Baccardi and Baroko, though never in Bramantip. Every moment that Celia spent away from Murphy seemed an eternity devoid of significance, and Murphy for his part expressed the same thought if possible more strongly in the words: "What is my life now but Celia?"

On the following Sunday, the moon being at conjunction, he proposed to her in the Battersea Park sub-tropical garden, immediately following the ringing of the bell.

Mr. Kelly groaned.

Celia accepted.

"Wretched girl," said Mr. Kelly, "most wretched."

Resting on Campanella's *City of the Sun*, Murphy said they must get married by hook or by crook before the moon came into opposition. Now it was September, the

sun was back in the Virgin, and their relationship had not
yet been regularised.

Mr. Kelly saw no reason why he should contain himself any longer. He started up in the bed, which opened
his eyes, as he knew perfectly well it would, and wanted
to know the who, what, where, by what means, why, in
what way and when. Scratch an old man and find a
Quintilian.

"Who is this Murphy," he cried, "for whom you have
been neglecting your work, as I presume? What is he?
Where does he come from? What is his family? What
does he do? Has he any money? Has he any prospects?
Has he any retrospects? Is he, has he, anything at all?"

Taking the first point first, Celia replied that Murphy
was Murphy. Continuing then in an orderly manner she
revealed that he belonged to no profession or trade; came
from Dublin—"My God!" said Mr. Kelly—knew of one
uncle, a Mr. Quigley, a well-to-do ne'er-do-well, resident
in Holland, with whom he strove to correspond; did nothing that she could discern; sometimes had the price of a
concert; believed that the future held great things in store
for him; and never ripped up old stories. He was Murphy.
He had Celia.

Mr. Kelly mustered all his hormones.

"What does he live on?" he shrieked.

"Small charitable sums," said Celia.

Mr. Kelly fell back. His bolt was shot. The heavens
were free to fall.

Celia now came to that part of her relation which she
rather despaired of explaining to Mr. Kelly, because she
did not properly understand it herself. She knew that if
by any means she could insert the problem into that immense cerebrum, the solution would be returned as
though by clockwork. Pacing to and fro at a slightly

faster rate, racking her brain which was not very large
for the best way to say it, she felt she had come to an
even more crucial junction in her affairs than that composed by Edith Grove, Cremorne Road and Stadium
Street.

"You are all I have in the world," she said.

"I," said Mr. Kelly, "and possibly Murphy."

"There is no one else in the world," said Celia, "least
of all Murphy, that I could speak to of this."

"You mollify me, said Mr. Kelly.

Celia halted, raised her clasped hands though she
knew his eyes were closed and said:

"Will you please pay attention to this, tell me what it
means and what I am to do?"

"Stop!" said Mr. Kelly. His attention could not be
mobilised like that at a moment's notice. His attention was
dispersed. Part was with its caecum, which was wagging
its tail again; part with his extremities, which were dragging anchor; part with his boyhood; and so on. All this
would have to be called in. When he felt enough had been
scraped together he said:

"Go!"

Celia spent every penny she earned and Murphy
earned no pennies. His honourable independence was
based on an understanding with his landlady, in pursuance
of which she sent exquisitely cooked accounts to Mr.
Quigley and handed over the difference, less a reasonable
commission, to Murphy. This superb arrangement enabled
him to consume away at pretty well his own gait, but was
inadequate for a domestic establishment, no matter how
frugal. The position was further complicated by the
shadows of a clearance area having fallen, not so much on
Murphy's abode as on Murphy's landlady. And it was
certain that the least appeal to Mr. Quigley would be

severely punished. "Shall I bite the hand that starves me," said Murphy, "to have it throttle me?"

Surely between them they could contrive to earn a little. Murphy thought so, with a look of such filthy intelligence as left her, self-aghast, needing him still. Murphy's respect for the imponderables of personality was profound, he took the miscarriage of his tribute very nicely. If she felt she could not, why then she could not, and that was all. Liberal to a fault, that was Murphy.

"So far I keep abreast," said Mr. Kelly. "There is just this tribute—"

"I have tried so hard to understand that," said Celia.

"But what makes you think a tribute was intended?" said Mr. Kelly.

"I tell you he keeps nothing from me," said Celia.

"Did it go something like this?" said Mr. Kelly. " 'I pay you the highest tribute that a man can pay a woman, and you throw a scene.' "

"Hark to the wind," said Celia.

"Damn your eyes," said Mr. Kelly, "did he or didn't he?"

"It's not a bad guess," said Celia.

"Guess my rump," said Mr. Kelly. "It is the formula."

"So long as one of us understands," said Celia.

In respecting what he called the Archeus, Murphy did no more than as he would be done by. He was consequently aggrieved when Celia suggested that he might try his hand at something more remunerative than apperceiving himself into a glorious grave and checking the starry concave, and would not take the anguish on his face for an answer. "Did I press you?" he said. "No. Do you press me? Yes. Is that equitable? My sweet."

"Will you conclude now as rapidly as possible," said Mr. Kelly. "I weary of Murphy."

He begged her to believe him when he said he could
not earn. Had he not already sunk a small fortune in
attempts to do so? He begged her to believe that he was
a chronic emeritus. But it was not altogether a question of
economy. There were metaphysical considerations, in
whose gloom it appeared that the night had come in which
no Murphy could work. Was Ixion under any contract to
keep his wheel in nice running order? Had any provision
been made for Tantalus to eat salt? Not that Murphy had
ever heard of.

"But we cannot go on without any money," said Celia.

"Providence will provide," said Murphy.

The imperturbable negligence of Providence to provide goaded them to such transports as West Brompton
had not known since the Earl's Court Exhibition. They
said little. Sometimes Murphy would begin to make a
point, sometimes he may have even finished making one,
it was hard to say. For example, early one morning he
said: "The hireling fleeth because he is an hireling." Was
that a point? And again: "What shall a man give in exchange for Celia?" Was that a point?

"Those were points undoubtedly," said Mr. Kelly.

When there was no money left and no bill to be cooked
for another week, Celia said that either Murphy got work
or she left him and went back to hers. Murphy said work
would be the end of them both.

"Points one and two," said Mr. Kelly.

Celia had not been long back on the street when
Murphy wrote imploring her to return. She telephoned to
say that she would return if he undertook to look for work.
Otherwise it was useless. He rang off while she was still
speaking. Then he wrote again saying he was starved out
and would do as she wished. But as there was no possibility of his finding in himself any reason for work taking

one form rather than another, would she kindly procure
a corpus of incentives based on the only system outside
his own in which he felt the least confidence, that of the
heavenly bodies. In Berwick Market there was a swami
who cast excellent nativities for sixpence. She knew the
year and date of the unhappy event, the time did not
matter. The science that had got over Jacob and Esau
would not insist on the precise moment of vagitus. He
would attend to the matter himself, were it not that he
was down to fourpence.

"And now I ring him up," concluded Celia, "to tell him
I have it, and he tries to choke me off."

"It?" said Mr. Kelly.

"What he told me to get," said Celia.

"Are you afraid to call it by its name?" said Mr. Kelly.

"That is all," said Celia. "Now tell me what to do,
because I have to go."

Drawing himself up for the third time in the bed
Mr. Kelly said:

"Approach, my child."

Celia sat down on the edge of the bed, their four
hands mingled on the counterpane, they gazed at one another in silence.

"You are crying, my child," said Mr. Kelly. Not a thing
escaped him.

"How can a person love you and go on like that?" said
Celia. "Tell me how it is possible."

"He is saying the same about you," said Mr. Kelly.

"To his funny old chap," said Celia.

"I beg your pardon," said Mr. Kelly.

"No matter," said Celia. "Hurry up and tell me what
to do."

"Approach, my child," said Mr. Kelly, slipping away
a little from his surroundings.

"Damn it, I am approached," said Celia. "Do you want me to get in beside you?"

The blue glitter of Mr. Kelly's eyes in the uttermost depths of their orbits became fixed, then veiled by the classical pythonic glaze. He raised his left hand, where Celia's tears had not yet dried, and seated it pronate on the crown of his skull—that was the position. In vain. He raised his right hand and laid the forefinger along his nose. He then returned both hands to their point of departure with Celia's on the counterpane, the glitter came back into his eye and he pronounced:

"Chuck him."

Celia made to rise, Mr. Kelly pinioned her wrists.

"Sever your connexion with this Murphy," he said, "before it is too late."

"Let me go," said Celia.

"Terminate an intercourse that must prove fatal," he said, "while there is yet time."

"Let me go," said Celia.

He let her go and she stood up. They gazed at each other in silence. Mr. Kelly missed nothing, his seams began to work.

"I bow to passion," he said.

Celia went to the door.

"Before you go," said Mr. Kelly, "you might hand me the tail of my kite. Some tassels have come adrift."

Celia went to the cupboard where he kept his kite, took out the tail and loose tassels and brought them over to the bed.

"As you say," said Mr. Kelly, "hark to the wind. I shall fly her out of sight to-morrow."

He fumbled vaguely at the coils of tail. Already he was in position, straining his eyes for the speck that was

he, digging in his heels against the immense pull sky-
ward. Celia kissed him and left him.

"God willing," said Mr. Kelly, "right out of sight."

Now I have no one, thought Celia, except possibly
Murphy.

3

The moon, by a striking coincidence full and at perigee,
was 29,000 miles nearer the earth than it had been for four
years. Exceptional tides were expected. The Port of London Authority was calm.

It was after ten when Celia reached the mew. There
was no light in his window, but that did not trouble her,
who knew how addicted he was to the dark. She had
raised her hand to knock the knock that he knew, when
the door flew open and a man smelling strongly of drink
rattled past her down the steps. There was only one way
out of the mew, and this he took after a brief hesitation.
He spurned the ground behind him in a spring-heeled
manner, as though he longed to run but did not dare. She
entered the house, her mind still tingling with the clash
of his leaden face and scarlet muffler, and switched on
the light in the passage. In vain, the bulb had been taken
away. She started to climb the stairs in the dark. On the
landing she paused to give herself a last chance, Murphy
and herself a last chance.

She had not seen him since the day he stigmatised
work as the end of them both, and now she came creeping
upon him in the dark to execute a fake jossy's sixpenny

writ to success and prosperity. He would be thinking of her as a Fury coming to carry him off, or even as a tipstaff with warrant to distrain. Yet it was not she, but Love, that was the bailiff. She was but the bumbailiff. This discrimination gave her such comfort that she sat down on the stairhead, in the pitch darkness excluding the usual auspices. How different it had been on the riverside, when the barges had waved, the funnel bowed, the tug and barge sung, yes to her. Or had they meant no? The distinction was so nice. What difference, for example, would it make now, whether she went on up the stairs to Murphy or back down them into the mew? The difference between her way of destroying them both according to him, and his way, according to her. The gentle passion.

No sound came from Murphy's room, but that did not trouble her, who knew how addicted he was to remaining still for long periods.

She fumbled in her bag for a coin. If her thumb felt the head she would go up; if her devil's finger, down. Her devil's finger felt the head and she rose to depart. An appalling sound issued from Murphy's room, a flurry of such despairing quality that she dropped the bag, followed after a short silence by a suspiration more lamentable than any groan. For a moment she did not move, the power to do so having deserted her. No sooner did this return than she snatched up the bag and flew to the rescue, as she supposed. Thus the omen of the coin was overruled.

Murphy was as last heard of, with this difference however, that the rocking-chair was now on top. Thus inverted his only direct contact with the floor was that made by his face, which was ground against it. His attitude roughly speaking was that of a very inexperienced diver about to enter the water, except that his arms were not extended to break the concussion, but fastened behind him. Only the most local movements were possible, a licking of the lips, a turning of the other cheek to the dust, and so on. Blood gushed from his nose.

Losing no time in idle speculation Celia undid the scarves and prised the chair off him with all possible speed. Part by part he subsided, as the bonds that held him fell away, until he lay fully prostrate in the crucified position, heaving. A huge pink nævus on the pinnacle of the right buttock held her spellbound. She could not understand how she had never noticed it before.

"Help," said Murphy.

Startled from her reverie she set to and rendered him every form of assistance known to an old Girl Guide. When she could think of nothing more she dragged him out of the corner, shovelled the rocking-chair under him, emptied him on to the bed, laid him out decently, covered him with a sheet and sat down beside him. The next move was his.

"Who are you?" said Murphy.

Celia mentioned her name. Murphy, unable to believe his ears, opened his eyes. The beloved features emerging from chaos were the face against the big blooming buzzing confusion of which Neary had spoken so highly. He closed his eyes and opened his arms. She sank down athwart his breast, their heads were side by side on the pillow but facing opposite ways, his fingers strayed through her yellow hair. It was the short circuit so earnestly desired by Neary, the glare of pursuit and flight extinguished.

In the morning he described in simple language how he came to be in that extraordinary position. Having gone to sleep, though sleep was hardly the word, in the chair, the next thing was he was having a heart attack. When this happened when he was normally in bed, nine times out of ten his struggles to subdue it landed him on the floor. It was therefore not surprising, given his trussed condition, that on this occasion they had caused the entire machine to turn turtle.

"But who tied you up?" said Celia.

She knew nothing of this recreation, in which Murphy had not felt the need to indulge while she was with him. He now gave her a full and frank account of its unique features.

"I was just getting it going when you rang up," he said.

Nor did she know anything of his heart attacks, which had not troubled him while she was with him. He now told her all about them, keeping back nothing that might alarm her.

"So you see," he said, "what a difference your staying with me makes."

Celia turned her face to the window. Clouds were moving rapidly across the sky. Mr. Kelly would be crowing.

"My bag is on the floor your side," she said.

The fall on the landing had cracked the mirror set in the flap. She stifled a cry, averted her head and handed him a large black envelope with the title in letters of various colours.

"What you told me to get," she said.

She felt him take it from her. When after some little time he still had not spoken nor made any movement she turned her head to see was anything amiss. All the colour (yellow) had ebbed from his face, leaving it ashen. A pale strand of blood scoring the jaw illustrated this neap. He kept her waiting a little longer and then said, in a voice unfamiliar to her:

"My life-warrant. Thank you."

It struck her that a merely indolent man would not be so affected by the prospect of employment.

"My little bull of incommunication," he said, "signed not with lead but with a jossy's spittle. Thank you."

Celia, hardening her heart, passed him a hairpin. Murphy's instinct was to treat this dun as he had those showered upon him in the days when he used to enjoy an income, namely, steam it open, marvel at its extravagance and return it undelivered. But then he had not been in bed with the collector.

"Why the black envelope," she said, "and the different-coloured letters?"

"Because Mercury," said Murphy, "god of thieves, planet *par excellence* and mine, has no fixed colour." He spread out the sheet folded in sixteen. "And because this is blackmail."

THEMA COELI

With Delineations
Compiled
By
RAMASWAMI KRISHNASWAMI NARAYANASWAMI SUK
Genethliac
Famous throughout Civilised World and Irish Free State

"Then I defy you, Stars."

THE GOAT

At time of Birth of this Native four degrees of the GOAT was rising, his highest attributes being Soul, Emotion, Clairaudience and Silence. Few Minds are better concocted than this Native's.

The Moon twenty-three degrees of the Serpent promotes great Magical Ability of the Eye, to which the lunatic would easy succumb. Avoid exhaustion by speech. Intense Love nature prominent, rarely suspicioning the Nasty, with inclinations to Purity. When Sensuality rules there is danger of Fits.

Mars having just set in the East denotes a great desire to engage in some pursuit, yet not. There has been persons of this description known to have expressed a wish to be in two places at a time.

When Health is below par, Regret may be entertained. May be termed a law-abiding character having a superior appearance. Should avoid drugs and resort to Harmony. Great care should be used in dealing with publishers, quadrupeds and tropical swamps, as these may terminate unprofitably for the Native.

Mercury sesquiquadrate with the Anarete is most malefic and will greatly conduce to Success terminating in the height of Glory, which may injure Native's prospects.

The Square of Moon and Solar Orb afflicts the Hyleg. Herschel in Aquarius stops the Water and he should guard against this. Neptune and Venus in the Bull denotes dealings with the Females only medium developed or of low organic quality. Companions or matrimonial Mate are recommended to be born under a fiery triplicity, when the Bowman should permit of a small family.

With regards to a Career, the Native should inspire and lead, as go between, promoter, detective, custodian, pioneer or, if possible, explorer, his motto in business being large profits and a quick turnover.

The Native should guard against Bright's disease and Grave's disease, also pains in the neck and feet.

Lucky Gems. Amethyst and Diamond. To ensure Success the Native should sport.

Lucky Colours. Lemon. To avert Calamity the Native should have a dash in apparel, also a squeeze in home decorations.

Lucky Days. Sunday. To attract the maximum Success the Native should begin new ventures.

Lucky Numbers. 4. The Native should commence new enterprises, for in so doing lies just that difference between Success and Calamity.

Lucky Years. 1936 and 1990. Successful and prosperous, though not without calamities and setbacks.

"Is it even so," said Murphy his yellow all revived by these prognostications. "Pandit Suk has never done anything better."

"Can you work now after that?" said Celia.

"Certainly I can," said Murphy. "The very first fourth to fall on a Sunday in 1936 I begin. I put on my gems and off I go, to custode, detect, explore, pioneer, promote or pimp, as occasion may arise."

"And in the meantime?" said Celia.

"In the meantime," said Murphy, "I must just watch out for fits, publishers, quadrupeds, the stone, Bright's—"

She gave a cry of despair intense while it lasted, then finished and done with, like an infant's.

"How you can be such a fool and a brute," she said, and did not bother to finish.

"But you wouldn't have me go against the diagram," said Murphy, "surely to God."

"A fool and a brute," she said.

"Surely that is rather severe," said Murphy.

"You tell me to get you this . . . this . . ."

"Corpus of deterrents," said Murphy.

"So that we can be together, and then you go and twist it into a . . . into a . . ."

"Separation order," said Murphy. Few minds were better concocted than this native's.

Celia opened her mouth to proceed, closed it without having done so. She despatched her hands on the gesture that Neary had made such a botch of at the thought of Miss Dwyer, and resolved it quite legitimately, as it

seemed to Murphy, by dropping them back into their
original position. Now she had nobody, except possibly
Mr. Kelly. She again opened and closed her mouth, then
began the slow business of going.

"You are not going," said Murphy.

"Before I'm kicked out," said Celia.

"But what is the good of going merely in body?" said
Murphy, thereby giving the conversation a twist that
brought it within her powers of comment.

"You are too modest," she said.

"Oh, do not let us fence," said Murphy, "at least let it
never be said that we fenced."

"I go as best I can," she said, "the same as I went last
time."

It really did look as though she were going, at her
present rate of adjustment she would be gone in twenty
minutes or half an hour. Already she was at work on her
face.

"I won't come back," she said. "I won't open your
letters. I'll move my pitch."

Convinced he had hardened his heart and would let
her go, she was taking her time.

"I'll be sorry I met you," she said.

"*Met* me!" said Murphy. "Met is magnificent."

He thought it wiser not to capitulate until it was certain that she would not. In the meantime, what about a
small outburst. It could do no harm, it might do good.
He did not feel really up to it, he knew that long before
the end he would wish he had not begun. But it was perhaps better than lying there silent, watching her lick her
lips, and waiting. He launched out.

"This love with a function gives me a pain in the
neck—"

"Not in the feet?" said Celia.

"What do you love?" said Murphy. "Me as I am. You can want what does not exist, you can't love it." This came well from Murphy. "Then why are you all out to change me? So that you won't have to love me," the voice rising here to a note that did him credit, "so that you won't be condemned to love me, so that you'll be reprieved from loving me." He was anxious to make his meaning clear. "Women are all the same bloody same, you can't love, you can't stay the course, the only feeling you can stand is being felt, you can't love for five minutes without wanting it abolished in brats and house bloody wifery. My God, how I hate the charVenus and her sausage and mash sex."

Celia put a foot to the ground.

"Avoid exhaustion by speech," she said.

"Have I wanted to change you? Have I pestered you to begin things that don't belong to you and stop things that do? How can I care what you DO?"

"I am what I do," said Celia.

"No," said Murphy. "You do what you are, you do a fraction of what you are, you suffer a dreary ooze of your being into doing." He threw his voice into an infant's whinge. " 'I cudden do annyting, Maaaammy.' That kind of doing. Unavoidable and tedious."

Celia was now fully seated on the edge of the bed, her back turned to him, making fast her Bollitoes.

"I have heard bilge," she said, and did not bother to finish.

"Hear a little more," said Murphy, "and then I expire. If I had to work out what you are from what you do, you could skip out of here now and joy be with you. First of all you starve me into terms that are all yours but the jossy, then you won't abide by them. The arrangement is that I enter the jaws of a job according to the celestial prescriptions of Professor Suk, then when I won't go against them you start to walk out on me. Is that the way you respect an agreement? What more can I do?"

He closed his eyes and fell back. It was not his habit to make out cases for himself. An atheist chipping the deity was not more senseless than Murphy defending his courses of inaction, as he did not require to be told. He had been carried away by his passion for Celia and by a most curious feeling that he should not collapse without at least the form of a struggle. This grisly relic from the days of nuts, balls and sparrows astonished himself. To die fighting was the perfect antithesis of his whole practice, faith and intention.

He heard her rise and go to the window, then come and stand at the foot of the bed. So far from opening his eyes he sucked in his cheeks. Was she perhaps subject to feelings of compassion?

"I'll tell you what more you can do," she said. "You can get up out of that bed, make yourself decent and walk the streets for work."

The gentle passion. Murphy lost all his yellow again.

"The streets!" he murmured. "Father forgive her."

He heard her go to the door.

"Not the slightest idea," he murmured, "of what her words mean. No more insight into their implications than a parrot into its profanities."

As he seemed likely to go on mumbling and marvelling to himself for some time, Celia said good-bye and opened the door.

"You don't know what you are saying," said Murphy. "Let me tell you what you are saying. Close the door."

Celia closed the door but kept her hand on the handle.

"Sit on the bed," said Murphy.

"No," said Celia.

"I can't talk against space," said Murphy, "my fourth highest attribute is silence. Sit on the bed."

The tone was that adopted by exhibitionists for their last words on earth. Celia sat on the bed. He opened his eyes, cold and unwavering as a gull's, and with great magical ability sunk their shafts into hers, greener than he had ever seen them and more hopeless than he had ever seen anybody's.

"What have I now?" he said. "I distinguish. You, my body and my mind." He paused for this monstrous proposition to be granted. Celia did not hesitate, she might never have occasion to grant him anything again. "In the mercantile gehenna," he said, "to which your words invite me, one of these will go, or two, or all. If you, then you only; if my body, then you also; if my mind, then all. Now?"

She looked at him helplessly. He seemed serious. But he had seemed serious when he spoke of putting on his gems and lemon, etc. She felt, as she felt so often with Murphy, spattered with words that went dead as soon as they sounded; each word obliterated, before it had time to make sense, by the word that came next; so that in the end she did not know what had been said. It was like difficult music heard for the first time.

"You twist everything," she said. "Work needn't mean any of that."

"Then is the position unchanged?" said Murphy. "Either I do what you want or you walk out. Is that it?"

She made to rise, he pinioned her wrists.

"Let me go," said Celia.

"Is it?" said Murphy.

"Let me go," said Celia.

He let her go. She rose and went to the window. The sky, cool, bright, full of movement, anointed her eyes, reminded her of Ireland.

"Yes or no?" said Murphy. The eternal tautology.

"Yes," said Celia. "Now you hate me."

"No," said Murphy. "Look is there a clean shirt."

From **Watt**

In the general introduction to this volume I related the details of my involvement in the original publication of *Watt* in Paris in 1953. Despite all efforts toward objectivity, I confess that that relationship may well account for the fact that it is one of my favorite works of fiction. Since that initial, collective reading of the work by the members of *Merlin* at our rue du Sabot headquarters, I have reread the work perhaps half a dozen times. And each time I discover formerly unperceived clues, nuances, insights, wordplays, that make it all the richer. The name of the title character himself, Watt, and that of the man into whose service he goes, Knott, lend themselves to all the obvious puns—and quite a few less obvious. Who is Watt? And what is Watt? And Mr. Knott is not, to mention only the negative and not the knot.

But *Watt* is not just fun. That it does contain so much mad, irrepressible humor is proof of how basic comedy is in Beckett's vision of the world, for one must remember the harsh, trying conditions under which it was written. He was living in Roussillon, in the unoccupied zone of France, working as a laborer, helping with the harvests, cutting wood, and even going so far as to glean the near-bare potato fields after the picking, in order to keep body, not to mention soul, alive.

Watt differs from the earlier prose in a number of ways. While the setting of *More Pricks Than Kicks* is clearly Dublin and environs, and *Murphy* evolves recognizably in London, with backward forays to the land of the Gaels, *Watt* lies in less certain country. The opening passage seems still identifiably Dublinesque, if not Dublin itself, and allusions abound throughout to the Ireland of the author's youth, yet Watt's journey, like those of the first-person protagonists of the French novels yet to come, is essentially an inner journey, through the landscape of the author's mind. From this point

on there will be a turning inward, away from the concrete
and visible.

Different, too, is the prose style itself. Here it is more
personal, tighter though no less poetic. Gone are the youthful exuberances of the Belacqua stories, and even of *Murphy;*
gone too the occasional Joycean mannerisms of those earlier
works. The prose here is not quite the lean, gleaming language of the *Trilogy,* but it is the bridge to that masterpiece.

The humor: *Watt,* I have always maintained, is one of
the funniest novels in the English language. But Beckett,
doubtless affected and influenced by the dark events through
which the world was passing, here offers a bleaker vision
than before: pain and despair temper the comedy, and the
asylum *is* at the end of the road.

If, as some critics have maintained, Murphy's mind is the
true hero of that work, Watt's mind may fairly be said to be
the hero of this. Jacqueline Hoefer, in one of the earliest
critical assessments of the novel, suggested that Watt is a
logical positivist in an illogical environment. Watt is a rationalist, and the incremental repetitions and seemingly endless permutations with which the novel abounds—to the
dismay of some, the joy of others—are his method of dealing
with the illogical, of proceeding on the assumption that the
empirical mind can get to the bottom of apparent mysteries
by patient analysis.

In construction, too, *Watt* is far more complex than the
earlier works. While it is Watt's story we are reading, there
is as well a narrator, Sam. And while Watt divided his story
into four parts, which he told in nonchronological order—
II, I, IV, III—it is only Sam's word we have for that. And
though Sam does rearrange them into chronological order,
we also learn, or deduce, that some doubt must be cast on
any order, for both Sam and Watt dwell in the mansions and
gardens of a mental asylum. Thus every statement, every
observation, every deduction and conclusion, and the most
logical permutations may indeed be but the results of the
illogical mind believing itself logical; or of Watt's flawed

memory; or of Sam's imperfect comprehension; or of Watt's mumbling; or of Sam's failing hearing: the possible permutations here are perhaps calculable, but I would assume can safely be said to be legion.

All of which adds to the maddening effect, or the general hilarity, as the case may be. You, sir or madam, are in the dock.

Mr Hackett turned the corner and saw, in the failing light, at some little distance, his seat. It seemed to be occupied. This seat, the property very likely of the municipality, or of the public, was of course not his, but he thought of it as his. This was Mr Hackett's attitude towards things that pleased him. He knew they were not his, but he thought of them as his. He knew were not his, because they pleased him.

Halting, he looked at the seat with greater care. Yes, it was not vacant. Mr Hackett saw things a little more clearly when he was still. His walk was a very agitated walk.

Mr Hackett did not know whether he should go on, or whether he should turn back. Space was open on his right hand, and on his left hand, but he knew that he would never take advantage of this. He knew also that he would not long remain motionless, for the state of his health rendered this unfortunately impossible. The dilemma was thus of extreme simplicity: to go on, or to turn, and return, round the corner, the way he had come. Was he, in other words, to go home at once, or was he to remain out a little longer?

Stretching out his left hand, he fastened it round a rail. This permitted him to strike his stick against the pavement. The feel, in his palm, of the thudding rubber appeased him, slightly.

But he had not reached the corner when he turned again and hastened towards the seat, as fast as his legs could carry him. When he was so near the seat, that he could have touched it with his stick, if he had wished, he

again halted and examined its occupants. He had the
right, he supposed, to stand and wait for the tram. They
too were perhaps waiting for the tram, for a tram, for
many trams stopped here, when requested, from without
or within, to do so.

Mr Hackett decided, after some moments, that if they
were waiting for a tram they had been doing so for some
time. For the lady held the gentleman by the ears, and
the gentleman's hand was on the lady's thigh, and the
lady's tongue was in the gentleman's mouth. Tired of
waiting for the tram, said* Mr Hackett, they strike up an
acquaintance. The lady now removing her tongue from
the gentleman's mouth, he put his into hers. Fair do, said
Mr Hackett. Taking a pace forward, to satisfy himself that
the gentleman's other hand was not going to waste, Mr
Hackett was shocked to find it limply dangling over the
back of the seat, with between its fingers the spent three
quarters of a cigarette.

I see no indecency, said the policeman.

We arrive too late, said Mr Hackett. What a shame.

Do you take me for a fool? said the policeman.

Mr Hackett recoiled a step, forced back his head until
he thought his throatskin would burst, and saw at last,
afar, bent angrily upon him, the red violent face.

Officer, he cried, as God is my witness, he had his
hand upon it.

God is a witness that cannot be sworn.

If I interrupted your beat, said Mr Hackett, a thousand pardons. I did so with the best intentions, for you,
for me, for the community at large.

---

* Much valuable space has been saved, in this work, that would
otherwise have been lost, by avoidance of the plethoric reflexive
pronoun after *say*.

The policeman replied briefly to this.

If you imagine that I have not your number, said Mr Hackett, you are mistaken. I may be infirm, but my sight is excellent. Mr Hackett sat down on the seat, still warm, from the loving. Good evening, and thank you, said Mr Hackett.

It was an old seat, low and worn. Mr Hackett's nape rested against the solitary backboard, beneath it unimpeded his hunch protruded, his feet just touched the ground. At the ends of the long outspread arms the hands held the armrests, the stick hooked round his neck hung between his knees.

So from the shadows he watched the last trams pass, oh not the last, but almost, and in the sky, and in the still canal, the long greens and yellows of the summer evening.

But now a gentleman passing, with a lady on his arm, espied him.

Oh, my dear, he said, there is Hackett.

Hackett, said the lady. What Hackett? Where?

You know Hackett, said the gentleman. You must have often heard me speak of Hackett. Hunchy Hackett. On the seat.

The lady looked attentively at Mr Hackett.

So that is Hackett, she said.

Yes, said the gentleman.

Poor fellow, she said.

Oh, said the gentleman, let us now stop, do you mind, and wish him the time of evening. He advanced, exclaiming, My dear fellow, my dear fellow, how are you?

Mr Hackett raised his eyes, from the dying day.

My wife, cried the gentleman. Meet my wife. My wife. Mr Hackett.

I have heard so much about you, said the lady, and now I meet you, at last. Mr Hackett!

I do not rise, not having the force, said Mr Hackett.

Why I should think not indeed, said the lady. She stooped towards him, quivering with solicitude. I should hope not indeed, she said.

Mr Hackett thought she was going to pat him on the head, or at least stroke his hunch. He called in his arms and they sat down beside him, the lady on the one side, and the gentleman on the other. As a result of this, Mr Hackett found himself between them. His head reached to the armpits. Their hands met above the hunch, on the backboard. They drooped with tenderness towards him.

You remember Grehan? said Mr Hackett.

The poisoner, said the gentleman.

The solicitor, said Mr Hackett.

I knew him slightly, said the gentleman. Six years, was it not.

Seven, said Mr Hackett. Six are rarely given.

He deserved ten, in my opinion, said the gentleman.

Or twelve, said Mr Hackett.

What did he do? said the lady.

Slightly overstepped his prerogatives, said the gentleman.

I received a letter from him this morning, said Mr Hackett.

Oh, said the gentleman, I did not know they might communicate with the outer world.

He is a solicitor, said Mr Hackett. He added, I am scarcely the outer world.

What rubbish, said the gentleman.

What nonsense, said the lady.

The letter contained an enclosure, said Mr Hackett, of which, knowing your love of literature, I would favour you with the primeur, if it were not too dark to see.

The primeur, said the lady.

That is what I said, said Mr Hackett.

I have a petrol-lighter, said the gentleman.

Mr Hackett drew a paper from his pocket and the gentleman lit his petrol-lighter.

Mr Hackett read:

TO NELLY

To Nelly, said the lady.

To Nelly, said Mr. Hackett.

There was a silence.

Shall I continue? said Mr Hackett.

My mother's name was Nelly, said the lady.

The name is not uncommon, said Mr Hackett, I have known several Nellies.

Read on, my dear fellow, said the gentleman.

Mr Hackett read:

TO NELLY

To thee, sweet Nell, when shadows fall
Jug-jug! Jug-jug!
I here in thrall
My wanton thoughts do turn.
Walks she out yet with Byrne?
Moves Hyde his hand amid her skirts
As erst? I ask, and Echo answers: Certes.

Tis well! Tis well! Far, far be it
Pu-we! Pu-we!
From me, my tit,
Such innocent joys to chide.
Burn, burn with Byrne, from Hyde
Hide naught—hide naught save what
Is Greh'n's. IT hide from Hyde, with Byrne
*   burn not.*

It! Peerless gage of maidenhood!
Cuckoo! Cuckoo!
Would that I could

Be certain in my mind
Upon discharge to find
Neath Cupid's flow'r, hey nonny O!
Diana's blushing bud in statu quo.

Then darkly kindle durst my soul
Tuwhit! Tuwhoo!
As on it stole
The murmur to become
Epithalamium,
And Hymen o'er my senses shed
The dewy forejoys of the marriage-bed.

Enough—

Ample, said the lady.

A woman in a shawl passed before them. Her belly could dimly be seen, sticking out, like a balloon.

I was never like that, my dear, said the lady, was I?

Not to my knowledge, my love, said the gentleman.

You remember the night that Larry was born, said the lady.

I do, said the gentleman.

How old is Larry now? said Mr Hackett.

How old is Larry, my dear? said the gentleman.

How old is Larry, said the lady. Larry will be forty years old next March, D.V.

That is the kind of thing Dee always vees, said Mr Hackett.

I wouldn't go as far as that, said the gentleman.

Would you care to hear, Mr Hackett, said the lady, about the night that Larry was born?

Oh do tell him, my dear, said the gentleman.

Well, said the lady, that morning at breakfast Goff turns to me and he says, Tetty, he says, Tetty, my pet, I should very much like to invite Thompson, Cream and Coulquhoun to help us eat the duck, if I felt sure you felt up to it. Why, my dear, says I, I never felt fitter in my life. Those were my words, were they not?

I believe they were, said Goff.

Well, said Tetty, when Thompson comes into the dining-room, followed by Cream and Berry (Coulquhoun I remember had a previous engagement), I was already seated at the table. There was nothing strange in that, seeing I was the only lady present. You did not find that strange, did you, my love?

Certainly not, said Goff, most natural.

The first mouthful of duck had barely passed my lips, said Tetty, when Larry leaped in my wom.

Your what? said Mr Hackett.

My wom, said Tetty.

You know, said Goff, her woom.

How embarrassing for you, said Mr Hackett.

I continued to eat, drink and make light conversation, said Tetty, and Larry to leap, like a salmon.

What an experience for you, said Mr Hackett.

There were moments, I assure you, when I thought he would tumble out on the floor, at my feet.

Merciful heavens, you felt him slipping, said Mr Hackett.

No trace of this dollar appeared on my face, said Tetty. Did it, my dear?

Not a trace, said Goff.

Nor did my sense of humour desert me. What rolypoly, said Mr Berry, I remember, turning to me with a smile, what delicious rolypoly, it melts in the mouth. Not only in the mouth, sir, I replied, without an instant's hesitation, not only in the mouth, my dear sir. Not too osy with the sweet, I thought.

Not too what? said Mr Hackett.

Osy, said Goff. You know, not too osy.

With the coffee and liquors, labour was in full swing, Mr Hackett, I give you my solemn word, under the groaning board.

Swing is the word, said Goff.

You knew she was pregnant, said Mr Hackett.

Why er, said Goff, you see er, I er, we er —

Tetty's hand fell heartily on Mr Hackett's thigh.

He thought I was coy, she cried. Hahahaha. Haha. Ha. Haha, said Mr Hackett.

I was greatly worried I admit, said Goff.

Finally they retired, did you not? said Tetty.

We did indeed, said Goff, we retired to the billiard-room, for a game of slosh.

I went up those stairs, Mr Hackett, said Tetty, on my hands and knees, wringing the carpetrods as though they were made of raffia.

You were in such anguish, said Mr Hackett.

Three minutes later I was a mother.

Unassisted, said Goff.

I did everything with my own hands, said Tetty, everything.

She severed the cord with her teeth, said Goff, not having a scissors to her hand. What do you think of that?

I would have snapped it across my knee, if necessary, said Tetty.

That is a thing I often wondered, said Mr Hackett, what it feels like to have the string cut.

For the mother or the child? said Goff.

For the mother, said Mr Hackett. I was not found under a cabbage, I believe.

For the mother, said Tetty, the feeling is one of relief, of great relief, as when the guests depart. All my subsequent strings were severed by Professor Cooper, but the feeling was always the same, one of riddance.

Then you dressed and came downstairs, said Mr Hackett, leading the infant by the hand.

We heard the cries, said Goff.

Judge of their surprise, said Tetty.

Cream's potting had been extraordinary, extraordinary, I remember, said Goff. I never saw anything like it. We were watching breathless, as he set himself for a long thin jenny, with the black of all balls.

What temerity, said Mr Hackett.

A quite impossible stroke, in my opinion, said Goff. He drew back his queue to strike, when the wail was heard. He permitted himself an expression that I shall not repeat.

Poor little Larry, said Tetty, as though it were his fault.

Tell me no more, said Mr Hackett, it is useless.

These northwestern skies are really extraordinary, said Goff, are they not.

So voluptuous, said Tetty. You think it is all over and then pop! up they flare, with augmented radiance.

Yes, said Mr Hackett, there are protuberances and protuberances.

Poor Mr Hackett, said Tetty, poor *dear* Mr Hackett.

Yes, said Mr Hackett.

Nothing to the Glencullen Hacketts, I suppose, said Tetty.

It was there I fell off the ladder, said Mr Hackett.

What age were you then? said Tetty.

One, said Mr Hackett.

And where was your dear mother? said Tetty.

She was out somewhere, said Mr Hackett.

And your papa? said Tetty.

Papa was out breaking stones on Prince William's Seat, said Mr Hackett.

You were all alone, said Tetty.

There was the goat, I am told, said Mr Hackett.

He turned away from the ladder fallen in the dark yard and his gaze moved down over the fields and the low tottering walls, across the stream and up the further slope to the bluff already in shadow, and the summer sky. He slipped down with the little sunlit fields, he toiled up with the foothills to the dark bluff, and he heard the distant clink of the hammers.

She left you all alone in the yard, said Tetty, with the goat.

It was a beautiful summer's day, said Mr Hackett.

And what possessed her to slip off like that? said Goff.

I never asked her, said Mr Hackett. The pub, or the chapel, or both.

Poor woman, God forgive her, said Tetty.

Faith I wouldn't put it past him, said Mr Hackett.

Night is now falling fast, said Goff, soon it will be quite dark.

Then we shall all go home, said Mr Hackett.

On the far side of the street, opposite to where they sat, a tram stopped. It remained stationary for some little time, and they heard the voice of the conductor, raised in anger. Then it moved on, disclosing, on the pavement, motionless, a solitary figure, lit less and less by the receding lights, until it was scarcely to be distinguished from the dim wall behind it. Tetty was not sure whether it was a man or a woman. Mr Hackett was not sure that it was not a parcel, a carpet for example, or a roll of tarpaulin, wrapped up in dark paper and tied about the middle with a cord. Goff rose, without a word, and rapidly crossed the street. Tetty and Mr Hackett could see his eager gestures, for his coat was light in colour, and hear his voice, raised in remonstrance. But Watt moved no more, as far as they

could see, than if he had been of stone, and if he spoke
he spoke so low that they did not hear him.

Mr Hackett did not know when he had been more
intrigued, nay, he did not know when he had been so intrigued. He did not know either what it was that so intrigued him. What is it that so intrigues me, he said, whom
even the extraordinary, even the supernatural, intrigue so
seldom, and so little. Here there is nothing in the least
unusual, that I can see, and yet I burn with curiosity, and
with wonder. The sensation is not disagreeable, I must
say, and yet I do not think I could bear it for more than
twenty minutes, or half an hour.

The lady also was an interested spectator.

Goff rejoined them, very cross. I recognised him at
once, he said. He made use, with reference to Watt, of an
expression that we shall not record.

For the past seven years, he said, he owes me five
shillings, that is to say, six and ninepence.

He does not move, said Tetty.

He refuses to pay, said Mr Hackett.

He does not refuse to pay, said Goff. He offers me four
shillings and fourpence. It is all the money he has in the
world.

Then he would owe you only two and threepence,
said Mr Hackett.

I cannot leave him without a penny in his pocket, said
Goff.

Why not? said Mr Hackett.

He is setting out on a journey, said Goff. If I accepted
his offer he would be obliged to turn back.

That might be the best thing for him, said Mr Hackett.
Perhaps some day, when we are all dead, looking back he
will say, if only Mr Nesbit had accepted—

Nixon, my name is, said Goff. Nixon.

If only Mr Nixon had accepted my four and fourpence that night, and I had turned back, instead of going on.

All lies, I suppose, in any case, said Mrs Nixon.

No no, said Mr Nixon, he is a most truthful man, really incapable, I believe, of telling an untruth.

You might at least have accepted a shilling, said Mr Hackett, or one and six.

There he is now, on the bridge, said Mrs Nixon.

He stood with his back towards them, from the waist up faintly outlined against the last wisps of day.

You haven't told us his name, said Mr Hackett.

Watt, said Mr Nixon.

I never heard you mention him, said Mrs Nixon.

Strange, said Mr Nixon.

Known him long? said Mr Hackett.

I cannot really say I know him, said Mr Nixon.

Like a sewer-pipe, said Mrs Nixon. Where are his arms?

Since when can't you really say you know him? said Mr Hackett.

My dear fellow, said Mr Nixon, why this sudden interest?

Do not answer if you prefer not to, said Mr Hackett.

It is difficult to answer, said Mr Nixon. I seem to have known him all my life, but there must have been a period when I did not.

How is that, said Mr Hackett.

He is considerably younger than I, said Mr Nixon.

And you never mention him, said Mr Hackett.

Why, said Mr Nixon, I may very well have mentioned him, there is really no reason why I should not. It is true—. He paused. He does not invite mention, he said, there are people like that.

Not like me, said Mr Hackett.

He is gone, said Mrs Nixon.

Is that so, said Mr Nixon. The curious thing is, my dear fellow, I tell you quite frankly, that when I see him, or think of him, I think of you, and that when I see you, or think of you, I think of him. I have no idea why this is so.

Well well, said Mr Hackett.

He is on his way now to the station, said Mr Nixon. Why I wonder did he get down here.

It is the end of the penny fare, said Mrs Nixon.

That depends where he got on, said Mr Nixon.

He can scarcely have got on at a point remoter than the terminus, said Mr Hackett.

But does the penny fare end here, said Mr Nixon, at a merely facultative stop? Surely it ends rather at the station.

I think you are right, said Mr Hackett.

Then why did he get off here? said Mr Nixon.

Perhaps he felt like a little fresh air, said Mr Hackett, before being pent up in the train.

Weighed down as he is, said Mr Nixon. Come come.

Perhaps he mistook the stop, said Mrs Nixon.

But this is not a stop, said Mr Nixon, in the ordinary sense of the word. Here the tram stops only by request. And since nobody else got off, and since nobody got on, the request must have come from Watt.

A silence followed these words. Then Mrs Nixon said:

I do not follow you, Goff, Why should he not have requested the tram to stop, if he wished to do so?

There is no reason, my dear, said Mr Nixon, no earthly reason, why he should not have requested the tram to stop, as he undoubtedly did. But the fact of his having requested the tram to stop proves that he did not mistake the stop, as you suggest. For if he had mistaken the stop, and thought himself already at the railway station, he would not have requested the tram to stop. For the tram always stops at the station.

Perhaps he is off his head, said Mr Hackett.

He is a little strange at times, said Mr. Nixon, but he is an experienced traveller.

Perhaps, said Mr Hackett, finding that he had a little time on his hands, he decided to while it away through the sweet cool evening air, rather than in the nasty railway station.

But he will miss his train, said Mr Nixon, he will miss the last train out, if he does not run.

Perhaps he wished to annoy the conductor, said Mrs Nixon, or the driver.

But a milder, more inoffensive creature does not exist, said Mr Nixon. He would literally turn the other cheek, I honestly believe, if he had the energy.

Perhaps, said Mr Hackett, he suddenly made up his mind not to leave town after all. Between the terminus and here he had time to reconsider the matter. Then, having made up his mind that it is better after all not to leave town just now, he stops the tram and gets down, for it is useless to go on.

But he went on, said Mr Nixon, he did not go back the way he came, but went on, towards the station.

Perhaps he is going home by a roundabout way, said Mrs Nixon.

Where does he live? said Mr Hackett.

He has no fixed address that I know of, said Mr Nixon.

Then his going on towards the station proves nothing, said Mrs Nixon. He may be fast asleep in Quin's hotel at the present moment.

With four and four in his pocket, said Mr Hackett.

Or on a bench somewhere, said Mrs Nixon. Or in the

park. Or on the football field. Or on the cricket field. Or on the bowling green.

Or on the tennis courts, said Mr Nixon.

I think not, said Mr Hackett. He gets off the tram, determined not to leave town after all. But a little further reflexion shows him the folly of such a course. This would explain his attitude after the tram had moved on, and left him.

The folly of what course? said Mr Nixon.

Of turning back so soon, said Mr Hackett, before he was well started on his way.

Did you see the accoutrement? said Mrs Nixon. What had he on his head?

His hat, said Mr Nixon.

The thought of leaving town was most painful to him, said Mr Hackett, but the thought of not doing so no less so. So he sets off for the station, half hoping he may miss his train.

You may be right, said Mr Nixon.

Too fearful to assume himself the onus of a decision, said Mr Hackett, he refers it to the frigid machinery of a time-space relation.

Very ingenious, said Mr Nixon.

And what do you suppose frightens him all of a sudden? said Mrs Nixon.

It can hardly be the journey itself, said Mr Hackett, since you tell me he is an experienced traveller.

A silence followed these words.

Now that I have made that clear, said Mr Hackett, you might describe your friend a little more fully.

I really know nothing, said Mr Nixon.

But you must know something, said Mr Hackett. One does not part with five shillings to a shadow. Nationality, family, birthplace, confession, occupation, means of existence, distinctive signs, you cannot be in ignorance of all this.

Utter ignorance, said Mr Nixon.

He is not a native of the rocks, said Mr Hackett.

I tell you nothing is known, cried Mr Nixon. Nothing.

A silence followed these angry words, by Mr Hackett resented, by Mr Nixon repented.

He had a huge big red nose, said Mr Nixon grudgingly.

Mr Hackett pondered this.

You are not asleep, my dear, said Mr Nixon.

I grow drowsy, said Mrs Nixon.

Here is a man you seem to have known all your life, said Mr Hackett, who owes you five shillings for the past seven years, and all you can tell me is that he has a huge big red nose and no fixed address. He paused. He added, And that he is an experienced traveller. He paused. He added, And that he is considerably younger than you, a common condition I must say. He paused. He added, And that he is truthful, gentle and sometimes a little strange. He glared up angrily at Mr Nixon's face. But Mr Nixon did not see this angry glare, for he was looking at something quite different.

I think it is time for us to be getting along, he said, is it not, my dear.

In an instant the last flowers will be engulfed, said Mrs Nixon.

Mr Nixon rose.

Here is a man you have known as long as you can remember, said Mr Hackett, to whom you lent five shillings seven years ago, whom you immediately recognize, at a considerable distance, in the dark. You say you know nothing of his antecedents. I am obliged to believe you.

Nothing obliges you, said Mr Nixon.

I choose to believe you, said Mr Hackett. And that you

are unable to tell what you do not know I am willing to believe also. It is a common failing.

Tetty, said Mr Nixon.

But certain things you must know, said Mr Hackett.

For example, said Mr Nixon.

How you met him, said Mr Hackett. In what circumstances he touched you. Where he is to be seen.

What does it matter who he is? said Mrs Nixon. She rose.

Take my arm, my dear, said Mr Nixon.

Or what he does, said Mrs Nixon. Or how he lives. Or where he comes from. Or where he is going to. Or what he looks like. What can it possibly matter, to us?

I ask myself the same question, said Mr Hackett.

How I met him, said Mr Nixon. I really do not remember, any more than I remember meeting my father.

Good God, said Mr Hackett.

In what circumstances he touched me, said Mr Nixon. I met him one day in the street. One of his feet was bare. I forget which. He drew me to one side and said he was in need of five shillings to buy himself a boot. I could not refuse him.

But one does not buy a boot, exclaimed Mr Hackett.

Perhaps he knew where he could have it made to measure, said Mrs Nixon.

I know nothing of that, said Mr Nixon. As to where he is to be seen, he is to be seen in the streets, walking about. But one does not see him often.

He is a university man, of course, said Mrs Nixon.

I should think it highly probable, said Mr Nixon.

Mr and Mrs Nixon moved off, arm in arm. But they had not gone far when they returned. Mr Nixon stooped and murmured in Mr Hackett's ear, Mr Nixon who did not like the sun to go down on the least hint of an estrangement.

Drink, said Mr Hackett.

Oh my goodness no, said Mr Nixon, he drinks nothing but milk.

Milk, exclaimed Mr Hackett.

Even water he will not touch, said Mr Nixon.

Well, said Mr Hackett wearily, I am obliged to you, I suppose.

Mr and Mrs Nixon moved off, arm in arm. But they had not gone far when they heard a cry. They stopped, and listened. It was Mr Hackett, crying, in the night, Pleased to have met you, Mrs Nisbet. Mrs Nixon tightening her hold on Mr Nixon's arm, cried back, The pleasure is mine, Mr Hackett.

What? cried Mr Hackett.

She said the pleasure is hers, cried Mr Nixon.

Mr Hackett resumed his holds on the armrests. Pulling himself forward, and letting himself fall back, several times in rapid succession, he scratched the crest of his hunch against the backboard. He looked towards the horizon that he had come out to see, of which he had seen so little. Now it was quite dark. Yes, now the western sky was as the eastern, which was as the southern, which was as the northern.

Poetry

Beckett had been in Paris for about two years, as *lecteur d'anglais* at l'Ecole Nomale Supérieure, when he heard tell of a contest that Nancy Cunard of the Hours Press was sponsoring. The none-too-piddling prize of £10 was to be awarded to the winning poem, which would, in addition, see the light of print courtesy of the sponsor.

Thomas MacGreevy, Beckett's Irish friend and his predecessor at l'Ecole Normale, told Beckett about the contest the day of the deadline, in mid-June. A hundred or so poems had already been entered, but Richard Aldington and Miss Cunard, the self-appointed judges, found none worthy of the award. MacGreevy challenged Beckett to try his luck. It was by then already late in the afternoon, but Beckett, perhaps tempted by the prize money but more likely by the imposed theme—Time—set about to write what was to become *Whoroscope*, a ninety-eight-line poem which has the dubious distinction of containing, as appendix, more footnotes than *The Waste Land*.

Beckett wrote the first half of the poem before dinner that evening, downed a hasty meal (as Nancy Cunard reports in her *Those Were the Hours*), then went back to l'Ecole Normale and finished it by three in the morning, at which point he walked down to Miss Cunard's and dropped it in her mailbox.

The competition had stipulated that the entries should not exceed one hundred lines, and *Whoroscope*, tailored to conform, made it just under the wire at ninety-eight lines. At the suggestion of Richard Aldington, Beckett added, in the manner of T. S. Eliot's *The Waste Land*, copious notes, meant to elucidate the poem itself. As some critics have pointed out, the notes are often more puzzling than the text. In any case,

they make it clear that we are dealing with a dramatic monologue, the subject of which is René Descartes.

Whoroscope appeared under the imprint of Miss Cunard's
Hours Press in the summer of 1930, in an edition of 300 copies,
on the cover of which was a white label that read:

> This poem was awarded the £10 prize for the best
> poem on Time in the competition judged by Richard
> Aldington and Nancy Cunard at the Hours Press, and
> is published in an edition of 100 signed copies at 5s.
> and 200 copies at 1s. This is also Mr. Samuel Beckett's
> first separately published work.

During the next five years scattered poems appeared,
but no new volume was published until 1935. If 1930 and
the year or two that followed had seemed auspicious for the
young Irishman, there followed a prolonged period of drought
and doubt, especially after the death of his father in 1933.
The year 1935 found Beckett down and out in London, eking
out a bare existence through a combination of his small
annuity, some reviewing, and a bit of translating. Still, by
the spring of that year, he felt he had enough for a slim
collection of poems, and in his faithful friend George Reavey
a young if impecunious publisher willing to bring them out.
As is the case with most young poets, the problem of publication was nigh insurmountable, and often in desperation the
young poets themselves turn publisher to see the light of
print. Reavey published not only Beckett and his fellow
Irish poets Denis Devlin and Brian Coffey, but also two
volumes of his own. Beckett's *Echo's Bones* appeared in 1935.

The following year, in the June, 1936, issue of *transition*,
Eugene Jolas reprinted a number of the poems in the volume,
thus giving the young Beckett a somewhat wider exposure.

Three decades after the publication of *Echo's Bones*,
the BBC Third Programme presented a selection of poems
by Samuel Beckett, produced by Martin Esslin, the choice of

poems having been made by critic John Fletcher. Beckett, who was present at the taping, happened to mention to Esslin that, had the choice been his, he would have chosen somewhat differently. As a result, a second program was broadcast later that year using the author's own preferences.

When I made the initial selection for the present volume, I was unaware of these 1966 programs; yet I was pleased to note that my selection differed from Beckett's in only two instances. I have incorporated these two poems in the following selection.

Whoroscope

What's that?
An egg?
By the brothers Boot it stinks fresh.
Give it to Gillot.

Galileo how are you
and his consecutive thirds!
The vile old Copernican lead-swinging son of a
        sutler!
We're moving he said we're off—Porca
        Madonna!
the way a boatswain would be, or a sack-of-
        potatoey charging Pretender.
That's not moving, that's *moving*.   10

What's that?
A little green fry or a mushroomy one?
Two lashed ovaries with prostisciutto?
How long did she womb it, the feathery one?
Three days and four nights?
Give it to Gillot.

Faulhaber, Beeckman and Peter the Red,
come now in the cloudy avalanche or Gassendi's
        sun-red crystally cloud

and I'll pebble you all your hen-and-a-half ones
or I'll pebble a lens under the quilt in the midst
        of day.   20

To think he was my own brother, Peter the
        Bruiser,
and not a syllogism out of him
no more than if Pa were still in it.
Hey! pass over those coppers,
sweet millèd sweat of my burning liver!
Them were the days I sat in the hot-cupboard
        throwing Jesuits out of the skylight.

Who's that? Hals?
Let him wait.

My squinty doaty!
I hid and you sook.   30
And Francine my precious fruit of a house-and-
        parlour foetus!
What an exfoliation!
Her little grey flayed epidermis and scarlet
        tonsils!
My one child
scourged by a fever to stagnant murky blood—
blood!
Oh Harvey belovèd
how shall the red and white, the many in the
        few,

(dear bloodswirling Harvey)
eddy through that cracked beater?   40
And the fourth Henry came to the crypt of the
              arrow.

What's that?
How long?
Sit on it.

A wind of evil flung my despair of ease
against the sharp spires of the one
lady:
not once or twice but . . . .
(Kip of Christ hatch it!)
in one sun's drowning   50
(Jesuitasters please copy).
So on with the silk hose over the knitted, and
              the morbid leather—
what am I saying! the gentle canvas—
and away to Ancona on the bright Adriatic,
and farewell for a space to the yellow key of
              the Rosicrucians.
They don't know what the master of them that
              do did,
that the nose is touched by the kiss of all foul
              and sweet air,
and the drums, and the throne of the fæcal
              inlet,
and the eyes by its zig-zags.
So we drink Him and eat Him   60

and the watery Beaune and the stale cubes of
        Hovis
because He can jig
as near or as far from His Jigging Self
and as sad or lively as the chalice or the tray asks.
How's that, Antonio?

In the name of Bacon will you chicken me up
        that egg.
Shall I swallow cave-phantoms?

Anna Maria!
She reads Moses and says her love is crucified.
Leider! Leider! she bloomed and withered,   70
a pale abusive parakeet in a mainstreet window.

No I believe every word of it I assure you.
Fallor, ergo sum!
The coy old frôleur!
He tolle'd and legge'd
and he buttoned on his redemptorist waistcoat.
No matter, let it pass.
I'm a bold boy I know
so I'm not my son
(even if I were a concierge)   80
nor Joachim my father's
but the chip of a perfect block that's neither old
        nor new,
the lonely petal of a great high bright rose.

Are you ripe at last,
my slim pale double-breasted turd?
How rich she smells,
this abortion of a fledgling!
I will eat it with a fish fork.
White and yolk and feathers.
Then I will rise and move moving   90
toward Rahab of the snows,
the murdering matinal pope-confessed amazon,
Christina the ripper.
Oh Weulles spare the blood of a Frank
who has climbed the bitter steps,
(René du Perron . . . . !)
and grant me my second
starless inscrutable hour.

                                                              1930

Notes

René Descartes, Seigneur du Perron, liked his ome-
lette made of eggs hatched from eight to ten days;
shorter or longer under the hen and the result, he says,
is disgusting.

He kept his own birthday to himself so that no astrol-
oger could cast his nativity.
The shuttle of a ripening egg combs the warp of his
days.

P. 80, l.   3 In 1640 the brothers Boot refuted Ar-
istotle in Dublin.

4 Descartes passed on the easier problems in analytical geometry to his
valet Gillot.

5-10 Refer to his contempt for Galileo Jr.,
(whom he confused with the more
musical Galileo Sr.), and to his expedi-
ent sophistry concerning the movement of the earth.

17 He solved problems submitted by
these mathematicians.

P. 81, l. 21-26 The attempt at swindling on the part
of his elder brother Pierre de la Bre-
taillière—The money he received as a
soldier.

27 Franz Hals.

29-30 As a child he played with a little cross-
eyed girl.

31-35 His daughter died of scarlet fever at
the age of six.

37-40 Honoured Harvey for his discovery
of the circulation of the blood, but
would not admit that he had explained
the motion of the heart.

P.82, l.   41 The heart of Henri iv was received at
the Jesuit college of La Flèche while
Descartes was still a student there.

45-53 His visions and pilgrimage to Loretto.

56-65 His Eucharistic sophistry, in reply to
the Jansenist Antoine Arnauld, who
challenged him to reconcile his doctrine of matter with the doctrine of
transubstantiation.

P.83, l.   68 Schurmann, the Dutch blue-stocking,
a pious pupil of Voët, the adversary of
Descartes.

73-76 Saint Augustine has a revelation in the
shrubbery and reads Saint Paul.

77-83 He proves God by exhaustion.

P.84, l. 91-93 Christina, queen of Sweden. At Stock-
holm, in November, she required Des-
cartes, who had remained in bed till
midday all his life, to be with her at
five o'clock in the morning.

94 Weulles, a Peripatetic Dutch physician at the Swedish court, and an
enemy of Descartes.

From Echo's Bones

The Vulture

dragging his hunger through the sky
of my skull shell of sky and earth

stooping to the prone who must
soon take up their life and walk

mocked by a tissue that may not serve
till hunger earth and sky be offal

Serena I

without the grand old British Museum
Thales and the Aretino
on the bosom of the Regent's Park the phlox
crackles under the thunder
scarlet beauty in our world dead fish adrift
all things full of gods
pressed down and bleeding
a weaver-bird is tangerine the harpy is past
              caring
the condor likewise in his mangy boa
they stare out across monkey-hill the elephants
Ireland
the light creeps down their old home canyon
sucks me aloof to that old reliable
the burning btm of George the drill
ah across the way a adder
broaches her rat
white as snow
in her dazzling oven strom of peristalsis
limae labor

ah father father that art in heaven

I find me taking the Crystal Palace
for the Blessed Isles from Primrose Hill
alas I must be that kind of person
hence in Ken Wood who shall find me
my breath held in the midst of thickets
none but the most quarried lovers

I surprise me moved by the many a funnel
            hinged
for the obeisance to Tower Bridge
the viper's curtsy to and from the City
till in the dusk a lighter
blind with pride
tosses aside the scarf of the bascules
then in the grey hold of the ambulance
throbbing on the brink ebb of sighs
then I hug me below among the canaille
until a guttersnipe blast his cernèd eyes
demanding 'ave I done with the Mirror
I stump off in a fearful rage under Married
            Men's Quarters
Bloody Tower
and afar off at all speed screw me up Wren's
            giant bully
and curse the day caged panting on the platform
under the flaring urn
I was not born Defoe

but in Ken Wood
who shall find me

my brother the fly
the common housefly
sidling out of darkness into light
fastens on his place in the sun
whets his six legs
revels in his planes his poisers
it is the autumn of his life
he could not serve typhoid and mammon

Serena III

fix this pothook of beauty on this palette
you never know it might be final

or leave her she is paradise and then
plush hymens on your eyeballs

or on Butt Bridge blush for shame
the mixed declension of those mammae
cock up thy moon thine and thine only
up up up to the star of evening
swoon upon the arch-gasometer
on Misery Hill brand-new carnation
swoon upon the little purple
house of prayer
something heart of Mary
the Bull and Pool Beg that will never meet
not in this world

whereas dart away through the cavorting scapes
bucket o'er Victoria Bridge that's the idea
slow down slink down the Ringsend Road
Irishtown Sandymount puzzle find the Hell
              Fire
the Merrion Flats scored with a thrillion sigmas

Jesus Christ Son of God Saviour His Finger
girls taken strippin that's the idea
on the Bootersgrad breakwind and water
the tide making the dun gulls in a panic
the sands quicken in your hot heart
hide yourself not in the Rock keep on the move
keep on the move

Sanies I

all the livelong way this day of sweet showers
        from Portrane on the seashore
Donabate sad swans of Turvey Swords
pounding along in three ratios like a sonata
like a Ritter with pommelled scrotum atra cura
        on the step
Botticelli from the fork down pestling the
        transmission
tires bleeding voiding zeep the highway
all heaven in the sphincter
the sphincter

müüüüüüüde now
potwalloping now through the promenaders
this trusty all-steel this super-real
bound for home like a good boy
where I was born with a pop with the green of
        the larches
ah to be back in the caul now with no trusts
no fingers no spoilt love
belting along in the meantime clutching the
        bike
the billows of the nubile the cere wrack
pot-valiant caulless waisted in rags hatless
for mamma papa chicken and ham

warm Grave too say the word
happy days snap the stem shed a tear
this day Spy Wedsday seven pentades past
oh the larches the pain drawn like a cork
the glans he took the day off up hill and down
            dale
with a ponderous fawn from the Liverpool
            London and Globe
back the shadows lengthen the sycomores are
            sobbing
to roly-poly oh to me a spanking boy
buckets of fizz childbed is thirsty work
for the midwife he is gory
for the proud parent he washes down a gob of
            gladness
for footsore Achates also he pants his pleasure
sparkling beestings for me
tired now hair ebbing gums ebbing ebbing
            home
good as gold now in the prime after a brief
            prodigality
yea and suave
suave urbane beyond good and evil
biding my time without rancour you may take
            your oath
distraught half-crooked courting the sneers of
            these fauns these smart nymphs
clipped like a pederast as to one trouser-end
sucking in my bloated lantern behind a Wild
            Woodbine

cinched to death in a filthy slicker
flinging the proud Swift forward breasting the
        swell of Stürmers
I see main verb at last
her whom alone in the accusative
I have dismounted to love
gliding towards me dauntless nautch-girl on the
        face of the waters
dauntless daughter of desires in the old black
        and flamingo
get along with you now take the six the seven
        the eight or the little single-decker
take a bus for all I care walk cadge a lift
home to the cob of your web in Holles Street
and let the tiger go on smiling
in our hearts that funds ways home

Sanies II

there was a happy land
the American Bar
in Rue Mouffetard
there were red eggs there
I have a dirty I say henorrhoids
coming from the bath
the steam the delight the sherbet
the chagrin of the old skinnymalinks
slouching happy body
loose in my stinking old suit
sailing slouching up to Puvis the gauntlet of
          tulips
lash lash me with yaller tulips I will let down
my stinking old trousers
my love she sewed up the pockets alive the live-
          oh she did she said that was better
spotless then within the brown rags gliding
frescoward free up the fjord of dyed eggs and
          thongbells
I disappear don't you know into the local
the mackerel are at billiards there they are
          crying the scores
the Barfrau makes a big impression with her
          mighty bottom

Dante and blissful Beatrice are there
prior to Vita Nuova
the balls splash no luck comrade
Gracieuse is there Belle-Belle down the drain
booted Percinet with his cobalt jowl
they are necking gobble-gobble
suck is not suck that alters
lo Alighieri has got off au revoir to all that
I break down quite in a titter of despite
hark
upon the saloon a terrible hush
a shiver convulses Madame de la Motte
it courses it peals down her collops
the great bottom foams into stillness
quick quick the cavaletto supplejacks for
                mumbo-jumbo
vivas puellas mortui incurrrrrsant boves
oh subito subito ere she recover the cang
                bamboo for bastinado
a bitter moon fessade à la mode
oh Becky spare me I have done thee no wrong
                spare me damn thee
spare me good Becky
call off thine adders Becky I will compensate
                thee in full
Lord have mercy upon us
Christ have mercy upon us

Lord have mercy upon us

Da Tagte Es

redeem the surrogate goodbyes
the sheet astream in your hand
who have no more for the land
and the glass unmisted above your eyes

Echo's Bones

asylum under my tread all this day
their muffled revels as the flesh falls
breaking without fear or favour wind
the gantelope of sense and nonsense run
taken by the maggots for what they are

1935

Cascando

1.

why not merely the despaired of
occasion of
wordshed

is it not better abort than be barren

the hours after you are gone are so leaden
they will always start dragging too soon
the grapples clawing blindly the bed of want
bringing up the bones the old loves
sockets filled once with eyes like yours
all always is it better too soon than never
the black want splashing their faces
saying again nine days never floated the loved
nor nine months
nor nine lives

2.

saying again
if you do not teach me I shall not learn

saying again there is a last
even of last times
last times of begging
last times of loving
of knowing not knowing pretending
a last even of last times of saying
if you do not love me I shall not be loved
if I do not love you I shall not love

the churn of stale words in the heart again
love love love thud of the old plunger
pestling the unalterable
whey of words

terrified again
of not loving
of loving and not you
of being loved and not by you
of knowing not knowing pretending
pretending

I and all the others that will love you
if they love you

3.

unless they love you

1936

Saint-Lô

Vire will wind in other shadows
unborn through the bright ways tremble
and the old mind ghost-forsaken
sink into its havoc

1946

Criticism

Dante . . . Bruno.
Vico . . Joyce.

In 1929, not long after his friend and predecessor at l'Ecole Normale, Thomas MacGreevy, had introduced the then twenty-two-year-old Beckett to James Joyce, Beckett was asked to contribute to the critical anthology then in preparation, dealing with the many levels and facets of Joyce's *Work in Progress*—later to become *Finnegans Wake*.

Joyce, of course, was closely involved with the critical work, and, in a very real sense, supervised both the selection of the contributors and the content of their pieces. In a letter to Adrienne Monnier dated September 3, 1928, Joyce speaks of the collection as comprising "eleven articles plus one other by Stuart Gilbert, bringing the total to twelve." In all likelihood, Beckett was not at that point among the twelve "apostles," since he did not arrive in Paris till October of that year and had not yet made Joyce's acquaintance. But sometime between September 1928 and the following May, when the volume was published by Shakespeare and Company under the title *Our Exagmination Round His Factification For Incamination Of Work In Progress*, Beckett joined the clan, probably as a last-minute substitute for one of the original twelve. The book appeared officially on May 27, 1929, with Beckett's essay the lead, and the entire contents was reprinted a month later in *transition* No. 16–17, thus bringing the young Beckett to the attention of the readership of that important review.

For years I had thought the peculiar ellipses of the title were just further typographical idiosyncrasies on the part of the French printers. But in reading a book on Beckett by Raymond Federman and John Fletcher I found that, here as always, Beckett's punctuation, as his every word, is absolutely precise: "From Dante to Bruno," the author explained, "is a jump of about three centuries, from Bruno to Vico about one, and from Vico to Joyce about two."

Other contributors to *Our Exagmination . . .* included William Carlos Williams, Eugene Jolas, Stuart Gilbert, Elliot Paul, Robert McAlmon, and Beckett's young friend Thomas MacGreevy.* If it is fair to say that all were laudatory, they did, to varying degrees, help explain and clarify the purpose and methods of Joyce's awesome endeavor. Beckett's piece, learned and at times bearing echoes of the Master's voice, is nonetheless remarkable not only for some cogent and original insights into Joyce's work but also for what it tells us about Beckett's views and esthetics at the time. Thus the opening sentence: "The danger is in the neatness of identifications." Or this, referring specifically to Joyce's new work: "Here words are not the polite contortions of 20th century printer's ink. They are alive. They elbow their way on to the page, and glow and blaze and fade and disappear." Or: "Must we wring the neck of a certain system in order to stuff it into a contemporary pigeon-hole, or modify the dimensions of that pigeon-hole for the satisfaction of the analogymongers? Literary criticism is not book-keeping."

Beckett often said that it is the work, not the artist, that is important. Thus one must, in general, perceive the mind of the artist through the work, and from the clues deduce as one can. In this early piece, it is possible to see, glittering in among the learned arguments, visible proof of a strong, original mind, still searching no doubt for its own territory but already, at age twenty-two, clearly aware of the landmarks that would guide it there.

---

* Joyce himself is believed to have contributed to the volume, under a pseudonym.

The danger is in the neatness of identifications. The conception of Philosophy and Philology as a pair of nigger minstrels out of the Teatro dei Piccoli is soothing, like the contemplation of a carefully folded ham-sandwich. Giambattista Vico himself could not resist the attractiveness of such coincidence of gesture. He insisted on complete identification between the philosophical abstraction and the empirical illustration, thereby annulling the absolutism of each conception—hoisting the real unjustifiably clear of its dimensional limits, temporalizing that which is extratemporal. And now here am I, with my handful of abstractions, among which notably: a mountain, the coincidence of contraries, the inevitability of cyclic evolution, a system of Poetics, and the prospect of self-extension in the world of Mr. Joyce's *Work in Progress*. There is the temptation to treat every concept like 'a bass dropt neck fust in till a bung crate,' and make a really tidy job of it. Unfortunately such an exactitude of application would imply distortion in one of two directions. Must we wring the neck of a certain system in order to stuff it into a contemporary pigeon-hole, or modify the dimensions of that pigeon-hole for the satisfaction of the analogymongers? Literary criticism is not book-keeping.

Giambattista Vico was a practical roundheaded Neapolitan. It pleases Croce to consider him as a mystic, essentially speculative, *"disdegnoso dell' empirismo."* It is a surprising interpretation, seeing that more than three-fifths of his *Scienza Nuova* is concerned with empirical investigation. Croce opposes him to the reformative materialistic school of Ugo Grozio, and absolves him from the utilitarian preoccupations of Hobbes, Spinoza, Locke, Bayle and Machiavelli. All this cannot be swallowed without protest. Vico defines Providence as: *"una mente spesso diversa ed alle volte tutta contraria e sempre superiore ad essi fini particolari che essi uomini si avevano proposti; dei quali fini ristretti fatti mezzi per servire a fini più ampi, gli ha sempre adoperati per conservare l'umana generazione in questa terra."* What could be more definitely utilitarianism? His treatment of the origin and functions of poetry, language and myth, as will appear later, is as far removed from the mystical as it is possible to imagine. For our immediate purpose, however, it matters little whether we consider him as a mystic or as a scientific investigator; but there are no two ways about considering him as an *innovator*. His division of the development of human society into three ages: Theocratic, Heroic, Human (civilized), with a corresponding classification of language: Hieroglyphic (sacred), Metaphorical (poetic), Philosophical (capable of abstraction and generalisation), was by no means new, although it must have appeared so to his contemporaries. He derived this convenient classification from the Egyptians, via Herodotus. At the same time it is impossible to deny the originality with which he applied and developed its implications. His exposition of the ineluctable circular progression of Society was completely new, although the germ of it was contained in Giordano Bruno's treatment of identified contraries. But it is in Book 2, described by himself as *"tutto il corpo . . . la chiave maestra . . . dell' opera,"* that appears the unqualified originality of his mind; here he evolved a theory of the origins of poetry and language, the significance of myth, and the nature of barbaric civilization that must

have appeared nothing less than an impertinent outrage
against tradition. These two aspects of Vico have their
reverberations, their reapplications—without, however, receiving the faintest explicit illustration—in *Work in Progress.*

It is first necessary to condense the thesis of Vico, the
scientific historian. In the beginning was the thunder: the
thunder set free Religion, in its most objective and un-
philosophical form—idolatrous animism: Religion produced Society, and the first social men were the cave-
dwellers, taking refuge from a passionate Nature: this
primitive family life receives its first impulse towards development from the arrival of terrified vagabonds; admitted, they are the first slaves: growing stronger, they
exact agrarian concessions, and a despotism has evolved
into a primitive feudalism: the cave becomes a city, and
the feudal system a democracy: then an anarchy: this is
corrected by a return to monarchy: the last stage is a
tendency towards interdestruction: the nations are dispersed, and the Phoenix of Society arises out of their ashes.
To this six-termed social progression corresponds a six-
termed progression of human motives: necessity, utility,
convenience, pleasure, luxury, abuse of luxury: and their
incarnate manifestations: Polyphemus, Achilles, Caesar
and Alexander, Tiberius, Caligula and Nero. At this point
Vico applies Bruno—though he takes very good care not
to say so—and proceeds from rather arbitrary data to
philosophical abstraction. There is no difference, says
Bruno, between the smallest possible chord and the smallest possible arc, no difference between the infinite circle
and the straight line. The maxima and minima of particular contraries are one and indifferent. Minimal heat equals
minimal cold. Consequently transmutations are circular.
The principle (minimum) of one contrary takes its move-

ment from the principle (maximum) of another. Therefore not only do the minima coincide with the minima, the
maxima with the maxima, but the minima with the
maxima in the succession of transmutations. Maximal
speed is a state of rest. The maximum of corruption and
the minimum of generation are identical: in principle,
corruption is generation. And all things are ultimately
identified with God, the universal monad, Monad of
monads. From these considerations Vico evolved a
Science and Philosophy of History. It may be an amusing
exercise to take an historical figure, such as Scipio, and
label him No. 3; it is of no ultimate importance. What is
of ultimate importance is the recognition that the passage
from Scipio to Caesar is as inevitable as the passage from
Caesar to Tiberius, since the flowers of corruption in Scipio
and Caesar are the seeds of vitality in Caesar and Tiberius.
Thus we have the spectacle of a human progression that
depends for its movement on individuals, and which at the
same time is independent of individuals in virtue of what
appears to be a preordained cyclicism. It follows that History is neither to be considered as a formless structure, due
exclusively to the achievements of individual agents, nor
as possessing reality apart from and independent of them,
accomplished behind their backs in spite of them, the
work of some superior force, variously known as Fate,
Chance, Fortune, God. Both these views, the materialistic
and the transcendental, Vico rejects in favour of the rational. Individuality is the concretion of universality, and
every individual action is at the same time superindi-
vidual. The individual and the universal cannot be considered as distinct from each other. History, then, is not
the result of Fate or Chance—in both cases the individual
would be separated from his product—but the result of a
Necessity that is not Fate, of a Liberty that is not Chance

(compare Dante's "yoke of liberty"). This force he called
Divine Providence, with his tongue, one feels, very much
in his cheek. And it is to this Providence that we must
trace the three institutions common to every society:
Church, Marriage, Burial. This is not Bossuet's Providence,
transcendental and miraculous, but immanent and the stuff
itself of human life, working by natural means. Humanity
is its work in itself. God acts on her, but by means of her.
Humanity is divine, but no man is divine. This social and
historical classification is clearly adapted by Mr. Joyce as
a structural convenience—or inconvenience. His position is
in no way a philosophical one. It is the detached attitude
of Stephen Dedalus in *Portrait of the Artist* . . . who
describes Epictetus to the Master of Studies as "an old
gentleman who said that the soul is very like a bucketful
of water." The lamp is more important than the lamplighter. By structural I do not only mean a bold outward
division, a bare skeleton for the housing of material. I
mean the endless substantial variations on these three
beats, and interior intertwining of these three themes into
a decoration of arabesques—decoration and more than
decoration. Part 1 is a mass of past shadow, corresponding
therefore to Vico's first human institution, Religion, or
to his Theocratic age, or simply to an abstraction—Birth.
Part 2 is the lovegame of the children, corresponding to
the second institution, Marriage, or to the Heroic age, or
to an abstraction—Maturity. Part 3 is passed in sleep,
corresponding to the third institution, Burial, or to the
Human age, or to an abstraction—Corruption. Part 4. is the
day beginning again, and corresponds to Vico's Providence, or to the transition from the Human to the Theocratic, or to an abstraction—Generation. Mr. Joyce does
not take birth for granted, as Vico seems to have done. So
much for the dry bones. The consciousness that there is

a great deal of the unborn infant in the lifeless octoge-
narian, and a great deal of both in the man at the apogee
of his life's curve, removes all the stiff interexclusiveness
that is often the danger in neat construction. Corruption
is not excluded from Part 1 nor maturity from Part 3.
The four "lovedroyd curdinals" are presented on the same
plane—"his element curdinal numen and his enement
curdinal marrying and his epulent curdinal weisswasch
and his eminent curdinal Kay o' Kay!" There are numerous
references to Vico's four human institutions—Providence
counting as one! "A good clap, a fore wedding, a bad
wake, tell hell's well": "their weatherings and their marry-
ings and their buryings and their natural selections": "the
lightning look, the birding cry, awe from the grave, ever-
flowing on our times": "by four hands of forethought the
first babe of reconcilement is laid in its last cradle of hume
sweet hume."

Apart from this emphasis on the tangible conveniences
common to Humanity, we find frequent expressions of
Vico's insistence on the inevitable character of every
progression—or retrogression: "The Vico road goes round
to meet where terms begin. Still onappealed to by the
cycles and onappalled by the recoursers, we feel all serene,
never you fret, as regards our dutyful cask. . . . before
there was a man at all in Ireland there was a lord at Lucan.
We only wish everyone was as sure of anything in this
watery world as we are of everything in the newlywet
fellow that's bound to follow. . . ." "The efferfresh-
painted livy in beautific repose upon the silence of the
dead from Pharoph the next first down to ramescheckles
the last bust thing." "In fact, under the close eyes of the
inspectors the traits featuring the chiaroscuro coalesce,
their contrarieties eliminated, in one stable somebody
similarly as by the providential warring of heartshaker

with housebreaker and of dramdrinker against freethinker
our social something bowls along bumpily, experiencing a
jolting series of prearranged disappointments, down the
long lane of (it's as semper as oxhousehumper) generations, more generations and still more generations"—this
last a case of Mr. Joyce's rare subjectivism. In a word, here
is all humanity circling with fatal monotony about the
Providential fulcrum—the "convoy wheeling encirculing
abound the gigantig's lifetree." Enough has been said, or
at least enough has been suggested, to show how Vico is
substantially present in the *Work in Progress*. Passing to
the Vico of the Poetics we hope to establish an even more
striking, if less direct, relationship.

Vico rejected the three popular interpretations of the
poetic spirit, which considered poetry as either an ingenious popular expression of philosophical conceptions,
or an amusing social diversion, or an exact science within
the research of everyone in possession of the recipe.
Poetry, he says, was born of curiosity, daughter of ignorance. The first men had to create matter by the force of
their imagination, and "poet" means "creator." Poetry was
the first operation of the human mind, and without it
thought could not exist. Barbarians, incapable of analysis
and abstraction, must use their fantasy to explain what
their reasons cannot comprehend. Before articulation
comes song; before abstract terms, metaphors. The figurative character of the oldest poetry must be regarded, not
as sophisticated confectionery, but as evidence of a
poverty-stricken vocabulary and of a disability to achieve
abstraction. Poetry is essentially the antithesis of Metaphysics: Metaphysics purge the mind of the senses and
cultivate the disembodiment of the spiritual; Poetry is all
passion and feeling and animates the inanimate; Metaphysics are most perfect when most concerned with uni-

versals; Poetry, when most concerned with particulars. Poets are the sense, philosophers the intelligence of humanity. Considering the Scholastics' axiom: *"niente è nell'intelletto che prima non sia nel senso,"* it follows that poetry is a prime condition of philosophy and civilization. The primitive animistic movement was a manifestation of the *"forma poetica dello spirito."*

His treatment of the origin of language proceeds along similar lines. Here again he rejected the materialistic and transcendental views: the one declaring that language was nothing but a polite and conventional symbolism; the other, in desperation, describing it as a gift from the Gods. As before, Vico is the rationalist, aware of the natural and inevitable growth of language. In its first dumb form, language was gesture. If a man wanted to say "sea," he pointed to the sea. With the spread of animism this gesture was replaced by the word: "Neptune." He directs our attention to the fact that every need of life, natural, moral and economic, has its verbal expression in one or other of the 30,000 Greek divinities. This is Homer's "language of the Gods." Its evolution through poetry to a highly civilized vehicle, rich in abstract and technical terms, was as little fortuitous as the evolution of society itself. Words have their progressions as well as social phases. "Forest-cabin-village-city-academy" is one rough progression. Another: "mountain-plain-riverbank." And every word expands with psychological inevitability. Take the Latin word: "Lex."

1.   Lex = Crop of acorns.
2.   Ilex = Tree that produces acorns.
3. Legere = To gather.
4. Aquilex = He that gathers the waters.
5.   Lex = Gathering together of peoples, public assembly.

6.   Lex = Law.
7.   Legere = To gather together letters into a word, to read.

The root of any word whatsoever can be traced back to some pre-lingual symbol. This early inability to abstract the general from the particular produced the Type-names. It is the child's mind over again. The child extends the names of the first familiar objects to other strange objects in which he is conscious of some analogy. The first men, unable to conceive the abstract idea of "poet" or "hero," named every hero after the first hero, every poet after the first poet. Recognizing this custom of designating a number of individuals by the names of their prototypes, we can explain various classical and mythological mysteries. Hermes is the prototype of the Egyptian inventor: so for Romulus, the great law-giver, and Hercules, the Greek hero: so for Homer. Thus Vico asserts the spontaneity of language and denies the dualism of poetry and language. Similarly, poetry is the foundation of writing. When language consisted of gesture, the spoken and written were identical. Hieroglyphics, or sacred language, as he calls it, were not the invention of philosophers for the mysterious expression of profound thought, but the common necessity of primitive peoples. Convenience only begins to assert itself at a far more advanced stage of civilization, in the form of alphabetism. Here Vico, implicitly at least, distinguishes between writing and direct expression. In such direct expression, form and content are inseparable. Examples are the medals of the Middle Ages, which bore no inscription and were a mute testimony to the feebleness of conventional alphabetic writing: and the flags of our own day. As with Poetry and Language, so with Myth. Myth, according to Vico, is neither an allegorical expression of general philosophical axioms (Conti, Bacon), nor a de-

rivative from particular peoples, as for instance the
Hebrews or Egyptians, nor yet the work of isolated poets,
but an historical statement of fact, of actual contemporary
phenomena, actual in the sense that they were created
out of necessity by primitive minds, and firmly believed.
Allegory implies a threefold intellectual operation: the
construction of a message of general significance, the preparation of a fabulous form, and an exercise of considerable
technical difficulty in uniting the two, an operation
totally beyond the reach of the primitive mind. Moreover,
if we consider the myth as being essentially allegorical,
we are not obliged to accept the form in which it is
cast as a statement of fact. But we know that the actual
creators of these myths gave full credence to their face-
value. Jove was no symbol: he was terribly real. It was
precisely their superficial metaphorical character that
made them intelligible to people incapable of receiving
anything more abstract than the plain record of objectivity.

Such is a painful exposition of Vico's dynamic treatment of Language, Poetry and Myth. He may still appear
as a mystic to some: if so, a mystic that rejects the transcendental in every shape and form as a factor in human
development, and whose Providence is not divine enough
to do without the cooperation of Humanity.

On turning to the *Work in Progress* we find that the
mirror is not so convex. Here is direct expression—pages
and pages of it. And if you don't understand it, Ladies and
Gentlemen, it is because you are too decadent to receive it.
You are not satisfied unless form is so strictly divorced
from content that you can comprehend the one almost
without bothering to read the other. The rapid skimming
and absorption of the scant cream of sense is made possible by what I may call a continuous process of copious

intellectual salivation. The form that is an arbitrary and independent phenomenon can fulfil no higher function than that of stimulus for a tertiary or quartary conditioned reflex of dribbling comprehension. When Miss Rebecca West clears her decks for a sorrowful deprecation of the Narcisstic element in Mr. Joyce by the purchase of 3 hats, one feels that she might very well wear her bib at all her intellectual banquets, or alternatively, assert a more noteworthy control over her salivary glands than is possible for Monsieur Pavlov's unfortunate dogs. The title of this book is a good example of a form carrying a strict inner determination. It should be proof against the usual volley of cerebral sniggers: and it may suggest to some a dozen incredulous Joshuas prowling around the Queen's Hall, springing their tuning-forks lightly against fingernails that have not yet been refined out of existence. Mr. Joyce has a word to say to you on the subject: "Yet to concentrate solely on the literal sense or even the psychological content of any document to the sore neglect of the enveloping facts themselves circumstantiating it is just as harmful; etc." And another: "Who in his heart doubts either that the facts of feminine clothiering are there all the time or that the feminine fiction, stranger than the facts, is there also at the same time, only a little to the rere? Or that one may be separated from the other? Or that both may be contemplated simultaneously? Or that each may be taken up in turn and considered apart from the other?"

Here form *is* content, content *is* form. You complain that this stuff is not written in English. It is not written at all. It is not to be read—or rather it is not only to be read. It is to be looked at and listened to. His writing is not *about* something; *it is that something itself.* (A fact that has been grasped by an eminent English novelist and his-

torian whose work is in complete opposition to Mr.
Joyce's.) When the sense is sleep, the words go to sleep.
(See the end of *Anna Livia*.) When the sense is dancing,
the words dance. Take the passage at the end of Shaun's
pastoral: "To stirr up love's young fizz I tilt with this bri-
dle's cup champagne, dimming douce from her peepair of
hide-seeks tight squeezed on my snowybreasted and while
my pearlies in their sparkling wisdom are nippling her
bubblets I swear (and let you swear) by the bumper round
of my poor old snaggletooth's solidbowel I ne'er will prove
I'm untrue to (theare!) you liking so long as my hole looks.
Down." The language is drunk. The very words are tilted
and effervescent. How can we qualify this general esthetic
vigilance without which we cannot hope to snare the sense
which is for ever rising to the surface of the form and becoming the form itself? St. Augustine puts us on the track
of a word with his *"intendere,"* Dante has: *"Donne
ch'avete intelletto d'amore,"* and *"Voi che, intendendo, il
terzo ciel movete";* but his *"intendere"* suggests a strictly
intellectual operation. When an Italian says to-day *"Ho
inteso,"* he means something between *"Ho udito"* and *"Ho
capito,"* a sensuous untidy art of intellection. Perhaps
"apprehension" is the most satisfactory English word.
Stephen says to Lynch: "Temporal or spatial, the esthetic
image is first luminously apprehended as selfbounded and
selfcontained upon the immeasurable background of space
or time which is not it. . . . You apprehend its whole-
ness." There is one point to make clear: the Beauty of
Work in Progress is not presented in space alone, since
its adequate apprehension depends as much on its visibility as on its audibility. There is a temporal as well as a
spatial unity to be apprehended. Substitute "and" for "or"
in the quotation, and it becomes obvious why it is as inadequate to speak of "reading" *Work in Progress* as it

would be extravagant to speak of "apprehending" the work
of the late Mr. Nat Gould. Mr. Joyce has desophisticated
language. And it is worth while remarking that no language is so sophisticated as English. It is abstracted to
death. Take the word "doubt": it gives us hardly any
sensuous suggestion of hesitancy, of the necessity for
choice, of static irresolution. Whereas the German "Zwei-
fel" does, and, in lesser degree, the Italian "dubitare." Mr.
Joyce recognises how inadequate "doubt" is to express a
state of extreme uncertainty, and replaces it by "in two-
some twiminds." Nor is he by any means the first to recognize the importance of treating words as something more
than mere polite symbols. Shakespeare uses fat, greasy
words to express corruption: "Duller shouldst thou be than
the fat weed that rots itself in death on Lethe wharf." We
hear the ooze squelching all through Dickens's description
of the Thames in *Great Expectations*. This writing that you
find so obscure is a quintessential extraction of language
and painting and gesture, with all the inevitable clarity of
the old inarticulation. Here is the savage economy of
hieroglyphics. Here words are not the polite contortions of
20th century printer's ink. They are alive. They elbow
their way on to the page, and glow and blaze and fade
and disappear. "Brawn is my name and broad is my nature
and I've breit on my brow and all's right with every fea-
ture and I'll brune this bird or Brown Bess's bung's gone
bandy." This is Brawn blowing with a light gust through
the trees or Brawn passing with the sunset. Because the
wind in the trees means as little to you as the evening
prospect from the Piazzale Michelangiolo—though you
accept them both because your non-acceptance would be
of no significance, this little adventure of Brawn means
nothing to you—and you do not accept it, even though
here also your non-acceptance is of no significance. H. C.

Earwigger, too, is not content to be mentioned like a
shilling-shocker villain, and then dropped until the exigencies of the narrative require that he be again referred
to. He continues to suggest himself for a couple of pages,
by means of repeated permutations on his "normative
letters," as if to say: "This is all about me, H. C. Earwigger: don't forget this is all about me!" This inner
elemental vitality and corruption of expression imparts a
furious restlessness to the form, which is admirably suited
to the purgatorial aspect of the work. There is an endless
verbal germination, maturation, putrefaction, the cyclic
dynamism of the intermediate. This reduction of various
expressive media to their primitive economic directness,
and the fusion of these primal essences into an assimilated
medium for the exteriorisation of thought, is pure Vico,
and Vico, applied to the problem of style. But Vico is
reflected more explicitly than by a distillation of disparate
poetic ingredients into a synthetical syrup. We notice
that there is little or no attempt at subjectivism or abstraction, no attempt at metaphysical generalisation. We are
presented with a statement of the particular. It is the old
myth: the girl on the dirt track, the two washerwomen on
the banks of the river. And there is considerable animism:
the mountain "abhearing," the river puffing her old doud-
heen. (See the beautiful passage beginning: "First she let
her hair fall and down it flussed.") We have Type-names:
Isolde—any beautiful girl: Earwigger—Guinness's Brewery,
the Wellington monument, the Phoenix Park, anything
that occupies an extremely comfortable position between
the two stools. Anna Livia herself, mother of Dublin, but
no more the only mother than Zoroaster was the only
oriental stargazer. "Teems of times and happy returns. The
same anew. Ordovico or viricordo. Anna was, Livia is,
Plurabelle's to be. Northmen's thing made Southfolk's

place, but howmultyplurators made eachone in person."
Basta! Vico and Bruno are here, and more substantially
than would appear from this swift survey of the question.
For the benefit of those who enjoy a parenthetical sneer,
we would draw attention to the fact that when Mr. Joyce's
early pamphlet *The Day of Rabblement* appeared, the
local philosophers were thrown into a state of some bewilderment by a reference in the first line to "The Nolan."
They finally succeeded in identifying this mysterious individual with one of the obscurer ancient Irish kings. In
the present work he appears frequently as "Browne &
Nolan," the name of a very remarkable Dublin Bookseller
and Stationer.

To justify our title, we must move North, *"Sovra'l
bel fiume d'Arno alla gran villa"* . . . Between *"colui per
lo cui verso—il meonio cantor non è più solo"* and the "still
to-day insufficiently malestimated notesnatcher, Shem the
Penman," there exists considerable circumstantial simi-
larity. They both saw how worn out and threadbare was
the conventional language of cunning literary artificers,
both rejected an approximation to a universal language.
If English is not yet so definitely a polite necessity as
Latin was in the Middle Ages, at least one is justified in
declaring that its position in relation to other European
languages is to a great extent that of mediaeval Latin to
the Italian dialects. Dante did not adopt the vulgar out of
any kind of local jingoism nor out of any determination to
assert the superiority to Tuscan to all its rivals as a form
of spoken Italian. On reading his *De Vulgari Eloquentia*
we are struck by his complete freedom from civic in-
tolerance. He attacks the world's Portadownians: *"Nam
quicumque tam obscenae rationis est, ut locum suae
nationis delitosissimm credat esse sub sole, huic etiam præ
cunctis propriam volgare licetur, idest maternam locu-*

tionem. Nos autem, cui mundus est patria . . . etc."
When he comes to examine the dialects he finds Tuscan:
*"turpissimum . . . fere omnes Tusci in suo turpiloquio
obtusi . . . non restat in dubio quin aliud sit vulgare
quod quaerimus quam quod attingit populus Tuscan-
orum."* His conclusion is that the corruption common to all
the dialects makes it impossible to select one rather than
another as an adequate literary form, and that he who
would write in the vulgar must assemble the purest
elements from each dialect and construct a synthetic
language that would at least possess more than a circum-
scribed local interest: which is precisely what he did. He
did not write in Florentine any more than in Neapolitan.
He wrote a vulgar that *could* have been spoken by an ideal
Italian who had assimilated what was best in all the
dialects of his country, but which in fact was certainly not
spoken nor ever had been. Which disposes of the capital
objection that might be made against this attractive
parallel between Dante and Mr. Joyce in the question of
language, i.e. that at least Dante wrote what was being
spoken in the streets of his own town, whereas no creature
in heaven or earth ever spoke the language of *Work in
Progress*. It is reasonable to admit that an international
phenomenon might be capable of speaking it, just as in
1300 none but an inter-regional phenomenon could have
spoken the language of the Divine Comedy. We are
inclined to forget that Dante's literary public was Latin,
that the form of his Poem was to be judged by Latin eyes
and ears, by a Latin Esthetic intolerant of innovation, and
which could hardly fail to be irritated by the substitution
of *"Nel mezzo del cammin di nostra vita"* with its "bar-
barous" directness for the suave elegance of: *"Ultima
regna canam, fluido contermina mundo,"* just as English
eyes and ears prefer: "Smoking his favourite pipe in the

sacred presence of ladies" to: "Rauking his flavourite turfco in the smukking precincts of lydias." Boccaccio did not jeer at the "*piedi sozzi*" of the peacock that Signora Alighieri dreamed about.

I find two well made caps in the "*Convivio,*" one to fit the collective noodle of the monodialectical arcadians whose fury is precipitated by a failure to discover "innoce-free" in the concise Oxford Dictionary and who qualify as the "ravings of a Bedlamite" the formal structure raised by Mr. Joyce after years of patient and inspired labour: "*Questi sono da chiamare pecore e non uomini; chè se una pecora si gittasse da una ripa di mille passi, tutte l'altre le adrebbono dietro; e se una pecore a per alcuna cagione al passare d'una strada salta, tutte le altre saltano, eziando nulla veggendo da saltare. E io ne vidi già molte in un pozzo saltare, per una che dentro vi salto, forse credendo di saltare un muro.*" And the other for Mr. Joyce, biologist in words: "*Questo* (formal innovation) *sarà luce nuova, sole nuovo, il quale sorgerà ore l'usato tramonterà e darà luce a coloro che sono in tenebre e in oscurità per lo usato sole che a loro non luce.*" And, lest he should pull it down over his eyes and laugh behind the peak, I translate "*in tenebre e in oscurità*" by "bored to extinction." (Dante makes a curious mistake speaking of the origin of language, when he rejects the authority of Genesis that Eve was the first to speak, when she addressed the Serpent. His incredulity is amusing: "*inconvenienter putatur tam egregium humani generis actum, vel prius quam a viro, foemina profluisse.*" But before Eve was born, "the animals were given names by Adam, the man who "first said goo to a goose." Moreover it is explicitly stated that the choice of names was left entirely to Adam, so that there is not the slightest Biblical authority for the conception of language as a direct gift of God, any more than there is any intellectual authority for conceiving that we are indebted for the "Concert" to the individual who used to buy paint for Giorgione.)

We know very little about the immediate reception accorded to Dante's mighty vindication of the "vulgar," but we can form our own opinions when, two centuries later, we find Castiglione splitting more than a few hairs concerning the respective advantages of Latin and Italian, and Poliziano writing the dullest of dull Latin Elegies to justify his existence as the author of "*Orfeo*" and the "*Stanze.*" We may also compare, if we think it worth while, the storm of ecclesiastical abuse raised by Mr. Joyce's work, and the treatment that the Divine Comedy must certainly have received from the same source. His Contemporary Holiness might have swallowed the crucifixion of "*lo sommo Giove,*" and all it stood for, but he could scarcely have looked with favour on the spectacle of three of his immediate predecessors plunged head-foremost in the fiery stone of Malebolge, nor yet the identification of the Papacy in the mystical procession of Terrestial Paradise with a "*puttana sciolta.*" The "*De Monarshia*" was burnt publicly under Pope Giovanni XXII at the instigation of Cardinal Beltrando and the bones of its author would have suffered the same fate but for the interference of an influential man of letters, Pino della Tosa. Another point of comparison is the preoccupation with the significance of numbers. The death of Beatrice inspired nothing less than a highly complicated poem dealing with the importance of the number 3 in her life. Dante never ceased to be obsessed by this number. Thus the poem is divided into three Cantiche, each composed of 33 Canti, and written in terza rima. Why, Mr. Joyce seems to say, should there be four legs to a table, and four to a horse, and four seasons and four Gospels and four Provinces in

Ireland? Why twelve Tables of the Law, and twelve
Apostles and twelve months and twelve Napoleonic mar-
shals and twelve men in Florence called Ottolenghi? Why
should the Armistice be celebrated at the eleventh hour of
the eleventh day of the eleventh month? He cannot tell
you because he is not God Almighty, but in a thousand
years he will tell you, and in the meantime must be content to know why horses have not five legs, nor three. He
is conscious that things with a common numerical characteristic tend towards a very significant interrelationship.
This preoccupation is freely translated in his present work,
see the "Question and Answer" chapter, and the Four
speaking through the child's brain. They are the four
winds as much as the four Provinces, and the four
Episcopal Sees as much as either.

A last word about the Purgatories. Dante's is conical
and consequently implies culmination. Mr. Joyce's is
spherical and excludes culmination. In the one there is an
ascent from real vegetation—Ante-Purgatory, to ideal
vegetation—Terrestial Paradise: in the other there is no
ascent and no ideal vegetation. In the one, absolute progression and a guaranteed consummation: in the other,
flux—progression or retrogression, and an apparent consummation. In the one movement is unidirectional, and a
step forward represents a net advance: in the other movement is non-directional—or multi-directional, and a step
forward is, by definition, a step back. Dante's Terrestial
Paradise is the carriage entrance to a Paradise that is not
terrestial: Mr. Joyce's Terrestial Paradise is the tradesmen's entrance on to the sea-shore. Sin is an impediment
to movement up the cone, and a condition of movement
round the sphere. In what sense, then, is Mr. Joyce's work
purgatorial? In the absolute absence of the Absolute. Hell
is the static lifelessness of unrelieved viciousness. Paradise

the static lifelessness of unrelieved immaculation. Purgatory a flood of movement and vitality released by the conjunction of these two elements. There is a continuous purgatorial process at work, in the sense that the vicious circle of humanity is being achieved, and this achievement depends on the recurrent predomination of one of two broad qualities. No resistance, no eruption, and it is only in Hell and Paradise that there are no eruptions, that there can be none, need be none. On this earth that is Purgatory, Vice and Virtue—which you may take to mean any pair of large contrary human factors—must in turn be purged down to spirits of rebelliousness. Then the dominant crust of the Vicious or Virtuous sets, resistance is provided, the explosion duly takes place and the machine proceeds. And no more than this; neither prize nor penalty; simply a series of stimulants to enable the kitten to catch its tail. And the partially purgatorial agent? The partially purged.

Part II

The Post-War Years
(1946–1960)

Fiction

First Love

This story emanates from that remarkable vintage year of 1946, which produced Beckett's first works written directly in French. The rich harvest included, in addition to "First Love," the stories "The Expelled," "The Calmative," and "The End," and the novel *Mercier and Camier*.

The stories, excepting "First Love," Beckett published in various literary magazines, first in French and later in translation. In 1955 he brought out, with Les Editions de Minuit, a volume containing these same three stories—"L'Expulsé" ("The Expelled"), "Le Calmant" ("The Calmative"), and "La Fin" ("The End")—and the thirteen "Textes pour rien" ("Texts for Nothing") written in 1950. Pointedly, "First Love" was omitted, and it was not until 1970 that Beckett consented to make this story public. In that year it was published in French; Beckett finally completed its translation into English in 1973; it appeared in 1974, almost thirty years after its composition.

Reading "First Love," one finds it hard to understand the author's reluctance, for it is marvelously funny and yet poignant, full of what Christopher Ricks in *The New Statesman* called "that bone-deep fatigue which gives Beckett's decrepit figures . . . their ruined strength, their rigor, not mortis, but of moribundity." And yet it stands apart from the other three stories, which have a unity of their own, and form a mini-trilogy, perhaps presaging the later, major trilogy of novels.

As Beckett moved from English to French, so he moved from a third-person to a first-person narrative, hero and narrator merging into one. Typically, the "first love" of the title is associated with death, for the memory is evoked by a visit by the narrator to his father's grave. Untypically—for most of Beckett's characters are past the climacteric—the hero

of "First Love" is a mere twenty-five, but he has, at least *in
posse*, all the attributes of those impossible, beloved tramps
who will soon people the rich canvases of Beckett's later
period.

I associate, rightly or wrongly, my marriage with the death of my father, in time. That other links exist, on other planes, between these two affairs, is not impossible. I have enough trouble as it is in trying to say what I think I know.

I visited, not so long ago, my father's grave, that I do know, and noted the date of his death, of his death alone, for that of his birth had no interest for me, on that particular day. I set out in the morning and was back by night, having lunched lightly in the graveyard. But some days later, wishing to know his age at death, I had to return to the grave, to note the date of his birth. These two limiting dates I then jotted down on a piece of paper, which I now carry about with me. I am thus in a position to affirm that I must have been about twenty-five at the time of my marriage. For the date of my own birth, I repeat, my own birth, I have never forgotten, I never had to note it down, it remains graven in my memory, the year at least, in figures that life will not easily erase. The day itself comes back to me, when I put my mind to it, and I often celebrate it, after my fashion, I don't say each time it comes back, for it comes back too often, but often.

Personally I have nothing against graveyards, I take the air there willingly, perhaps more willingly than elsewhere, when take the air I must. The smell of corpses, distinctly perceptible under those of grass and humus mingled, I do not find unpleasant, a trifle on the sweet side perhaps, a trifle heady, but how infinitely preferable to what the living emit, their feet, teeth, armpits, arses, sticky foreskins and frustrated ovules. And when my father's remains join in, however modestly, I can almost shed a tear. The living wash in vain, in vain perfume themselves, they stink. Yes, as a place for an outing, when out I must, leave me my grave-yards and keep—you—to your public parks and beauty-spots. My sandwich, my banana, taste sweeter when I'm sitting on a tomb, and when the time comes to piss again, as it so often does, I have my pick. Or I wander, hands clasped behind my back, among the slabs, the flat, the leaning and the upright, culling the inscriptions. Of these I never weary, there are always three or four of such drollery that I have to hold on to the cross, or the stele, or the angel, so as not to fall. Mine I composed long since and am still pleased with it, tolerably pleased. My other writings are no sooner dry than they revolt me, but my epitaph still meets with my ap-proval. There is little chance unfortunately of its ever being reared above the skull that conceived it, unless the State takes up the matter. But to be unearthed I must first be found, and I greatly fear those gentlemen will have as much trouble finding me dead as alive. So I hasten to record it here and now, while there is yet time:

Hereunder lies the above who up below
So hourly died that he survived till now.

The second and last or rather latter line limps a little per-haps, but that is no great matter, I'll be forgiven more than that when I'm forgotten. Then with a little luck you hit on a genuine interment, with real live mourners and the odd relict rearing to throw herself into the pit. And nearly always

that charming business with the dust, though in my experience there is nothing less dusty than holes of this type, verg-
ing on muck for the most part, nor anything particularly
powdery about the deceased, unless he happen to have died,
or she, by fire. No matter, their little gimmick with the dust
is charming. But my father's yard was not among my favourite. To begin with it was too remote, way out in the
wilds of the country on the side of a hill, and too small, far
too small, to go on with. Indeed it was almost full, a few
more widows and they'd be turning them away. I infinitely
preferred Ohlsdorf, particularly the Linne section, on Prus-
sian soil, with its nine hundred acres of corpses packed tight,
though I knew no one there, except by reputation the wild
animal collector Hagenbeck. A lion, if I remember right, is
carved on his monument, death must have had for Hagenbeck the countenance of a lion. Coaches ply to and fro,
crammed with widows, widowers, orphans and the like.
Groves, rottoes, artificial lakes with swans, purvey consolation to the inconsolable. It was December, I had never felt
so cold, the eel soup lay heavy on my stomach, I was afraid
I'd die, I turned aside to vomit, I envied them.

But to pass on to less melancholy matters, on my
father's death I had to leave the house. It was he who wanted
me in the house. He was a strange man. One day he said,
Leave him alone, he's not disturbing anyone. He didn't
know I was listening. This was a view he must have often
voiced, but the other times I wasn't by. They would never
let me see his will, they simply said he had left me such a
sum. I believed then, and still believe, that he had stipulated

in his will for me to be left the room I had occupied in his lifetime and for food to be brought me there, as hitherto. He may even have given this the force of condition precedent. Presumably he liked to feel me under his roof, otherwise he would not have opposed my eviction. Perhaps he merely pitied me. But somehow I think not. He should have left me the entire house, then I'd have been all right, the others too for that matter, I'd have summoned them and said, Stay, stay by all means, your home is here. Yes, he was properly had, my poor father, if his purpose was really to go on protecting me from beyond the tomb. With regard to the money it is only fair to say they gave it to me without delay, on the very day following the inhumation. Perhaps they were legally bound to. I said to them, Keep this money and let me live on here, in my room, as in Papa's lifetime. I added, God rest his soul, in the hope of melting them. But they refused. I offered to place myself at their disposal, a few hours every day, for the little odd maintenance jobs every dwelling requires, if it is not to crumble away. Pottering is still just possible, I don't know why. I proposed in particular to look after the hothouse. There I would have gladly whiled away the hours, in the heat, tending the tomatoes, hyacinths, pinks and seedlings. My father and I alone, in that household, understood tomatoes. But they refused. One day, on my return from stool, I found my room locked and my belongings in a heap before the door. This will give you some idea how constipated I was, at this juncture. It was, I am now convinced, anxiety constipation. But was I genuinely constipated? Somehow I think not. Softly, softly. And yet I must

have been, for how otherwise account for those long, those
cruel sessions in the necessary house? At such times I never
read, any more than at other times, never gave way to revery
or meditation, just gazed dully at the almanac hanging from
a nail before my eyes, with its chromo of a bearded stripling
in the midst of sheep, Jesus no doubt, parted the cheeks with
both hands and strained, heave! ho! heave! ho!, with the
motions of one tugging at the oar, and only one thought in
my mind, to be back in my room and flat on my back again.
What can that have been but constipation? Or am I confusing it with the diarrhoea? It's all a muddle in my head,
graves and nuptials and the different varieties of motion. Of
my scanty belongings they had made a little heap, on the
floor, against the door. I can still see that little heap, in the
kind of recess full of shadow between the landing and my
room. It was in this narrow space, guarded on three sides
only, that I had to change, I mean exchange my dressing-
gown and nightgown for my travelling costume, I mean
shoes, socks, trousers, shirt, coat, greatcoat and hat, I can
think of nothing else. I tried other doors, turning the knobs
and pushing, or pulling, before I left the house, but none
yielded. I think if I'd found one open I'd have barricaded
myself in the room, they would have had to gas me out. I
felt the house crammed as usual, the usual pack, but saw no
one. I imagined them in their various rooms, all bolts
drawn, every sense on the alert. Then the rush to the window, each holding back a little, hidden by the curtain, at the
sound of the street door closing behind me, I should have
left it open. Then the doors fly open and out they pour, men,

women and children, and the voices, the sighs, the smiles, the hands, the keys in the hands, the blessed relief, the precautions rehearsed, if this then that, but if that then this, all clear and joy in every heart, come let's eat, the fumigation can wait. All imagination to be sure, I was already on my way, things may have passed quite differently, but who cares how things pass, provided they pass. All those lips that had kissed me, those hearts that had loved me (it is with the heart one loves, is it not, or am I confusing it with something else?), those hands that had played with mine and those minds that had almost made their own of me! Humans are truly strange. Poor Papa, a nice mug he must have felt that day if he could see me, see us, a nice mug on my account I mean. Unless in his great disembodied wisdom he saw further than his son whose corpse was not yet quite up to scratch.

But to pass on to less melancholy matters, the name of the woman with whom I was soon to be united was Lulu. So at least she assured me and I can't see what interest she could have had in lying to me, on this score. Of course one can never tell. She also disclosed her family name, but I've forgotten it. I should have made a note of it, on a piece of paper, I hate forgetting a proper name. I met her on a bench, on the bank of the canal, one of the canals, for our town boasts two, though I never knew which was which. It was a well situated bench, backed by a mound of solid earth and garbage, so that my rear was covered. My flanks too, partially, thanks to a pair of venerable trees, more than venerable, dead, at either end of the bench. It was no doubt these

trees one fine day, aripple with all their foliage, that had
sown the idea of a bench, in someone's fancy. To the fore,
a few yards away, flowed the canal, if canals flow, don't ask
me, so that from that quarter too the risk of surprise was
small. And yet she surprised me. I lay stretched out, the
night being warm, gazing up through the bare boughs inter-
locking high above me, where the trees clung together for
support, and through the drifting cloud, at a patch of starry
sky as it came and went. Shove up, she said. My first movement was to go, but my fatigue, and my having nowhere to
go, dissuaded me from acting on it. So I drew back my feet
a little way and she sat. Nothing more passed between us
that evening and she soon took herself off, without another
word. All she had done was sing, *sotto voce,* as to herself,
and without the words fortunately, some old folk songs, and
so disjointedly, skipping from one to another and finishing
none, that even I found it strange. The voice, though out of
tune, was not unpleasant. It breathed of a soul too soon
wearied ever to conclude, that perhaps least arse-aching soul
of all. The bench itself was soon more than she could bear
and as for me, one look had been enough for her. Whereas
in reality she was a most tenacious woman. She came back
next day and the day after and all went off more or less as
before. Perhaps a few words were exchanged. The next day
it was raining and I felt in security. Wrong again. I asked
her if she was resolved to disturb me every evening. I disturb
you? she said. I felt her eyes on me. They can't have seen
much, two eyelids at the most, with a hint of nose and brow,
darkly, because of the dark. I thought we were easy, she

said. You disturb me, I said, I can't stretch out with you there. The collar of my greatcoat was over my mouth and yet she heard me. Must you stretch out? she said. The mistake one makes is to speak to people. You have only to put your feet on my knees, she said. I didn't wait to be asked twice, under my miserable calves I felt her fat thighs. She began stroking my ankles. I considered kicking her in the cunt. You speak to people about stretching out and they immediately see a body at full length. What mattered to me in my dispeopled kingdom, that in regard to which the disposition of my carcass was the merest and most futile of accidents, was supineness in the mind, the dulling of the self and of that residue of execrable frippery known as the non-self and even the world, for short. But man is still today, at the age of twenty-five, at the mercy of an erection, physically too, from time to time, it's the common lot, even I was not immune, if that may be called an erection. It did not escape her naturally, women smell a rigid phallus ten miles away and wonder, How on earth did he spot me from there? One is no longer oneself, on such occasions, and it is painful to be no longer oneself, even more painful if possible than when one is. For when one is one knows what to do to be less so, whereas when one is not one is any old one irredeemably. What goes by the name of love is banishment, with now and then a postcard from the homeland, such is my considered opinion, this evening. When she had finished and my self been resumed, mine own, the mitigable, with the help of a brief torpor, it was alone. I sometimes wonder if that is not all invention, if in reality things did not take quite a different course, one I had no choice but to forget. And yet her image remains bound, for me, to that of the bench, not the bench by day, nor yet the bench by night, but the bench at evening, in such sort that to speak of the bench, as it appeared to me at evening, is to speak of her, for me. That proves nothing, but there is nothing I wish to prove. On the subject of the bench by day no words need be wasted, it never knew me, gone before morning and never back till dusk. Yes, in the daytime I foraged for food and marked down likely cover. Were you to inquire, as undoubtedly you itch, what I had done with the money my father had left me, the answer would be I had done nothing with it but leave it lie in my pocket. For I knew I would not be always young, and that summer does not last for ever either, nor even autumn, my mean soul told me so. In the end I told her I'd had enough. She disturbed me exceedingly, even absent. Indeed she still disturbs me, but no worse now than the rest. And it matters nothing to me now, to be disturbed, or so little, what does it mean, disturbed, and what would I do with myself if I wasn't? Yes, I've changed my system, it's the winning one at last, for the ninth or tenth time, not to mention not long now, not long till curtain down, on disturbers and disturbed, no more tattle about that, all that, her and the others, the shitball and heaven's high halls. So you don't want me to come any more, she said. It's incredible the way they repeat what you've just said to them, as if they risked faggot and fire in believing their ears. I told her to come just the odd time. I didn't understand women at that period. I still don't for that matter. Nor men either. Nor animals either. What I understand best, which is not saying much, are my pains. I think them through daily, it doesn't take long, thought moves so fast, but they are not only in my thought, not all. Yes, there are moments, particularly in the afternoon, when I go all syncretist, à la Reinhold. What equilibrium! But even them, my pains, I understand ill. That must come from my not being all pain and nothing else. There's the rub. Then they recede, or I, till they fill me with amaze and wonder, seen from a better planet. Not often, but I ask no more. Catch-cony life! To be nothing but pain, how that would simplify matters! Omnidolent! Impious dream. I'll tell them to you some day none the less, if I think of it, if I can, my strange pains, in detail, distinguishing between the different kinds, for the sake of clarity, those of the mind, those of the heart or emotional conative, those of the soul (none prettier than these) and finally those of the frame proper, first the inner or latent, then those affecting the surface, beginning with the hair and scalp and moving methodically down, without haste, all the way down to the feet beloved of the corn, the cramp, the kibe, the bunion, the hammer toe, the nail ingrown, the fallen arch, the common blain, the club foot, duck foot, goose foot, pigeon foot, flat foot, trench foot and other curiosities. And I'll tell by the same token, for those kind enough to listen, in accordance with a system whose inventor I forget, of those instants when, neither drugged, nor drunk, nor in ecstasy, one feels nothing. Next of course she desired to know what I meant by the odd time, that's what you get for opening your mouth. Once a week? Once in ten days? Once a fortnight? I replied

less often, far less often, less often to the point of no more
if she could, and if she could not the least often possible.
And the next day (what is more) I abandoned the bench,
less I must confess on her account than on its, for the site
no longer answered my requirements, modest though they
were, now that the air was beginning to strike chill, and for
other reasons better not wasted on cunts like you, and took
refuge in a deserted cowshed marked on one of my forays.
It stood in the corner of a field richer on the surface in nettles than in grass and in mud than in nettles, but whose sub-
soil was perhaps possessed of exceptional qualities. It was
in this byre, littered with dry and hollow cowclaps subsiding
with a sigh at the poke of my finger, that for the first time in
my life, and I would not hesitate to say the last if I had not
to husband my cyanide, I had to contend with a feeling
which gradually assumed, to my dismay, the dread name of
love. What constitutes the charm of our country, apart of
course from its scant population, and this without help of
the meanest contraceptive, is that all is derelict, with the sole
exception of history's ancient faeces. These are ardently
sought after, stuffed and carried in procession. Wherever
nauseated time has dropped a nice fat turd you will find our
patriots, sniffing it up on all fours, their faces on fire. Ely-
sium of the roofless. Hence my happiness at last. Lie down,
all seems to say, lie down and stay down. I see no connexion
between these remarks. But that one exists, and even more
than one, I have little doubt, for my part. But what? Which?
Yes, I loved her, it's the name I gave, still give alas, to what
I was doing then. I had nothing to go by, having never loved

before, but of course had heard of the thing, at home, in school, in brothel and at church, and read romances, in prose and verse, under the guidance of my tutor, in six or seven languages, both dead and living, in which it was handled at length. I was therefore in a position, in spite of all, to put a label on what I was about when I found myself inscribing the letters of Lulu in an old heifer pat or flat on my face in the mud under the moon trying to tear up the nettles by the roots. They were giant nettles, some full three foot high, to tear them up assuaged my pain, and yet it's not like me to do that to weeds, on the contrary, I'd smother them in manure if I had any. Flowers are a different matter. Love brings out the worst in man and no error. But what kind of love was this, exactly? Love-passion? Somehow I think not. That's the priapic one, is it not? Or is this a different variety? There are so many, are there not? All equally if not more delicious, are they not? Platonic love, for example, there's another just occurs to me. It's disinterested. Perhaps I loved her with a platonic love? But somehow I think not. Would I have been tracing her name in old cowshit if my love had been pure and disinterested? And with my devil's finger into the bargain, which I then sucked. Come now! My thoughts were all of Lulu, if that doesn't give you some idea nothing will. Anyhow I'm sick and tired of this name Lulu, I'll give her another, more like her, Anna for example, it's not more like her but no matter. I thought of Anna then, I who had learnt to think of nothing, nothing except my pains, a quick think through, and of what steps to take not to perish off-hand of hunger, or cold, or shame,

but never on any account of living beings as such (I wonder what that means) whatever I may have said, or may still
say, to the contrary or otherwise, on this subject. But I have
always spoken, no doubt always shall, of things that never
existed, or that existed if you insist, no doubt always will,
but not with the existence I ascribe to them. Kepis, for example, exist beyond a doubt, indeed there is little hope of
their ever disappearing, but personally I never wore a kepi. I
wrote somewhere, They gave me . . . a hat. Now the truth
is they never gave me a hat, I have always had my own hat,
the one my father gave me, and I have never had any other
hat than that hat. I may add it has followed me to the grave.
I thought of Anna then, long long sessions, twenty minutes,
twenty-five minutes and even as long as half an hour daily.
I obtain these figures by the addition of other, lesser figures.
That must have been my way of loving. Are we to infer
from this I loved her with that intellectual love which drew
from me such drivel, in another place? Somehow I think
not. For had my love been of this kind would I have stooped
to inscribe the letters of Anna in time's forgotten cowplats?
To divellicate urtica *plenis manibus?* And felt, under my
tossing head, her thighs to bounce like so many demon
bolsters? Come now! In order to put an end, to try and put
an end, to this plight, I returned one evening to the bench,
at the hour she had used to join me there. There was no sign
of her and I waited in vain. It was December already, if not
January, and the cold was seasonable, that is to say reasonable, like all that is seasonable. But one is the hour of the
dial, and another that of changing air and sky, and another

yet again the heart's. To this thought, once back in the straw, I owed an excellent night. The next day I was earlier to the bench, much earlier, night having barely fallen, winter night, and yet too late, for she was there already, on the bench, under the boughs tinkling with rime, her back to the frosted mound, facing the icy water. I told you she was a highly tenacious woman. I felt nothing. What interest could she have in pursuing me thus? I asked her, without sitting down, stumping to and fro. The cold had embossed the path. She replied she didn't know. What could she see in me, would she kindly tell me that at least, if she could. She replied she couldn't. She seemed warmly clad, her hands buried in a muff. As I looked at this muff, I remember, tears came to my eyes. And yet I forget what colour it was. The state I was in then! I have always wept freely, without the least benefit to myself, till recently. If I had to weep this minute I could squeeze till I was blue, I'm convinced not a drop would fall. The state I am in now! It was things made me weep. And yet I felt no sorrow. When I found myself in tears for no apparent reason it meant I had caught sight of something unbeknownst. So I wonder if it was really the muff that evening, if it was not rather the path, so iron hard and bossy as perhaps to feel like cobbles to my tread, or some other thing, some chance thing glimpsed below the threshold, that so unmanned me. As for her, I might as well never have laid eyes on her before. She sat all huddled and muffled up, her head sunk, the muff with her hands in her lap, her legs pressed tight together, her heels clear of the ground. Shapeless, ageless, almost lifeless, it might have been anything or anyone, an old woman or a little girl. And the way she kept on saying, I don't know, I can't. I alone did not know and could not. Is it on my account you came? I said. She managed yes to that. Well here I am, I said. And I? Had I not come on hers? Here we are, I said. I sat down beside her but sprang up again immediately as though scalded. I longed to be gone, to know if it was over. But before going, to be on the safe side, I asked her to sing me a song. I thought at first she was going to refuse, I mean simply not sing, but no, after a moment she began to sing and sang for some time, all the time the same song it seemed to me, without change of attitude. I did not know the song, I had never heard it before and shall never hear it again. It had something to do with lemon trees, or orange trees, I forget, that is all I remember, and for me that is no mean feat, to remember it had something to do with lemon trees, or orange trees, I forget, for of all the other songs I have ever heard in my life, and I have heard plenty, it being apparently impossible, physically impossible short of being deaf, to get through this world, even my way, without hearing singing, I have retained nothing, not a word, not a note, or so few words, so few notes, that, that what, that nothing, this sentence has gone on long enough. Then I started to go and as I went I heard her singing another song, or perhaps more verses of the same, fainter and fainter the further I went, then no more, either because she had come to an end or because I was gone too far to hear her. To have to harbour such a doubt was something I preferred to avoid, at that period. I lived of course in doubt, on doubt, but such trivial doubts as

this, purely somatic as some say, were best cleared up without delay, they could nag at me like gnats for weeks on end.
So I retraced my steps a little way and stopped. At first I
heard nothing, then the voice again, but only just, so faintly
did it carry. First I didn't hear it, then I did, I must therefore have begun hearing it, at a certain point, but no, there
was no beginning, the sound emerged so softly from the
silence and so resembled it. When the voice ceased at last
I approached a little nearer, to make sure it had really
ceased and not merely been lowered. Then in despair, saying, No knowing, no knowing, short of being beside her,
bent over her, I turned on my heel and went, for good, full
of doubt. But some weeks later, even more dead than alive
than usual, I returned to the bench, for the fourth or fifth
time since I had abandoned it, at roughly the same hour, I
mean roughly the same sky, no, I don't mean that either, for
it's always the same sky and never the same sky, what words
are there for that, none I know, period. She wasn't there,
then suddenly she was, I don't know how, I didn't see her
come, nor hear her, all ears and eyes though I was. Let us
say it was raining, nothing like a change, if only of weather.
She had her umbrella up, naturally, what an outfit. I asked
if she came every evening. No, she said, just the odd time.
The bench was soaking wet, we paced up and down, not
daring to sit. I took her arm, out of curiosity, to see if it
would give me pleasure, it gave me none, I let it go. But why
these particulars? To put off the evil hour. I saw her face a
little clearer, it seemed normal to me, a face like millions of
others. The eyes were crooked, but I didn't know that till

later. It looked neither young nor old, the face, as though
stranded between the vernal and the sere. Such ambiguity I
found difficult to bear, at that period. As to whether it was
beautiful, the face, or had once been beautiful, or could conceivably become beautiful, I confess I could form no opinion. I had seen faces in photographs I might have found
beautiful had I known even vaguely in what beauty was supposed to consist. And my father's face, on his death-bolster,
had seemed to hint at some form of aesthetics relevant to
man. But the faces of the living, all grimace and flush, can
they be described as objects? I admired in spite of the dark,
in spite of my fluster, the way still or scarcely flowing water
reaches up, as though athirst, to that falling from the sky.
She asked if I would like her to sing something. I replied no,
I would like her to say something. I thought she would say
she had nothing to say, it would have been like her, and so
was agreeably surprised when she said she had a room, most
agreeably surprised, though I suspected as much. Who has
not a room? Ah I hear the clamour. I have two rooms, she
said. Just how many rooms do you have? I said. She said
she had two rooms and a kitchen. The premises were ex-
panding steadily, given time she would remember a bath-
room. Is it two rooms I heard you say? I said. Yes, she
said. Adjacent? I said. At last conversation worthy of the
name. Separated by the kitchen, she said. I asked her why
she had not told me before. I must have been beside myself,
at this period. I did not feel easy when I was with her, but
at least free to think of something else than her, of the old
trusty things, and so little by little, as down steps towards a

deep, of nothing. And I knew that away from her I would
forfeit this freedom.

There were in fact two rooms, separated by a kitchen,
she had not lied to me. She said I should have fetched my
things. I explained I had no things. It was at the top of an
old house, with a view of the mountains for those who cared.
She lit an oil-lamp. You have no current? I said. No, she
said, but I have running water and gas. Ha, I said, you have
gas. She began to undress. When at their wit's end they undress, no doubt the wisest course. She took off everything,
with a slowness fit to enflame an elephant, except her stock-
ings, calculated presumably to bring my concupiscence to
the boil. It was then I noticed the squint. Fortunately she
was not the first naked woman to have crossed my path, so I
could stay, I knew she would not explode. I asked to see the
other room which I had not yet seen. If I had seen it already
I would have asked to see it again. Will you not undress?
she said. Oh you know, I said, I seldom undress. It was the
truth, I was never one to undress indiscriminately. I often
took off my boots when I went to bed, I mean when I composed myself (composed!) to sleep, not to mention this or
that outer garment according to the outer temperature. She
was therefore obliged, out of common savoir faire, to
throw on a wrap and light me the way. We went via the
kitchen. We could just as well have gone via the corridor, as
I realized later, but we went via the kitchen, I don't know
why, perhaps it was the shortest way. I surveyed the room
with horror. Such density of furniture defeats imagination.
Not a doubt, I must have seen that room somewhere. What's

this? I cried. The parlour, she said. The parlour! I began
putting out the furniture through the door to the corridor.
She watched, in sorrow I suppose, but not necessarily. She
asked me what I was doing. She can't have expected an
answer. I put it out piece by piece, and even two at a time,
and stacked it all up in the corridor, against the outer wall.
They were hundreds of pieces, large and small, in the end
they blocked the door, making egress impossible, and *a
fortiori* ingress, to and from the corridor. The door could be
opened and closed, since it opened inwards, but had become
impassable. To put it wildly. At least take off your hat, she
said. I'll treat of my hat some other time perhaps. Finally
the room was empty but for a sofa and some shelves fixed
to the wall. The former I dragged to the back of the room,
near the door, and next day took down the latter and put
them out, in the corridor, with the rest. As I was taking
them down, strange memory, I heard the word fibrome, or
brone, I don't know which, never knew, never knew what it
meant and never had the curiosity to find out. The things
one recalls! And records! When all was in order at last I
dropped on the sofa. She had not raised her little finger to
help me. I'll get sheets and blankets, she said. But I wouldn't
hear of sheets. You couldn't draw the curtain? I said. The
window was frosted over. The effect was not white, because
of the night, but faintly luminous none the less. This faint
cold sheen, though I lay with my feet towards the door, was
more than I could bear. I suddenly rose and changed the
position of the sofa, that is to say turned it round so that
the back, hitherto against the wall, was now on the outside

and consequently the front, or way in, on the inside. Then
I climbed back, like a dog into its basket. I'll leave you the
lamp, she said, but I begged her to take it with her. And
suppose you need something in the night, she said. She was
going to start quibbling again, I could feel it. Do you know
where the convenience is? she said. She was right, I was forgetting. To relieve oneself in bed is enjoyable at the time,
but soon a source of discomfort. Give me a chamber-pot, I
said. But she did not possess one. I have a close-stool of
sorts, she said. I saw the grandmother on it, sitting up very
stiff and grand, having just purchased it, pardon, picked it
up, at a charity sale, or perhaps won it in a raffle, a period
piece, and now trying it out, doing her best rather, almost
wishing someone could see her. That's the idea, procrasti-
nate. Any old recipient, I said, I don't have the flux. She
came back with a kind of saucepan, not a true saucepan for
it had no handle, it was oval in shape with two lugs and a
lid. My stewpan, she said. I don't need the lid, I said. You
don't need the lid? she said. If I had said I needed the lid
she would have said, You need the lid? I drew this utensil
down under the blanket, I like something in my hand when
sleeping, it reassures me, and my hat was still wringing. I
turned to the wall. She caught up the lamp off the mantelpiece where she had set it down, that's the idea, every particular, it flung her waving shadow over me, I thought she
was off, but no, she came stooping down towards me over
the sofa back. All family possessions, she said. I in her shoes
would have tiptoed away, but not she, not a stir. Already
my love was waning, that was all that mattered. Yes, already

I felt better, soon I'd be up to the slow descents again, the long submersions, so long denied me through her fault. And I had only just moved in! Try and put me out now, I said. I seemed not to grasp the meaning of these words, nor even hear the brief sound they made, till some seconds after having uttered them. I was so unused to speech that my mouth would sometimes open, of its own accord, and void some phrase or phrases, grammatically unexceptionable but entirely devoid if not of meaning, for on close inspection they would reveal one, and even several, at least of foundation. But I heard each word no sooner spoken. Never had my voice taken so long to reach me as on this occasion. I turned over on my back to see what was going on. She was smiling. A little later she went away, taking the lamp with her. I heard her steps in the kitchen and then the door of her room close behind her. Why behind her? I was alone at last, in the dark at last. Enough about that. I thought I was all set for a good night, in spite of the strange surroundings, but no, my night was most agitated. I woke next morning quite spent, my clothes in disorder, the blanket likewise, and Anna beside me, naked naturally. One shudders to think of her exertions. I still had the stewpan in my grasp. It had not served. I looked at my member. If only it could have spoken! Enough about that. It was my night of love.

Gradually I settled down, in this house. She brought my meals at the appointed hours, looked in now and then to see if all was well and make sure I needed nothing, emptied the stewpan once a day and did out the room once a month. She could not always resist the temptation to speak to me, but on the whole gave me no cause to complain. Sometimes I heard her singing in her room, the song traversed her door, then the kitchen, then my door, and in this way won to me, faint but indisputable. Unless it travelled by the corridor. This did not greatly incommode me, this occasional sound of singing. One day I asked her to bring me a hyacinth, live, in a pot. She brought it and put it on the mantelpiece, now the only place in my room to put things, unless you put them on the floor. Not a day passed without my looking at it. At first all went well, it even put forth a bloom or two, then it gave up and was soon no more than a limp stem hung with limp leaves. The bulb, half clear of the clay as though in search of oxygen, smelt foul. She wanted to remove it, but I told her to leave it. She wanted to get me another, but I told her I didn't want another. I was more seriously disturbed by other sounds, stifled giggles and groans, which filled the dwelling at certain hours of the night, and even of the day. I had given up thinking of her, quite given up, but still I needed silence, to live my life. In vain I tried to listen to such reasonings as that air is made to carry the clamours of the world, including inevitably much groan and giggle, I obtained no relief. I couldn't make out if it was always the same gent or more than one. Lovers' groans are so alike, and lovers' giggles. I had such horror then of these paltry perplexities that I always fell into the same error, that of seeking to clear them up. It took me a long time, my lifetime so to speak, to realize that the colour of an eye half seen, or the source of some distant sound, are closer to Giudecca in the hell of unknowing than the exist-

ence of God, or the origins of protoplasm, or the existence
of self, and even less worthy than these to occupy the wise.
It's a bit much, a lifetime, to achieve this consoling conclusion, it doesn't leave you much time to profit by it. So a fat
lot of help it was when, having put the question to her, I was
told they were clients she received in rotation. I could obviously have got up and gone to look through the keyhole.
But what can you see, I ask you, through holes the likes of
those? So you live by prostitution, I said. We live by prostitution, she said. You couldn't ask them to make less noise? I
said, as if I believed her. I added, Or a different kind of
noise. They can't help but yap and yelp, she said. I'll have to
leave, I said. She found some old hangings in the family
junk and hung them before our doors, hers and mine. I
asked her if it would not be possible, now and then, to have
a parsnip. A parsnip! she cried, as if I had asked for a dish
of sucking Jew. I reminded her that the parsnip season was
fast drawing to a close and that if, before it finally got there,
she could feed me nothing but parsnips I'd be grateful. I
like parsnips because they taste like violets and violets
because they smell like parsnips. Were there no parsnips on
earth violets would leave me cold and if violets did not exist
I would care as little for parsnips as I do for turnips, or
radishes. And even in the present state of their flora, I mean
on this planet where parsnips and violets contrive to coexist,
I could do without both with the utmost ease, the uttermost
ease. One day she had the impudence to announce she was
with child, and four or five months gone into the bargain,
by me of all people! She offered me a side view of her belly.

She even undressed, no doubt to prove she wasn't hiding a cushion under her skirt, and then of course for the pure pleasure of undressing. Perhaps it's mere wind, I said, by way of consolation. She gazed at me with her big eyes whose colour I forget, with one big eye rather, for the other seemed riveted on the remains of the hyacinth. The more naked she was the more cross-eyed. Look, she said, stooping over her breasts, the haloes are darkening already. I summoned up my remaining strength and said, Abort, abort, and they'll blush like new. She had drawn back the curtain for a clear view of all her rotundities. I saw the mountain, impassible, cavernous, secret, where from morning to night I'd hear nothing but the wind, the curlews, the clink like distant silver of the stone-cutters' hammers. I'd come out in the daytime to the heather and gorse, all warmth and scent, and watch at night the distant city lights, if I chose, and the other lights, the lighthouses and lightships my father had named for me, when I was small, and whose names I could find again, in my memory, if I chose, that I knew. From that day forth things went from bad to worse, to worse and worse. Not that she neglected me, she could never have neglected me enough, but the way she kept plaguing me with *our* child, exhibiting her belly and breasts and saying it was due any moment, she could feel it lepping already. If it's lepping, I said, it's not mine. I might have been worse off than I was, in that house, that was certain, it fell short of my ideal naturally, but I wasn't blind to its advantages. I hesitated to leave, the leaves were falling already, I dreaded the winter. One should not dread the winter, it too has its

bounties, the snow gives warmth and deadens the tumult
and its pale days are soon over. But I did not yet know, at
that time, how tender the earth can be for those who have
only her and how many graves in her giving, for the living.
What finished me was the birth. It woke me up. What that
infant must have been going through! I fancy she had a
woman with her, I seemed to hear steps in the kitchen, on
and off. It went to my heart to leave a house without being
put out. I crept out over the back of the sofa, put on my
coat, greatcoat and hat, I can think of nothing else, laced
up my boots and opened the door to the corridor. A mass of
junk barred my way, but I scrabbled and barged my way
through it in the end, regardless of the clatter. I used the
word marriage, it was a kind of union in spite of all. Precautions would have been superfluous, there was no com-
peting with those cries. It must have been her first. They
pursued me down the stairs and out into the street. I stopped
before the house door and listened. I could still hear them.
If I had not known there was crying in the house I might
not have heard them. But knowing it I did. I was not sure
where I was. I looked among the stars and constellations for
the Wains, but could not find them. And yet they must have
been there. My father was the first to show them to me. He
had shown me others, but alone, without him beside me, I
could never find any but the Wains. I began playing with
the cries, a little in the same way as I had played with the
song, on, back, on, back, if that may be called playing. As
long as I kept walking I didn't hear them, because of the
footsteps. But as soon as I halted I heard them again, a little

fainter each time, admittedly, but what does it matter, faint
or loud, cry is cry, all that matters is that it should cease. For
years I thought they would cease. Now I don't think so any
more. I could have done with other loves perhaps. But there
it is, either you love or you don't.

From
Mercier and Camier

This, Beckett's first novel written directly in French, was composed between July and September of 1946. Its full title, originally, was *Le Voyage de Mercier et Camier autour du pot dans les bosquets de Bondy*, about which a few words seem necessary. In French, *tourner autour du pot* means "to beat around the bush," or "not come to the point," which is a pretty fair description of what happens, or does not happen, in the novel. The "Bondy" of the title refers to a village not far from Paris famous, in times past, for being infested with highwaymen. Thus, roughly translated, the full title, in English, might be: *The Pointless Voyage of Mercier and Camier into the Den of Thieves*. Or, rather, might have been, for Beckett, when finally he consented to publication, shortened it to the present title.

The novel opens with a narrator's comment: "The journey of Mercier and Camier is one I can tell, if I will, for I was with them all the time." That is the last we hear of the narrator, who apparently does "will," for the voyage proceeds apace. About the voyagers we learn very little, except that Mercier is tall and gaunt, Camier short and fat (the music-hall pair incarnate); Mercier grizzled and gray-eyed, Camier red-faced; Mercier a family man, Camier some kind of detective ("F. X. Camier, Private Investigator, Soul of Discretion," his card reads). As for the purpose of the voyage, or the reason behind it, we know only that they have undertaken it after years of evasion and procrastination, "driven by a need now clear and now obscure."

Reviewing the book for the *London Observer*, A. Alvarez described it thus:

> The two heroes meet and, after much hesitation, set off on a vague journey which only twice manages to get them briefly clear of town. They spend a good deal of time in bars and with a friendly prostitute

called Helen. They kill a policeman. They curse God
and their various ailments and indulge in a little metaphysics. Finally, they drift apart and are brought together again at the close by Watt, making a useful
guest appearance.

All of which goes to show how pointless it is ever to
summarize the plot of any Beckett novel, for it is the method,
the style, the high humor and low comedy, the fusion of
form and content that turn the commonplace into art. A. Alvarez goes on to say that it is "funnier than any of his other
novels," an opinion I do not necessarily share, but it is
surely high on the list. More important—and I suspect this
is why Beckett hesitated for almost twenty-five years to allow
it in print—it can be thought of as a bridge to *Waiting for
Godot*. Certainly no earlier work of Beckett's fiction is so
replete with the brisk exchanges of dialogue that constantly
occur between Mercier and Camier, prefiguring by several
years those to come between Didi and Gogo. A number of
critics, notably John Fletcher and Colin Duckworth, have
demonstrated convincingly the debt of the play to this earlier
novel, in case anyone needs convincing.

If in the dialogue, the situations, and the music-hall rou-
tines and accoutrements, Beckett had clearly moved into new
territory, it is now clear—in retrospect—that at this juncture
he needed a new form. Still immersed in the novel form, he
was using more and more frequently methods and techniques
that required dramatic presentation. Until the appearance of
Mercier and Camier in French in 1970, and four years later
in English, Beckett's movement into drama in the early
fifties seemed somehow abrupt and unexplainable. Reading
this novel, we can see clearly that he was heading, almost
ineluctably, for the theater. By the time he arrived there, he
had already prepared himself, not only through *Mercier
and Camier* but also the jettisoned 1947 play, *Eleuthéria*, for
that form which he would make so quickly and compellingly
his own: the drama.

1

The journey of Mercier and Camier is one I can tell, if I will, for I was with them all the time.

Physically it was fairly easy going, without seas or frontiers to be crossed, through regions untormented on the whole, if desolate in parts. Mercier and Camier did not remove from home, they had that great good fortune. They did not have to face, with greater or less success, outlandish ways, tongues, laws, skies, foods, in surroundings little resembling those to which first childhood, then boyhood, then manhood had inured them. The weather, though often inclement (but they knew no better), never exceeded the limits of the temperate, that is to say of what could still be borne, without danger if not without discomfort, by the average native fittingly clad and shod. With regard to money, if it did not run to first class transport or the palatial hotel, still there was enough to keep them going, to and fro, without recourse to alms. It may be said therefore that in this respect too they were fortunate, up to a point. They had to struggle, but less than many must, less perhaps than most of those who venture forth, driven by a need now clear and now obscure.

They had consulted together at length, before embarking

on this journey, weighing with all the calm at their command what benefits they might hope from it, what ills apprehend, maintaining turn about the dark side and the rosy. The only certitude they gained from these debates was that of not lightly launching out, into the unknown.

Camier was first to arrive at the appointed place. That is to say that on his arrival Mercier was not there. In reality Mercier had forestalled him by a good ten minutes. Not Camier then, but Mercier, was first to arrive. He possessed himself in patience for five minutes, with his eye on the various avenues of approach open to his friend, then set out for a saunter destined to last full fifteen minutes. Meantime Camier, five minutes having passed without sight or sign of Mercier, took himself off in his turn for a little stroll. On his return to the place, fifteen minutes later, it was in vain he cast about him, and understandably so. For Mercier, after cooling his heels for a further five minutes, had wandered off again for what he pleased to call a little stretch. Camier hung around for five more minutes, then again departed, saying to himself, Perhaps I'll run into him in the street. It was at this moment that Mercier, back from his breather, which as chance this time would have it had not exceeded ten minutes, glimpsed receding in the morning mist a shape suggestive of Camier's and which was indeed none other. Unhappily it vanished as though swallowed up by the cobbles, leaving Mercier to resume his vigil. But on expiry of what is beginning to look like the regulation five minutes he abandoned it again, feeling the need of a little motion. Their joy was thus for an instant unbounded, Mercier's joy and Camier's joy,

when after five and ten minutes respectively of uneasy
prowl, debouching simultaneously on the square, they
found themselves face to face for the first time since the
evening before. The time was nine fifty in the morning.
In other words:

Arr.	Dep.	Arr.	Dep.	Arr.	Dep.	Arr.
Mercier . 9.05	9.10	9.25	9.30	9.40	9.45	9.50
Camier . 9.15	9.20	9.35	9.40	9.50		

What stink of artifice.

They were still in each other's arms when the rain
began to fall, with quite oriental abruptness. They made
therefore with all speed to the shelter which, in the
form of a pagoda, had been erected here as protection
from the rain and other inclemencies, in a word from
the weather. Shadowy and abounding in nooks and
crannies it was a friend to lovers also and to the aged of
either sex. Into this refuge, at the same instant as our
heroes, bounded a dog, followed shortly by a second.
Mercier and Camier, irresolute, exchanged a look. They
had not finished in each other's arms and yet felt awkward about resuming. The dogs for their part were
already copulating, with the utmost naturalness.

The place where they now found themselves, where
they had agreed, not without pains, that they should
meet, was not properly speaking a square, but rather a
small public garden at the heart of a tangle of streets and
lanes. It displayed the usual shrubberies, flower-beds,
pools, fountains, statues, lawns and benches in strangu-
lating profusion. It had something of the maze, irksome
to perambulate, difficult of egress, for one not in its
secrets. Entry was of course the simplest thing in the

world. In the centre, roughly, towered huge a shining
copper beech, planted several centuries earlier, according to the sign rudely nailed to the bole, by a Field
Marshal of France peacefully named Saint-Ruth. Hardly
had he done so, in the words of the inscription, when he
was struck dead by a cannon-ball, faithful to the last to
the same hopeless cause, on a battlefield having little in
common, from the point of view of landscape, with
those on which he had won his spurs, first as brigadier,
then as lieutenant, if that is the order in which spurs are
won, on the battlefield. It was no doubt to this tree that
the garden owed its existence, a consequence which can
scarcely have occurred to the Field Marshal as on that
distant day, well clear of the quincunxes, before an
elegant and replete assistance, he held the frail sapling
upright in the hole gorged with evening dew. But to
have done with this tree and hear no more about it,
from it the garden derived what little charm it still
possessed, not to mention of course its name. The
stifled giant's days were numbered, it would not cease
henceforward to pine and rot till finally removed, bit by
bit. Then for a while, in the garden mysteriously named,
people would breathe more freely.

Mercier and Camier did not know the place. Hence
no doubt their choice of it for their meeting. Certain
things shall never be known for sure.

Through the orange panes the rain to them seemed
golden and brought back memories, determined by the
hazard of their excursions, to the one of Rome, of
Naples to the other, mutually unavowed and with a
feeling akin to shame. They should have felt the better
for this glow of distant days when they were young, and

warm, and loved art, and mocked marriage, and did not know each other, but they felt no whit the better.

Let us go home, said Camier.

Why? said Mercier.

It won't stop all day, said Camier.

Long or short, tis but a shower, said Mercier.

I can't stand there doing nothing, said Camier.

Then let us sit, said Mercier.

Worse still, said Camier.

Then let us walk up and down, said Mercier, yes, arm in arm let us pace to and fro. There is not much room, but there might be even less. Lay down our umbrella, there, help me off with our knapsack, so, thanks, and off we go.

Camier submitted.

Every now and then the sky lightened and the rain abated. Then they would halt before the door. This was the signal for the sky to darken again and the rain to redouble in fury.

Don't look, said Mercier.

The sound is enough, said Camier.

True, said Mercier.

After a moment of silence Mercier said:

The dogs don't trouble you?

Why does he not withdraw? said Camier.

He cannot, said Mercier.

Why? said Camier.

One of nature's little gadgets, said Mercier, no doubt to make insemination double sure.

They begin astraddle, said Camier, and finish arsy-versy.

What would you? said Mercier. The ecstasy is past,

they yearn to part, to go and piss against a post or eat a
morsel of shit, but cannot. So they turn their backs on
each other. You'd do as much, if you were they.

Delicacy would restrain me, said Camier.

And what would you do? said Mercier.

Feign regret, said Camier, that I could not renew such
pleasure incontinent.

After a moment of silence Camier said:

Let us sit us down, I feel all sucked off.

You mean sit down, said Mercier.

I mean sit us down, said Camier.

Then let us sit us down, said Mercier.

On all hands already the workers were at it again, the
air waxed loud with cries of pleasure and pain and with
the urbaner notes of those for whom life had exhausted
its surprises, as well on the minus side as on the plus.
Things too were getting ponderously under way. It was
in vain the rain poured down, the whole business was
starting again with apparently no less ardour than if the
sky had been a cloudless blue.

You kept me waiting, said Mercier.

On the contrary, said Camier.

I arrived at nine five, said Mercier.

And I at nine fifteen, said Camier.

You see, said Mercier.

Waiting, said Camier, and keeping waiting can only
be with reference to a pre-arranged terminus.

And for what hour was our appointment, according to
you? said Mercier.

Nine fifteen, said Camier.

Then you are grievously mistaken, said Mercier.

Meaning? said Camier.

Will you never have done astounding me? said
Mercier.

Explain yourself, said Camier.

I close my eyes and live it over again, said Mercier,
your hand in mine, tears rising to my eyes and the sound
of my faltering voice, So be it, tomorrow at nine. A
drunken woman passed by, singing a ribald song and
hitching up her skirts.

She went to your head, said Camier. He took a notebook from his pocket, turned the leaves and read:
Monday 15, St. Macarius, 9.15, St. Ruth, collect
umbrella at Helen's.

And what does that prove? said Mercier.

My good faith, said Camier.

True, said Mercier.

We shall never know, said Camier, at what hour we
arranged to meet today, so let us drop the subject.

In all this confusion one thing alone is sure, said
Mercier, and that is that we met at ten to ten, at the
same time as the hands, or rather a moment later.

There is that to be thankful for, said Camier.

The rain had not yet begun, said Mercier.

The morning fervour was intact, said Camier.

Don't lose our agenda, said Mercier.

At this moment suddenly appeared from nowhere the
first of a long line of maleficent beings. His uniform,
sickly green in colour, its place of honour rife with
heroic emblems and badges, suited him down to the
ground. Inspired by the example of the great Sarsfield he
had risked his life without success in defence of a
territory which in itself must have left him cold and
considered as a symbol cannot have greatly heated him

either. He carried a stick at once elegant and massive
and even leaned on it from time to time. He suffered
torment with his hip, the pain shot down his buttock
and up his rectum deep into the bowels and even as far
north as the pyloric valve, culminating as a matter of
course in uretro-scrotal spasms with quasi-incessant
longing to micturate. Invalided out with a grudging
pension, whence the sour looks of nearly all those, male
and female, with whom his duties and remnants of
bonhomie brought him daily in contact, he sometimes
felt it would have been wiser on his part, during the
great upheaval, to devote his energies to the domestic
skirmish, the Gaelic dialect, the fortification of his faith
and the treasures of a folklore beyond compare. The
bodily danger would have been less and the benefits
more certain. But this thought, when he had relished all
its bitterness, he would banish from his mind, as un-
worthy of it. His moustache, once stiff as the lip it was
grown to hide, was no longer so. From time to time,
when he remembered, with a blast from below of fetid
breath mingled with spittle, he straightened it moment-
arily. Motionless at the foot of the pagoda steps, his cape
agape, streaming with rain, he darted his eyes to and
fro, from Mercier and Camier to the dogs, from the
dogs to Mercier and Camier.

Who owns that bicycle? he said.

Mercier and Camier exchanged a look.

We could have done without this, said Camier.

Shift her, said the ranger.

It may prove diverting, said Mercier.

Who owns them dogs? said the ranger.

I don't see how we can stay, said Camier.

Can it I wonder be the fillip we needed, to get us moving? said Mercier.

The ranger mounted the steps of the shelter and stood stock-still in the doorway. The air darkened immediately and turned a deeper yellow.

I think he is about to attack us, said Camier.

I leave the balls to you, as usual, said Mercier.

Dear sergeant, said Camier, what exactly can we do for you?

You see that bicycle? said the ranger.

I see nothing, said Camier. Mercier, do you see a bicycle?

Is she yours? said the ranger.

A thing we do not see, said Camier, for whose existence we have only your word, how are we to tell if it is ours, or another's?

Why would it be ours? said Mercier. Are these dogs ours? No. We see them today for the first time. And you would have it that the bicycle, assuming it exists, is ours? And yet the dogs are not ours.

Bugger the dogs, said the ranger.

But as if to give himself the lie he fell on them with stick and boot and drove them cursing from the pagoda. Tied together as they still were, by the post-coitus, their retreat was no easy matter. For the efforts they made to escape, acting equally in opposite directions, could not but annul each other. They must have greatly suffered.

He has now buggered the dogs, said Mercier.

He has driven them from the shelter, said Camier, there is no denying that, but by no means from the garden.

The rain will soon wash them loose, said Mercier.

Less rut-besotted they would have thought of it themselves.

The fact is he has done them a service, said Camier.

Let us show him a little kindness, said Mercier, he's a
hero of the great war. Here we were, high and dry,
masturbating full pelt without fear of interruption, while
he was crawling in the Flanders mud, shitting in his
puttees.

Conclude nothing from those idle words, Mercier and
Camier were old young.

It's an idea, said Camier.

Will you look at that clatter of decorations, said
Mercier. Do you realize the gallons of diarrhoea that
represents?

Darkly, said Camier, as only one so costive can.

Let us suppose this alleged bicycle is ours, said
Mercier. Where lies the harm?

A truce to dissembling, said Camier, it is ours.

Shift her out of here, said the ranger.

The day has dawned at last, said Camier, after years of
shilly-shally, when we must go, we know not whither,
perhaps never to return . . . alive. We are simply
waiting for the day to lift, then full speed ahead. Try and
understand.

What is more, said Mercier, we have still thought to
take, before it is too late.

Thought to take? said Camier.

Those were my words, said Mercier.

I thought all thought was taken, said Camier, and all
in order.

All is not, said Mercier.

Will you shift her or won't you? said the ranger.

Are you venal, said Mercier, since you are deaf to reason?

Silence.

Can you be bought off? said Mercier.

Certainly, said the ranger.

Give him a bob, said Mercier. To think our first disbursement should be a sop to bribery and extortion.

The ranger vanished with a curse.

How of a piece they all are, said Mercier.

Now he'll prowl around, said Camier.

What can that matter to us? said Mercier.

I don't like being prowled around, said Camier.

Mercier took exception to this turn. Camier maintained it. This little game soon palled. It must have been near noon.

And now, said Mercier, the time is come for us.

For us? said Camier.

Precisely, said Mercier, for us, for serious matters.

What about a bite to eat? said Camier.

Thought first, said Mercier, then sustenance.

A long debate ensued, broken by long silences in which thought took place. At such times they would sink, now Mercier, now Camier, to such depths of meditation that the voice of one, resuming its drift, was powerless to bring the other back, or passed unheard. Or they would arrive simultaneously at often contrary conclusions and simultaneously begin to state them. Nor was it rare for one to lapse into a brood before the other had concluded his exposé. And there were times they would look long at each other, unable to utter a word, their minds two blanks. It was fresh from one such daze they decided to abandon their inquiry, for the time being. The afternoon was well advanced, the rain was falling still, the short winter day was drawing to a close.

It is you have the provisions, said Mercier.

On the contrary, said Camier.

True, said Mercier.

My hunger is gone, said Camier.

One must eat, said Mercier.

I see no point, said Camier.

We have a long hard road before us still, said Mercier.

The sooner we drop the better, said Camier.

True, said Mercier.

The ranger's head appeared in the doorway. Believe it or not, only his head was to be seen. It was to say, in his quaint way, they were free to spend the night for half-a-crown.

Is thought now taken, said Camier, and all in order?

No, said Mercier.

Will all ever be? said Camier.

I believe so, said Mercier, yes, I believe, not firmly, no, but I believe, yes, the day is coming when all will be in order, at last.

That will be delightful, said Camier.

Let us hope so, said Mercier.

A long look passed between them. Camier said to himself, Even him I cannot see. A like thought agitated his vis-à-vis.

Two points seemed nevertheless established as a result of this consultation.

1. Mercier would set off alone, awheel, with the raincoat. Wherever he should stop for the night, at the first stage, he would get all in readiness to receive

Camier. Camier would take the road as soon as the weather permitted. Camier would keep the umbrella. No mention of the sack.

2. It so chanced that Mercier, up to now, had shown himself the live wire, Camier the dead weight. The reverse was to be expected at any moment. On the less weak let the weaker always lean, for the course to follow. They might conceivably be valiant together. That would be the day. Or the great weakness might overtake them simultaneously. Let them in this case not give way to despair, but wait with confidence for the evil moment to pass. In spite of the vagueness of these expressions they understood each other, more or less.

Not knowing what to think, said Camier, I look away.

It would seem to be lifting, said Mercier.

The sun comes out at last, said Camier, that we may admire it sink, below the horizon.

That long moment of brightness, said Mercier, with its thousand colours, always stirs my heart.

The day of toil is ended, said Camier, a kind of ink rises in the east and floods the sky.

The bell rang, announcing closing time.

I sense vague shadowy shapes, said Camier, they come and go with muffled cries.

I too have the feeling, said Mercier, we have not gone unobserved since morning.

Are we by any chance alone now? said Camier.

I see no one, said Mercier.

Let us then go together, said Camier.

They left the shelter.

The sack, said Mercier.

The umbrella, said Camier.

The raincoat, said Mercier.

It I have, said Camier.

Is there nothing else? said Mercier.

I see nothing else, said Camier.

I'll get them, said Mercier, you mind the bicycle.

It was a woman's bicycle, without free wheel unfortunately. To brake one pedalled backwards.

The ranger, his bunch of keys in his hand, watched them recede. Mercier held the handlebar, Camier the saddle. The pedals rose and fell.

He cursed them on their way.

2

In the show windows the lights came on, went out, according to the show. Through the slippery streets the crowd pressed on as towards some unquestioned goal. A strange well-being, wroth and weary, filled the air. Close the eyes and not a voice is heard, only the onward panting of the feet. In this throng silence they advanced as best they could, at the edge of the sidewalk, Mercier in front, his hand on the handlebar, Camier behind, his hand on the saddle, and the bicycle slithered in the gutter by their side.

You hinder me more than you help me, said Mercier.

I'm not trying to help you, said Camier, I'm trying to help myself.

Then all is well, said Mercier.

I'm cold, said Camier.

It was indeed cold.

It is indeed cold, said Mercier.

Where do our feet think they're taking us? said Camier.

They would seem to be heading for the canal, said Mercier.

Already? said Camier.

Perhaps we shall be tempted, said Mercier, to strike

out along the towpath and follow it till boredom doth
ensue. Before us, beckoning us on, without our having
to lift our eyes, the dying tints we love so well.

Speak for yourself, said Camier.

The very water, said Mercier, will linger livid, which
is not to be despised either. And then the whim, who
knows, may take us to throw ourselves in.

The little bridges slip by, said Camier, ever fewer and
farther between. We pore over the locks, trying to
understand. From the barges made fast to the bank waft
the watermen's voices, bidding us good-night. Their
day is done, they smoke a last pipe before turning in.

Every man for himself, said Mercier, and God for one
and all.

The town lies far behind, said Camier. Little by little
night overtakes us, blueblack. We splash through
puddles left by the rain. It is no longer possible to
advance. Retreat is equally out of the question.

He added, some moments later:

What are you musing on, Mercier?

On the horror of existence, confusedly, said Mercier.

What about a drink? said Camier.

I thought we had agreed to abstain, said Mercier,
except in the event of accident, or indisposition. Does
not that figure among our many conventions?

I don't call drink, said Camier, a quick nip to put
some life in us.

They stopped at the first pub.

No bikes here, said the publican.

Perhaps after all he was a mere hireling.

And now? said Camier.

We might chain it to a lamppost, said Mercier.

That would give us more freedom, said Camier. He added, Of movement.

In the end they fell back on a railing. It came to the same.

And now? said Mercier.

Back to no bikes? said Camier.

Never! said Mercier.

Never say that, said Camier.

So they adjourned across the way.

Sitting at the bar they discoursed of this and that, brokenly, as was their custom. They spoke, fell silent, listened to each other, stopped listening, each as he fancied or as bidden from within. There were moments, minutes on end, when Camier lacked the strength to raise his glass to his mouth. Mercier was subject to the same failing. Then the less weak of the two gave the weaker to drink, inserting between his lips the rim of his glass. A press of sombre shaggy bulks hemmed them about, thicker and thicker as the hour wore on. From their conversation there emerged in spite of all, among other points, the following.

1. It would be useless, nay, madness, to venture any further for the moment.

2. They need only ask Helen to put them up for the night.

3. Nothing would prevent them from setting out on the morrow, hail, rain or shine, at the crack of dawn.

4. They had nothing to reproach themselves with.

5. Did what they were looking for exist?

6. What were they looking for?

7. There was no hurry.

8. All their judgements relating to the expedition called for revision, in tranquillity.

9. Only one thing mattered: depart.

10. To hell with it all anyway.

Back in the street they linked arms. After a few hundred yards Mercier drew Camier's attention to the fact that they were not in step.

You have your gait, said Camier, I have mine.

I'm not accusing anyone, said Mercier, but it's wearing. We advance in jerks.

I'd prefer you to ask me straight out, said Camier, straight out plump and plain, either to let go your arm and move away or else to fall in with your titubations.

Camier, Camier, said Mercier, squeezing his arm.

They came to a crossroads and stopped.

Which way do we drag ourselves now? said Camier.

Our situation is no ordinary one, said Mercier, I mean in relation to Helen's home, if I know where we are. For these different ways all lead there with equal success.

Then let us turn back, said Camier.

And lose ground we can ill afford? said Mercier.

We can't stay stuck here all night, said Camier, like a couple of clots.

Let us toss our umbrella, said Mercier. It will fall in a certain way, according to laws of which we know nothing. Then all we have to do is press forward in the designated direction.

The umbrella answered, Left! It resembled a great wounded bird, a great bird of ill omen shot down by hunters and awaiting quivering the coup de grâce. The likeness was striking. Camier picked it up and hung it from his pocket.

It is not broken, I trust, said Mercier.

Here their attention was drawn to a strange figure, that of a gentleman wearing, despite the rawness of the air, a simple frock-coat and top-hat. He seemed, for the moment, to be going their way, for their view was of his rear. His hands, in a gesture coquettishly demential, held high and wide apart the skirts of his cutaway. He advanced warily, with stiff and open tread.

Do you feel like singing? said Camier.

Not to my knowledge, said Mercier.

The rain was beginning again. But had it ever ceased?

Let us make haste, said Camier.

Why do you ask me that? said Mercier.

Camier seemed in no hurry to reply. Finally he said:

I hear singing.

They halted, the better to listen.

I hear nothing, said Mercier.

And yet you have good ears, said Camier, so far as I know.

Very fair, said Mercier.

Strange, said Camier.

Do you hear it still? said Mercier.

For all the world a mixed choir, said Camier.

Perhaps it's a delusion, said Mercier.

Possibly, said Camier.

Let's run, said Mercier.

They ran some little way in the dark and wet, without meeting a soul. When they had done running Mercier deplored the nice state, soaked to the buff, in which they would arrive at Helen's, to which in reply Camier described how they would immediately strip and put their things to dry, before the fire or in the hot-cupboard with the boiler and hot water pipes.

Come to think of it, said Mercier, why didn't we use our umbrella?

Camier looked at the umbrella, now in his hand. He had placed it there that he might run more freely.

We might have indeed, he said.

Why burden oneself with an umbrella, said Mercier, and not put it up as required?

Quite, said Camier.

Put it up now, in the name of God, said Mercier.

But Camier could not put it up.

Give it here, said Mercier.

But Mercier could not put it up either.

This was the moment chosen by the rain, acting on behalf of the universal malignity, to come down in buckets.

It's stuck, said Camier, don't strain it whatever you do.

Mercier used a nasty expression.

Meaning me? said Camier.

With both hands Mercier raised the umbrella high above his head and dashed it to the ground. He used another nasty expression. And to crown all, lifting to the sky his convulsed and streaming face, he said, As for thee, fuck thee.

Decidedly Mercier's grief, heroically contained since morning, could be no longer so.

Is it our little omniomni you are trying to abuse? said Camier. You should know better. It's he on the contrary fucks thee. Omniomni, the all-unfuckable.

Kindly leave Mrs Mercier outside this discussion, said Mercier.

The mind has snapped, said Camier.

The first thing one noticed at Helen's was the carpet.

Will you look at that pile, said Camier.

Prime moquette, said Mercier.

Unbelievable, said Camier.

You'd think you never saw it till now, said Mercier, and you wallowing on it all these years.

I never did see it till now, said Camier, and now I can't forget it.

So one says, said Mercier.

If that evening the carpet in particular caught the eye, it was not alone in catching it, for a cockatoo caught it too. It clung shakily to its perch hung from a corner of the ceiling and dizzily rocked by conflicting swing and spin. It was wide awake, in spite of the late hour. Feebly and fitfully its breast rose and fell, faint quiverings ruffled up the down at every expiration. Every now and then the beak would gape and for what seemed whole seconds fishlike remain agape. Then the black spindle of the tongue was seen to stir. The eyes, averted from the light, filled with unspeakable bewilderment and distress, seemed all ears. Shivers of anguish rippled the plumage, blazing in ironic splendour. Beneath it, on the carpet, a great news-sheet was spread.

There's my bed and there's the couch, said Helen.

They're all yours, said Mercier. For my part I'll sleep with none.

A nice little suck-off, said Camier, not too prolonged, by all means, but nothing more.

Terminated, said Helen, the nice little suck-offs but nothing more.

I'll lie on the floor, said Mercier, and wait for dawn.

Scenes and faces will unfold before my gaze, the rain on the skylight sound like claws and night rehearse its colours. The longing will take me to throw myself out of the window, but I'll master it. He repeated, in a roar, I'll master it!

Back in the street they wondered what they had done with the bicycle. The sack too had disappeared.

Did you see the polly? said Mercier.

Pretty thing, said Camier.

It groaned in the night, said Mercier.

Camier questioned this.

It will haunt me till my dying day, said Mercier.

I didn't know she had one, said Camier, what haunts me is the Kidderminster.

Nor I, said Mercier. She says she's had it for years.

She's lying of course, said Camier.

It was still raining. They took shelter in an archway, not knowing where to go.

When exactly did you notice the sack was gone? said Mercier.

This morning, said Camier, when I went to get my sulfamides.

I see no sign of the umbrella, said Mercier.

Camier inspected himself, stooping and spreading out his arms as if concerned with a button.

We must have left it at Helen's, he said.

My feeling is, said Mercier, that if we don't leave this town today we never shall. So let us think twice before we start trying to———.

He almost said recoup.

What exactly was there in the sack? said Camier.

Toilet requisites and necessaries, said Mercier.

Superfluous luxury, said Camier.

A few pairs of socks, said Mercier, and one of drawers.

God, said Camier.

Some eatables, said Mercier.

Rotten ripe for the muckheap, said Camier.

On condition we retrieve them, said Mercier.

Let us board the first express southward bound! cried Camier. He added, more soberly, And so not be tempted to get out at the nearest stop.

And why south, said Mercier, rather than north, or east, or west?

I prefer south, said Camier.

Is that sufficient ground? said Mercier.

It's the nearest terminus, said Camier.

True, said Mercier.

He went out into the street and looked up at the sky, a grey pall, look where he would.

The sky is uniformly leaden, he said, resuming his place under the arch, we'll drown like rats without the umbrella.

Camier criticized this simile.

Like rats, said Mercier.

Even if we had the umbrella, said Camier, we could not use it, for it is broken.

What fresh extravagance is this? said Mercier.

We broke it yesterday, said Camier. Your idea.

Mercier took his head between his hands. Little by little the scene came back to him. Proudly he drew himself up, to his full height.

Come, he said, regrets are vain.

We'll wear the raincoat turn and turn about, said Camier.

We'll be in the train, said Mercier, speeding south.

Through the streaming panes, said Camier, we try to number the cows, shivering pitiably in the scant shelter of the hedges. Rooks take wing, all dripping and bedraggled. But gradually the day lifts and we arrive in the brilliant sunlight of a glorious winter's afternoon. It seems like Monaco.

I don't seem to have eaten for forty-eight hours, said Mercier. And yet I am not hungry.

One must eat, said Camier. He went on to compare the stomach with the bladder.

Apropos, said Mercier, how is your cyst?

Dormant, said Camier, but under the surface mischief is brewing.

What will you do then? said Mercier.

I dread to think, said Camier.

I could just manage a cream puff, said Mercier.

Wait here, said Camier.

No no! cried Mercier. Don't leave me! Don't let us leave each other!

Camier left the archway and began to cross the street. Mercier called him back and an altercation ensued, too foolish to be recorded, so foolish was it.

Another would take umbrage, said Camier. Not I, all things considered. For I say to myself, The hour is grave and Mercier . . . well . . . He advanced towards Mercier who promptly recoiled. I was only going to embrace you, said Camier. I'll do it some other time, when you're less yourself, if I think of it.

He went out into the rain and disappeared. Alone in the archway Mercier began pacing to and fro, deep in bitter thought. It was their first separation since the morning of the day before. Raising suddenly his eyes, as from a vision no longer to be borne, he saw two children, a little boy and a little girl, standing gazing at him. They wore little black oilskins with hoods, identical, and the boy had a little satchel on his back. They held each other by the hand.

Papa! they said, with one voice or nearly.

Good evening, my children, said Mercier, get along with you now.

But they did not get along with them, no, but stood their ground, their little clasped hands lightly swinging back and forth. Finally the little girl drew hers away and advanced towards him they had addressed as papa. She stretched out her little arms towards him, as if to invite a kiss, or at least a caress. The little boy followed suit, with visible misgiving. Mercier raised his foot and dashed it against the pavement. Be off with you! he cried. He bore down on them, wildly gesturing and his face contorted. The children backed away to the sidewalk and there stood still again. Fuck off out of here! screamed Mercier. He flew at them in a fury and they took to their heels. But soon they halted and looked back. What they saw then must have impressed them strongly, for they ran on and bolted down the first sidestreet. As for the unfortunate Mercier, satisfied after a few minutes of fuming tenterhooks that the danger was past, he returned dripping to the archway and resumed his reflections, if not at the point where they had been interrupted, at least at one near by.

Mercier's reflections were peculiar in this, that the same swell and surge swept through them all and cast the mind away, no matter where it embarked, on the same rocks invariably. They were perhaps not so much reflections as a dark torrent of brooding where past and future merged in a single flood and closed, over a present for ever absent. Ah well.

Here, said Camier, I hope you haven't been fretting.

Mercier extracted the cake from its paper wrapping and placed it on the palm of his hand. He bent forward and down till his nose was almost touching it and the eyes not far behind. He darted towards Camier, while still in this position, a sidelong look full of mistrust.

A cream horn, said Camier, the best I could find.

Mercier, still bent double, moved forward to the verge of the archway, where the light was better, and examined the cake again.

It's full of cream, said Camier.

Mercier slowly clenched his fist and the cake gushed between his fingers. The staring eyes filled with tears. Camier advanced to get a better view. The tears flowed, overflowed, all down the furrowed cheeks and vanished in the beard. The face remained unmoved. The eyes, still streaming and no doubt blinded, seemed intent on some object stirring on the ground.

If you didn't want it, said Camier, you had better given it to a dog, or to a child.

I'm in tears, said Mercier, don't intrude.

When the flow stopped Camier said:

Let me offer you our handkerchief.

There are days, said Mercier, one is born every minute. Then the world is full of shitty little Merciers. It's hell. Oh but to cease!

Enough, said Camier. You look like a capital S. Ninety if a day.

Would I were, said Mercier. He wiped his hand on the seat of his trousers. He said, I'll start crawling any minute.

I'm off, said Camier.

Leaving me to my fate, said Mercier. I knew it.

You know my little ways, said Camier.

No, said Mercier, but I was counting on your affection to help me serve my time.

I can help you, said Camier, I can't resurrect you.

Take me by the hand, said Mercier, and lead me far away from here. I'll trot along at your side like a little puppy dog, or a tiny tot. And the day will come——.

A terrible screech of brakes rent the air, followed by a scream and a resounding crash. Mercier and Camier made a rush (after a moment's hesitation) for the open street and were rewarded by the vision, soon hidden by a concourse of gapers, of a big fat woman writhing feebly on the ground. The disorder of her dress revealed an amazing mass of billowing underclothes, originally white in colour. Her lifeblood, streaming from one or more wounds, had already reached the gutter.

Ah, said Mercier, that's what I needed, I feel a new man already.

He was in fact transfigured.

Let this be a lesson to us, said Camier.

Meaning? said Mercier.

Never to despair, said Camier, or lose our faith in life.

Ah, said Mercier with relief, I was afraid you meant something else.

As they went their way an ambulance passed, speeding towards the scene of the mishap.

I beg your pardon? said Camier.

A crying shame, said Mercier.

I don't follow you, said Camier.

A six cylinder, said Mercier.

And what of it? said Camier.

And they talk about the petrol shortage, said Mercier.

There are perhaps more victims than one, said Camier.

It might be an infant child, said Mercier, for all they care.

The rain was falling gently, as from the fine rose of a watering pot. Mercier advanced with upturned face. Now and then he wiped it, with his free hand. He had not had a wash for some time.

Summary
of two preceding chapters

I

Outset.
Meeting of Mercier and Camier.
Saint Ruth Square.
The beech.
The rain.
The shelter.
The dogs.
Distress of Camier.
The ranger.
The bicycle.
Words with the ranger.
Mercier and Camier confer.
Results of this conference.
Bright too late.
The bell.
Mercier and Camier set out.

II

The town at twilight.
Mercier and Camier on the way to the canal.
Vision of the canal.
The bicycle.

First bar.
Mercier and Camier confer.
Results of this conference.
Mercier and Camier on the way to Helen's.
Doubts as to the way.
The umbrella.
The man in the frockcoat.
The rain.
Camier hears singing.
Mercier and Camier run.
The umbrella.
The downpour.
Distress of Mercier.
At Helen's.
The cockatoo.
The Kidderminster.
The second day.
The rain.
Disappearance of sack, bicycle and umbrella.
The archway.
Mercier and Camier confer.
Results of this conference.
Departure of Camier.
Distress of Mercier.
Mercier and the children.
Return of Camier.
The cream horn.
Distress of Mercier.
The fat woman.
Mercier and Camier depart.
Rain on Mercier's face.

The Expelled

Beckett once told John Fletcher that the three 1946 stories later published together in volume form—"The Expelled," "The Calmative," and "The End"—might also have been called "Prime," "Death," and "Limbo." I have read them a dozen times; singly and collectively they rank, in my opinion, among the finest short works of fiction of the twentieth century. They are so taut, both in language and concept, so funny and yet so incredibly sad, so beautifully conceived and adapted to the exigencies of the short-story form, that I marvel at them continually, as one might marvel at three near-perfect gems.

All three are first-person narratives; the narrator/intruder/ironic commentator of earlier Beckett fiction has withered away and disappeared, leaving only three nameless protagonists to tell their own tales as best they can. I think, perhaps wrongly, of all three as one and the same; only the situations differ.

In the first a man is thrown out of a house where he lived, expelled for some unexplained reasons, and the story relates his efforts to find new lodgings. He falls in with a cabman he has engaged to help him in his search, the cabman befriends him and takes him home to his house, or rather his stable, whence the narrator makes his escape at first light.

"The Calmative" begins with the unforgettable line, "I don't know when I died," and from that post-mortem point the nameless narrator, who judges that he died old—"about ninety years old, and what years, and that my body bore it out, from head to foot"—decides to fill the void by telling himself a story.

It is his own story he tells, of a hopeless voyage through forest and town, until he can go no more and falls, "first to his knees, as cattle do, then on my face," in the midst of a throng who ignore him but, politely, are careful not to walk on him. The temptation to remain on the friendly stone ("well, indifferent") is strong, but even in death the calm which the mind desires refuses to come, and he is, at the last, up on his feet, heading west, since the sea lies east.

The hero of "The End" is tossed out of what appears to be a home, perhaps an asylum, in any event a refuge of some sort, and spends the rest of the story searching for another shelter, alternately finding momentary relief in a cave, a cabin in the mountains, a shed, and finally in an abandoned boat to which he affixes a casketlike lid. There, in his make-shift tomb, he conjures up a liquid world on which to float the boat, creates a vision filled with calm memories of his father and childhood, and prepares to drown by swallowing his calmative. Then:

> The sea, the sky, the mountains and the islands closed in and crushed me in a mighty systole, then scattered to the uttermost confines of space. The memory came faint and cold of the story I might have told, a story in the likeness of my life, I mean without the courage to end or the strength to go on.

It is in these stories Beckett's prose assumes a new leanness even as the vision broadens and darkens. As Beckett has found a new language, so he has found his true landscape within the confines of his own mind. Henceforth narrator and protagonist become one, that extraordinary "I" whose name will be, alternately, Molloy or Malone or the Unnamable, Didi or Gogo or Krapp, and who over the next thirty years will tell some of the most powerful, moving, and heart-rend-ing stories ever told.

There were not many steps. I had counted them a thousand times, both going up and coming down, but the figure has gone from my mind. I have never known whether you should say one with your foot on the sidewalk, two with the following foot on the first step, and so on, or whether the sidewalk shouldn't count. At the top of the steps I fell foul of the same dilemma. In the other direction, I mean from top to bottom, it was the same, the word is not too strong. I did not know where to begin nor where to end, that's the truth of the matter. I arrived therefore at three totally different figures, without ever knowing which of them was right. And when I say that the figure has gone from my mind, I mean that none of the three figures is with me any more, in my mind. It is true that if I were to find, in my mind, where it is certainly to be found, one of these figures, I would find it and it alone, without being able to deduce from it the other two. And even were I to recover two, I would not know the third. No, I would have to find all three, in my mind, in order to know all three. Memories are killing. So you must not think of certain things, of those that are dear to you, or rather you must think of them, for if you don't there is the danger of finding them, in your mind, little by little. That is to say, you must think of them for a while, a good while, every day several times a day, until they sink forever in the mud. That's an order.

After all it is not the number of steps that matters. The important thing to remember is that there were not many, and that I have remembered. Even for the child there were not many, compared to other steps he knew, from seeing them every day, from going up and coming down, and from playing on them at knuckle-bones and other games the very names of which he has forgotten. What must it have been like then for the man I had overgrown into?

The fall was therefore not serious. Even as I fell I heard the door slam, which brought me a little comfort, in the midst of my fall. For that meant they were not pursuing me down into the street, with a stick, to beat me in full view of the passers-by. For if that had been their intention they would not have shut the door, but left it open, so that the persons assembled in the vestibule might enjoy my chastisement and be edified. So, for once, they had confined themselves to throwing me out and no more about it. I had time, before coming to rest in the gutter, to conclude this piece of reasoning.

Under these circumstances nothing compelled me to get up immediately. I rested my elbow on the sidewalk, funny the things you remember, settled my ear in the cup of my hand and began to reflect on my situation, notwithstanding its familiarity. But the sound, fainter but unmistakable, of the door slammed again, roused me from my reverie, in which already a whole landscape was taking form, charming with hawthorn and wild roses, most dreamlike, and made me look up in alarm, my hands flat on the sidewalk and my legs braced for flight. But it was merely my hat sailing towards me through the air, rotating as it came. I caught it and put it on. They were most correct, according to their god.

They could have kept this hat, but it was not theirs, it was mine, so they gave it back to me. But the spell was broken.

How describe this hat? And why? When my head had attained I shall not say its definitive but its maximum dimensions, my father said to me, Come, son, we are going to buy your hat, as though it had pre-existed from time immemorial in a pre-established place. He went straight to the hat. I personally had no say in the matter, nor had the hatter. I have often wondered if my father's purpose was not to humiliate me, if he was not jealous of me who was young and handsome, fresh at least, while he was already old and all bloated and purple. It was forbidden me, from that day forth, to go out bareheaded, my pretty brown hair blowing in the wind. Sometimes, in a secluded street, I took it off and held it in my hand, but trembling. I was required to brush it morning and evening. Boys my age with whom, in spite of everything, I was obliged to mix occasionally, mocked me. But I said to myself, It is not really the hat, they simply make merry at the hat because it is a little more glaring than the rest, for they have no finesse. I have always been amazed at my contemporaries' lack of finesse, I whose soul writhed from morning to night, in the mere quest of itself. But perhaps they were simply being kind, like those who make game of the hunchback's big nose. When my father died I could have got rid of this hat, there was nothing more to prevent me, but not I. But how describe it? Some other time, some other time.

I got up and set off. I forget how old I can have been. In what had just happened to me there was nothing in the least memorable. It was neither the cradle nor the grave of anything whatever. Or rather it resembled so many other cradles, so many other graves, that I'm lost. But I don't believe I exaggerate when I say that I was in the prime of life, what I believe is called the full possession of one's faculties. Ah yes, them I possessed all right. I crossed the street and turned back towards the house that had just ejected me, I who never turned back when leaving. How beautiful it was! There were geraniums in the windows. I have brooded over geraniums for years. Geraniums are artful customers, but in the end I was able to do what I liked with them. I have always greatly admired the door of this house, up on top of its little flight of steps. How describe it? It was a massive green door, encased in summer in a kind of green and white striped housing, with a hole for the thunderous wrought-iron knocker and a slit for letters, this latter closed to dust, flies and tits by a brass flap fitted with springs. So much for that description. The door was set between two pillars of the same colour, the bell being on that to the right. The curtains were in unexceptionable taste. Even the smoke rising from one of the chimney-pots seemed to spread and vanish in the air more sorrowful than the neighbours', and bluer. I looked up at the third and last floor and saw my window outrageously open. A thorough cleaning was in full swing. In a few hours they would close the window, draw the curtains and spray the whole place with disinfectant. I knew them. I would have gladly died in that house. In a sort of vision I saw the door open and my feet come out.

I wasn't afraid to look, for I knew they were not spying on me from behind the curtains, as they could have done if they had wished. But I knew them. They had all gone back into their dens and resumed their occupations.

And yet I had done them no harm.

I did not know the town very well, scene of my birth and of my first steps in this world, and then of all the others, so many that I thought all trace of me was lost, but I was wrong. I went out so little! Now and then I would go to the window, part the curtains and look out. But then I hastened back to the depths of the room, where the bed was. I felt ill at ease with all this air about me, lost before the confusion of innumerable prospects. But I still knew how to act at this period, when it was absolutely necessary. But first I raised my eyes to the sky, whence cometh our help, where there are no roads, where you wander freely, as in a desert, and where nothing obstructs your vision, wherever you turn your eyes, but the limits of vision itself. It gets monotonous in the end. When I was younger I thought life would be good in the middle of a plain, and I went to the Lüneburg heath. With the plain in my head I went to the heath. There were other heaths far less remote, but a voice kept saying to me, It's the Lüneburg heath you need. The element lüne must have had something to do with it. As it turned out the Lüneburg heath was most unsatisfactory, most unsatisfactory. I came home disappointed, and at the same time relieved. Yes, I don't know why, but I have never been disappointed, and I often was in the early days, without feeling at the same time, or a moment later, an undeniable relief.

I set off. What a gait. Stiffness of the lower limbs, as if nature had denied me knees, extraordinary splaying of the feet to right and left of the line of march. The trunk, on the contrary, as if by the effect of a compensatory mechanism, was as flabby as an old ragbag, tossing wildly to the unpredictable jolts of the pelvis. I have often tried to correct these defects, to stiffen my bust, flex my knees

and walk with my feet in front of one another, for I had
at least five or six, but it always ended in the same way,
I mean with a 'loss of equilibrium, followed by a fall. A
man must walk without paying attention to what he's
doing, as he sighs, and when I walked without paying
attention to what I was doing I walked in the way I have
just described, and when I began to pay attention I managed a few steps of creditable execution and then fell. I
decided therefore to be myself. This carriage is due, in
my opinion, in part at least, to a certain leaning from
which I have never been able to free myself completely
and which left its stamp, as was only to be expected, on
my impressionable years, those which govern the fabri-
cation of character, I refer to the period which extends,
as far as the eye can see, from the first totterings, behind
a chair, to the third form, in which I concluded my
studies. I had then the deplorable habit, having pissed
in my trousers, or shat there, which I did fairly regularly early in the morning, about ten or half past
ten, of persisting in going on and finishing my day as if
nothing had happened. The very idea of changing my
trousers, or of confiding in mother, who goodness knows
asked nothing better than to help me, was unbearable, I
don't know why, and till bedtime I dragged on with
burning and stinking between my little thighs, or sticking to my bottom, the result of my incontinence. Whence
this wary way of walking, with the legs stiff and wide
apart, and this desperate rolling of the bust, no doubt
intended to put people off the scent, to make them think
I was full of gaiety and high spirits, without a care in
the world, and to lend plausibility to my explanations
concerning my nether rigidity, which I ascribed to hered-
itary rheumatism. My youthful ardour, in so far as I

had any, spent itself in this effort, I became sour and
mistrustful, a little before my time, in love with hiding
and the prone position. Poor juvenile solutions, explaining nothing. No need then for caution, we may reason
on to our heart's content, the fog won't lift.

The weather was fine. I advanced down the street,
keeping as close as I could to the sidewalk. The widest
sidewalk is never wide enough for me, once I set myself
in motion, and I hate to inconvenience strangers. A
policeman stopped me and said, The street for vehicles,
the sidewalk for pedestrians. Like a bit of Old Testament. So I got back on the sidewalk, almost apologetically, and persevered there, in spite of an indescribable jostle, for a good twenty steps, till I had to fling
myself to the ground to avoid crushing a child. He was
wearing a little harness, I remember, with little bells,
he must have taken himself for a pony, or a Clydesdale,
why not. I would have crushed him gladly, I loathe
children, and it would have been doing him a service, but
I was afraid of reprisals. Everyone is a parent, that is
what keeps you from hoping. One should reserve, on
busy streets, special tracks for these nasty little creatures,
their prams, hoops, sweets, scooters, skates, grandpas,
grandmas, nannies, balloons and balls, all their foul little
happiness in a word. I fell then, and brought down with
me an old lady covered with spangles and lace, who must
have weighed about sixteen stone. Her screams soon
drew a crowd. I had high hopes she had broken her
femur, old ladies break their femur easily, but not
enough, not enough. I took advantage of the confusion
to make off, muttering unintelligible oaths, as if I were
the victim, and I was, but I couldn't have proved it. They
never lynch children, babies, no matter what they do

they are whitewashed in advance. I personally would
lynch them with the utmost pleasure, I don't say I'd lend
a hand, no, I am not a violent man, but I'd encourage the
others and stand them drinks when it was done. But no
sooner had I begun to reel on than I was stopped by a second policeman, similar in all respects to the first, so much
so that I wondered whether it was not the same one. He
pointed out to me that the sidewalk was for every one, as
if it was quite obvious that I could not be assimilated to
that category. Would you like me, I said, without thinking for a single moment of Heraclitus, to get down in the
gutter? Get down wherever you want, he said, but leave
some room for others. If you can't bloody well get about
like every one else, he said, you'd do better to stay at
home. It was exactly my feeling. And that he should
attribute to me a home was no small satisfaction. At that
moment a funeral passed, as sometimes happens. There
was a great flurry of hats and at the same time a flutter
of countless fingers. Personally if I were reduced to
making the sign of the cross I would set my heart on
doing it right, nose, navel, left nipple, right nipple. But
the way they did it, slovenly and wild, he seemed crucified all of a heap, no dignity, his knees under his chin and
his hands anyhow. The more fervent stopped dead and
muttered. As for the policeman, he stiffened to attention,
closed his eyes and saluted. Through the windows of the
cabs I caught a glimpse of the mourners conversing with
animation, no doubt scenes from the life of their late
dear brother in Christ, or sister. I seem to have heard
that the hearse trappings are not the same in both cases,
but I never could find out what the difference consists in.
The horses were farting and shitting as if they were going to the fair. I saw no one kneeling.

But with us the last journey is soon done, it is in vain you quicken your pace, the last cab containing the domestics soon leaves you behind, the respite is over, the bystanders go their ways, you may look to yourself again. So I stopped a third time, of my own free will, and entered a cab. Those I had just seen pass, crammed with people hotly arguing, must have made a strong impression on me. It's a big black box, rocking and swaying on its springs, the windows are small, you curl up in a corner, it smells musty. I felt my hat grazing the roof. A little later I leant forward and closed the windows. Then I sat down again with my back to the horse. I was dozing off when a voice made me start, the cabman's. He had opened the door, no doubt despairing of making himself heard through the window. All I saw was his moustache. Where to? he said. He had climbed down from his seat on purpose to ask me that. And I who thought I was far away already. I reflected, searching in my memory for the name of a street, or a monument. Is your cab for sale? I said. I added, Without the horse. What would I do with a horse? But what would I do with a cab? Could I as much as stretch out in it? Who would bring me food? To the Zoo, I said. It is rare for a capital to be without a Zoo. I added, Don't go too fast. He laughed. The suggestion that he might go too fast to the Zoo must have amused him. Unless it was the prospect of being cabless. Unless it was simply myself, my own person, whose presence in the cab must have transformed it, so much so that the cabman, seeing me there with my head in the shadows of the roof and my knees against the window, had wondered perhaps if it was really his cab, really a cab. He hastens to look at his horse, and is reassured. But does one ever know oneself why one laughs? His laugh in any case was brief, which suggested I was not the joke. He closed the door and climbed back to his seat. It was not long then before the horse got under way.

Yes, surprising though it may seem, I still had a little money at this time. The small sum my father had left me as a gift, with no restrictions, at his death, I still wonder if it wasn't stolen from me. Then I had none. And yet my life went on, and even in the way I wanted, up to a point. The great disadvantage of this condition, which might be defined as the absolute impossibility of all purchase, is that it compels you to bestir yourself. It is rare, for example, when you are completely penniless, that you can have food brought to you from time to time in your retreat. You are therefore obliged to go out and bestir yourself, at least one day a week. You can hardly have a home address under these circumstances, it's inevitable. It was therefore with a certain delay that I learnt they were looking for me, for an affair concerning me. I forget through what channel. I did not read the newspapers, nor do I remember having spoken with anyone during these years, except perhaps three or four times, on the subject of food. At any rate, I must have had wind of the affair one way or another, otherwise I would never have gone to see the lawyer, Mr Nidder, strange how one fails to forget certain names, and he would never have received me. He verified my identity. That took some time. I showed him the metal initials in the lining of my hat, they proved nothing but they increased the probabilities. Sign, he said. He played with a cylindrical ruler, you could have felled an ox with it. Count, he said. A young woman, perhaps venal, was present at this interview, as a witness no doubt. I stuffed the wad in my pocket.

You shouldn't do that, he said. It occurred to me that
he should have asked me to count before I signed, it
would have been more in order. Where can I reach
you, he said, if necessary? At the foot of the stairs I
thought of something. Soon after I went back to ask
him where this money came from, adding that I had
a right to know. He gave me a woman's name that I've
forgotten. Perhaps she had dandled me on her knees
while I was still in swaddling clothes and there had
been some lovey-dovey. Sometimes that suffices. I repeat, in swaddling clothes, for any later it would have
been too late, for lovey-dovey. It is thanks to this money
then that I still had a little. Very little. Divided by my
life to come it was negligible, unless my conjectures
were unduly pessimistic. I knocked on the partition
beside my hat, right in the cabman's back if my calculations were correct. A cloud of dust rose from the
upholstery. I took a stone from my pocket and knocked
with the stone, until the cab stopped. I noticed that,
unlike most vehicles, which slow down before stopping,
the cab stopped dead. I waited. The whole cab shook.
The cabman, on his high seat, must have been listening. I saw the horse as with my eyes of flesh. It had
not lapsed into the drooping attitude of its briefest
halts, it remained alert, its ears pricked up. I looked
out of the window, we were again in motion. I banged
again on the partition, until the cab stopped again.
The cabman got down cursing from his seat. I lowered
the window to prevent his opening the door. Faster,
faster. He was redder than ever, purple in other words.
Anger, or the rushing wind. I told him I was hiring him
for the day. He replied that he had a funeral at three
o'clock. Ah the dead. I told him I had changed my

mind and no longer wished to go to the Zoo. Let us
not go to the Zoo, I said. He replied that it made no
difference to him where we went, provided it wasn't
too far, because of his beast. And they talk to us about
the specificity of primitive peoples' speech. I asked
him if he knew of an eating-house. I added, You'll eat
with me. I prefer being with a regular customer in
such places. There was a long table with two benches
of exactly the same length on either side. Across the
table he spoke to me of his life, of his wife, of his beast,
then again of his life, of the atrocious life that was
his, chiefly because of his character. He asked me if I
realized what it meant to be out of doors in all
weathers. I learnt there were still some cabmen who
spent their day snug and warm inside their cabs on
the rank, waiting for a customer to come and rouse
them. Such a thing was possible in the past, but nowadays other methods were necessary, if a man was to
have a little laid up at the end of his days. I described
my situation to him, what I had lost and what I was
looking for. We did our best, both of us, to understand, to explain. He understood that I had lost my
room and needed another, but all the rest escaped
him. He had taken it into his head, whence nothing
could ever dislodge it, that I was looking for a fur-
nished room. He took from his pocket an evening paper
of the day before, or perhaps the day before that again,
and proceeded to run through the advertisements, five
or six of which he underlined with a tiny pencil, the
same that hovered over the likely outsiders. He underlined no doubt those he would have underlined if he
had been in my shoes, or perhaps those concentrated
in the same district, because of his beast. I would

only have confused him by saying that I could tolerate
no furniture in my room except the bed, and that all
the other pieces, and even the very night table, had to
be removed before I would consent to set foot in it.
About three o'clock we roused the horse and set off
again. The cabman suggested I climb up beside
him on the seat, but for some time already I had been
dreaming of the inside of the cab and I got back inside.
We visited, methodically I hope, one after another, the
addresses he had underlined. The short winter's day
was drawing to a close. It seems to me sometimes that
these are the only days I have ever known, and especially that most charming moment of all, just before
night wipes them out. The addresses he had underlined, or rather marked with a cross, as common people
do, proved fruitless one by one, and one by one he
crossed them out with a diagonal stroke. Later he
showed me the paper, advising me to keep it safe so
as to be sure not to look again where I had already
looked in vain. In spite of the closed windows, the
creaking of the cab and the traffic noises, I heard him
singing, all alone aloft on his high seat. He had preferred me to a funeral, this was a fact which would
endure forever. He sang, *She is far from the land where
her young hero,* those are the only words I remember.
At each stop he got down from his seat and helped
me get down from mine. I rang at the door he directed
me to, and sometimes I disappeared inside the house.
It was a strange feeling, I remember, a house all about
me again, after so long. He waited for me on the sidewalk and helped me climb back into the cab. I was sick
and tired of this cabman. He clambered back to his seat
and we set off again. At a certain moment there occurred

this. He stopped. I shook off my torpor and made ready to
get down. But he did not come to open the door and offer
me his arm, so that I was obliged to get down by myself.
He was lighting the lamps. I love oil lamps, in spite of
their having been, with candles, and if I except the
stars, the first lights I ever knew. I asked him if I
might light the second lamp, since he had already lit
the first himself. He gave me his box of matches,
I swung open on its hinges the little convex glass, lit
and closed at once, so that the wick might burn steady
and bright snug in its little house, sheltered from the
wind. I had this joy. We saw nothing, by the light of
these lamps, save the vague outlines of the horse, but
the others saw them from afar, two yellow glows sailing
slowly through the air. When the equipage turned an
eye could be seen, red or green as the case might be, a
bossy rhomb as clear and keen as stained glass.

After we had verified the last address the cabman
suggested bringing me to a hotel he knew where I
would be comfortable. That makes sense, cabman,
hotel, it's plausible. With his recommendation I would
want for nothing. Every convenience, he said, with a
wink. I place this conversation on the sidewalk, in
front of the house from which I had just emerged. I
remember, beneath the lamp, the flank of the horse,
hollow and damp, and on the handle of the door the
cabman's hand in its woollen glove. The roof of the cab
was on a level with my neck. I suggested we have a
drink. The horse had neither eaten nor drunk all day.
I mentioned this to the cabman, who replied that his
beast would take no food till it was back in the stable.
If it ate anything whatever, during work, were it but
an apple or a lump of sugar, it would have stomach

pains and colics that would root it to the spot and might
even kill it. That was why he was compelled to tie its
jaws together with a strap whenever for one reason or
another he had to let it out of his sight, so that it would
not have to suffer from the kind hearts of the passers-
by. After a few drinks the cabman invited me to do
his wife and him the honour of spending the night in
their home. It was not far. Recollecting these emotions,
with the celebrated advantage of tranquillity, it seems
to me he did nothing else, all that day, but turn about
his lodging. They lived above a stable, at the back
of a yard. Ideal location, I could have done with it.
Having presented me to his wife, extraordinarily full-
bottomed, he left us. She was manifestly ill at ease,
alone with me. I could understand her, I don't stand
on ceremony on these occasions. No reason for this to
end or go on. Then let it end. I said I would go down
to the stable and sleep there. The cabman protested. I
insisted. He drew his wife's attention to the pustule on
top of my skull, for I had removed my hat out of civility.
He should have that removed, she said. The cabman
named a doctor he held in high esteem who had
rid him of an induration of the seat. If he wants to
sleep in the stable, said his wife, let him sleep in the
stable. The cabman took the lamp from the table and
preceded me down the stairs, or rather ladder, which
descended to the stable, leaving his wife in the dark.
He spread a horse blanket on the ground in a corner
on the straw and left me a box of matches in case I
needed to see clearly in the night. I don't remember
what the horse was doing all this time. Stretched out
in the dark I heard the noise it made as it drank, a
noise like no other, the sudden gallop of the rats, and

above me the muffled voices of the cabman and his
wife as they criticized me. I held the box of matches
in my hand, a big box of safety matches. I got up
during the night and struck one. Its brief flame enabled
me to locate the cab. I was seized, then abandoned,
by the desire to set fire to the stable. I found the cab
in the dark, opened the door, the rats poured out, I
climbed in. As I settled down I noticed that the cab
was no longer level, it was inevitable, with the shafts
resting on the ground. It was better so, that allowed
me to lie well back, with my feet higher than my head
on the other seat. Several times during the night I felt
the horse looking at me through the window and the
breath of its nostrils. Now that it was unharnessed it
must have been puzzled by my presence in the cab. I
was cold, having forgotten to take the blanket, but not
quite enough to go and get it. Through the window of
the cab I saw the window of the stable, more and more
clearly. I got out of the cab. It was not so dark now
in the stable, I could make out the manger, the rack, the
harness hanging, what else, buckets and brushes. I
went to the door but couldn't open it. The horse didn't
take its eyes off me. Don't horses ever sleep? It seemed
to me the cabman should have tied it, to the manger
for example. So I was obliged to leave by the window.
It wasn't easy. But what is easy? I went out head first,
my hands were flat on the ground of the yard while
my legs were still thrashing to get clear of the frame.
I remember the tufts of grass on which I pulled with
both hands, in my efforts to extricate myself. I should
have taken off my greatcoat and thrown it through
the window, but that would have meant thinking of
it. No sooner had I left the yard than I thought of

something. Weakness. I slipped a banknote in the match box, went back to the yard and placed the box on the sill of the window through which I had just come. The horse was at the window. But after I had taken a few steps in the street I returned to the yard and took back my banknote. I left the matches, they were not mine. The horse was still at the window. I was sick and tired of this cabhorse. Dawn was just breaking. I did not know where I was. I made towards the rising sun, towards where I thought it should rise, the quicker to come into the light. I would have liked a sea horizon, or a desert one. When I am abroad in the morning, I go to meet the sun, and in the evening, when I am abroad, I follow it, till I am down among the dead. I don't know why I told this story. I could just as well have told another. Perhaps some other time I'll be able to tell another. Living souls, you will see how alike they are.

—*Translated by* RICHARD SEAVER
in collaboration with the author

Molloy (Part 1)

Beckett is reported to have once declared to a critic: "I conceived of *Molloy* and what followed the day I became aware of my stupidity. Then I began to write the things I feel." If the declaration seems falsely modest, one must remember that this is the same man who wrote, in *From an Abandoned Work:*

> Fortunately my father died when I was a boy, otherwise I might have been a professor, he had his heart set on it. A very fair scholar I was, too, no thought, but a great memory.

The same man, too, who did indeed give up teaching, to the disappointment of his family and colleagues at Trinity College; after he resigned at the end of 1931, he later confessed to several friends that he did so because he found it impossible to stand up before a class dispensing knowledge when he felt his own was so inadequate.

But however erudite Beckett was—and is—he must have come to the realization that this accumulation of knowledge, far from helping him plumb the depths of his own soul and write what he really felt, might well be a hindrance.

Molloy was written in 1947, hard after *Mercier and Camier* and the four short stories written the year before. It is without doubt a key work, his first major effort in what the narrator in *Mercier and Camier* called "the battle of the soliloquy." Henceforth Beckett's struggle takes place in the "hollow sphere hermetically closed to the world without" that Murphy refers to, namely, "the inside of my distant skull where once I wandered, now am fixed, lost for tininess, or straining against the walls," as the Unnamable describes it.

In the course of the three works, there are four soliloquys: those of Molloy and Moran in the first, that of Malone in the second, and that of the Unnamable in the last.

The two parts of *Molloy* complement and reinforce each other, Molloy's story, and journey, relating organically to Moran's. Molloy, the reluctant Cartesian, as one critic has called him, "rejects the world not because he is idle but because he is conscious of the vacuity of an existence that is denied a complete immortality . . . . He detects the absurdity of those substitutes with which reason has replaced immortality." Therefore, the mortal Molloy waits in the room which once was his mother's for the onset of death. He is "saying his good-byes," he wants to "finish dying," but meanwhile is under the obligation to set down the story of the events which have brought him to this room.

Moran, the unreluctant rationalist, a creature of habit, of worldly possessions, whose vision is turned outward to the world even as Molloy's is turned inward, is commanded to go find Molloy, who, at the end of Part I, has crawled painfully out of the forest into which he had ventured on the last leg of his journey in search of his mother, and has fallen into a ditch at the edge of a plain. Part II then is Moran's monologue, and however opposed the two creatures, however diametrically different their orientations, their lives are inextricably joined, and their journeys but two stations of the same Calvary.

Molloy was published in France on March 15, 1951, and *Malone meurt* (*Malone Dies*), which Beckett had written a year after *Molloy*, seven months later, on October 8, 1951, in printings of 3000 copies each. It would take some time before the printings were exhausted, and recognition was far from immediate. But it is safe to say that with the publication of these two works, and *The Unnamable* three years later, Beckett had already assured himself of a very special place in the annals of twentieth-century literature.

English-language editions of the works appeared in 1951 (*Molloy*), 1956 (*Malone Dies*), and 1958 (*The Unnamable*).

I am in my mother's room.   It's I who live there now.
I don't know how I got there.   Perhaps in an ambulance, certainly a vehicle of some kind.   I was helped.
I'd never have got there alone.   There's this man who
comes every week.   Perhaps I got here thanks to him.
He says not.   He gives me money and takes away the
pages.   So many pages, so much money.   Yes, I work
now, a little like I used to, except that I don't know how
to work any more.   That doesn't matter apparently.
What I'd like now is to speak of the things that are left,
say my good-byes, finish dying.   They don't want that.
Yes, there is more than one, apparently.   But it's always
the same one that comes.   You'll do that later, he says.
Good.   The truth is I haven't much will left.   When
he comes for the fresh pages he brings back the previous
week's.   They are marked with signs I don't understand.   Anyway I don't read them.   When I've done
nothing he gives me nothing, he scolds me.   Yet I don't
work for money.   For what then?   I don't know.   The

truth is I don't know much. For example my mother's
death. Was she already dead when I came? Or did
she only die later? I mean enough to bury. I don't
know. Perhaps they haven't buried her yet. In any
case I have her room. I sleep in her bed. I piss and
shit in her pot. I have taken her place. I must resemble
her more and more. All I need now is a son. Perhaps
I have one somewhere. But I think not. He would be
old now, nearly as old as myself. It was a little chambermaid. It wasn't true love. The true love was in
another. We'll come to that. Her name? I've forgotten it again. It seems to me sometimes that I even
knew my son, that I helped him. Then I tell myself
it's impossible. It's impossible I could ever have helped
anyone. I've forgotten how to spell too, and half the
words. That doesn't matter apparently. Good. He's
a queer one the one who comes to see me. He comes
every Sunday apparently. The other days he isn't free.
He's always thirsty. It was he told me I'd begun all
wrong, that I should have begun differently. He must
be right. I began at the beginning, like an old ballocks,
can you imagine that? Here's my beginning. Because
they're keeping it apparently. I took a lot of trouble
with it. Here it is. It gave me a lot of trouble. It
was the beginning, do you understand? Whereas now
it's nearly the end. Is what I do now any better? I
don't know. That's beside the point. Here's my beginning. It must mean something, or they wouldn't keep
it. Here it is.

This time, then once more I think, then perhaps a
last time, then I think it'll be over, with that world too.
Premonition of the last but one but one. All grows

dim. A little more and you'll go blind. It's in the
head. It doesn't work any more, it says, I don't work
any more. You go dumb as well and sounds fade. The
threshold scarcely crossed that's how it is. It's the head.
It must have had enough. So that you say, I'll manage
this time, then perhaps once more, then perhaps a last
time, then nothing more. You are hard set to formulate
this thought, for it is one, in a sense. Then you try
to pay attention, to consider with attention all those
dim things, saying to yourself, laboriously, It's my fault.
Fault? That was the word. But what fault? It's not
goodbye, and what magic in those dim things to which
it will be time enough, when next they pass, to say goodbye·
For you must say goodbye, it would be madness not to
say goodbye, when the time comes. If you think of
the forms and light of other days it is without regret.
But you seldom think of them, with what would you
think of them? I don't know. People pass too, hard
to distinguish from yourself. That is discouraging. So
I saw A and C going slowly towards each other, uncon-
scious of what they were doing. It was on a road remark-
ably bare, I mean without hedges or ditches or any
kind of edge, in the country, for cows were chewing in
enormous fields, lying and standing, in the evening
silence. Perhaps I'm inventing a little, perhaps embel-
lishing, but on the whole that's the way it was. They
chew, swallow, then after a short pause effortlessly bring
up the next mouthful. A neck muscle stirs and the
jaws begin to grind again. But perhaps I'm remembering things. The road, hard and white, seared the tender
pastures, rose and fell at the whim of hills and hollows.
The town was not far. It was two men, unmistakably,

one small and one tall. They had left the town, first
one, then the other, and then the first, weary or remembering a duty, had retraced his steps. The air was sharp
for they wore greatcoats. They looked alike, but no
more than others do. At first a wide space lay between
them. They couldn't have seen each other, even had
they raised their heads and looked about, because of
this wide space, and then because of the undulating land,
which caused the road to be in waves, not high, but
high enough, high enough. But the moment came when
together they went down into the same trough and in
this trough finally met. To say they knew each other,
no, nothing warrants it. But perhaps at the sound of
their steps, or warned by some obscure instinct, they
raised their heads and observed each other, for a good
fifteen paces, before they stopped, breast to breast. Yes;
they did not pass each other by, but halted, face to face,
as in the country, of an evening, on a deserted road,
two wayfaring strangers will, without there being anything extraordinary about it. But they knew each other
perhaps. Now in any case they do, now I think they
will know each other, greet each other, even in the depths
of the town. They turned towards the sea which, far
in the east, beyond the fields, loomed high in the waning
sky, and exchanged a few words. Then each went on
his way. Each went on his way, A back towards the
town, C on by ways he seemed hardly to know, or not
at all, for he went with uncertain step and often stopped
to look about him, like someone trying to fix landmarks
in his mind, for one day perhaps he may have to retrace
his steps, you never know. The treacherous hills where
fearfully he ventured were no doubt only known to him

from afar, seen perhaps from his bedroom window or from the summit of a monument which, one black day, having nothing in particular to do and turning to height for solace, he had paid his few coppers to climb, slower and slower, up the winding stones. From there he must have seen it all, the plain, the sea, and then these selfsame hills that some call mountains, indigo in places in the evening light, their serried ranges crowding to the skyline, cloven with hidden valleys that the eye divines from sudden shifts of colour and then from other signs for which there are no words, nor even thoughts. But all are not divined, even from that height, and often where only one escarpment is discerned, and one crest, in reality there are two, two escarpments, two crests, riven by a valley. But now he knows these hills, that is to say he knows them better, and if ever again he sees them from afar it will be I think with other eyes, and not only that but the within, all that inner space one never sees, the brain and heart and other caverns where thought and feeling dance their sabbath, all that too quite differently disposed. He looks old and it is a sorry sight to see him solitary after so many years, so many days and nights unthinkingly given to that rumour rising at birth and even earlier, What shall I do ? What shall I do? now low, a murmur, now precise as the headwaiter's And to follow? and often rising to a scream. And in the end, or almost, to be abroad alone, by unknown ways, in the gathering night, with a stick. It was a stout stick, he used it to thrust himself onward, or as a defence, when the time came, against dogs and marauders. Yes, night was gathering, but the man was innocent, greatly innocent, he had nothing to fear, though he went in fear,

he had nothing to fear, there was nothing they could do
to him, or very little. But he can't have known it. I
wouldn't know it myself, if I thought about it. Yes, he
saw himself threatened, his body threatened, his reason
threatened, and perhaps he was, perhaps they were,
in spite of his innocence. What business has innocence
here? What relation to the innumerable spirits of darkness? It's not clear. It seemed to me he wore a cocked
hat. I remember being struck by it, as I wouldn't have
been for example by a cap or by a bowler. I watched
him recede, overtaken (myself) by his anxiety, at least
by an anxiety which was not necessarily his, but of which
as it were he partook. Who knows if it wasn't my own
anxiety overtaking him. He hadn't seen me. I was
perched higher than the road's highest point and flattened
what is more against a rock the same colour as myself,
that is grey. The rock he probably saw. He gazed
around as if to engrave the landmarks on his memory
and must have seen the rock in the shadow of which I
crouched like Belacqua, or Sordello, I forget. But a
man, a fortiori myself, isn't exactly a landmark, because.
I mean if by some strange chance he were to pass that
way again, after a long lapse of time, vanquished, or to
look for some lost thing, or to destroy something, his
eyes would search out the rock, not the haphazard in its
shadow of that unstable fugitive thing, still living flesh.
No, he certainly didn't see me, for the reasons I've given
and then because he was in no humour for that, that
evening, no humour for the living, but rather for all that
doesn't stir, or stirs so slowly that a child would scorn it,
let alone an old man. However that may be, I mean
whether he saw me or whether he didn't, I repeat I watch-

ed him recede, at grips (myself) with the temptation
to get up and follow him, perhaps even to catch up with
him one day, so as to know him better, be myself less
lonely. But in spite of my soul's leap out to him, at the
end of its elastic, I saw him only darkly, because of the
dark and then because of the terrain, in the folds of which
he disappeared from time to time, to re-emerge further
on, but most of all I think because of other things calling
me and towards which too one after the other my soul
was straining, wildly.   I mean of course the fields, whiten-
ing under the dew, and the animals, ceasing from
wandering and settling for the night, and the sea, of which
nothing, and the sharpening line of crests, and the sky
where without seeing them I felt the first stars tremble,
and my hand on my knee and above all the other wayfarer,
A or C, I don't remember, going resignedly home.   Yes,
towards my hand also, which my knee felt tremble and of
which my eyes saw the wrist only, the heavily veined back,
the pallid rows of knuckles. But that is not, I mean my
hand, what I wish to speak of now, everything in due
course, but A or C returning to the town he had just
left.   But after all what was there particularly urban in
his   aspect?   He   was   bare-headed,   wore   sand-shoes,
smoked a cigar.   He moved with a kind of loitering indolence which rightly or wrongly seemed to me expressive.
But all that proved nothing, refuted nothing. Perhaps
he had come from afar, from the other end of the island
even, and was approaching the town for the first time
or returning to it after a long absence. A little dog
followed him, a pomeranien I think, but I don't think
so. I wasn't sure at the time and I'm still not sure,
though I've hardly thought about it. The little dog

followed wretchedly, after the fashion of pomeranians, stopping, turning in slow circles, giving up and then, a little further on, beginning all over again. Constipation is a sign of good health in pomeranians. At a given moment, pre-established if you like, I don't much mind, the gentleman turned back, took the little creature in his arms, drew the cigar from his lips and buried his face in the orange fleece, for it was a gentleman, that was obvious. Yes, it was an orange pomeranian, the less I think of it the more certain I am. And yet. But would he have come from afar, bare-headed, in sand-shoes, smoking a cigar, followed by a pomeranian? Did, he not seem rather to have issued from the ramparts, after a good dinner, to take his dog and himself for a walk, like so many citizens, dreaming and farting, when the weather is fine? But was not perhaps in reality the cigar a cutty, and were not the sand-shoes boots, hobnailed, dust-whitened, and what prevented the dog from being one of those stray dogs that you pick up and take in your arms, from compassion or because you have long been straying with no other company than the endless roads, sands, shingle, bogs and heather, than this nature answerable to another court, than at long intervals the fellow-convict you long to stop, embrace, suck, suckle and whom you pass by, with hostile eyes, for fear of his familiarities? Until the day when, your endurance gone, in this world for you without arms, you catch up in yours the first mangy cur you meet, carry it the time needed for it to love you and you it, then throw it away. Perhaps he had come to that, in spite of appearances. He disappeared, his head on his chest, the smoking object in his hand. Let me try and explain. From things about to

disappear I turn away in time. To watch them out of
sight, no, I can't do it. It was in this sense he disappeared. Looking away I thought of him, saying, He is
dwindling, dwindling. I knew what I meant. I knew
I could catch him, lame as I was. I had only to want to·
And yet no, for I did want to. To get up, to get down
on the road, to set off hobbling in pursuit of him, to hail
him, what could be easier? He hears my cries, turns,
waits for me. I am up against him, up against the dog,
gasping, between my crutches. He is a little frightened
of me, a little sorry for me, I disgust him not a little.
I am not a pretty sight, I don't smell good. What is
it I want? Ah that tone I know, compounded of pity,
of fear, of disgust. I want to see the dog, see the man,
at close quarters, know what smokes, inspect the shoes,
find out other things. He is kind, tells me of this and that
and other things, whence he comes, whither he goes.
I believe him, I know it's my only chance to — my only
chance, I believe all I'm told, I've disbelieved only too
much in my long life, now I swallow everything, greedily.
What I need now is stories, it took me a long time to
know that, and I'm not sure of it. There I am then,
informed as to certain things, knowing certain things
about him, things I didn't know, things I had craved to
know, things I had never thought of. What rigmarole.
I am even capable of having learnt what his profession
is, I who am so interested in professions. And to think
I try my best not to talk about myself. In a moment I
shall talk about the cows, about the sky, if I can. There
I am then, he leaves me, he's in a hurry. He didn't
seem to be in a hurry, he was loitering, I've already said
so, but after three minutes of me he is in a hurry, he has

to hurry. I believe him. And once again I am I will
not say alone, no, that's not like me, but, how shall I
say, I don't know, restored to myself, no, I never left
myself, free, yes, I don't know what that means but it's
the word I mean to use, free to do what, to do nothing,
to know, but what, the laws of the mind perhaps, of my
mind, that for example water rises in proportion as it
drowns you and that you would do better, at least no
worse, to obliterate texts than to blacken margins, to
fill in the holes of words till all is blank and flat and the
whole ghastly business looks like what it is, senseless,
speechless, issueless misery. So I doubtless did better,
at least no worse, not to stir from my observation post.
But instead of observing I had the weakness to return in
spirit to the other, the man with the stick. Then the
murmurs began again. To restore silence is the role of
objects. I said, Who knows if he hasn't simply come out
to take the air, relax, stretch his legs, cool his brain by
stamping the blood down to his feet, so as to make sure
of a good night, a joyous awakening, an enchanted morrow.
Was he carrying so much as a scrip? But the way of
walking, the anxious looks, the club, could these be
reconciled with one's conception of what is called a little
turn? But the hat, a town hat, an old-fashioned town
hat, which the least gust would carry far away. Unless
it was attached under the chin, by means of a string or an
elastic. I took off my hat and looked at it. It is fastened, it has always been fastened, to my buttonhole,
always the same buttonhole, at all seasons, by a long
lace. I am still alive then. That may come in useful.
The hand that held the hat I thrust as far as possible from
me and moved in an arc, to and fro. As I did so, I

watched the lapel of my greatcoat and saw it open and
close. I understand now why I never wore a flower in
my buttonhole, though it was large enough to hold a
whole nosegay. My buttonhole was set aside for my
hat. It was my hat that I beflowered. But it is neither
of my hat nor of my greatcoat that I hope to speak at
present, it would be premature. Doubtless I shall speak
of them later, when the time comes to draw up the inventory of my goods and possessions. Unless I lose them
between now and then. But even lost they will have
their place, in the inventory of my possessions. But I am
easy in my mind, I shall not lose them. Nor my crutches,
I shall not lose my crutches either. But I shall perhaps
one day throw them away. I must have been on the
top, or on the slopes, of some considerable eminence,
for otherwise how could I have seen, so far away, so near
at hand, so far beneath, so many things, fixed and moving.
But what was an eminence doing in this land with hardly
a ripple? And I, what was I doing there, and why come?
These are things that we shall try and discover. But
these are things we must not take seriously. There is a
little of everything, apparently, in nature, and freaks
are common. And I am perhaps confusing several
different occasions, and different times, deep down,
and deep down is my dwelling, oh not deepest down,
somewhere between the mud and the scum. And perhaps
it was A one day at one place, then C another at another,
then a third the rock and I, and so on for the other compo-
nents, the cows, the sky, the sea, the mountains. I
can't believe it. No, I will not lie, I can easily conceive
it. No matter, no matter, let us go on, as if all arose from
one and the same weariness, on and on heaping up and

up, until there is no room, no light, for any more.   What
is certain is that the man with the stick did not pass by
again that night, because I would have heard him, if
he had.   I don't say I would have seen him, I say I
would have heard him.   I sleep little and that little by
day.   Oh not systematically, in my life without end I
have dabbled with every kind of sleep, but at the time
now coming back to me I took my doze in the daytime
and, what is more, in the morning.   Let me hear nothing
of the moon, in my night there is no moon, and if it
happens that I speak of the stars it is by mistake.   Now
of all the noises that night not one was of those heavy
uncertain steps, or of that club with which he sometimes
smote the earth until it quaked.   How agreeable it is
to be confirmed, after a more or less long period of vacil-
lation, in one's first impressions.   Perhaps that is what
tempers the pangs of death.   Not that I was so conclus-
ively, I mean confirmed, in my first impressions with
regard to — wait — C.   For the wagons and carts
which a little before dawn went thundering by, on their
way to market with fruit, eggs, butter and perhaps cheese,
in one of these perhaps he would have been found, overcome by fatigue or discouragement, perhaps even dead.
Or he might have gone back to the town by another way
too far away for me to hear its sounds, or by little paths
through the fields, crushing the silent grass, pounding the
silent ground.   And so at last I came out of that distant
night, divided between the murmurs of my little world,
its dutiful confusions, and those so different (so different?)
of all that between two suns abides and passes away.
Never once a human voice.   But the cows, when the
peasants passed, crying in vain to be milked.   A and

C I never saw again.   But perhaps I shall see them again.
But shall I be able to recognise them?   And am I sure I
never saw them again?   And what do I mean by seeing
and seeing again?   An instant of silence, as when the
conductor taps on his stand, raises his arms, before the
unanswerable clamour.   Smoke, sticks, flesh, hair, at
evening, afar, flung about the craving for a fellow.   I
know how to summon these rags to cover my shame.   I
wonder what that means.   But I shall not always be in
need.   But talking of the craving for a fellow let me
observe that having waked between eleven o'clock and
midday (I heard the angelus, recalling the incarnation,
shortly after) I resolved to go and see my mother.   I
needed, before I could resolve to go and see that woman,
reasons of an urgent nature, and with such reasons,
since I did not know what to do, or where to go, it was
child's play for me, the play of an only child, to fill my
mind until it was rid of all other preoccupation and I
seized with a trembling at the mere idea of being hind-
ered from going there, I mean to my mother, there and
then.   So I got up, adjusted my crutches and went down
to the road, where I found my bicycle (I didn't know I
had one) in the same place I must have left it.   Which
enables me to remark that, crippled though I was, I
was no mean cyclist, at that period.   This is how I went
about it.   I fastened my crutches to the cross-bar, one
on either side, I propped the foot of my stiff leg (I forget
which, now they're both stiff) on the projecting front
axle, and I pedalled with the other.   It was a chainless
bicycle, with a free-wheel, if such a bicycle exists.   Dear
bicycle, I shall not call you bike, you were green, like so
many of your generation, I don't know why.   It is a

pleasure to meet it again. To describe it at length would
be a pleasure. It had a little red horn instead of the bell
fashionable in your days. To blow this horn was for me
a real pleasure, almost a vice. I will go further and
declare that if I were obliged to record, in a roll of honour,
those activities which in the course of my interminable
existence have given me only a mild pain in the balls,
the blowing of a rubber horn—toot!—would figure
among the first. And when I had to part from my bicycle
I took off the horn and kept it about me. I believe I
have it still, somewhere, and if I blow it no more it is
because it has gone dumb. Even motor-cars have no
horns nowadays, as I understand the thing, or rarely.
When I see one, through the lowered window of a stationary car, I often stop and blow it. This should all
be re-written in the pluperfect. What a rest to speak
of bicycles and horns. Unfortunately it is not of them
I have to speak, but of her who brought me into the world,
through the hole in her arse if my memory is correct.
First taste of the shit. So I shall only add that every
hundred yards or so I stopped to rest my legs, the good
one as well as the bad, and not only my legs, not only my
legs. I didn't properly speaking get down off the machine,
I remained astride it, my feet on the ground, my arms on
the handle-bars, my head on my arms, and I waited
until I felt better. But before I leave this earthly paradise,
suspended between the mountains and the sea, sheltered
from certain winds and exposed to all that Auster vents,
in the way of scents and langours, on this accursed country,
it would ill become me not to mention the awful cries
of the corncrakes that run in the corn, in the meadows,
all the short summer night long, dinning their rattles.

And this enables me, what is more, to know when that unreal journey began, the second last but one of a form fading among fading forms, and which I here declare without further ado to have begun in the second or third week of June, at the moment that is to say most painful of all when over what is called our hemisphere the sun is at its pitilessmost and the arctic radiance comes pissing on our midnights. It is then the corncrakes are heard. My mother never refused to see me, that is she never refused to receive me, for it was many a long day since she had seen anything at all. I shall try and speak calmly. We were so old, she and I, she had had me so young, that we were like a couple of old cronies, sexless, unrelated, with the same memories, the same rancours, the same expectations. She never called me son, fortunately, I couldn't have borne it, but Dan, I don't know why, my name is not Dan. Dan was my father's name perhaps, yes, perhaps she took me for my father. I took her for my mother and she took me for my father. Dan, you remember the day I saved the swallow. Dan, you remember the day you buried the ring. I remembered, I remembered, I mean I knew more or less what she was talking about, and if I hadn't always taken part personally in the scenes she evoked, it was just as if I had. I called her Mag, when I had to call her something. And I called her Mag because for me, without my knowing why, the letter g abolished the syllable Ma, and as it were spat on it, better than any other letter would have done. And at the same time I satisfied a deep and doubtless unacknowledged need, the need to have a Ma, that is a mother, and to proclaim it, audibly. For before you say mag you say ma, inevitably. And da, in my part of the world, means father. Besides for me the question did not arise, at the period I'm worming into now, I mean the question of whether to call her Ma, Mag or the Countess Caca, she having for countless years been as deaf as a post. I think she was quite incontinent, both of faeces and water, but a kind of prudishness made us avoid the subject when we met, and I could never be certain of it. In any case it can't have amounted to much, a few niggardly wetted goat-droppings every two or three days. The room smelt of ammonia, oh not merely of ammonia, but of ammonia, ammonia. She knew it was me, by my smell. Her shrunken hairy old face lit up, she was happy to smell me. She jabbered away with a rattle of dentures and most of the time didn't realize what she was saying. Anyone but myself would have been lost in this clattering gabble, which can only have stopped during her brief instants of unconsciousness. In any case I didn't come to listen to her. I got into communication with her by knocking on her skull. One knock meant yes, two no, three I don't know, four money, five goodbye. I was hard put to ram this code into her ruined and frantic understanding, but I did it, in the end. That she should confuse yes, no, I don't know and goodbye, was all the same to me, I confused them myself. But that she should associate the four knocks with anything but money was something to be avoided at all costs. During the period of training therefore, at the same time as I administered the four knocks on her skull, I stuck a bank-note under her nose or in her mouth. In the innocence of my heart! For she seemed to have lost, if not absolutely all notion of mensuration, at least the faculty of counting beyond two. It was too far for her,

yes, the distance was too great, from one to four. By
the time she came to the fourth knock she imagined she
was only at the second, the first two having been erased
from her memory as completely as if they had never been
felt, though I don't quite see how something never felt
can be erased from the memory, and yet it is a common
occurrence. She must have thought I was saying no
to her all the time, whereas nothing was further from my
purpose. Enlightened by these considerations I looked
for and finally found a more effective means of putting the
idea of money into her head. This consisted in repla-
cing the four knocks of my index-knuckle by one or more
(according to my needs) thumps of the fist, on her skull.
That she understood. In any case I didn't come for
money. I took her money, but I didn't come for that.
My mother. I don't think too harshly of her. I know
she did all she could not to have me, except of course
the one thing, and if she never succeeded in getting
me unstuck, it was that fate had earmarked me for less
compassionate sewers. But it was well-meant and that's
enough for me. No it is not enough for me, but I give
her credit, though she is my mother, for what she tried
to do for me. And I forgive her for having jostled me a
little in the first months and spoiled the only endurable,
just endurable, period of my enormous history. And I
also give her credit for not having done it again, thanks
to me, or for having stopped in time, when she did. And
if ever I'm reduced to looking for a meaning to my life,
you never can tell, it's in that old mess I'll stick my nose
to begin with, the mess of that poor old uniparous whore
and myself the last of my foul brood, neither man nor
beast. I should add, before I get down to the facts,

you'd swear they were facts, of that distant summer
afternoon, that with this deaf blind impotent mad old
woman, who called me Dan and whom I called Mag,
and with her alone, I—no, I can't say it. That is to
say I could say it but I won't say it, yes, I could say it
easily, because it wouldn't be true. What did I see of
her? A head always, the hands sometimes, the arms
rarely. A head always. Veiled with hair, wrinkles,
filth, slobber. A head that darkened the air. Not that
seeing matters, but it's something to go on with. It
was I who took the key from under the pillow, who took
the money out of the drawer, who put the key back under
the pillow. But I didn't come for money. I think
there was a woman who came each week. Once I
touched with my lips, vaguely, hastily, that little grey
wizened pear. Pah. Did that please her? I don't
know. Her babble stopped for a second, then began
again. Perhaps she said to herself, Pah. I smelt a
terrible smell. It must have come from the bowels.
Odour of antiquity. Oh I'm not criticizing her, I don't
diffuse the perfumes of Araby myself. Shall I describe
the room? No. I shall have occasion to do so later
perhaps. When I seek refuge there, bet to the world,
all shame drunk, my prick in my rectum, who knows.
Good. Now that we know where we're going, let's go
there. It's so nice to know where you're going, in the
early stages. It almost rids you of the wish to go there.
I was distraught, who am so seldom distraught, from what
should I be distraught, and as to my motions even more
uncertain than usual. The night must have tired me,
at least weakened me, and the sun, hoisting itself higher
and higher in the east, had poisoned me, while I slept.

I ought to have put the bulk of the rock between it and
me before closing my eyes. I confuse east and west,
the poles too, I invert them readily. I was out of sorts.
They are deep, my sorts, a deep ditch, and I am not
often out of them. That's why I mention it. Nevertheless I covered several miles and found myself under
the ramparts. There I dismounted in compliance with
the regulations. Yes, cyclists entering and leaving town
are required by the police to dismount, cars to go into
bottom gear and horsedrawn vehicles to slow down to a
walk. The reason for this regulation is I think this,
that the ways into and of course out of this town are
narrow and darkened by enormous vaults, without
exception. It is a good rule and I observe it religiously,
in spite of the difficulty I have in advancing on my crutches
pushing my bicycle at the same time. I managed somehow. Being ingenious. Thus we cleared these difficult
straits, my bicycle and I, together. But a little further on
I heard myself hailed. I raised my head and saw a
policeman. Elliptically speaking, for it was only later,
by way of induction, or deduction, I forget which, that I
knew what it was. What are you doing there? he
said. I'm used to that question, I understood it immediately. Resting, I said. Resting, he said. Resting,
I said. Will you answer my question? he cried. So
it always is when I'm reduced to confabulation, I honestly
believe I have answered the question I am asked and in
reality I do nothing of the kind. I won't reconstruct
the conversation in all its meanderings. It ended in my
understanding that my way of resting, my attitude when
at rest, astride my bicycle, my arms on the handlebars,
my head on my arms, was a violation of I don't know

what, public order, public decency. Modestly I pointed
to my crutches and ventured one or two noises regarding
my infirmity, which obliged me to rest as I could, rather
than as I should. But there are not two laws, that was
the next thing I thought I understood, not two laws,
one for the healthy, another for the sick, but one only
to which all must bow, rich and poor, young and old,
happy and sad. He was eloquent. I pointed out that
I was not sad. That was a mistake. Your papers,
he said, I knew it a moment later. Not at all, I said,
not at all. Your papers! he cried. Ah my papers.
Now the only papers I carry with me are bits of newspaper.
to wipe myself, you understand, when I have a stool.
Oh I don't say I wipe myself every time I have a stool,
no, but I like to be in a position to do so, if I have to.
Nothing strange about that, it seems to me. In a panic
I took this paper from my pocket and thrust it under
his nose. The weather was fine. We took the little
side streets, quiet, sunlit, I springing along between my
crutches, he pushing my bicycle, with the tips of his
white-gloved fingers. I wasn't—I didn't feel unhappy.
I stopped a moment, I made so bold, to lift my hand and
touch the crown of my hat. It was scorching. I felt
the faces turning to look after us, calm faces and joyful
faces, faces of men, of women and of children. I seemed
to hear, at a certain moment, a distant music. I stopped,
the better to listen. Go on, he said. Listen, I said.
Get on, he said. I wasn't allowed to listen to the music.
It might have drawn a crowd. He gave me a shove. I
had been touched, oh not my skin, but none the less
my skin had felt it, it had felt a man's hard fist, through
its coverings. While still putting my best foot foremost

I gave myself up to that golden moment, as if I had been someone else. It was the hour of rest, the forenoon's toil ended, the afternoon's to come. The wisest perhaps, lying in the squares or sitting on their doorsteps, were savouring its languid ending, forgetful of recent cares, indifferent to those at hand. Others on the contrary were using it to hatch their plans, their heads in their hands. Was there one among them to put himself in my place, to feel how removed I was then from him I seemed to be, and in that remove what strain, as of hawsers about to snap? It's possible. Yes, I was straining towards those spurious deeps, their lying promise of gravity and peace, from all my old poisons I struggled towards them, safely bound. Under the blue sky, under the watchful gaze. Forgetful of my mother, set free from the act, merged in this alien hour, saying, Respite, respite. At the police station I was haled before a very strange official. Dressed in plain-clothes, in his shirt-sleeves, he was sprawling in an arm-chair, his feet on his desk, a straw hat on his head and protruding from his mouth a thin flexible object I could not identify. I had time to become aware of these details before he dismissed me. He listened to his subordinate's report and then began to interrogate me in a tone which, from the point of view of civility, left increasingly to be desired, in my opinion. Between his questions and my answers, I mean those deserving of consideration, the intervals were more or less long and turbulent. I am so little used to being asked anything that when I am asked something I take some time to know what. And the mistake I make then is this, that instead of quietly reflecting on what I have just heard, and heard distinctly, not being hard of hearing, in spite of all I have heard, I hasten to answer blindly, fearing perhaps lest my silence fan their anger to fury. I am full of fear, I have gone in fear all my life, in fear of blows. Insults, abuse, these I can easily bear, but I could never get used to blows. It's strange. Even spits still pain me. But they have only to be a little gentle, I mean refrain from hitting me, and I seldom fail to give satisfaction, in the long run. Now the sergeant, content to threaten me with a cylindrical ruler, was little by little rewarded for his pains by the discovery that I had no papers in the sense this word had a sense for him, nor any occupation, nor any domicile, that my surname escaped me for the moment and that I was on my way to my mother, whose charity kept me dying. As to her address, I was in the dark, but knew how to get there, even in the dark. The district? By the shambles your honour, for from my mother's room, through the closed windows, I had heard, stilling her chatter, the bellowing of the cattle, that violent raucous tremulous bellowing not of the pastures but of the towns, their shambles and cattle-markets. Yes, after all, I had perhaps gone too far in saying that my mother lived near the shambles, it could equally well have been the cattle-market, near which she lived. Never mind, said the sergeant, it's the same district. I took advantage of the silence which followed these kind words to turn towards the window, blindly or nearly, for I had closed my eyes, proffering to that blandness of blue and gold my face and neck alone, and my mind empty too, or nearly, for I must have been wondering if I did not feel like sitting down, after such a long time standing, and remembering what I had learnt in that connexion, namely that the sitting posture was not for me any more, because of my short stiff leg, and that there were only two postures for me any more, the vertical, drooping between my crutches, sleeping on my feet, and the horizontal, down on the ground. And yet the desire to sit down came upon me from time to time, back upon me from a vanished world. And I did not always resist it, forewarned though I was. Yes, my mind felt it surely, this tiny sediment, incomprehensibly stirring like grit at the bottom of a puddle, while on my face and great big Adam's apple the air of summer weighed and the splendid summer sky. And suddenly I remembered my name, Molloy. My name is Molloy, I cried, all of a sudden, now I remember. Nothing compelled me to give this information, but I gave it, hoping to please I suppose. They let me keep my hat on, I don't know why. Is it your mother's name? said the sergeant, it must have been a sergeant. Molloy, I cried, my name is Molloy. Is that your mother's name? said the sergeant. What? I said. Your name is Molloy, said the sergeant. Yes, I said, now I remember. And your mother? said the sergeant. I didn't follow. Is your mother's name Molloy too? said the sergeant. I thought it over. Your mother, said the sergeant, is your mother's—Let me think! I cried. At least I imagine that's how it was. Take your time, said the sergeant. Was mother's name Molloy? Very likely. Her name must be Molloy too, I said. They took me away, to the guardroom I suppose, and there I was told to sit down. I must have tried to explain. I won't go into it. I obtained permission, if not to lie down on a bench, at least to remain standing, propped against the wall. The room was dark

and full of people hastening to and fro, malefactors,
policemen, lawyers, priests and journalists I suppose.
All that made a dark, dark forms crowding in a dark
place. They paid no attention to me and I repaid the
compliment. Then how could I know they were paying
no attention to me, and how could I repay the compliment, since they were paying no attention to me? I
don't know. I knew it and I did it, that's all I know.
But suddenly a woman rose up before me, a big fat woman
dressed in black, or rather in mauve. I still wonder
today if it wasn't the social worker. She was holding
out to me, on an odd saucer, a mug full of a greyish
concoction which must have been green tea with saccharine
and powdered milk. Nor was that all, for between
mug and saucer a thick slab of dry bread was precariously
lodged, so that I began to say, in a kind of anguish,
It's going to fall, it's going to fall, as if it mattered whether
it fell or not. A moment later I myself was holding,
in my trembling hands, this little pile of tottering dispar-
ates, in which the hard, the liquid and the soft were
joined, without understanding how the transfer had been
effected. Let me tell you this, when social workers
offer you, free, gratis and for nothing, something to hinder
you from swooning, which with them is an obsession,
it is useless to recoil, they will pursue you to the ends of
the earth, the vomitory in their hands. The Salvation
Army is no better. Against the charitable gesture there
is no defence, that I know of. You sink your head,
you put out your hands all trembling and twined together
and you say, Thank you, thank you lady, thank you
kind lady. To him who has nothing it is forbidden not
to relish filth. The liquid overflowed, the mug rocked

with a noise of chattering teeth, not mine, I had none,
and the sodden bread sagged more and more. Until,
panicstricken, I flung it all far from me. I did not let
it fall, no, but with a convulsive thrust of both my hands
I threw it to the ground, where it smashed to smithereens,
or against the wall, far from me, with all my strength.
I will not tell what followed, for I am weary of this place,
I want to go. It was late afternoon when they told me
I could go. I was advised to behave better in future.
Conscious of my wrongs, knowing now the reasons for
my arrest, alive to my irregular situation as revealed by
the enquiry, I was surprised to find myself so soon at
freedom once again, if that is what it was, unpenalised.
Had I, without my knowledge, a friend at court? Had I,
without knowing it, favourably impressed the sergeant?
Had they succeeded in finding my mother and obtaining
from her, or from the neighbours, partial confirmation
of my statements? Were they of the opinion that it
was useless to prosecute me? To apply the letter of
the law to a creature like me is not an easy matter. It
can be done, but reason is against it. It is better to
leave things to the police. I don't know. If it is unlaw-
ful to be without papers, why did they not insist on my
getting them. Because that costs money and I had none?
But in that case could they not have appropriated my
bicycle? Probably not, without a court order. All
that is incomprehensible. What is certain is this, that I
never rested in that way again, my feet obscenely resting
on the earth, my arms on the handlebars and on my
arms my head, rocking and abandoned. It is indeed a
deplorable sight, a deplorable example, for the people,
who so need to be encouraged, in their bitter toil, and to

have before their eyes manifestations of strength only, of courage and of joy, without which they might collapse, at the end of the day, and roll on the ground. I have only to be told what good behaviour is and I am well-behaved, within the limits of my physical possibilities. And so I have never ceased to improve, from this point of view, for I—I used to be intelligent and quick. And as far as good-will is concerned, I had it to overflowing, the exasperated good-will of the overanxious. So that my repertory of permitted attitudes has never ceased to grow, from my first steps until my last, executed last year. And if I have always behaved like a pig, the fault lies not with me but with my superiors, who corrected me only on points of detail instead of showing me the essence of the system, after the manner of the great English schools, and the guiding principles of good manners, and how to proceed, without going wrong, from the former to the latter, and how to trace back to its ultimate source a given comportment. For that would have allowed me, before parading in public certain habits such as the finger in the nose, the scratching of the balls, digital emunction and the peripatetic piss, to refer them to the first rules of a reasoned theory. On this subject I had only negative and empirical notions, which means that I was in the dark, most of the time, and all the more completely as a lifetime of observations had left me doubting the possibility of systematic decorum, even within a limited area. But it is only since I have ceased to live that I think of these things and the other things. It is in the tranquillity of decomposition that I remember the long confused emotion which was my life, and that I judge it, as it is said that God will judge me, and with no less impertinence. To decompose is to live too, I know, I know, don't torment me, but one sometimes forgets. And of that life too I shall tell you perhaps one day, the day I know that when I thought I knew I was merely existing and that passion without form or stations will have devoured me down to the rotting flesh itself and that when I know that I know nothing, am only crying out as I have always cried out, more or less piercingly, more or less openly. Let me cry out then, it's said to be good for you. Yes, let me cry out, this time, then another time perhaps, then perhaps a last time. Cry out that the declining sun fell full on the white wall of the barracks. It was like being in China. A confused shadow was cast. It was I and my bicycle. I began to play, gesticulating, waving my hat, moving my bicycle to and fro before me, blowing the horn, watching the wall. They were watching me through the bars, I felt their eyes upon me. The policeman on guard at the door told me to go away. He needn't have, I was calm again. The shadow in the end is no better than the substance. I asked the man to help me, to have pity on me. He didn't understand. I thought of the food I had refused. I took a pebble from my pocket and sucked it. It was smooth, from having been sucked so long, by me, and beaten by the storm. A little pebble in your mouth, round and smooth, appeases, soothes, makes you forget your hunger, forget your thirst. The man came towards me, angered by my slowness. Him too they were watching, through the windows. Somewhere someone laughed. Inside me too someone was laughing. I took my sick leg in my hands and passed it over the frame. I went. I had forgotten where I was going.

I stopped to think. It is difficult to think riding, for me. When I try and think riding I lose my balance and fall. I speak in the present tense, it is so easy to speak in the present tense, when speaking of the past. It is the mythological present, don't mind it. I was already settling in my raglimp stasis when I remembered it wasn't done. I went on my way, that way of which I knew nothing, qua way, which was nothing more than a surface, bright or dark, smooth or rough, and always dear to me, in spite of all, and the dear sound of that which goes and is gone, with a brief dust, when the weather is dry. There I am then, before I knew I had left the town, on the canal-bank. The canal goes through the town, I know I know, there are even two. But then these hedges, these fields? Don't torment yourself, Molloy. Suddenly I see, it was my right leg the stiff one, then. Toiling towards me along the tow-path I saw a team of little grey donkeys, on the far bank, and I heard angry cries and dull blows. I got down. I put my foot to the ground the better to see the approaching barge, so gently approaching that the water was unruffled. It was a cargo of nails and timber, on its way to some carpenter I suppose. My eyes caught a donkey's eyes, they fell to his little feet, their brave fastidious tread. The boatman rested his elbow on his knee, his head on his hand. He had a long white beard. Every three or four puffs, without taking his pipe from his mouth, he spat into the water. I could not see his eyes. The horizon was burning with sulphur and phosphorus, it was there I was bound. At last I got right down, hobbled down to the ditch and lay down, beside my bicycle. I lay at full stretch, with outspread arms. The white hawthorn stooped

towards me, unfortunately I don't like the smell of hawthorn. In the ditch the grass was thick and high, I took
off my hat and pressed about my face the long leafy stalks.
Then I could smell the earth, the smell of the earth was
in the grass that my hands wove round my face till I was
blinded. I ate a little too, a little grass. It came back
to my mind, from nowhere, as a moment before my name,
that I had set out to see my mother, at the beginning
of this ending day. My reasons? I had forgotten them.
But I knew them, I must have known them, I had only
to find them again and I would sweep, with the clipped
wings of necessity, to my mother. Yes, it's all easy when
you know why, a mere matter of magic. Yes, the whole
thing is to know what saint to implore, any fool can
implore him. For the particulars, if you are interested
in particulars, there is no need to despair, you may
scrabble on the right door, in the right way, in the end.
It's for the whole there seems to be no spell. Perhaps
there is no whole, before you're dead. An opiate for
the life of the dead, that should be easy. What am I
waiting for then, to exorcize mine? It's coming, it's
coming. I hear from here the howl resolving all, even
if it is not mine. Meanwhile there's no use knowing
you are gone, you are not, you are writhing yet, the hair
is growing, the nails are growing, the entrails emptying,
all the morticians are dead. Someone has drawn the
blinds, you perhaps. Not the faintest sound. Where
are the famous flies? Yes, there is no denying it, any
longer, it is not you who are dead, but all the others.
So you get up and go to your mother, who thinks she is
alive. That's my impression. But now I shall have to
get myself out of this ditch. How joyfully I would vanish

there, sinking deeper and deeper under the rains. No
doubt I'll come back some day, here, or to a similar
slough, I can trust my feet for that, as no doubt some day
I'll meet again the sergeant and his merry men. And
if, too changed to know it is they, I do not say it is they,
make no mistake, it will be they, though changed. For
to contrive a being, a place, I nearly said an hour, but
I would not hurt anyone's feelings, and then to use them
no more, that would be, how shall I say, I don't know.
Not to want to say, not to know what you want to say,
not to be able to say what you think you want to say,
and never to stop saying, or hardly ever, that is the thing
to keep in mind, even in the heat of composition. That
night was not like the other night, if it had been I would
have known. For when I try and think of that night,
on the canal-bank, I find nothing, no night properly
speaking, nothing but Molloy in the ditch, and perfect
silence, and behind my closed lids the little night and its little
lights, faint at first, then flaming and extinguished, now
ravening, now fed, as fire by filth and martyrs. I say
that night, but there was more than one perhaps. The lie,
the lie, to lying thought. But I find the morning, a morning,
and the sun already high, and the little sleep I had then,
according to my custom, and space with its sounds again,
and the shepherd watching me sleep and under whose
eyes I opened my eyes. Beside him a panting dog,
watching me too, but less closely than his master, for
from time to time he stopped watching me to gnaw at
his flesh, furiously, where the ticks were in him I suppose.
Did he take me for a black sheep entangled in the brambles
and was he waiting for an order from his master to drag
me out? I don't think so. I don't think so. I don't smell like a sheep, I

wish I smelt like a sheep, or a buck-goat. When I wake I see the first things quite clearly, the first things that offer, and I understand them, when they are not too difficult. Then in my eyes and in my head a fine rain begins to fall, as from a rose, highly important. So I knew at once it was a shepherd and his dog I had before me, above me rather, for they had not left the path. And I identified the bleating too, without any trouble, the anxious bleating of the sheep, missing the dog at their heels. It is then too that the meaning of words is least obscure to me, so that I said, with tranquil assurance, Where are you taking them, to the fields or to the shambles? I must have completely lost my sense of direction, as if direction had anything to do with the matter. For even if he was going towards the town, what prevented him from skirting it, or from leaving it again by another gate, on his way to new pastures, and if he was going away from it that meant nothing either, for slaughter-houses are not confined to towns, no, they are everywhere, the country is full of them, every butcher has his slaughter-house and the right to slaughter, according to his lights. But whether it was he didn't understand, or didn't want to reply, he didn't reply, but went on his way without a word, without a word for me I mean, for he spoke to his dog who listened attentively, cocking his ears. I got to my knees, no, that doesn't work, I got up and watched the little procession recede. I heard the shepherd whistle, and I saw him flourishing his crook, and the dog bustling about the herd, which but for him would no doubt have fallen into the canal. All that through a glittering dust, and soon through that mist too which rises in me every day and veils the world

from me and veils me from myself. The bleating grew
faint, because the sheep were less anxious, or because they
were further away, or because my hearing was worse
than a moment before, which would surprise me, for my
hearing is still very good, scarcely blunted coming up
to dawn, and if I sometimes hear nothing for hours on end
it is for reasons of which I know nothing, or because about
me all goes really silent, from time to time, whereas for
the righteous the tumult of the world never stops. That
then is how that second day began, unless it was the third,
or the fourth, and it was a bad beginning, because it
left me with persisting doubts, as to the destination of
those sheep, among which there were lambs, and often
wondering if they had safely reached some commonage
or fallen, their skulls shattered, their thin legs crumpl-
ing, first to their knees, then over on their fleecy sides,
under the pole-axe, though that is not the way they
slaughter sheep, but with a knife, so that they bleed
to death. But there is much to be said too for these
little doubts. Good God, what a land of breeders,
you see quadrupeds everywhere. And it's not over yet,
there are still horses and goats, to mention only them,
I feel them watching out for me, to get in my path. I
have no need of that. But I did not lose sight of my
immediate goal, which was to get to my mother as quickly
as possible, and standing in the ditch I summoned to
my aid the good reasons I had for going there, without a
moment's delay. And though there were many things
I could do without thinking, not knowing what I was
going to do until it was done, and not even then, going
to my mother was not one of them. My feet, you see,
never took me to my mother unless they received a defin-

ite order to do so. The glorious, the truly glorious
weather would have gladdened any other heart than mine.
But I have no reason to be gladdened by the sun and I
take good care not to be. The Aegean, thirsting for
heat and light, him I killed, he killed himself, early on,
in me. The pale gloom of rainy days was better fitted
to my taste, no, that's not it, to my humour, no, that's
not it either, I had neither taste nor humour, I lost them
early on. Perhaps what I mean is that the pale gloom
etc., hid me better, without its being on that account
particularly pleasing to me. Chameleon in spite of
himself, there you have Molloy, viewed from a certain
angle. And in winter, under my greatcoat, I wrapped
myself in swathes of newspaper, and did not shed them
until the earth awoke, for good, in April. The Times
Literary Supplement was admirably adapted to this
purpose, of a neverfailing toughness and impermeability.
Even farts made no impression on it. I can't help it,
gas escapes from my fundament on the least pretext,
it's hard not to mention it now and then, however great
my distaste. One day I counted them. Three hundred
and fifteen farts in nineteen hours, or an average of over
sixteen farts an hour. After all it's not excessive. Four
farts every fifteen minutes. It's nothing. Not even
one fart every four minutes. It's unbelievable. Damn
it, I hardly fart at all, I should never have mentioned it.
Extraordinary how mathematics help you to know yourself. In any case this whole question of climate left me
cold, I could stomach any mess. So I will only add that
the mornings were often sunny, in that part of the world,
until ten o'clock or coming up to eleven, and that then
the sky darkened and the rain fell, fell till evening.

Then the sun came out and went down, the drenched
earth sparkled an instant, then went out, bereft of light.
There I am then back in the saddle, in my numbed heart
a prick of misgiving, like one dying of cancer obliged to
consult his dentist. For I did not know if it was the
right road. All roads were right for me, a wrong road
was an event, for me. But when I was on my way to
my mother only one road was right, the one that led
to her, or one of those that led to her, for all did not
lead to her. I did not know if I was on one of those
right roads and that disturbed me, like all recall to life.
Judge then of my relief when I saw, ahead of me, the
familiar ramparts loom. I passed beyond them, into a
district I did not know. And yet I knew the town well,
for I was born there and had never succeeded in putting
between it and me more than ten or fifteen miles, such
was its grasp on me, I don't know why. So that I came
near to wondering if I was in the right town, where I
first saw the murk of day and which still harboured my
mother, somewhere or other, or if I had not stumbled,
as a result of a wrong turn, on a town whose very name I
did not know. For my native town was the only one
I knew, having never set foot in any other. But I had
read with care, while I still could read, accounts of travellers more fortunate than myself, telling of other towns
as beautiful as mine, and even more beautiful, though
with a different beauty. And now it was a name I
sought, in my memory, the name of the only town it
had been given me to know, with the intention, as soon
as I had found it, of stopping, and saying to a passer-by,
doffing my hat, I beg your pardon, Sir, this *is* X, is it
not?, X being the name of my town. And this name

that I sought, I felt sure that it began with a B or with a
P, but in spite of this clue, or perhaps because of its
falsity, the other letters continued to escape me. I
had been living so far from words so long, you understand,
that it was enough for me to see my town, since we're
talking of my town, to be unable, you understand. It's
too difficult to say, for me. And even my sense of identity
was wrapped in a namelessness often hard to penetrate,
as we have just seen I think. And so on for all the other
things which made merry with my senses. Yes, even
then, when already all was fading, waves and particles,
there could be no things but nameless things, no names
but thingless names. I say that now, but after all what
do I know now about then, now when the icy words
hail down upon me, the icy meanings, and the world dies
too, foully named. All I know is what the words know,
and the dead things, and that makes a handsome little
sum, with a beginning, a middle and an end as in the
well-built phrase and the long sonata of the dead. And
truly it little matters what I say, this or that or any other
thing. Saying is inventing. Wrong, very rightly
wrong. You invent nothing, you think you are inventing, you think you are escaping, and all you do is stammer
out your lesson, the remnants of a pensum one day got
by heart and long forgotten, life without tears, as it is
wept. To hell with it anyway. Where was I. Unable
to remember the name of my town I resolved to stop
by the kerb, to wait for a passer-by with a friendly and
intelligent air and then to whip off my hat and say,
with my smile, I beg your pardon Sir, excuse me Sir,
what is the name of this town, if you please? For the
word once let fall I would know if it was the right word

the one I was seeking, in my memory, or another, and so
where I stood. This resolution, actually formed as I
rode along, was never to be carried out, an absurd mishap
prevented it. Yes, my resolutions were remarkable in
this, that they were no sooner formed than something
always happened to prevent their execution. That
must be why I am even less resolute now than then,
just as then I was even less so than I once had been.
But to tell the truth (to tell the truth!) I have never
been particularly resolute, I mean given to resolutions,
but rather inclined to plunge headlong into the shit,
without knowing who was shitting against whom or on
which side I had the better chance of skulking with
success. But from this leaning too I derived scant satisfaction and if I have never quite got rid of it it is not for
want of trying. The fact is, it seems, that the most you
can hope is to be a little less, in the end, the creature you
were in the beginning, and the middle. For I had
hardly perfected my plan, in my head, when my bicycle
ran over a dog, as subsequently appeared, and fell to the
ground, an ineptness all the more unpardonable as the
dog, duly leashed, was not out on the road, but in on the
pavement, docile at its mistress's heels. Precautions are
like resolutions, to be taken with precaution. The lady
must have thought she had left nothing to chance, so
far as the safety of her dog was concerned, whereas in
reality she was setting the whole system of nature at
naught, no less surely than I myself with my insane
demands for more light. But instead of grovelling in
my turn, invoking my great age and infirmities, I made
things worse by trying to run away. I was soon overtaken, by a bloodthirsty mob of both sexes and all ages,

for I caught a glimpse of white beards and little almost
angelfaces, and they were preparing to tear me to pieces
when the lady intervened.   She said in effect, she told
me so later on and I believed her, Leave this poor old
man alone.   He has killed Teddy, I grant you that,
Teddy whom I loved like my own child, but it is not so
serious as it seems, for as it happens I was taking him to
the veterinary surgeon, to have him put out of his misery.
For Teddy was old, blind, deaf, crippled with rheumatism and perpetually incontinent, night and day, indoors
and out of doors.   Thanks then to this poor old man I
have been spared a painful task, not to mention the
expense which I am ill able to afford, having no other
means of support than the pension of my dear departed,
fallen in defence of a country that called itself his and
from which in his lifetime he never derived the smallest
benefit, but only insults and vexations.   The crowd
was beginning to disperse, the danger was past, but the
lady in her stride.   You may say, she said, that he did
wrong to run away, that he should have explained,
asked to be forgiven.   Granted.   But it is clear he has
not all his wits about him, that he is beside himself,
for reasons of which we know nothing and which might
put us all to shame, if we did know them.   I even wonder
if he knows what he has done.   There emanated such
tedium from this droning voice that I was making ready
to move on when the unavoidable police constable rose
up before me.   He brought down heavily on my handle-
bars his big red hairy paw, I noticed it myself, and had
it appears with the lady the following conversation.
Is this the man who ran over your dog, Madam?   He is,
sergeant, and what of it?   No, I can't record this fatuous

colloquy. So I will merely observe that finally in his
turn the constable too dispersed, the word is not too
strong, grumbling and growling, followed by the last
idlers who had given up all hope of my coming to a bad
end. But he turned back and said, Remove that dog.
Free at last to go I began to do so. But the lady, a
Mrs Loy, I might as well say it now and be done with
it, or Lousse, I forget, Christian name something like
Sophie, held me back, by the tail of my coat, and said,
assuming the words were the same when I heard them
as when first spoken, Sir, I need you. And seeing I
suppose from my expression, which frequently betrays
me, that she had made herself understood, she must
have said, If he understands that he can understand
anything. And she was not mistaken, for after some
time I found myself in possession of certain ideas or
points of view which could only have come to me from her,
namely that having killed her dog I was morally obliged
to help her carry it home and bury it, that she did not
wish to prosecute me for what I had done, but that it
was not always possible to do as one did not wish, that
she found me likeable enough in spite of my hideous
appearance and would be happy to hold out to me a
helping hand, and so on, I've forgotten the half of it.
Ah yes, I too needed her, it seemed. She needed me to
help her get rid of her dog, and I needed her, I've forgotten for what. She must have told me, for that was
an insinuation I could not decently pass over in silence
as I had the rest, and I made no bones about telling
her I needed neither her nor anyone else, which was
perhaps a slight exaggeration, for I must have needed my
mother, otherwise why this frenzy of wanting to get

to her? That is one of the many reasons why I avoid
speaking as much as possible. For I always say either
too much or too little, which is a terrible thing for a man
with a passion for truth like mine. And I shall not
abandon this subject, to which I shall probably never
have occasion to return, with such a storm blowing up,
without making this curious observation, that it often
happened to me, before I gave up speaking for good,
to think I had said too little when in fact I had said too
much and in fact to have said too little when I thought
I had said too much. I mean that on reflexion, in the
long run rather, my verbal profusion turned out to be
penury, and inversely. So time sometimes turns the
tables. In other words, or perhaps another thing,
whatever I said it was never enough and always too
much. Yes, I was never silent, whatever I said I was
never silent. Divine analysis that conduces thus to
knowledge of yourself, and of your fellow-men, if you
happen to have any. For to say I needed no one was
not to say too much, but an infinitesimal part of what I
should have said, could not have said, should never have
said. Need of my mother! No, there were no words
for the want of need in which I was perishing. So that
she, I mean Sophie, must have told me the reasons why
I needed her, since I had dared to disagree. And perhaps
if I took the trouble I might find them again, but trouble,
many thanks, some other time. And now enough of
this boulevard, it must have been a boulevard, of all
these righteous ones, these guardians of the peace, all
these feet and hands, stamping, clutching, clenched in
vain, these bawling mouths that never bawl out of season,
this sky beginning to drip, enough of being abroad,

trapped, visible. Someone was poking the dog, with a malacca. The dog was uniformly yellow, a mongrel I suppose, or a pedigree, I can never tell the difference. His death must have hurt him less than my fall me. And he at least was dead. We slung him across the saddle and set off like an army in retreat, helping each other I suppose, to keep the corpse from falling, to keep the bicycle moving, to keep ourselves moving, through the jeering crowd. The house where Sophie—no, I can't call her that any more, I'll try calling her Lousse, without the Mrs—the house where Lousse lived was not far away. Oh it was not nearby either, I had my bellyful by the time I got there. That is to say I didn't have it really. You think you have your bellyful but you seldom have it really. It was because I knew I was there that I had my bellyful, a mile more to go and I would only have had my bellyful an hour later. Human nature. Marvellous thing. The house where Lousse lived. Must I describe it? I don't think so. I won't, that's all I know, for the moment. Perhaps later on, if I get to know it. And Lousse? Must I describe her? I suppose so. Let's first bury the dog. It was she dug the hole, under a tree. You always bury your dog under a tree, I don't know why. But I have my suspicions. It was she dug the hole because I couldn't, though I was the gentleman, because of my leg. That is to say I could have dug with a trowel, but not with a spade. For when you dig a grave one leg supports the weight of the body while the other, flexing and unflexing, drives the spade into the earth. Now my sick leg, I forget which, it's immaterial here, was in a condition neither to dig, because it was rigid, nor alone to support me,

because it would have collapsed. I had so to speak only
one leg at my disposal, I was virtually onelegged, and
I would have been happier, livelier, amputated at the
groin. And if they had removed a few testicles into the
bargain I wouldn't have objected. For from such
testicles as mine, dangling at mid-thigh at the end of a
meagre cord, there was nothing more to be squeezed,
not a drop. So that non che la speme il desiderio, and
I longed to see them gone, from the old stand where
they bore false witness, for and against, in the lifelong
charge against me. For if they accused me of having made
a balls of it, of me, of them, they thanked me for it too,
from the depths of their rotten bag, the right lower than
the left, or inversely, I forget, decaying circus clowns.
And, worse still, they got in my way when I tried to walk,
when I tried to sit down, as if my sick leg was not enough,
and when I rode my bicycle they bounced up and down.
So the best thing for me would have been for them to
go, and I would have seen to it myself, with a knife or
secateurs, but for my terror of physical pain and festered
wounds, so that I shook. Yes, all my life I have gone in
terror of festered wounds, I who never festered, I was
so acid. My life, my life, now I speak of it as of something over, now as of a joke which still goes on, and it
is neither, for at the same time it is over and it goes on,
and is there any tense for that? Watch wound and buried
by the watchmaker, before he died, whose ruined works
will one day speak of God, to the worms. But those
cullions, I must be attached to them after all, cherish
them as others do their scars, or the family album. In
any case it wasn't their fault I couldn't dig, but my
leg's. It was Lousse dug the hole while I held the dog

in my arms. He was heavy already and cold, but he
had not yet begun to stink. He smelt bad, if you like,
but bad like an old dog, not like a dead dog. He too
had dug holes, perhaps at this very spot. We buried
him as he was, no box or wrapping of any kind, like a
Carthusian monk, but with his collar and lead. It was
she put him in the hole, though I was the gentleman.
For I cannot stoop, neither can I kneel, because of my
infirmity, and if ever I stoop, forgetting who I am, or
kneel, make no mistake, it will not be me, but another.
To throw him in the hole was all I could have done,
and I would have done it gladly. And yet I did not
do it. All the things you would do gladly, oh without
enthusiasm, but gladly, all the things there seems no
reason for your not doing, and that you do not do! Can
it be we are not free? It might be worth looking into.
But what was my contribution to this burial? It was
she dug the hole, put in the dog, filled up the hole. On
the whole I was a mere spectator, I contributed my
presence. As if it had been my own burial. And it
was. It was a larch. It is the only tree I can identify,
with certainty. Funny she should have chosen, to
bury her dog beneath, the only tree I can identify, with
certainty. The sea-green needles are like silk and speckled,
it always seemed to me, with little red, how shall I say,
with little red specks. The dog had ticks in his ears, I
have an eye for such things, they were buried with him.
When she had finished her grave she handed me the
spade and began to muse, or brood. I thought she
was going to cry, it was the thing to do, but on the contrary
she laughed. It was perhaps her way of crying. Or
perhaps I was mistaken and she was really crying, with the

noise of laughter. Tears and laughter, they are so much
Gaelic to me. She would see him no more, her Teddy
she had loved like an only child. I wonder why, since
she had obviously made up her mind to bury the dog
at home, she had not asked the vet to call and destroy the
brute on the premises. Was she really on her way to
the vet at the moment her path crossed mine? Or had
she said so solely in order to attenuate my guilt? Private
calls are naturally more expensive. She ushered me
into the drawing-room and gave me food and drink,
good things without a doubt. Unfortunately I didn't
much care for good things to eat. But I quite liked
getting drunk. If she lived in embarrassed circumstances
there was no sign of it. That kind of embarrassment I
feel at once. Seeing how painful the sitting posture was
for me she fetched a chair for my stiff leg. Without
ceasing to ply me with delicacies she kept up a chatter
of which I did not understand the hundredth part. With
her own hand she took off my hat, and carried it away,
to hang it up somewhere, on a hat-rack I suppose, and
seemed surprised when the lace pulled her up in her
stride. She had a parrot, very pretty, all the most
approved colours. I understood him better than his
mistress. I don't mean I understood him better than she
understood him, I mean I understood him better than I
understood her. He exclaimed from time to time,
Fuck the son of a bitch, fuck the son of a bitch. He must
have belonged to an American sailor, before he belonged
to Lousse. Pets often change masters. He didn't say
much else. No, I'm wrong, he also said, Putain de merde!
He must have belonged to a French sailor before he
belonged to the American sailor. Putain de merde!

Unless he had hit on it alone, it wouldn't surprise me.
Lousse tried to make him say, Pretty Polly! I think
it was too late. He listened, his head on one side, pondered, then said, Fuck the son of a bitch. It was clear
he was doing his best. Him too one day she would bury.
In his cage probably. Me too, if I had stayed, she would
have buried. If I had her address I'd write to her, to
come and bury me. I fell asleep. I woke up in a bed,
in my skin. They had carried their impertinence to the
point of washing me, to judge by the smell I gave off,
no longer gave off. I went to the door. Locked. To
the window. Barred. It was not yet quite dark. What
is there left to try when you have tried the door and the
window? The chimney perhaps. I looked for my
clothes. I found a light switch and switched it on. No
result. What a story! All that left me cold, or nearly.
I found my crutches, against an easy chair. It may seem
strange that I was able to go through the motions I have
described without their help. I find it strange. You
don't remember immediately who you are, when you
wake. On a chair I found a white chamber pot with
a roll of toilet-paper in it. Nothing was being left to
chance. I recount these moments with a certain minute-
ness, it is a relief from what I feel coming. I set a
pouffe against the easy chair, sat down in the latter and
on the former laid my stiff leg. The room was chock-full
of pouffes and easy chairs, they thronged all about me,
in the gloom. There were also occasional tables, footstools,
tallboys, etc., in abundance. Strange feeling of congest-
ion that the night dispersed, though it lit the chandelier,
which I had left turned on. My beard was missing,
when I felt for it with anguished hand. They had

shaved me, they had shorn me of my scant beard. How
had my sleep withstood such liberties? My sleep as a
rule so uneasy. To this question I found a number of
replies. But I did not know which of them was right.
Perhaps they were all wrong. My beard grows properly
only on my chin and dewlap. Where the pretty bristles
grow on other faces, on mine there are none. But such
as it was they had docked my beard. Perhaps they had
dyed it too, I had no proof they had not. I thought I
was naked, in the easy chair, but I finally realized I was
wearing a nightdress, very flimsy. If they had come
and told me I was to be sacrificed at sunrise I would not
have been taken aback. How foolish one can be. It
seemed to me too that I had been perfumed, lavender
perhaps. I said, If only your poor mother could see
you now. I am no enemy of the commonplace. She
seemed far away, my mother, far away from me, and yet
I was a little closer to her than the night before, if my
reckoning was accurate. But was it? If I was in the
right town, I had made progress. But was I? If on the
other hand I was in the wrong town, from which my
mother would necessarily be absent, then I had lost
ground. I must have fallen asleep, for all of a sudden
there was the moon, a huge moon framed in the window.
Two bars divided it in three segments, of which the middle
remained constant, while little by little the right gained
what the left lost. For the moon was moving from
left to right, or the room was moving from right to left,
or both together perhaps, or both were moving from
left to right, but the room not so fast as the moon, or
from right to left, but the moon not so fast as the room.
But can one speak of right and left in such circumstances?

That movements of an extreme complexity were taking place seemed certain, and yet what a simple thing it seemed, that vast yellow light sailing slowly behind my bars and which little by little the dense wall devoured, and finally eclipsed. And now its tranquil course was written on the walls, a radiance scored with shadow, then a brief quivering of leaves, if they were leaves, then that too went out, leaving me in the dark. How difficult it is to speak of the moon and not lose one's head, the witless moon. It must be her arse she shows us always. Yes, I once took an interest in astronomy, I don't deny it. Then it was geology that killed a few years for me. The next pain in the balls was anthropology and the other disciplines, such as psychiatry, that are connected with it, disconnected, then connected again, according to the latest discoveries. What I liked in anthropology was its inexhaustible faculty of negation, its relentless definition of man, as though he were no better than God, in terms of what he is not, But my ideas on this subject were always horribly confused, for my knowledge of men was scant and the meaning of being beyond me. Oh I've tried everything. In the end it was magic that had the honour of my ruins, and still today, when I walk there, I find its vestiges. But mostly they are a place with neither plan nor bounds and of which I understand nothing, not even of what it is made, still less into what. And the thing in ruins. I don't know what it is, what it was, nor whether it is not less a question of ruins than the indestructible chaos of timeless things, if that is the right expression. It is in any case a place devoid of mystery, deserted by magic, because devoid of mystery. And if I do not go there gladly, I go perhaps more gladly there than anywhere else, astonished and at peace, I nearly said as in a dream, but no, no. But it is not the kind of place where you go, but where you find yourself, sometimes, not knowing how, and which you cannot leave at will, and where you find yourself without any pleasure, but with more perhaps than in those places you can escape from, by making an effort, places full of mystery, full of the familiar mysteries. I listen and the voice is of a world collapsing endlessly, a frozen world, under a faint untroubled sky, enough to see by, yes, and frozen too. And I hear it murmur that all wilts and yields, as if loaded down, but here there are no loads, and the ground too, unfit for loads, and the light too, down towards an end it seems can never come. For what possible end to these wastes where true light never was, nor any upright thing, nor any true foundation, but only these leaning things, forever lapsing and crumbling away, beneath a sky without memory of morning or hope of night. These things, what things, come from where, made of what? And it says that here nothing stirs, has never stirred, will never stir, except myself, who do not stir either, when I am there, but see and am seen. Yes, a world at an end, in spite of appearances, its end brought it forth, ending it began, is it clear enough? And I too am at an end, when I am there, my eyes close, my sufferings cease and I end, I wither as the living can not. And if I went on listening to that far whisper, silent long since and which I still hear, I would learn still more, about this. But I will listen no longer, for the time being, to that far whisper, for I do not like it, I fear it. But it is not a sound like the other sounds, that you listen

to, when you choose, and can sometimes silence, by going
away or stopping your ears, no, but it is a sound which
begins to rustle in your head, without your knowing
how, or why. It's with your head you hear it, not your
ears, you can't stop it, but it stops itself, when it chooses.
It makes no difference therefore whether I listen to it
or not, I shall hear it always, no thunder can deliver
me, until it stops. But nothing compels me to speak
of it, when it doesn't suit me. And it doesn't suit me,
at the moment. No, what suits me, at the moment,
is to be done with this business of the moon which was
left unfinished, by me, for me. And if I get done with
it less successfully than if I had all my wits about me,
I shall none the less get done with it, as best I can, at least I
think so. That moon then, all things considered, filled
me suddenly with amaze, with surprise, perhaps better.
Yes, I was considering it, after my fashion, with indifference, seeing it again, in a way, in my head, when a great
fright came suddenly upon me. And deeming this
deserved to be looked into I looked into it and quickly
made the following discovery, among others, but I confine
myself to the following, that this moon which had just
sailed gallant and full past my window had appeared to
me the night before, or the night before that, yes, more
likely, all young and slender, on her back, a shaving.
And then I had said, Now I see, he has waited for the
new moon before launching forth on unknown ways,
leading south. And then a little later, Perhaps I should
go to mother tomorrow. For all things hang together,
by the operation of the Holy Ghost, as the saying is.
And if I failed to mention this detail in its proper place,
it is because you cannot mention everything in its proper

place, you must choose, between the things not worth mentioning and those even less so. For if you set out to mention everything you would never be done, and that's what counts, to be done, to have done. Oh I know, even when you mention only a few of the things there are, you do not get done either, I know, I know. But it's a change of muck. And if all muck is the same muck that doesn't matter, it's good to have a change of muck, to move from one heap to another a little further on, from time to time, fluttering you might say, like a butterfly, as if you were ephemeral. And if you are wrong, and you are wrong, I mean when you record circumstances better left unspoken, and leave unspoken others, rightly, if you like, but how shall I say, for no good reason, yes, rightly, but for no good reason, as for example that new moon, it is often in good faith, excellent faith. Had there then elapsed, between that night on the mountain, that night when I saw A and C and then made up my mind to go and see my mother, and this other night, more time than I had thought, namely fourteen full days, or nearly? And if so, what had happened to those fourteen days, or nearly, and where had they flown? And what possible chance was there of finding a place for them, no matter what their burden, in the so rigorous chain of events I had just undergone? Was it not wiser to suppose either that the moon seen two nights before, far from being new as I had thought, was on the eve of being full, or else that the moon seen from Lousse's house, far from being full, as it had appeared to me, was in fact merely entering on its first quarter, or else finally that here I had to do with two moons, as far from the new as from the full and so alike in outline that the

naked eye could hardly tell between them, and that
whatever was at variance with these hypotheses was so
much smoke and delusion. It was at all events with
the aid of these considerations that I grew calm again
and was restored, in the face of nature's pranks, to my
old ataraxy, for what it was worth. And it came back
also to my mind, as sleep stole over it again, that my
nights were moonless and the moon foreign, to my nights,
so that I had never seen, drifting past the window, carrying
me back to other nights, other moons, this moon I had
just seen, I had forgotten who I was (excusably) and
spoken of myself as I would have of another, if I had
been compelled to speak of another. Yes it sometimes
happens and will sometimes happen again that I forget
who I am and strut before my eyes, like a stranger. Then
I see the sky different from what it is and the earth too
takes on false colours. It looks like rest, it is not, I vanish
happy in that alien light, which must have once been
mine, I am willing to believe it, then the anguish of
return, I won't say where, I can't, to absence perhaps,
you must return, that's all I know, it's misery to stay,
misery to go. The next day I demanded my clothes.
The valet went to find out. He came back with the news
they had been burnt. I continued my inspection of the
room. It was at first sight a perfect cube. Through the
lofty window I saw boughs. They rocked gently, but
not all the time, shaken now and then by sudden spasms.
I noticed the chandelier was burning. My clothes,
I said, my crutches, forgetting my crutches were there,
against the chair. He left me alone again, leaving
the door open. Through the door I saw a big window,
bigger than the door which it overlapped entirely, and

opaque. The valet came back with the news my clothes
had been sent to the dyers, to have the shine taken off.
He held my crutches, which should have seemed strange
to me, but seemed natural to me, on the contrary. I took
hold of one and began to strike the pieces of furniture
with it, not very hard, just hard enough to overturn them,
without breaking them. They were fewer than in the
night. To tell the truth I pushed them rather than
struck them, I thrust at them, I lunged, and that is
not pushing either, but it's more like pushing than striking. But recalling who I was I soon threw away my
crutch and came to a standstill in the middle of the room,
determined to stop asking for things, to stop pretending
to be angry. For to want my clothes, and I thought I
wanted them, was no reason for pretending be to angry,
when they were refused. And alone once more I resumed
my inspection of the room and was on the point of endow-
ing it with other properties when the valet came back
with the news my clothes had been sent for and I would
have them soon. Then he began to straighten the
tables and chairs I had overturned and to put them
back into place, dusting them as he did so with a feather
duster which suddenly appeared in his hand. And so
I began to help him as best I could, by way of proving
that I bore no grudge against anyone. And though I
could not do much, because of my stiff leg, yet I did what
I could, that is to say I took each object as he straightened
it and proceeded with excruciating meticulousness to
restore it to its proper place, stepping back with raised
arms the better to assess the result and then springing
forward to effect minute improvements. And with
the tail of my nightdress as with a duster I petulantly

flicked them one by one. But of this little game too I
soon wearied and suddenly stood stock still in the middle
of the room. But seeing him ready to go I took a step
forward and said, My bicycle. And I said it again, and
again, the same words, until he appeared to understand.
I don't know to what race he belonged, he was so tiny and
ageless, assuredly not to mine. He was an oriental
perhaps, a vague oriental, a child of the Rising Sun.
He wore white trousers, a white shirt and a yellow waistcoat, like a chamois he was, with brass buttons and sandals.
It is not often that I take cognizance so clearly of the
clothes that people wear and I am happy to give you the
benefit of it. The reason for that was perhaps this,
that all morning the talk had been of clothes, of mine.
And perhaps I had been saying, to myself, words to this
effect, Look at him, peaceful in his own clothes, and
look at me, floating about inside another man's nightdress, another woman's probably, for it was pink and
transparent and adorned with ribands and frills and
lace. Whereas the room, I saw the room but darkly,
at each fresh inspection it seemed changed, and that is
known as seeing darkly, in the present state of our knowledge. The boughs themselves seemed to shift, as though
endowed with an orbital velocity of their own, and in
the big frosted window the door was no longer inscribed,
but had slightly shifted to the right, or to the left, I forget,
so that there now appeared within its frame a panel of
white wall, on which I succeeded in casting faint shadows
when I moved. But that there were natural causes
to all these things I am willing to concede, for the resources
of nature are infinite apparently. It was I who was not
natural enough to enter into that order of things, and

appreciate its niceties. But I was used to seeing the sun
rise in the south, used to not knowing where I was going,
what I was leaving, what was going with me, all things
turning and twisting confusedly about me. It is difficult,
is it not, to go to one's mother with things in such a state,
more difficult than to the Lousses of this world, or to its
police-stations, or to the other places that are waiting
for me, I know. But the valet having brought my clothes,
in a paper which he unwrapped in front of me, I saw that
my hat was not among them, so that I said, My hat.
And when he finally understood what I wanted he went
away and came back a little later with my hat. Nothing
was missing then except the lace to fasten my hat to my
buttonhole, but that was something I could not hope
to make him understand, and so I did not mention it.
An old lace, you can always find an old lace, no lace
lasts for ever, the way clothes do, real clothes. As for
the bicycle, I had hopes that it was waiting for me somewhere below stairs, perhaps even before the front door,
ready to carry me away from these horrible scenes. And
I did not see what good it would do to ask for it again,
to submit him and myself to this fresh ordeal, when it
could be avoided. These considerations crossed my mind
with a certain rapidity. Now with regard to the pockets,
four in all, of my clothes, I verified their contents in front
of the valet and discovered that certain things were
missing. My sucking-stone in particular was no longer
there. But sucking-stones abound on our beaches,
when you know where to look for them, and I deemed it
wiser to say nothing about it, all the more so as he would
have been capable, after an hour's argument, of going
and fetching me from the garden a completely unsuck-

able stone. This was a decision too which I took almost instantaneously. But of the other objects which had disappeared why speak, since I did not know exactly what they were. And perhaps they had been taken from me at the police-station, without my knowing it, or scattered and lost, when I fell, or at some other time, or thrown away, for I would sometimes throw away all I had about me, in a burst of irritation. So why speak of them? I resolved nevertheless to declare loudly that a knife was missing, a noble knife, and I did so to such effect that I soon received a very fine vegetable knife, so-called stainless, but it didn't take me long to stain it, and which opened and shut into the bargain, unlike all the vegetable knives I had ever known, and which had a safety catch, highly dangerous as soon appeared and the cause of innumerable cuts, all over my fingers caught between the handle of so-called genuine Irish horn and the blade red with rust and so blunted that it was less a matter of cuts than of contusions. And if I deal at such length with this knife it is because I have it somewhere still I think, among my possessions, and because having dealt with it here at such length I shall not have to deal with it again, when the moment comes, if it ever comes, to draw up the list of my possessions, and that will be a relief, a welcome relief, when that moment comes, I know. For it is natural I should dilate at lesser length on what I lost than on what I could not lose, that goes without saying. And if I do not always appear to observe this principle it is because it escapes me, from time to time, and vanishes, as utterly as if I had never educed it. Mad words, no matter. For I no longer know what I am doing, nor why, those are things I under-

stand less and less, I don't deny it, for why deny it, and
to whom, to you, to whom nothing is denied? And then
doing fills me with such a, I don't know, impossible
to express, for me, now, after so long, yes, that I don't
stop to enquire in virtue of what principle. And all
the less so as whatever I do, that is to say whatever I
say, it will always as it were be the same thing, yes, as
it were. And if I speak of principles, when there are
none, I can't help it, there must be some somewhere.
And if always doing the same thing as it were is not the
same as observing the same principle, I can't help it
either. And then how can you know whether you
are observing it or not? And how can you want to know?
No, all that is not worth while, not worth while bothering
about, and yet you do bother about it, your sense of
values gone. And the things that are worth while you
do not bother about, you let them be, for the same reason,
or wisely, knowing that all these questions of worth and
value have nothing to do with you, who don't know what
you're doing, nor why, and must go on not knowing it,
on pain of, I wonder what, yes, I wonder. For anything worse than what I do, without knowing what,
or why, I have never been able to conceive, and that
doesn't surprise me, for I never tried. For had I been
able to conceive something worse than what I had I
would have known no peace until I got it, if I know
anything about myself. And what I have, what I am,
is enough, was always enough for me, and as far as my
dear little sweet little future is concerned I have no qualms,
I have a good time coming. So I put on my clothes,
having first made sure they had not been tampered with
that is to say I put on my trousers, my great coat, my hat

and my boots. My boots. They came up to where
my calves would have been if I had had calves, and
partly they buttoned, or would have buttoned, if they
had had buttons, and partly they laced, and I have
them still, I think, somewhere. Then I took my crutches
and left the room. The whole day had gone in this
tomfoolery and it was dusk again. Going down the
stairs I inspected the window I had seen through the
door. It lit the staircase with its wild tawny light.
Lousse was in the garden, fussing around the grave.
She was sowing grass on it, as if grass wouldn't have sown
itself on it. She was taking advantage of the cool of
evening. Seeing me, she came warmly towards me and
gave me food and drink. I ate and drank standing,
casting about me in search of my bicycle. She talked
and talked. Soon sated, I began the search for my
bicycle. She followed me. In the end I found it,
half buried in a soft bush. I threw aside my crutches
and took it in my hands, by the saddle and the handle-
bars, intending to wheel it a little, back and forth,
before getting on and leaving for ever this accursed place.
But I pushed and pulled in vain, the wheels would not
turn. It was as though the brakes were jammed, and
heaven knows they were not, for my bicycle had no
brakes. And suddenly overcome by a great weariness,
in spite of the dying day when I always felt most alive,
I threw the bicycle back in the bush and lay down on
the ground, on the grass, careless of the dew, I never
feared the dew. It was then that Lousse, taking advantage of my weakness, squatted down beside me and
began to make me propositions, to which I must confess
I listened, absent-mindedly, I had nothing else to do, I

could do nothing else, and doubtless she had poisoned my
beer with something intended to mollify me, to mollify
Molloy, with the result that I was nothing more than a
lump of melting wax, so to speak.   And from these propositions, which she enunciated slowly and distinctly,
repeating each clause several times, I finally elicited the
following, or gist.   I could not prevent her having a
weakness for me, neither could she.   I would live in
her home, as though it were my own.   I would have
plenty to eat and drink, to smoke too if I smoked, for
nothing, and my remaining days would glide away
without a care.   I would as it were take the place of the
dog I had killed, as it for her had taken the place of a
child.   I would help in the garden, in the house, when
I wished, if I wished.   I would not go out on the street,
for once out I would never find my way in again.   I
would adopt the rhythm of life which best suited me,
getting up, going to bed and taking my meals at whatsoever hours I pleased.   If I did not choose to be clean,
to wear nice clothes, to wash and so on, I need not.
She would be grieved, but what was her grief, compared
to my grief?   All she asked was to feel me near her,
with her, and the right to contemplate from time to time
this extraordinary body both at rest and in motion.
Every now and then I interrupted her, to ask what town
I was in.   But either because she did not understand me,
or because she preferred to leave me in ignorance, she did
not reply to my question, but went on with her soliloquy,
reiterating tirelessly each new proposition, then expound-
ing further, slowly, gently, the benefits for both of us
if I would make my home with her.   Till nothing was
left but this monotonous voice, in the deepening night

and the smell of the damp earth and of a strongly scented flower which at the time I could not identify, but which later I identified as spike-lavender. There were beds of it everywhere, in this garden, for Lousse loved spike, she must have told me herself, otherwise I would not have known, she loved it above all other herbs and flowers, because of its smell, and then also because of its spikes, and its colour. And if I had not lost my sense of smell the smell of lavender would always make me think of Lousse, in accordance with the well-known mechanism of association. And she gathered this lavender when it bloomed I presume, left it to dry and then made it up into lavender-bags that she put in her cupboards to perfume her handkerchiefs, her underclothing and house-linen. But none the less from time to time I heard the chiming of the hours, from the clocks and belfries, chiming out longer and longer, then suddenly briefly, then longer and longer again. This will give some idea of the time she took to cozen me, of her patience and physical endurance, for all the time she was squatting or kneeling beside me, whereas I was stretched out at my ease on the grass, now on my back, now on my stomach, now on one side, now on the other. And all the time she never stopped talking, whereas I only opened my mouth to ask, at long intervals, more and more feebly, what town we were in. And sure of her victory at last, or simply feeling she had done all she could and that further insistence was useless, she got up and went away, I don't know where, for I stayed where I was, with regret, mild regret. For in me there have always been two fools, among others, one asking nothing better than to stay where he is and the other imagining that life might be slightly less horrible a little further on. So that I was never disappointed, so to speak, whatever I did, in this domain. And these inseparable fools I indulged turn about, that they might understand their foolishness. And that night there was no question of moon, nor any other light, but it was a night of listening, a night given to the faint soughing and sighing stirring at night in little pleasure gardens, the shy sabbath of leaves and petals and the air that eddies there as it does not in other places, where there is less constraint, and as it does not during the day, when there is more vigilance, and then something else that is not clear, being neither the air nor what it moves, perhaps the far unchanging noise the earth makes and which other noises cover, but not for long. For they do not account for that noise you hear when you really listen, when all seems hushed. And there was another noise, that of my life become the life of this garden as it rode the earth of deeps and wildernesses. Yes, there were times when I forgot not only who I was, but that I was, forgot to be. Then I was no longer that sealed jar to which I owed my being so well preserved, but a wall gave way and I filled with roots and tame stems for example, stakes long since dead and ready for burning, the recess of night and the imminence of dawn, and then the labour of the planet rolling eager into winter, winter would rid it of these contemptible scabs. Or of that winter I was the precarious calm, the thaw of the snows which make no difference and all the horrors of it all all over again. But that did not happen to me often, mostly I stayed in my jar which knew neither seasons nor gardens. And a good thing too. But in there you have to be careful, ask yourself questions, as for example whether

you still are, and if no when it stopped, and if yes how
long it will still go on, anything at all to keep you from
losing the thread of the dream.   For my part I willingly
asked myself questions, one after the other, just for the
sake of looking at them.   No, not willingly, wisely, so
that I might believe I was still there.   And yet it mean.
nothing to me to be still there.   I called that thinking.
I thought almost without stopping, I did not dare stop
Perhaps that was the cause of my innocence.   It was a
little the worse for wear, a little threadbare perhaps,
but I was glad to have it, yes, I suppose.   Thanks I
suppose, as the urchin said when I picked up his marble,
I don't know why, I didn't have to, and I suppose he
would have preferred to pick it up himself.   Or perhaps
it wasn't to be picked up.   And the effort it cost me,
with my stiff leg.   The words engraved themselves for
ever on my memory, perhaps because I understood
them at once, a thing I didn't often do.   Not that I
was hard of hearing, for I had quite a sensitive ear,
and sounds unencumbered with precise meaning were
registered perhaps better by me than by most.   What
was it then?   A defect of the understanding perhaps,
which only began to vibrate on repeated solicitations,
or which did vibrate, if you like, but at a lower frequency,
or a higher, than that of ratiocination, if such a thing is
conceivable, and such a thing is conceivable, since I
conceive it.   Yes, the words I heard, and heard distinctly,
having quite a sensitive ear, were heard a first time,
then a second, and often even a third, as pure sounds,
free of all meaning, and this is probably one of the reasons
why conversation was unspeakably painful to me.   And
the words I uttered myself, and which must nearly always

have gone with an effort of the intelligence, were often to me as the buzzing of an insect. And this is perhaps one of the reasons I was so untalkative, I mean this trouble I had in understanding not only what others said to me, but also what I said to them. It is true that in the end, by dint of patience, we made ourselves understood, but understood with regard to what, I ask of you, and to what purpose? And to the noises of nature too, and of the works of men, I reacted I think in my own way and without desire of enlightenment. And my eye too, the seeing one, must have been ill-connected with the spider, for I found it hard to name what was mirrored there, often quite distinctly. And without going so far as to say that I saw the world upside down (that would have been too easy) it is certain I saw it in a way inordinately formal, though I was far from being an aesthete, or an artist. And of my two eyes only one functioning more or less correctly, I misjudged the distance separating me from the other world, and often I stretched out my hand for what was far beyond my reach, and often I knocked against obstacles scarcely visible on the horizon. But I was like that even when I had my two eyes, it seems to me, but perhaps not, for it is long since that era of my life, and my recollection of it is more than imperfect. And now I come to think of it, my attempts at taste and smell were scarcely more fortunate, I smelt and tasted without knowing exactly what, nor whether it was good, nor whether it was bad, and seldom twice running the same thing. I would have been I think an excellent husband, incapable of wearying of my wife and committing adultery only from absent-mindedness. Now as to telling you why I stayed a good while with Lousse, no,

I cannot. That is to say I could I suppose, if I took
the trouble. But why should I? In order to establish
beyond all question that I could not do otherwise? For
that is the conclusion I would come to, fatally. I who
had loved the image of old Geulincx, dead young, who
left me free, on the black boat of Ulysses, to crawl towards
the East, along the deck. That is a great measure of
freedom, for him who has not the pioneering spirit.
And from the poop, poring upon the wave, a sadly rejoic-
ing slave, I follow with my eyes the proud and futile
wake. Which, as it bears me from no fatherland away,
bears me onward to no shipwreck. A good while then
with Lousse. It's vague, a good while, a few months
perhaps, a year perhaps. I know it was warm again
the day I left, but that meant nothing, in my part of the
world, where it seemed to be warm or cold or merely
mild at any moment of the year and where the days did
not run gently up and down, no, not gently. Perhaps
things have changed since. So all I know is that it
was much the same weather when I left as when I came,
so far as I was capable of knowing what the weather
was. And I had been under the weather so long, under
all weathers, that I could tell quite well between them,
my body could tell between them and seemed even to
have its likes, its dislikes. I think I stayed in several
rooms one after the other, or alternately, I don't know.
In my head there are several windows, that I do know,
but perhaps it is always the same one, open variously
on the parading universe. The house was fixed, that is
perhaps what I mean by these different rooms. House
and garden were fixed, thanks to some unknown mechanism of compensation, and I, when I stayed still, as I

did most of the time, was fixed too, and when I moved, from place to place, it was very slowly, as in a cage out of time, as the saying is, in the jargon of the schools, and out of space too to be sure. For to be out of one and not out of the other was for cleverer than me, who was not clever, but foolish. But I may be quite wrong. And these different windows that open in my head, when I grope again among those days, really existed perhaps and perhaps do still, in spite of my being no longer there, I mean there looking at them, opening them and shutting them, or crouched in a corner of the room marvelling at the things they framed. But I will not dwell on this episode, so ludicrously brief when you think of it and so poor in substance. For I helped neither in the house nor the garden and knew nothing of what work was going forward, day and night, nothing save the sounds that came to me, dull sounds and sharp ones too, and then often the roar of air being vigorously churned, it seemed to me, and which perhaps was nothing more than the sound of burning. I preferred the garden to the house, to judge by the long hours I spent there, for I spent there the greater part of the day and of the night, whether it was wet or whether it was fine. Men were always busy there, working at I know not what. For the garden seemed hardly to change, from day to day, apart from the tiny changes due to the customary cycle of birth, life and death. And in the midst of those men I drifted like a dead leaf on springs, or else I lay down on the ground, and then they stepped gingerly over me as though I had been a bed of rare flowers. Yes, it was doubtless in order to preserve the garden from apparent change that they laboured at it thus.

My bicycle had disappeared again. Sometimes I felt
the wish to look for it again, to find it again and find out
what was wrong with it or even go for a little ride on the
walks and paths connecting the different parts of the
garden. But instead of trying to satisfy this wish I stayed
where I was looking at it, if I may say so, looking at it
as it shrivelled up and finally disappeared, like the famous
fatal skin, only much quicker. For there seem to be
two ways of behaving in the presence of wishes, the active
and the contemplative, and though they both give the
same result it was the latter I preferred, matter of temperament I presume. The garden was surrounded with
a high wall, its top bristling with broken glass like fins.
But what must have been absolutely unexpected was
this, that this wall was broken by a wicket-gate giving
free access to the road, for it was never locked, of that I
was all but convinced, having opened and closed it
without the least trouble on more than one occasion,
both by day and by night, and seen it used by others
than myself, for the purpose as well of entrance as of
exit. I would stick out my nose, then hastily call it in
again. A few further remarks. Never did I see a
woman within these precincts, and by precincts I do not
merely mean the garden, as I probably should, but the
house too, but only men, with the obvious exception of
Lousse. What I saw and did not see did not matter
much admittedly, but I mention it all the same. Lousse
herself I saw but little, she seldom showed herself, to me,
out of tact perhaps, fearing to alarm me. But I think
she spied on me a great deal, hiding behind the bushes,
or the curtains, or skulking in the shadows of a first-
floor room, with a spy-glass perhaps. For had she not

said she desired above all to see me, both coming and
going and rooted to the spot. And to get a good view
you need the keyhole, the little chink among the leaves,
and so on, whatever prevents you from being seen and
from seeing more than a little at a time. No? I don't
know. Yes, she inspected me, little by little, and even
in my very going to bed, my sleeping and my getting up,
the mornings that I went to bed. For in this matter
I remained faithful to my custom, which was to sleep
in the morning, when I slept at all. For it sometimes
happened that I did not sleep at all, for several days,
without feeling at all the worse for it. For my waking
was a kind of sleeping. And I did not always sleep
in the same place, but now I slept in the garden, which
was large, and now I slept in the house, which was large
too, really extremely spacious. And this uncertainty
as to the hour and place of my sleeping must have entranc-
ed her, I imagine, and made the time pass pleasantly.
But it is useless to dwell on this period of my life. If
I go on long enough calling that my life I'll end up by
believing it. It's the principle of advertising. This
period of my life. It reminds me, when I think of it,
of air in a water-pipe. So I will only add that this
woman went on giving me slow poison, slipping I know
not what poisons into the drink she gave me, or into the
food she gave me, or both, or one day one, the next the
other. That is a grave charge to bring and I do not
bring it lightly. And I bring it without ill-feeling,
yes, I accuse her without ill-feeling of having drugged my
food and drink with noxious and insipid powders and
potions. But even sipid they would have made no difference, I would have swallowed it all down with the same

whole-heartedness. That celebrated whiff of almonds for example would never have taken away my appetite. My appetite! What a subject. For conversation. I had hardly any. I ate like a thrush. But the little I did eat I devoured with a voracity usually attributed to heavy eaters, and wrongly, for heavy eaters as a rule eat ponderously and with method, that follows from the very notion of heavy eating. Whereas I flung myself at the mess, gulped down the half or the quarter of it in two mouthfuls without chewing (with what would I have chewed?), then pushed it from me with loathing. One would have thought I ate to live! Similarly I would engulf five or six mugs of beer with one swig, then drink nothing for a week. What do you expect, one is what one is, partly at least. Nothing or little to be done. Now as to the substances she insinuated thus into my various systems, I could not say whether they were stimulants or whether they were not rather depressants. The truth is, coenaesthetically speaking of course, I felt more or less the same as usual, that is to say, if I may give myself away, so terror-stricken that I was virtually bereft of feeling, not to say of consciousness, and drowned in a deep and merciful torpor shot with brief abominable gleams, I give you my word. Against such harmony of what avail the miserable molys of Lousse, administered in infinitesimal doses probably, to draw the pleasure out. Not that they remained entirely without effect, no, that would be an exaggeration. For from time to time I caught myself making a little bound in the air, two or three feet off the ground at least, at least, I who never bounded. It looked like levitation. And it happened too, less surprisingly, when I was walking, or even

propped up against something, that I suddenly collapsed,
like a puppet when its strings are dropped, and lay long
where I fell, literally boneless. Yes, that struck me as
less strange, for I was used to collapsing thus, but with
this difference, that I felt it coming, and prepared myself
accordingly, as an epileptic does when he feels the fit
coming. I mean that knowing I was going to fall I lay
down, or I wedged myself where I stood so firmly that
nothing short of an earthquake could have dislodged me,
and I waited. But these were precautions I did not always
take, preferring the fall to the trouble of having to lie
down or stand fast. Whereas the falls I suffered when
with Lousse did not give me a chance to circumvent
them. But all the same they surprised me less, they
were more in keeping with me, than the little bounds.
For even as a child I do not remember ever having
bounded, neither rage nor pain ever made me bound,
even as a child, however ill-qualified I am to speak of
that time. Now with regard to my food, it seems to me
I ate it as, when and where it best suited me. I never
had to call for it. It was brought to me, wherever I
happened to be, on a tray. I can still see the tray,
almost at will, it was round, with a low rim, to keep the
things from falling off, and coated with red lacquer,
cracking here and there. It was small too, as became a
tray having to hold a single dish and one slab of bread
For the little I ate I crammed into my mouth with my
hands, and the bottles I drank from the bottle were brought
to me separately, in a basket. But this basket made no
impression on me, good or bad, and I could not tell
you what it was like. And many a time, having strayed
for one reason or another from the place where the meal

had been brought to me, I couldn't find it again, when I felt the desire to eat. Then I searched high and low, often with success, being fairly familiar with the places where I was likely to have been, but often too in vain. Or I did not search at all, preferring hunger and thirst to the trouble of having to search without being sure of finding, or of having to ask for another tray to be brought, and another basket, or the same, to the place where I was. It was then I regretted my sucking-stone. And when I talk of preferring, for example, or regretting, it must not be supposed that I opted for the least evil, and adopted it, for that would be wrong. But not knowing exactly what I was doing or avoiding, I did it and avoided it all unsuspecting that one day, much later, I would have to go back over all these acts and omissions, dimmed and mellowed by age, and drag them into the eudemonistic slop. But I must say that with Lousse my health got no worse, or scarcely. By which I mean that what was already wrong with me got worse and worse, little by little, as was only to be expected. But there was kindled no new seat of suffering or infection, except of course those arising from the spread of existing plethoras and deficiencies. But I may very well be wrong. For of the disorders to come, as for example the loss of the toes of my left foot, no, I am wrong, my right foot, who can say exactly when on my helpless clay the fatal seeds were sown. So all I can say, and I do my best to say no more, is that during my stay with Lousse no more new symptoms appeared, of a patholo-gical nature, I mean nothing new or strange, nothing I could not have foreseen if I could have, nothing at all comparable to the sudden loss of half my toes. For

that is something I could never have foreseen and the
meaning of which I have never fathomed, I mean its
connexion with my other discomforts, from my ignorance
of medical matters, I suppose. For all things run together,
in the body's long madness, I feel it. But it is useless
to drag out this chapter of my, how shall I say, my existence, for it has no sense, to my mind. It is a dug at
which I tug in vain, it yields nothing but wind and
spatter. So I will confine myself to the following brief
additional remarks, and the first of which is this, that
Lousse was a woman of an extraordinary flatness, physically speaking of course, to such a point that I am still
wondering this evening, in the comparative silence of
my last abode, if she was not a man rather or at least an
androgyne. She had a somewhat hairy face, or am I
imagining it, in the interests of the narrative? The poor
woman, I saw her so little, so little looked at her. And
was not her voice suspiciously deep? So she appears
to me today. Don't be tormenting yourself, Molloy,
man or woman, what does it matter? But I cannot help
asking myself the following question. Could a woman
have stopped me as I swept towards mother? Probably.
Better still, was such an encounter possible, I mean
between me and a woman? Now men, I have rubbed up
against a few men in my time, but women? Oh well,
I may as well confess it now, yes, I once rubbed up against
one. I don't mean my mother, I did more than rub up
against her. And if you don't mind we'll leave my
mother out of all this. But another who might have
been my mother, and even I think my grandmother,
if chance had not willed otherwise. Listen to him now
talking about chance. It was she made me acquainted

with love. She went by the peaceful name of Ruth I
think, but I can't say for certain. Perhaps the name was
Edith. She had a hole between her legs, oh not the
bunghole I had always imagined, but a slit, and in this I
put, or rather she put, my so-called virile member, not
without difficulty, and I toiled and moiled until I dis-
charged or gave up trying or was begged by her to stop.
A mug's game in my opinion and tiring on top of that, in
the long run. But I lent myself to it with a good enough
grace, knowing it was love, for she had told me so. She
bent over the couch, because of her rheumatism, and in
I went from behind. It was the only position she could
bear, because of her lumbago. It seemed all right
to me for I had seen dogs, and I was astonished when
she confided that you could go about it differently.
I wonder what she meant exactly. Perhaps after all she
put me in her rectum. A matter of complete indifference
to me, I needn't tell you. But is it true love, in the rectum? That's what bothers me sometimes. Have I never
known true love, after all? She too was an eminently
flat woman and she moved with short stiff steps, leaning
on an ebony stick. Perhaps she too was a man, yet
another of them. But in that case surely our testicles
would have collided, while we writhed. Perhaps she
held hers tight in her hand, on purpose to avoid it. She
favoured voluminous tempestuous shifts and petticoats
and other undergarments whose names I forget. They
welled up all frothing and swishing and then, congress
achieved, broke over us in slow cascades. And all I
could see was her taut yellow nape which every now and
then I set my teeth in, forgetting I had none, such is
the power of instinct. We met in a rubbish dump,

unlike any other, and yet they are all alike, rubbish dumps. I don't know what she was doing there. I was limply poking about in the garbage saying probably, for at that age I must still have been capable of general ideas, This is life. She had no time to lose, I had nothing to lose, I would have made love with a goat, to know what love was She had a dainty flat, no, not dainty, it made you want to lie down in a corner and never get up again. I liked it. It was full of dainty furniture, under our desperate strokes the couch moved forward on its castors, the whole place fell about our ears, it was pandemonium. Our commerce was not without tenderness, with trembling hands she cut my toe-nails and I rubbed her rump with winter cream. This idyll was of short duration. Poor Edith, I hastened her end perhaps. Anyway it was she who started it, in the rubbish dump, when she laid her hand upon my fly. More precisely, I was bent double over a heap of muck, in the hope of finding something to disgust me for ever with eating, when she, undertaking me from behind, thrust her stick between my legs and began to titillate my privates. She gave me money after each session, to me who would have consented to know love, and probe it to the bottom, without charge. But she was an idealist. I would have preferred it seems to me an orifice less arid and roomy, that would have given me a higher opinion of love it seems to me. However. Twixt finger and thumb tis heaven in comparison. But love is no doubt above such base contingencies. And not when you are comfortable, but when your frantic member casts about for a rubbing-place, and the unction of a little mucous membrane, and meeting with none does not beat in retreat, but retains its tumefaction, it is then no doubt that true love comes to pass, and wings away, high above the tight fit and the loose. And when you add a little pedicure and massage, having nothing to do with the instant of bliss strictly speaking, then I feel no further doubt is justified, in this connexion. The other thing that bothers me, in this connexion, is the indifference with which I learnt of her death, one black night I was crawling towards her, an indifference softened indeed by the pain of losing a source of revenue. She died taking a warm tub, as her custom was before receiving me. It limbered her up. When I think she might have expired in my arms! The tub overturned and the dirty water spilt all over the floor and down on top of the lodger below, who gave the alarm. Well, well, I didn't think I knew this story so well. She must have been a woman after all, if she hadn't been it would have got around, in the neighbourhood. It is true they were extraordinarily reserved, in my part of the world, about everything connected with sexual matters. But things have perhaps changed since my time. And it is quite possible that the fact of having found a man when they should have found a woman was immediately repressed and forgotten, by the few unfortunate enough to know about it. As it is quite possible that everybody knew about it, and spoke about it, with the sole exception of myself. But there is one thing that torments me, when I delve into all this, and that is to know whether all my life has been devoid of love or whether I really met with it, in Ruth. What I do know for certain is that I never sought to repeat the experience, having I suppose the intuition that it had been unique and perfect, of its kind, achieved and inimitable, and that it behoved me to preserve its memory, pure of all pastiche, in my heart, even if it meant my resorting from time to time to the alleged joys of so-called self-abuse. Don't talk to me about the chambermaid, I should never have mentioned her, she was long before, I was sick, perhaps there was no chambermaid, ever, in my life. Molloy, or life without a chambermaid. All of which goes to demonstrate that the fact of having met Lousse and even frequented her, in a way, proved nothing as to her sex. And I am quite willing to go on thinking of her as an old woman, widowed and withered, and of Ruth as another, for she too used to speak of her defunct husband and of his inability to satisfy her legitimate cravings. And there are days, like this evening, when my memory confuses them and I am tempted to think of them as one and the same old hag, flattened and crazed by life. And God forgive me, to tell you the horrible truth, my mother's image sometimes mingles with theirs, which is literally unendurable, like being crucified, I don't know why and I don't want to. But I left Lousse at last, one warm airless night, without saying goodbye, as I might at least have done, and without her trying to hold me back, except perhaps by spells. But she must have seen me go, get up, take my crutches and go away, springing on them through the air. And she must have seen the wicket close behind me, for it closed by itself, with the help of a spring, and known me gone, for ever. For she knew the way I had of going to the wicket and peeping out, then quickly drawing back. And she did not try and hold me back but she went and sat down on her dog's grave, perhaps, which was mine too in a way, and which by the way she had not sown with grass,

as I had thought, but with all kinds of little many-coloured
flowers and herbacious plants, selected I imagine in such
a way that when some went out others lit up. I left
her my bicycle which I had taken a dislike to, suspecting
it to be the vehicle of some malignant agency and perhaps
the cause of my recent misfortunes. But all the same I
would have taken it with me if I had known where it
was and that it was in running order. But I did not.
And I was afraid, if I tried to find out, of wearing out
the small voice saying, Get out of here, Molloy, take your
crutches and get out of here and which I had taken so
long to understand, for I had been hearing it for a long
time. And perhaps I understood it all wrong, but I
understood it and that was the novelty. And it seemed to
me I was not necessarily going for good and that I might
come back one day, by devious winding ways, to the place
I was leaving. And perhaps my course is not yet fully
run. Outside in the road the wind was blowing, it was
another world. Not knowing where I was nor consequently what way I ought to go I went with the wind.
And when, well slung between my crutches, I took off,
then I felt it helping me, that little wind blowing from
what quarter I could not tell. And don't come talking
at me of the stars, they look all the same to me, yes, I
cannot read the stars, in spite of my astronomical studies.
But I entered the first shelter I came to and stayed there
till dawn, for I knew I was bound to be stopped by the
first policeman and asked what I was doing, a question
to which I have never been able to find the correct reply.
But it cannot have been a real shelter and I did not stay
till dawn, for a man came in soon after me and drove
me out. And yet there was room for two. I think he

was a kind of nightwatchman, a man of some kind certainly, he must have been employed to watch over some
kind of public works, digging I suppose. I see a brazier.
There must have been a touch of autumn in the air, as
the saying is. I therefore moved on and ensconced
myself on a flight of stairs, in a mean lodging-house,
because there was no door or it didn't shut, I don't know.
Long before dawn this lodging-house began to empty.
People came down the stairs, men and women. I glued
myself against the wall. They paid no heed to me,
nobody interfered with me. In the end I too went
away, when I deemed it prudent, and wandered about
the town in search of a familiar monument, so that I
might say, I am in my town, after all, I have been there
all the time. The town was waking, doors opening and
shutting, soon the noise would be deafening. But espying
a narrow alley between two high buildings I looked about
me, then slipped into it. Little windows overlooked it,
on either side, on every floor, facing one another. Lavatory lights I suppose. There are things from time to
time, in spite of everything, that impose themselves on
the understanding with the force of axioms, for unknown
reasons. There was no way out of the alley, it was not so
much an alley as a blind alley. At the end there were two
recesses, no, that's not the word, opposite each other,
littered with miscellaneous rubbish and with excrements,
of dogs and masters, some dry and odourless, others still
moist. Ah those papers never to be read again, perhaps
never read. Here lovers must have lain at night and
exchanged their vows. I entered one of the alcoves,
wrong again, and leaned against the wall. I would have
preferred to lie down and there was no proof that I

would not. But for the moment I was content to lean
against the wall, my feet far from the wall, on the verge of
slipping, but I had other props, the tips of my crutches.
But a few minutes later I crossed the alley into the other
chapel, that's the word, where I felt I might feel better,
and settled myself in the same hypotenusal posture.
And at first I did actually seem to feel a little better, but
little by little I acquired the conviction that such was not
the case. A fine rain was falling and I took off my hat
to give my skull the benefit of it, my skull all cracked and
furrowed and on fire, on fire. But I also took it off because
it was digging into my neck, because of the thrust of the
wall. So I had two good reasons for taking it off and they
were none too many, neither alone would ever have
prevailed I feel. I threw it from me with a careless lavish
gesture and back it came, at the end of its string or lace,
and after a few throes came to rest against my side. At
last I began to think, that is to say to listen harder. Little
chance of my being found there, I was in peace for as
long as I could endure peace. For the space of an instant
I considered settling down there, making it my lair and
sanctuary, for the space of an instant. I took the vegetable knife from my pocket and set about opening my
wrist. But pain soon got the better of me. First I
cried out, then I gave up, closed the knife and put it
back in my pocket. I wasn't particularly disappointed,
in my heart of hearts I had not hoped for anything better.
So much for that. And backsliding has always depressed
me, but life seems made up of backsliding, and death
itself must be a kind of backsliding, I wouldn't be surprised. Did I say the wind had fallen? A fine rain
falling, somehow that seems to exclude all idea of wind.

My knees are enormous, I have just caught a glimpse of
them, when I got up for a second. My two legs are
as stiff as a life-sentence and yet I sometimes get up.
What can you expect? Thus from time to time I shall
recall my present existence compared to which this is a
nursery tale. But only from time to time, so that it
may be said, if necessary, whenever necessary, Is it possible
that thing is still alive? Or again, Oh it's only a diary,
it'll soon be over. That my knees are enormous, that
I still get up from time to time, these are things that do
not seem at first sight to signify anything in particular.
I record them all the more willingly. In the end I left
the impasse, where half-standing half-lying I may have
had a little sleep, my little morning sleep, and I set off,
believe it or not, towards the sun, why not, the wind
having fallen. Or rather towards the least gloomy quarter of the heavens which a vast cloud was shrouding from
the zenith to the skylines. It was from this cloud the
above rain was falling. See how all things hang together.
And as to making up my mind which quarter of the heavens was the least gloomy, it was no easy matter. For at
first sight the heavens seemed uniformly gloomy. But by
taking a little pains, for there were moments in my life
when I took a little pains, I obtained a result, that is to
say I came to a decision, in this matter. So I was able to
continue on my way, saying, I am going towards the sun,
that is to say in theory towards the East, or perhaps
the South-East, for I am no longer with Lousse, but out
in the heart again of the pre-established harmony, which
makes so sweet a music, which is so sweet a music, for
one who has an ear for music. People were hastening
angrily to and fro, most of them, some in the shelter of

the umbrella, others in that perhaps a little less effective of the rainproof coat. A few had taken refuge under trees and archways. And among those who, more courageous or less delicate, came and went, and among those who had stopped, to avoid getting wet, many a one must have said, They are right, I am wrong, meaning by they the category to which he did not belong, or so I imagine. As many a one too must have said, I am right, they are wrong, while continuing to storm against the foul weather that was the occasion of his superiority. But at the sight of a young old man of wretched aspect, shivering all alone in a narrow doorway, I suddenly remembered the project conceived the day of my encounter with Lousse and her dog and which this encounter had prevented me from carrying out. So I went and stood beside him, with the air I hoped of one who says, Here's a clever fellow, let me follow his example. But before I should make my little speech, which I wished to seem spontaneous and so did not make at once, he went out into the rain and away. For this speech was one liable, in virtue of its content, if not to offend at least to astonish. And that was why it was important to deliver it at the right moment and in the right tone. I apologize for these details, in a moment we'll go faster, much faster. And then perhaps relapse again into a wealth of filthy circumstance. But which in its turn again will give way to vast frescoes, dashed off with loathing. Homo mensura can't do without staffage. There I am then in my turn alone, in the doorway. I could not hope for anyone to come and stand beside me, and yet it was a possibility I did not exclude. That's a fairly good caricature of my state of mind at that instant. Net result, I stayed where

I was.   I had stolen from Lousse a little silver, oh nothing much, massive teaspoons for the most part, and other small objects whose utility I did not grasp but which seemed as if they might have some value.   Among these latter there was one which haunts me still, from time to time.   It consisted of two crosses joined, at their points of intersection, by a bar, and resembled a tiny sawing-horse, with this difference however, that the crosses of the true sawing-horse are not perfect crosses, but truncated at the top, whereas the crosses of the little object I am referring to were perfect, that is to say composed each of two identical V's, one upper with its opening above, like all V's for that matter, and the other lower with its opening below, or more precisely of four rigorously identical V's, the two I have just named and then two more, one on the right hand, the other on the left, having their openings on the right and the left respectively.   But perhaps it is out of place to speak here of right and left, of upper and lower.   For this little object did not seem to have any base properly so-called, but stood with equal stability on any one of its four bases, and without any change of appearance, which is not true of the sawing-horse.   This strange instrument I think I still have somewhere, for I could never bring myself to sell it, even in my worst need, for I could never understand what possible purpose it could serve, nor even contrive the faintest hypothesis on the subject.   And from time to time I took it from my pocket and gazed upon it, with an astonished and affectionate gaze, if I had not been incapable of affection.   But for a certain time I think it inspired me with a kind of veneration, for there was no doubt in my mind that it was not an object of virtu, but

that it had a most specific function always to be hidden
from me. I could therefore puzzle over it endlessly
without the least risk. For to know nothing is nothing,
not to want to know anything likewise, but to be beyond
knowing anything, to know you are beyond knowing
anything, that is when peace enters in, to the soul of
the incurious seeker. It is then the true division begins,
of twenty-two by seven for example, and the pages fill
with the true ciphers at last. But I would rather not
affirm anything on this subject. What does seem undeniable to me on the contrary is this, that giving in to
the evidence, to a very strong probability rather, I left
the shelter of the doorway and began levering myself
forward, swinging slowly through the sullen air. There
is rapture, or there should be, in the motion crutches
give. It is a series of little flights, skimming the ground.
You take off, you land, through the thronging sound
in wind and limb, who have to fasten one foot to the
ground before they dare lift up the other. And even
their most joyous hastening is less aerial than my hobble.
But these are reasonings, based on analysis. And though
my mind was still taken up with my mother, and with
the desire to know if I was near her, it was gradually
less so, perhaps because of the silver in my pockets, but
I think not, and then too because these were ancient
cares and the mind cannot always brood on the same
cares, but needs fresh cares from time to time, so as to
revert with renewed vigour, when the time comes, to
ancient cares. But can one speak here of fresh and
ancient cares? I think not. But it would be hard for
me to prove it. What I can assert, without fear of—
without fear, is that I gradually lost interest in knowing,

among other things, what town I was in and if I should
soon find my mother and settle the matter between us.
And even the nature of that matter grew dim, for me,
without however vanishing completely. For it was
no small matter and I was bent on it. All my life, I
think, I had been bent on it. Yes, so far as I was capable
of being bent on anything all a lifetime long, and what
a lifetime, I had been bent on settling this matter between my mother and me, but had never succeeded.
And while saying to myself that time was running out,
and that soon it would be too late, was perhaps too late
already, to settle the matter in question, I felt myself
drifting towards other cares, other phantoms. And far
more than to know what town I was in, my haste was now
to leave it, even were it the right one, where my mother
had waited so long and perhaps was waiting still. And
it seemed to me that if I kept on in a straight line I was
bound to leave it, sooner or later. So I set myself to
this as best I could, making allowance for the drift to
the right of the feeble light that was my guide. And my
pertinacity was such that I did indeed come to the ramparts
as night was falling, having described a good quarter
of a circle, through bad navigation. It is true I stopped
many times, to rest, but not for long, for I felt harried,
wrongly perhaps. But in the country there is another
justice, other judges, at first. And having cleared the
ramparts I had to confess the sky was clearing, prior to
its winding in the other shroud, night. Yes, the great
cloud was ravelling, discovering here and there a pale
and dying sky, and the sun, already down, was manifest
in the livid tongues of fire darting towards the zenith,
falling and darting again, ever more pale and languid,

and doomed no sooner lit to be extinguished. This phenomenon, if I remember rightly, was characteristic of my region. Things are perhaps different today. Though I fail to see, never having left my region, what right I have to speak of its characteristics. No, I never escaped, and even the limits of my region were unknown to me. But I felt they were far away. But this feeling was based on nothing serious, it was a simple feeling. For if my region had ended no further than my feet could carry me, surely I would have felt it changing slowly. For regions do not suddenly end, as far as I know, but gradually merge into one another. And I never noticed anything of the kind, but however far I went, and in no matter what direction, it was always the same sky, always the same earth, precisely, day after day and night after night. On the other hand, if it is true that regions gradually merge into one another, and this remains to be proved, then I may well have left mine many times, thinking I was still within it. But I preferred to abide by my simple feeling and its voice that said, Molloy, your region is vast, you have never left it and you never shall. And wheresoever you wander, within its distant limits, things will always be the same, precisely. It would thus appear, if this is so, that my movements owed nothing to the places they caused to vanish, but were due to something else, to the buckled wheel that carried me, in unforeseeable jerks, from fatigue to rest, and inversely, for example. But now I do not wander any more, anywhere any more, and indeed I scarcely stir at all, and yet nothing is changed. And the confines of my room, of my bed, of my body, are as remote from me as were those of my region, in the days of my splendour.

And the cycle continues, joltingly, of flight and bivouac, in an Egypt without bounds, without infant, without mother. And when I see my hands, on the sheet, which they love to floccillate already, they are not mine, less than ever mine, I have no arms, they are a couple, they play with the sheet, love-play perhaps, trying to get up perhaps, one on top of the other. But it doesn't last, I bring them back, little by little, towards me, it's resting time. And with my feet it's the same, sometimes, when I see them at the foot of the bed, one with toes, the other without. And that is more deserving of mention. For my legs, corresponding here to my arms of a moment ago, are both stiff now and very sore, and I shouldn't be able to forget them as I can my arms, which are more or less sound and well. And yet I do forget them and I watch the couple as they watch each other, a great way off. But my feet are not like my hands, I do not bring them back to me, when they become my feet again, for I cannot, but they stay there, far from me, but not so far as before. End of the recall. But you'd think that once well clear of the town, and having turned round to look at it, what there was to see of it, you'd think that then I should have realized whether it was really my town or not. But no, I looked at it in vain, and perhaps unquestioningly, and simply to give the gods a chance, by turning round. Perhaps I only made a show of looking at it. I didn't feel I missed my bicycle, no, not really, I didn't mind going on my way the way I said, swinging low in the dark over the earth, along the little empty country roads. And I said there was little like-lihood of my being molested and that it was more likely I should molest them, if they saw me.

Morning is the time to hide. They wake up, hale and
hearty, their tongues hanging out for order, beauty and
justice, baying for their due. Yes, from eight or nine
till noon is the dangerous time. But towards noon
things quiet down, the most implacable are sated, they
go home, it might have been better but they've done a
good job, there have been a few survivors but they'll
give no more trouble, each man counts his rats. It may
begin again in the early afternoon, after the banquet,
the celebrations, the congratulations, the orations, but
it's nothing compared to the morning, mere fun. Coming
up to four or five of course there is the night-shift, the
watchmen, beginning to bestir themselves. But already
the day is over, the shadows lengthen, the walls multiply,
you hug the walls, bowed down like a good boy, oozing
with obsequiousness, having nothing to hide, hiding
from mere terror, looking neither right nor left, hiding
but not provocatively, ready to come out, to smile, to
listen, to crawl, nauseating but not pestilent, less rat
than toad. Then the true night, perilous too but sweet
to him who knows it, who can open to it like the flower
to the sun, who himself is night, day and night. No there
is not much to be said for the night either, but compared
to the day there is much to be said for it, and notably
compared to the morning there is everything to be said
for it. For the night purge is in the hands of technicians,
for the most part. They do nothing else, the bulk of
the population have no part in it, preferring their warm
beds, all things considered. Day is the time for lynching,
for sleep is sacred, and especially the morning, between
breakfast and lunch. My first care then, after a few
miles in the desert dawn, was to look for a place to sleep,

for sleep too is a kind of protection, strange as it may seem. For sleep, if it excites the lust to capture, seems to appease the lust to kill, there and then and bloodily, any hunter will tell you that. For the monster on the move, or on the watch, lurking in his lair, there is no mercy, whereas he taken unawares, in his sleep, may sometimes get the benefit of milder feelings, which deflect the barrel, sheathe the kris. For the hunter is weak at heart and sentimental, overflowing with repressed treasures of gentleness and compassion. And it is thanks to this sweet sleep of terror or exhaustion that many a foul beast, and worthy of extermination, can live on till he dies in the peace and quiet of our zoological gardens, broken only by the innocent laughter, the knowing laughter, of children and their elders, on Sundays and Bank Holidays. And I for my part have always preferred slavery to death, I mean being put to death. For death is a condition I have never been able to conceive to my satisfaction and which therefore cannot go down in the ledger of weal and woe. Whereas my notions on being put to death inspired me with confidence, rightly or wrongly, and I felt I was entitled to act on them, in certain emergencies. Oh they weren't notions like yours, they were notions like mine, all spasm, sweat and trembling, without an atom of common sense or lucidity. But they were the best I had. Yes, the confusion of my ideas on the subject of death was such that I sometimes wondered, believe me or not, if it wasn't a state of being even worse than life. So I found it natural not to rush into it and, when I forgot myself to the point of trying, to stop in time. It's my only excuse. So I crawled into some hole somewhere I suppose and waited, half

sleeping, half sighing, groaning and laughing, or feeling
my body, to see if anything had changed, for the morning
frenzy to abate. Then I resumed my spirals. And as
to saying what became of me, and where I went, in the
months and perhaps the years that followed, no. For
I weary of these inventions and others beckon to me.
But in order to blacken a few more pages may I say I
spent some time at the seaside, without incident. There
are people the sea doesn't suit, who prefer the mountains
or the plain. Personally I feel no worse there than anywhere else. Much of my life has ebbed away before
this shivering expanse, to the sound of the waves in storm
and calm, and the claws of the surf. Before, no, more
than before, one with, spread on the sand, or in a cave.
In the sand I was in my element, letting it trickle between
my fingers, scooping holes that I filled in a moment later
or that filled themselves in, flinging it in the air by handfuls, rolling in it. And in the cave, lit by the beacons
at night, I knew what to do in order to be no worse off
than elsewhere. And that my land went no further,
in one direction at least, did not displease me. And
to feel there was one direction at least in which I could
go no further, without first getting wet, then drowned,
was a blessing. For I have always said, First learn to
walk, then you can take swimming lessons. But don't
imagine my region ended at the coast, that would be
a grave mistake. For it was this sea too, its reefs and
distant islands, and its hidden depths. And I too once
went forth on it, in a sort of oarless skiff, but I paddled
with an old bit of driftwood. And I sometimes wonder
if I ever came back, from that voyage. For if I see myself
putting to sea, and the long hours without landfall, I do

not see the return, the tossing on the breakers, and I do not hear the frail keel grating on the shore. I took advantage of being at the seaside to lay in a store of sucking stones. They were pebbles but I call them stones. Yes, on this occasion I laid in a considerable store. I distributed them equally between my four pockets, and sucked them turn and turn about. This raised a problem which I first solved in the following way. I had say sixteen stones, four in each of my four pockets these being the two pockets of my trousers and the two pockets of my greatcoat. Taking a stone from the right pocket of my greatcoat, and putting it in my mouth, I replaced it in the right pocket of my greatcoat by a stone from the right pocket of my trousers, which I replaced by a stone from the left pocket of my trousers, which I replaced by a stone from the left pocket of my greatcoat, which I replaced by the stone which was in my mouth, as soon as I had finished sucking it. Thus there were still four stones in each of my four pockets, but not quite the same stones. And when the desire to suck took hold of me again, I drew again on the right pocket of my greatcoat, certain of not taking the same stone as the last time. And while I sucked it I rearranged the other stones in the way I have just described. And so on. But this solution did not satisfy me fully. For it did not escape me that, by an extraordinary hazard, the four stones circulating thus might always be the same four. In which case, far from sucking the sixteen stones turn and turn about, I was really only sucking four, always the same, turn and turn about. But I shuffled them well in my pockets, before I began to suck, and again, while I sucked, before transferring them, in the hope of obtaining a more general

circulation of the stones from pocket to pocket. But
this was only a makeshift that could not long content
a man like me. So I began to look for something else.
And the first thing I hit upon was that I might do better
to transfer the stones four by four, instead of one by one,
that is to say, during the sucking, to take the three stones
remaining in the right pocket of my greatcoat and replace
them by the four in the right pocket of my trousers, and
these by the four in the left pocket of my trousers, and
these by the four in the left pocket of my greatcoat, and
finally these by the three from the right pocket of my
greatcoat, plus the one, as soon as I had finished sucking
it, which was in my mouth. Yes, it seemed to me at
first that by so doing I would arrive at a better result.
But on further reflection I had to change my mind and
confess that the circulation of the stones four by four
came to exactly the same thing as their circulation one
by one. For if I was certain of finding each time, in the
right pocket of my greatcoat, four stones totally different
from their immediate predecessors, the possibility nevertheless remained of my always chancing on the same
stone, within each group of four, and consequently of
my sucking, not the sixteen turn and turn about as I
wished, but in fact four only, always the same, turn and
turn about. So I had to seek elsewhere than in the mode
of circulation. For no matter how I caused the stones
to circulate, I always ran the same risk. It was obvious
that by increasing the number of my pockets I was bound
to increase my chances of enjoying my stones in the way
I planned, that is to say one after the other until their
number was exhausted. Had I had eight pockets, for
example, instead of the four I did have, then even the

most diabolical hazard could not have prevented me from sucking at least eight of my sixteen stones, turn and turn about.   The truth is I should have needed sixteen pockets in order to be quite easy in my mind.   And for a long time I could see no other conclusion than this, that short of having sixteen pockets, each with its stone, I could never reach the goal I had set myself, short of an extraordinary hazard.   And if at a pinch I could double the number of my pockets, were it only by dividing each pocket in two, with the help of a few safety-pins let us say, to quadruple them seemed to be more than I could manage. And I did not feel inclined to take all that trouble for a half-measure.   For I was beginning to lose all sense of measure, after all this wrestling and wrangling, and to say, All or nothing.   And if I was tempted for an instant to establish a more equitable proportion between my stones and my pockets, by reducing the former to the number of the latter, it was only for an instant.   For it would have been an admission of defeat.   And sitting on the shore, before the sea, the sixteen stones spread out before my eyes, I gazed at them in anger and per-plexity.   For just as I had difficulty in sitting on a chair, or in an arm-chair, because of my stiff leg you understand, so I had none in sitting on the ground, because of my stiff leg and my stiffening leg, for it was about this time that my good leg, good in the sense that it was not stiff, began to stiffen.   I needed a prop under the ham you understand, and even under the whole length of the leg, the prop of the earth.   And while I gazed thus at my stones, revolving interminable martingales all equally defective, and crush-ing handfuls of sand, so that the sand ran through my fingers and fell back on the strand, yes, while thus I lulled my mind and part of my body, one day suddenly it dawned on the former, dimly, that I might perhaps achieve my purpose without increasing the number of my pockets, or reducing the number of my stones, but simply by sacrificing the principle of trim. The meaning of this illumination, which suddenly began to sing within me, like a verse of Isaiah, or of Jeremiah, I did not penetrate at once, and notably the word trim, which I had never met with, in this sense, long remained obscure. Finally I seemed to grasp that this word trim could not here mean anything else, anything better, than the distribution of the sixteen stones in four groups of four, one group in each pocket, and that it was my refusal to consider any distribution other than this that had vitiated my calculations until then and rendered the problem literally insoluble. And it was on the basis of this interpretation, whether right or wrong, that I finally reached a solution, inelegant assuredly, but sound, sound. Now I am willing to believe, indeed I firmly believe, that other solutions to this problem might have been found, and indeed may still be found, no less sound, but much more elegant, than the one I shall now describe, if I can. And I believe too that had I been a little more insistent, a little more resistant, I could have found them myself. But I was tired, but I was tired, and I contented myself ingloriously with the first solution that was a solution, to this problem. But not to go over the heartbreaking stages through which I passed before I came to it, here it is, in all its hideousness. All (all !) that was necessary was to put for example, to begin with, six stones in the right pocket of my greatcoat, or supply-pocket, five in the right pocket of my trousers, and five in the left pocket of my trousers, that makes the lot, twice five ten plus six sixteen, and none, for none remained, in the left pocket of my greatcoat, which for the time being remained empty, empty of stones that is, for its usual contents remained, as well as occasional objects. For where do you think I hid my vegetable knife, my silver, my horn and the other things that I have not yet named, perhaps shall never name. Good. Now I can begin to suck. Watch me closely. I take a stone from the right pocket of my greatcoat, suck it, stop sucking it, put it in the left pocket of my greatcoat, the one empty (of stones). I take a second stone from the right pocket of my greatcoat, suck it, put it in the left pocket of my greatcoat. And so on until the right pocket of my greatcoat is empty (apart from its usual and casual contents) and the six stones I have just sucked, one after the other, are all in the left pocket of my greatcoat. Pausing then, and concentrating, so as not to make a balls of it, I transfer to the right pocket of my greatcoat, in which there are no stones left, the five stones in the right pocket of my trousers, which I replace by the five stones in the left pocket of my trousers, which I replace by the six stones in the left pocket of my greatcoat. At this stage then the left pocket of my greatcoat is again empty of stones, while the right pocket of my greatcoat is again supplied, and in the right way, that is to say with other stones than those I have just sucked. These other stones I then begin to suck, one after the other, and to transfer as I go along to the left pocket of my greatcoat, being absolutely certain, as far as one can be in an affair of this kind, that I am not sucking the same stones as a moment before, but others. And when the right pocket of my greatcoat is again empty (of stones), and the five I have just sucked are all without exception in the left pocket of my greatcoat, then I proceed to the same redistribution as a moment before, or a similar redestribution, that is to say I transfer to the right pocket of my greatcoat, now again available, the five stones in the right pocket of my trousers, which I replace by the six stones in the left pocket of my trousers, which I replace by the five stones in the left pocket of my greatcoat. And there I am ready to begin again. Do I have to go on? No, for it is clear that after the next series, of sucks and transfers, I shall be back where I started, that is to say with the first six stones back in the supply pocket, the next five in the right pocket of my stinking old trousers and finally the last five in left pocket of same, and my sixteen stones will have been sucked once at least in impeccable succession, not one sucked twice, not one left unsucked. It is true that the next time I could scarcely hope to suck my stones in the same order as the first time and that the first, seventh and twelfth for example of the first cycle might very well be the sixth, eleventh and sixteenth respectively of the second, if the worst came to the worst. But that was a drawback I could not avoid. And if in the cycles taken together utter confusion was bound to reign, at least within each cycle taken separately I could be easy in my mind, at least as easy as one can be, in a proceeding of this kind. For in order for each cycle to be identical, as to the succession of stones in my mouth, and God knows I had set my heart on it, the only means were numbered stones or sixteen pockets. And rather than make twelve more pockets or number my stones, I preferred to make the best of the comparative peace of mind

I enjoyed within each cycle taken separately. For it was
not enough to number the stones, but I would have had
to remember, every time I put a stone in my mouth, the
number I needed and look for it in my pocket. Which
would have put me off stone for ever, in a very short
time. For I would never have been sure of not making
a mistake, unless of course I had kept a kind of register,
in which to tick off the stones one by one, as I sucked
them. And of this I believed myself incapable. No,
the only perfect solution would have been the sixteen
pockets, symmetrically disposed, each one with its stone.
Then I would have needed neither to number nor to
think, but merely, as I sucked a given stone, to move
on the fifteen others, each to the next pocket, a delicate
business admittedly, but within my power, and to call
always on the same pocket when I felt like a suck. This
would have freed me from all anxiety, not only within
each cycle taken separately, but also for the sum of all
cycles, though they went on forever. But however imperfect my own solution was, I was pleased at having found
it all alone, yes, quite pleased. And if it was perhaps
less sound than I had thought in the first flush of discovery, its inelegance never diminished. And it was above
all inelegant in this, to my mind, that the uneven distribution was painful to me, bodily. It is true that a kind
of equilibrium was reached, at a given moment, in the
early stages of each cycle, namely after the third suck
and before the fourth, but it did not last long, and the
rest of the time I felt the weight of the stones dragging
me now to one side, now to the other. So it was something more than a principle I abandoned, when I abandoned the equal distribution, it was a bodily need. But to

suck the stones in the way I have described, not haphazard, but with method, was also I think a bodily need.
Here then were two incompatible bodily needs, at log-
gerheads. Such things happen. But deep down I
didn't give a tinker's curse about being off my balance,
dragged to the right hand and the left, backwards and
forwards. And deep down it was all the same to me
whether I sucked a different stone each time or always
the same stone, until the end of time. For they all tasted
exactly the same. And if I had collected sixteen, it
was not in order to ballast myself in such and such a
way, or to suck them turn about, but simply to have a
little store, so as never to be without. But deep down
I didn't give a fiddler's curse about being without, when
they were all gone they would be all gone, I wouldn't
be any the worse off, or hardly any. And the solution
to which I rallied in the end was to throw away all the
stones but one, which I kept now in one pocket, now in
another, and which of course I soon lost, or threw away,
or gave away, or swallowed. It was a wild part of the
coast. I don't remember having been seriously molested.
The black speck I was, in the great pale stretch of sand,
who could wish it harm? Some came near, to see what
it was, whether it wasn't something of value from a wreck,
washed up by the storm. But when they saw the jetsam
was alive, decently if wretchedly clothed, they turned
away. Old women and young ones, yes, too, come to
gather wood, came and stared, in the early days. But
they were always the same and it was in vain I moved
from one place to another, in the end they all knew what I
was and kept their distance. I think one of them one
day, detaching herself from her companions, came and

offered me something to eat and that I looked at her
in silence, until she went away. Yes, it seems to me
some such incident occurred about this time. But perhaps I am thinking of another stay, at an earlier time,
for this will be my last, my last but one, or two, there is
never a last, by the sea. However that may be I see a
young woman coming towards me and stopping from time
to time to look back at her companions. Huddled together like sheep they watch her recede, urging her on,
and laughing no doubt, I seem to hear laughter, far away.
Then it is her back I see, as she goes away, now it is towards me she looks back, but without stopping. But
perhaps I am merging two times in one, and two women,
one coming towards me, shyly, urged on by the cries
and laughter of her companions, and the other going
away from me, unhesitatingly. For those who came
towards me I saw coming from afar, most of the time,
that is one of the advantages of the seaside. Black specks
in the distance I saw them coming, I could follow all
their manœuvres, saying, It's getting smaller, or, it's
getting bigger. Yes, to be taken unawares was so to
speak impossible, for I turned often towards the land
too. Let me tell you something, my sight was better
at the seaside ! Yes, ranging far and wide over these vast
flats, where nothing lay, nothing stood, my good eye
saw more clearly and there were even days when the
bad one too had to look away. And not only did I see
more clearly, but I had less difficulty in saddling with
a name the rare things I saw. These are some of the
advantages and disadvantages of the seaside. Or perhaps it was I who was changing, why not ? And in the
morning, in my cave, and even sometimes at night,

when the storm raged, I felt reasonably secure from the
elements and mankind. But there too there is a price
to pay. In your box, in your caves, there too there is
a price to pay. And which you pay willingly, for a
time, but which you cannot go on paying forever. For
you cannot go on buying the same thing forever, with
your little pittance. And unfortunately there are other
needs than that of rotting in peace, it's not the word,
I mean of course my mother whose image, blunted for
some time past, was beginning now to harrow me again.
So I went back inland, for my town was not strictly
speaking on the sea, whatever may have been said to
the contrary. And to get to it you had to go inland,
I at least knew of no other way. For between my town
and the sea there was a kind of swamp which, as far back
as I can remember, and some of my memories have their
roots deep in the immediate past, there was always talk
of draining, by means of canals I suppose, or of trans-
forming into a vast port and docks, or into a city on piles
for the workers, in a word of redeeming somehow or
other. And with the same stone they would have killed
the scandal, at the gates of their metropolis, of a stinking
steaming swamp in which an incalculable number of
human lives were yearly engulfed, the statistics escape
me for the moment and doubtless always will, so complete is my indifference to this aspect of the question.
It is true they actually began to work and that work is
still going on in certain areas in the teeth of adversity,
setbacks, epidemics and the apathy of the Public Works
Department, far from me to deny it. But from this to
proclaiming that the sea came lapping at the ramparts
of my town, there was a far cry. And I for my part

will never lend myself to such a perversion (of the truth), until such time as I am compelled or find it convenient to do so. And I knew this swamp a little, having risked my life in it, cautiously, on several occasions, at a period of my life richer in illusions than the one I am trying to patch together here, I mean richer in certain illusions, in others poorer. So there was no way of coming at my town directly, by sea, but you had to disembark well to the north or the south and take to the roads, just imagine that, for they had never heard of Watt, just imagine that too. And now my progress, slow and painful at all times, was more so than ever, because of my short stiff leg, the same which I thought had long been as stiff as a leg could be, but damn the bit of it, for it was growing stiffer than ever, a thing I would not have thought possible, and at the same time shorter every day, but above all because of the other leg, supple hitherto and now growing rapidly stiff in its turn but not yet shortening, unhappily. For when the two legs shorten at the same time, and at the same speed, then all is not lost, no. But when one shortens, and the other not, then you begin to be worried. Oh not that I was exactly worried, but it was a nuisance, yes, a nuisance. For I didn't know which foot to land on, when I came down. Let us try and get this dilemma clear. Follow me carefully. The stiff leg hurt me, admittedly, I mean the old stiff leg, and it was the other which I normally used as a pivot, or prop. But now this latter, as a result of its stiffening I suppose, and the ensuing commotion among nerves and sinews, was beginning to hurt me even more than the other. What a story, God send I don't make a balls of it. For the old pain, do you follow me, I had got used to it, in a way, yes, in a kind of way. Whereas to the new pain, though of the same family exactly, I had not yet had time to adjust myself. Nor should it be forgotten that having one bad leg plus another more or less good, I was able to nurse the former, and reduce its sufferings to the minimum, to the maximum, by using the former exclusively, with the help of my crutches. But I no longer had this resource ! For I no longer had one bad leg plus another more or less good, but now both were equally bad. And the worse, to my mind, was that which till now had been good, at least comparatively good, and whose change for the worse I had not yet got used to. So in a way, if you like, I still had one bad leg and one good, or rather less bad, with this difference however, that the less bad now was the less good of heretofore. It was therefore on the old bad leg that I often longed to lean, between one crutchstroke and the next. For while still extremely sensitive, it was less so than the other, or it was equally so, if you like, but it did not seem so, to me, because of its seniority. But I couldn't ! What ? Lean on it. For it was shortening, don't forget, whereas the other, though stiffening, was not yet shortening, or so far behind its fellow that to all intents and purposes, intents and purposes, I'm lost, no matter. If I could even have bent it, at the knee, or even at the hip, I could have made it seem as short as the other, long enough to land on the true short one, before taking off again. But I couldn't. What? Bend it. For how could I bend it, when it was stiff? I was therefore compelled to work the same old leg as heretofore, in spite of its having become, at least as far as the pain was concerned, the worse of the two and the more in need of

nursing.   Sometimes to be sure, when I was lucky enough
to chance on a road conveniently cambered, or by taking
advantage of a not too deep ditch or any other breach
of surface, I managed to lengthen my short leg, for a
short time.   But it had done no work for so long that
it did not know how to go about it.   And I think a pile
of dishes would have better supported me than it, which
had so well supported me, when I was a tiny tot.   And
another factor of disequilibrium was here involved, I
mean when I thus made the best of the lie of the land,
I mean my crutches, which would have needed to be
unequal, one short and one long, if I was to remain vertical.   No?   I don't know.   In any case the ways I
went were for the most part little forest paths, that's
understandable, where differences of level, though abounding, were too confused and too erratic to be of any help
to me.   But did it make such a difference after all, as
far as the pain was concerned, whether my leg was free
to rest or whether it had to work?   I think not.   For
the suffering of the leg at rest was constant and monotonous.   Whereas the leg condemned to the increase
of pain inflicted by work knew the decrease of pain dispensed by work suspended, the space of an instant.   But
I am human, I fancy, and my progress suffered, from
this state of affairs, and from the slow and painful progress it had always been, whatever may have been said
to the contrary, was changed, saving your presence, to
a veritable calvary, with no limit to its stations and no
hope of crucifixion, though I say it myself, and no Simon,
and reduced me to frequent halts.   Yes, my progress
reduced me to stopping more and more often, it was
the only way to progress, to stop.   And though it is no

part of my tottering intentions to treat here in full, as
they deserve, these brief moments of the immemorial
expiation, I shall nevertheless deal with them briefly,
out of the goodness of my heart, so that my story, so clear
till now, may not end in darkness, the darkness of these
towering forests, these giant fronds, where I hobble,
listen, fall, rise, listen and hobble on, wondering sometimes,
need I say, if I shall ever see again the hated light, at
least unloved, stretched palely between the last boles,
and my mother, to settle with her, and if I would not
do better, at least just as well, to hang myself from a
bough, with a liane. For frankly light meant nothing
to me now, and my mother could scarcely be waiting
for me still, after so long. And my leg, my legs. But
the thought of suicide had little hold on me, I don't
know why, I thought I did, but I see I don't. The idea
of strangulation in particular, however tempting, I always
overcame, after a short struggle. And between you
and me there was never anything wrong with my respir-
atory tracts, apart of course from the agonies intrinsic
to that system. Yes, I could count the days when I
could neither breathe in the blessed air with its life-giving
oxygen nor, when I had breathed it in, breathe out the
bloody stuff, I could have counted them. Ah yes, my
asthma, how often I was tempted to put an end to it,
by cutting my throat. But I never succumbed. The
noise betrayed me, I turned purple. It came on mostly
at night, fortunately, or unfortunately, I could never
make up my mind. For if sudden changes of colour
matter less at night, the least unusual noise is then more
noticeable, because of the silence of the night. But
these were mere crises, and what are crises compared to

all that never stops, knows neither ebb nor flow, its surface leaden above infernal depths. Not a word, not a
word against the crises that seized me, wrung me, and
finally threw me away, mercifully, safe from help. And
I wrapped my head in my coat, to stifle the obscene noise
of choking, or I disguised it as a fit of coughing, universally accepted and approved and whose only disadvantage
is this, that it is liable to let you in for pity. And this is
perhaps the moment to observe, better late than never,
that when I speak of my progress being slowed down,
consequent on the defection of my good leg, I express
only an infinitesimal part of the truth. For the truth
is I had other weak points, here and there, and they too
were growing weaker and weaker, as was only to be
expected. But what was not to be expected was the
speed at which their weakness had increased, since my
departure from the seaside. For as long as I had remained at the seaside my weak points, while admittedly increasing in weakness, as was only to be expected, only
increased imperceptibly, in weakness I mean. So that
I would have hesitated to exclaim, with my finger up
my arse-hole for example, Jesus-Christ, it's much worse
than yesterday, I can hardly believe it is the same hole.
I apologise for having to revert to this lewd orifice, 'tis my
muse will have it so. Perhaps it is less to be thought of
as the eyesore here called by its name than as the symbol
of those passed over in silence, a distinction due perhaps
to its centrality and its air of being a link between me
and the other excrement. We underestimate this little
hole, it seems to me, we call it the arse-hole and affect
to despise it. But is it not rather the true portal of our
being and the celebrated mouth no more than the kitchen-

door. Nothing goes in, or so little, that is not rejected
on the spot, or very nearly. Almost everything revolts
it that comes from without and what comes from within
does not seem to receive a very warm welcome either.
Are not these significant facts. Time will tell. But
I shall do my utmost none the less to keep it in the background, in the future. And that will be easy, for the
future is by no means uncertain, the unspeakable future.
And when it comes to neglecting fundamentals, I think
I have nothing to learn, and indeed I confuse them with
accidentals. But to return to my weak points, let me
say again that at the seaside they had developed normally,
yes, I had noticed nothing abnormal. Either because
I did not pay enough attention to them, absorbed as I
was in the metamorphosis of my excellent leg, or because
there was in fact nothing special to report, in this connection. But I had hardly left the shore, harried by the
dread of waking one fine day, far from my mother, with
my two legs as stiff as my crutches, when they suddenly
began to gallop, my weak points did, and their weakness
became literally the weakness of death, with all the
disadvantages that this entails, when they are not vital
points. I fix at this period the dastardly desertion of my
toes, so to speak in the thick of the fray. You may object
that this is covered by the business of my legs, that it
has no importance, since in any case I could not put to
the ground the foot in question. Quite, quite. But
do you as much as know what foot we're talking about?
No. Nor I. Wait till I think. But you are right,
that wasn't a weak point properly speaking, I mean my
toes, I thought they were in excellent fettle, apart from
a few corns, bunions, ingrowing nails and a tendency

to cramp. No, my true weak points were elsewhere.
And if I do not draw up here and now the impressive
list of them it is because I shall never draw it up. No,
I shall never draw it up, yes, perhaps I shall. And then
I should be sorry to give a wrong idea of my health which,
if it was not exactly rude, to the extent of my bursting
with it, was at bottom of an incredible robustness. For
otherwise how could I have reached the enormous age
I have reached. Thanks to moral qualities? Hygienic
habits? Fresh air? Starvation? Lack of sleep? Solitude? Persecution? The long silent screams (dangerous
to scream)? The daily longing for the earth to swallow
me up? Come come. Fate is rancorous, but not to that
extent. Look at Mammy. What rid me of her, in the
end? I sometimes wonder. Perhaps they buried her
alive, it wouldn't surprise me. Ah the old bitch, a nice
dose she gave me, she and her lousy unconquerable
genes. Bristling with boils ever since I was a brat, a
fat lot of good that ever did me. The heart beats, and
what a beat. That my ureters—no, not a word on that
subject. And the capsules. And the bladder. And
the urethra. And the glans. Santa Maria. I give you
my word, I cannot piss, my word of honour, as a gentleman. But my prepuce, sat verbum, oozes urine, day
and night, at least I think it's urine, it smells of kidney.
What's all this, I thought I had lost the sense of smell.
Can one speak of pissing, under these conditions? Rubbish! My sweat too, and God knows I sweat, has a
queer smell. I think it's in my dribble as well, and
heaven knows I dribble. How I eliminate, to be sure,
uremia will never be the death of me. Me too they
would bury alive, in despair, if there was any justice in

the world. And this list of my weak points I shall never
draw up, for fear of its finishing me, I shall perhaps, one
day, when the time comes for the inventory of my goods
and chattels. For that day, if it ever dawns, I shall be
less afraid, of being finished, than I am today. For
today, if I do not feel precisely at the beginning of my
career, I have not the presumption either to think I
am near the end. So I husband my strength, for the
spurt. For to be unable to spurt, when the hour strikes,
no, you might as well give up. But it is forbidden to
give up and even to stop an instant. So I wait, jogging
along, for the bell to say, Molloy, one last effort, it's
the end. That's how I reason, with the help of images
little suited to my situation. And I can't shake off the
feeling, I don't know why, that the day will come for me
to say what is left of all I had. But I must first wait,
to be sure there is nothing more I can acquire, or lose,
or throw away, or give away. Then I can say, without
fear of error, what is left, in the end, of my possessions.
For it will be the end. And between now and then I
may get poorer, or richer, oh not to the extent of being
any better off, or any worse off, but sufficiently to pre-
clude me from announcing, here and now, what is left
of all I had, for I have not yet had all. But I can make
no sense of this presentiment, and that I understand is
very often the case with the best presentiments, that you
can make no sense of them. So perhaps it is a true presentiment, apt to be borne out. But can any more sense
be made of false presentiments? I think so, yes, I think
that all that is false may more readily be reduced, to
notions clear and distinct, distinct from all other notions.
But I may be wrong. But I was not given to presenti-

ments, but to sentiments sweet and simple, to episenti-
ments rather, if I may venture to say so. For I knew
in advance, which made all presentiment superfluous.
I will even go further (what can I lose?), I knew only in
advance, for when the time came I knew no longer, you
may have noticed it, or only when I made a superhuman
effort, and when the time was past I no longer knew either,
I regained my ignorance. And all that taken together,
if that is possible, should serve to explain many things,
and notably my astonishing old age, still green in places,
assuming the state of my health, in spite of all I have
said about it, is insufficient to account for it. Simple
supposition, committing me to nothing. But I was
saying that if my progress, at this stage, was becoming
more and more slow and painful, this was not due solely
to my legs, but also to innumerable so-called weak points,
having nothing to do with my legs. Unless one is to
suppose, gratuitously, that they and my legs were part
of the same syndrome, which in that case would have
been of a diabolical complexity. The fact is, and I
deplore it, but it is too late now to do anything about it,
that I have laid too much stress on my legs, throughout
these wanderings, to the detriment of the rest. For I
was no ordinary cripple, far from it, and there were
days when my legs were the best part of me, with the
exception of the brain capable of forming such a judge-
ment. I was therefore obliged to stop more and more
often, I shall never weary of repeating it, and to lie down,
in defiance of the rules, now prone, now supine, now on
one side, now on the other, and as much as possible with
the feet higher than the head, to dislodge the clots. And
to lie with the feet higher than the head, when your legs

are stiff, is no easy matter. But don't worry, I did it.
When my comfort was at stake there was no trouble I
would not go to. The forest was all about me and the
boughs, twining together at a prodigious height, compared
to mine, sheltered me from the light and the elements.
Some days I advanced no more than thirty or forty
paces, I give you my oath. To say I stumbled in impenetrable darkness, no, I cannot. I stumbled, but the
darkness was not impenetrable. For there reigned a
kind of blue gloom, more than sufficient for my visual
needs. I was astonished this gloom was not green,
rather than blue, but I saw it blue and perhaps it was.
The red of the sun, mingling with the green of the leaves,
gave a blue result, that is how I reasoned. But from time
to time. From time to time. What tenderness in these
little words, what savagery. But from time to time I
came on a kind of crossroads, you know, a star, or circus,
of the kind to be found in even the most unexplored of
forests. And turning then methodically to face the
radiating paths in turn, hoping for I know not what, I
described a complete circle, or less than a circle, or
more than a circle, so great was the resemblance between
them. Here the gloom was not so thick and I made
haste to leave it. I don't like gloom to lighten, there's
something shady about it. I had a certain number of
encounters in this forest, naturally, where does one not,
but nothing to signify. I notably encountered a charcoal-
burner. I might have loved him, I think, if I had been
seventy years younger. But it's not certain. For then
he too would have been younger by as much, oh not
quite as much, but much younger. I never really had
much love to spare, but all the same I had my little quota,

when I was small, and it went to the old men, when it
could. And I even think I had time to love one or
two, oh not with true love, no, nothing like the old woman,
I've lost her name again, Rose, no, anyway you see who
I mean, but all the same, how shall I say, tenderly, as
those on the brink of a better earth. Ah I was a precocious child, and then I was a precocious man. Now
they all give me the shits, the ripe, the unripe and the
rotting from the bough. He was all over me, begging
me to share his hut, believe it or not. A total stranger.
Sick with solitude probably. I say charcoal-burner, but
I really don't know. I see smoke somewhere. That's
something that never escapes me, smoke. A long dialogue ensued, interspersed with groans. I could not ask
him the way to my town, the name of which escaped me
still. I asked him the way to the nearest town, I found
the neccessary words, and accents. He did not know.
He was born in the forest probably and had spent his
whole life there. I asked him to show me the nearest
way out of the forest. I grew eloquent. His reply was
exceedingly confused. Either I didn't understand a
word he said, or he didn't understand a word I said, or
he knew nothing, or he wanted to keep me near him.
It was towards this fourth hypothesis that in all modesty
I leaned, for when I made to go, he held me back by the
sleeve. So I smartly freed a crutch and dealt him a
good dint on the skull. That calmed him. The dirty
old brute. I got up and went on. But I hadn't gone
more than a few paces, and for me at this time a few
paces meant something, when I turned and went back
to where he lay, to examine him. Seeing he had not
ceased to breathe I contented myself with giving him

a few warm kicks in the ribs, with my heels. This is how I went about it. I carefully chose the most favourable position, a few paces from the body, with my back of course turned to it. Then, nicely balanced on my crutches, I began to swing, backwards, forwards, feet pressed together, or rather legs pressed together, for how could I press my feet together, with my legs in the state they were? But how could I press my legs together, in the state they were? I pressed them together, that's all I can tell you. Take it or leave it. Or I didn't press them together. What can that possibly matter? I swung, that's all that matters, in an ever-widening arc, until I decided the moment had come and launched myself forward with all my strength and consequently, a moment later, backward, which gave the desired result. Where did I get this access of vigour? From my weakness perhaps. The shock knocked me down. Naturally. I came a cropper. You can't have everything, I've often noticed it. I rested a moment, then got up, picked up my crutches, took up my position on the other side of the body and applied myself with method to the same exercise. I always had a mania for symmetry. But I must have aimed a little low and one of my heels sank in something soft. However. For if I had missed the ribs, with that heel, I had no doubt landed in the kidney, oh not hard enough to burst it, no, I fancy not. People imagine, because you are old, poor, crippled, terrified, that you can't stand up for yourself, and generally speaking that is so. But given favourable conditions, a feeble and awkward assailant, in your own class what, and a lonely place, and you have a good chance of showing what stuff you are made of. And it is doubtless in order

to revive interest in this possibility, too often forgotten,
that I have delayed over an incident of no interest in
itself, like all that has a moral. But did I at least eat,
from time to time? Perforce, perforce, roots, berries,
sometimes a little mulberry, a mushroom from time to
time, trembling, knowing nothing about mushrooms.
What else, ah yes, carobs, so dear to goats. In a word
whatever I could find, forests abound in good things.
And having heard, or more probably read somewhere,
in the days when I thought I would be well advised to
educate myself, or amuse myself, or stupefy myself, or
kill time, that when a man in a forest thinks he is going
forward in a straight line, in reality he is going in a circle,
I did my best to go in a circle, hoping in this way to go
in a straight line. For I stopped being half-witted and
became sly, whenever I took the trouble. And my head
was a storehouse of useful knowledge. And if I did not
go in a rigorously straight line, with my system of going
in a circle, at least I did not go in a circle, and that was
something. And by going on doing this, day after day,
and night after night, I looked forward to getting out of
the forest, some day. For my region was not all forest,
far from it. But there were plains too, mountains and
sea, and some towns and villages, connected by highways
and byways. And I was all the more convinced that
I would get out of the forest some day as I had already
got out of it, more than once, and I knew how difficult
it was not to do again what you have done before. But
things had been rather different then. And yet I did
not despair of seeing the light tremble, some day, through
the still boughs, the strange light of the plain, its pale
wild eddies, through the bronze-still boughs, which no

breath ever stirred. But it was a day I dreaded too.
So that I was sure it would come sooner or later. For
it was not so bad being in the forest, I could imagine
worse, and I could have stayed there till I died, unre-
pining, yes, without pining for the light and the plain
and the other amenities of my region. For I knew them
well, the amenities of my region, and I considered that
the forest was no worse. And it was not only no worse,
to my mind, but it was better, in this sense, that I was there.
That is a strange way, is it not, of looking at things.
Perhaps less strange than it seems. For being in the
forest, a place neither worse nor better than the others,
and being free to stay there, was it not natural I should
think highly of it, not because of what it was, but because
I was there. For I was there. And being there I did
not have to go there, and that was not to be despised,
seeing the state of my legs and my body in general. That
is all I wished to say, and if I did not say it at the outset
it is simply that something was against it. But I could
not, stay in the forest I mean, I was not free to. That
is to say I could have, physically nothing could have been
easier, but I was not purely physical, I lacked something,
and I would have had the feeling, if I had stayed in the
forest, of going against an imperative, at least I had that
impression. But perhaps I was mistaken, perhaps I
would have been better advised to stay in the forest,
perhaps I could have stayed there, without remorse,
without the painful impression of committing a fault,
almost a sin. For I have greatly sinned, at all times,
greatly sinned against my prompters. And if I cannot
decently be proud of this I see no reason either to be sorry.
But imperatives are a little different, and I have always

been inclined to submit to them, I don't know why.
For they never led me anywhere, but tore me from places
where, if all was not well, all was no worse than anywhere else, and then went silent, leaving me stranded.
So I knew my imperatives well, and yet I submitted to
them. It had become a habit. It is true they nearly
all bore on the same question, that of my relations with
my mother, and on the importance of bringing as soon
as possible some light to bear on these and even on the
kind of light that should be brought to bear and the most
effective means of doing so. Yes, these imperatives
were quite explicit and even detailed until, having set
me in motion at last, they began to falter, then went
silent, leaving me there like a fool who neither knows
where he is going nor why he is going there. And they
nearly all bore, as I may have said already, on the same
painful and thorny question. And I do not think I
could mention even one having a different purport. And
the one enjoining me then to leave the forest without
delay was in no way different from those I was used to,
as to its meaning. For in its framing I thought I noticed
something new. For after the usual blarney there followed this solemn warning, Perhaps it is already too late.
It was in Latin, nimis sero, I think that's Latin. Charming things, hypothetical imperatives. But if I had never
succeeded in liquidating this matter of my mother, the
fault must not be imputed solely to that voice which
deserted me, prematurely. It was partly to blame,
that's all it can be reproached with. For the outer
world opposed my succeeding too, with its wiles, I have
given some examples. And even if the voice could have
harried me to the very scene of action, even then I might

well have succeeded no better, because of the other
obstacles barring my way. And in this command which
faltered, then died, it was hard not to hear the unspoken
entreaty, Don't do it, Molloy. In forever reminding
me thus of my duty was its purpose to show me the folly
of it? Perhaps. Fortunately it did no more than stress,
the better to mock if you like, an innate velleity. And
of myself, all my life, I think I had been going to my mother,
with the purpose of establishing our relations on a less
precarious footing. And when I was with her, and I
often succeeded, I left her without having done anything.
And when I was no longer with her I was again on my
way to her, hoping to do better the next time. And when
I appeared to give up and to busy myself with something
else, or with nothing at all any more, in reality I was
hatching my plans and seeking the way to her house.
This is taking a queer turn. So even without this so-
called imperative I impugn, it would have been difficult
for me to stay in the forest, since I was forced to assume
my mother was not there. And yet it might have been
better for me to try and stay. But I also said, Yet a
little while, at the rate things are going, and I won't
be able to move, but will have to stay, where I happen
to be, unless someone comes and carries me. Oh I did
not say it in such limpid language. And when I say I
said, etc., all I mean is that I knew confusedly things
were so, without knowing exactly what it was all about.
And every time I say, I said this, or, I said that, or speak
of a voice saying, far away inside me, Molloy, and then
a fine phrase more or less clear and simple, or find myself
compelled to attribute to others intelligible words, or
hear my own voice uttering to others more or less artic-

ulate sounds, I am merely complying with the con-
vention that demands you either lie or hold your peace.
For what really happened was quite different. And
I did not say, Yet a little while, at the rate things are
going, etc., but that resembled perhaps what I would
have said, if I had been able. In reality I said nothing
at all, but I heard a murmur, something gone wrong
with the silence, and I pricked up my ears, like an animal
I imagine, which gives a start and pretends to be dead.
And then sometimes there arose within me, confusedly,
a kind of consciousness, which I express by saying, I
said, etc., or, Don't do it Molloy, or, Is that your mother's
name? said the sergeant, I quote from memory. Or
which I express without sinking to the level of oratio
recta, but by means of other figures quite as deceitful,
as for example, It seemed to me that, etc., or, I had the
impression that, etc., for it seemed to me nothing at all,
and I had no impression of any kind, but simply somewhere
something had changed, so that I too had to change,
or the world too had to change, in order for nothing
to be changed. And it was these little adjustments,
as between Galileo's vessels, that I can only express by
saying, I feared that, or, I hoped that, or, Is that your
mother's name? said the sergeant, for example, and that
I might doubtless have expressed otherwise and better,
if I had gone to the trouble. And so I shall perhaps
some day when I have less horror of trouble than today.
But I think not. So I said, Yet a little while, at the
rate things are going, and I won't be able to move, but
will have to stay, where I happen to be, unless some kind
person comes and carries me. For my marches got
shorter and shorter and my halts in consequence more

and more frequent and I may add prolonged. For
the notion of the long halt does not necessarily follow
from that of the short march, nor that of the frequent
halt either, when you come to think of it, unless you give
frequent a meaning it does not possess, and I could never
bring myself to do a thing like that. And it seemed
to me all the more important to get out of this forest
with all possible speed as I would very soon be powerless to get out of anything whatsoever, were it but a
bower. It was winter, it must have been winter, and
not only many trees had lost their leaves, but these lost
leaves had gone all black and spongy and my crutches
sank into them, in places right up to the fork. Strange
to say I felt no colder than usual. Perhaps it was only
autumn. But I was never very sensitive to changes
of temperature. And the gloom, if it seemed less blue
than before, was as thick as ever. Which made me say
in the end, It is less blue because there is less green, but
it is no less thick thanks to the leaden winter sky. Then
something about the black dripping from the black
boughs, something in that line. The black slush of leaves
slowed me down even more. But leaves or no leaves
I would have abandoned erect motion, that of man.
And I still remember the day when, flat on my face by
way of rest, in defiance of the rules, I suddenly cried,
striking my brow, Christ, there's crawling, I never thought
of that. But could I crawl, with my legs in such a state,
and my trunk? And my head. But before I go on,
a word about the forest murmurs. It was in vain I
listened, I could hear nothing of the kind. But rather,
with much goodwill and a little imagination, at long
intervals a distant gong. A horn goes well with the forest,

you expect it. It is the huntsman. But a gong! Even
a tom-tom, at a pinch, would not have shocked me.
But a gong! It was mortifying, to have been looking
forward to the celebrated murmurs if to nothing else,
and to succeed only in hearing, at long intervals, in the
far distance, a gong. For a moment I dared hope it
was only my heart, still beating. But only for a moment.
For it does not beat, not my heart, I'd have to refer you
to hydraulics for the squelch that old pump makes. To
the leaves too I listened, before their fall, attentively in
vain. They made no sound, motionless and rigid, like
brass, have I said that before? So much for the forest
murmurs. From time to time I blew my horn, through
the cloth of my pocket. Its hoot was fainter every time.
I had taken it off my bicycle. When? I don't know.
And now, let us have done. Flat on my belly, using
my crutches like grapnels, I plunged them ahead of me
into the undergrowth, and when I felt they had a hold,
I pulled myself forward, with an effort of the wrists.
For my wrists were still quite strong, fortunately, in spite
of my decrepitude, though all swollen and racked by a
kind of chronic arthritis probably. That then briefly
is how I went about it. The advantage of this mode of
locomotion compared to others, I mean those I have
tried, is this, that when you want to rest you stop and
rest, without further ado. For standing there is no rest,
nor sitting either. And there are men who move about
sitting, and even kneeling, hauling themselves to right
and left, forward and backward, with the help of hooks.
But he who moves in this way, crawling on his belly, like
a reptile, no sooner comes to rest than he begins to rest,
and even the very movement is a kind of rest, compared

to other movements, I mean those that have worn me
out.   And in this way I moved onward in the forest, slowly, but with a certain regularity, and I covered my fifteen
paces, day in, day out, without killing myself.   And I
even crawled on my back, plunging my crutches blindly
behind me into the thickets, and with the black boughs
for sky to my closing eyes.   I was on my way to mother.
And from time to time I said, Mother, to encourage me
I suppose.   I kept losing my hat, the lace had broken
long ago, until in a fit of temper I banged it down on my
skull with such violence that I couldn't get it off again.
And if I had met any lady friends, if I had had any lady
friends, I would have been powerless to salute them
correctly.   But there was always present to my mind,
which was still working, if laboriously, the need to turn,
to keep on turning, and every three or four jerks I altered
course, which permitted me to describe, if not a circle,
at least a great polygon, perfection is not of this world,
and to hope that I was going forward in a straight line,
in spite of everything, day and night, towards my mother.
And true enough the day came when the forest ended
and I saw the light, the light of the plain, exactly as I
had foreseen.   But I did not see it from afar, trembling
beyong the harsh trunks, as I had foreseen, but suddenly
I was in it, I opened my eyes and saw I had arrived.
And the reason for that was probably this, that for some
time past I had not opened my eyes, or seldom.   And
even my little changes of course were made blindly, in
the dark.   The forest ended in a ditch, I don't know why,
and it was in this ditch that I became aware of what had
happened to me.   I suppose it was the fall into the ditch
that opened my eyes, for why would they have opened

otherwise? I looked at the plain rolling away as far as the eye could see. No, not quite so far as that. For my eyes having got used to the light I fancied I saw, faintly outlined against the horizon, the towers and steeples of a town, which of course I could not assume was mine, on such slight evidence. It is true the plain seemed familiar, but in my region all the plains looked alike, when you knew one you knew them all. In any case, whether it was my town or not, whether somewhere under that faint haze my mother panted on or whether she poisoned the air a hundred miles away, were ludicrously idle questions for a man in my position, though of undeniable interest on the plane of pure knowledge. For how could I drag myself over that vast moor, where my crutches would fumble in vain. Rolling perhaps. And then? Would they let me roll on to my mother's door? Fortunately for me at this painful juncture, which I had vaguely foreseen, but not in all its bitterness, I heard a voice telling me not to fret, that help was coming. Literally. These words struck it is not too much to say as clearly on my ear, and on my understanding, as the urchin's thanks I suppose when I stooped and picked up his marble. Don't fret Molloy, we're coming. Well, I suppose you have to try everything once, succour included, to get a complete picture of the resources of their planet. I lapsed down to the bottom of the ditch. It must have been spring, a morning in spring. I thought I heard birds, skylarks perhaps. I had not heard a bird for a long time. How was it I had not heard any in the forest? Nor seen any. It had not seemed strange to me. Had I heard any at the seaside? Mews? I could not remember. I remembered the corn-crakes.

The two travellers came back to my memory. One had
a club. I had forgotten them. I saw the sheep again.
Or so I say now. I did not fret, other scenes of my life
came back to me. There seemed to be rain, then sun-
shine, turn about. Real spring weather. I longed to
go back into the forest. Oh not a real longing. Molloy
could stay, where he happened to be.

—Translated by PATRICK BOWLES
in collaboration with the author

From The Unnamable

"I began to write *Waiting for Godot*," Beckett once confessed to critic Colin Duckworth, "to get away from the awful prose I was writing at that time." The "awful prose" was that which graces *Molloy* and *Malone Dies*. Still, one can understand how, after that prodigious act of creation, Beckett felt the need to turn away from fiction, at least for a time.

When he turned back to it the following year, 1949, there was a marked difference in the prose, though the purpose to which it was put was still the same. In fact, through every work, from *Murphy* onward, the Beckettian quest has always been the same: we have only ourselves with which to know ourselves, and the world; and only words with which to conduct the search. And we know, however much we deceive, that these same words, our tools toward knowledge, are also the traitors that thwart us and prevent us from realizing our goal.

In the original conception of the work, the Unnamable had a name, Mahood, or at least *Mahood* was the projected title of the third volume. But as the specifics of time and space dissolved the further Beckett went, so too did the specifics of self.

Though he himself is nameless, and unnamable, the narrator of this volume brings in—or back—most of the other characters in the *Trilogy*, and others from without: Molloy, Moran, and Malone, of course; but also Watt, Mercier, Camier, Murphy; and new characters, Mahood, Basil, Worm.

There is another essential difference too: in contrast to so many of the protagonist-narrators of Beckett's fiction, who journey toward some goal, specified or not, *The Unnamable* —whose six opening words pose three rapierlike questions: "Where now? Who now? When now?"—moves ineluctably toward silence. Before silence certain things must be said, attempted. But when all the games are done, all the detours and side roads trod, all the fables and stories used up, silence will come. At last.

Throughout the extraordinary final section of the book, as the syntax bends and threatens to break, the short gasping phrases that will recur in much of the later prose take over (though here still with benefit of the ubiquitous comma): it is then that the word "silence" dominates, after "the words fail, the voice fails, so be it, I know that well, it will be the silence." It may be a silence "full of murmurs, distant cries," but silence nonetheless.

The words are prophetic: after *The Unnamable*, and the thirteen brief texts written the next year, 1950, silence would indeed be Beckett's lot in the realm of fiction for over a decade. Did that mean he had given up the impossible task? The last lines of *The Unnamable* give the answer:

> . . . it will be the silence, where I am, I don't know, I'll never know, in the silence you don't know, you must go on, I can't go on, I'll go on.

Where now? Who now? When now? Unquestioning. I, say I. Unbelieving. Questions, hypotheses, call them that. Keep going, going on, call that going, call that on. Can it be that one day, off it goes on, that one day I simply stayed in, in where, instead of going out, in the old way, out to spend day and night as far away as possible, it wasn't far. Perhaps that is how it began. You think you are simply resting, the better to act when the time comes, or for no reason, and you soon find yourself powerless ever to do anything again. No matter how it happened. It, say it, not knowing what. Perhaps I simply assented at last to an old thing. But I did nothing. I seem to speak, it is not I, about me, it is not about me. These few general remarks to begin with. What am I to do, what shall I do, what should I do, in my situation, how proceed? By aporia pure and simple? Or by affirmations and negations invalidated as uttered, or sooner or later? Generally speaking. There

must be other shifts. Otherwise it would be quite hopeless. But it is quite hopeless. I should mention before
going any further, any further on, that I say aporia
without knowing what it means. Can one be ephectic
otherwise than unawares? I don't know. With the yesses
and noes it is different, they will come back to me as
I go along and how, like a bird, to shit on them all
without exception. The fact would seem to be, if in
my situation one may speak of facts, not only that I
shall have to speak of things of which I cannot speak,
but also, which is even more interesting, but also that
I, which is if possible even more interesting, that I
shall have to, I forget, no matter. And at the same
time I am obliged to speak. I shall never be silent.
Never.

I shall not be alone, in the beginning. I am of course
alone. Alone. That is soon said. Things have to be soon
said. And how can one be sure, in such darkness? I
shall have company. In the beginning. A few puppets.
Then I'll scatter them, to the winds, if I can. And
things, what is the correct attitude to adopt towards
things? And, to begin with, are they necessary? What
a question. But I have few illusions, things are to be
expected. The best is not to decide anything, in this
connexion, in advance. If a thing turns up, for some
reason or another, take it into consideration. Where
there are people, it is said, there are things. Does this
mean that when you admit the former you must also
admit the latter? Time will tell. The thing to avoid, I
don't know why, is the spirit of system. People with
things, people without things, things without people,

what does it matter, I flatter myself it will not take
me long to scatter them, whenever I choose, to the
winds. I don't see how. The best would be not to begin.
But I have to begin. That is to say I have to go on.
Perhaps in the end I shall smother in a throng. Inces-
sant comings and goings, the crush and bustle of a
bargain sale. No, no danger. Of that.

Malone is there. Of his mortal liveliness little trace
remains. He passes before me at doubtless regular intervals, unless it is I who pass before him. No, once
and for all, I do not move. He passes, motionless. But
there will not be much on the subject of Malone, from
whom there is nothing further to be hoped. Personally
I do not intend to be bored. It was while watching
him pass that I wondered if we cast a shadow. Impossible to say. He passes close by me, a few feet away,
slowly, always in the same direction. I am almost sure
it is he. The brimless hat seems to me conclusive. With
his two hands he props up his jaw. He passes without
a word. Perhaps he does not see me. One of these days
I'll challenge him. I'll say, I don't know, I'll say something, I'll think of something when the time comes.
There are no days here, but I use the expression. I see
him from the waist up, he stops at the waist, as far as
I am concerned. The trunk is erect. But I do not know
whether he is on his feet or on his knees. He might also
be seated. I see him in profile. Sometimes I wonder if
it is not Molloy. Perhaps it is Molloy, wearing Malone's
hat. But it is more reasonable to suppose it is Malone,
wearing his own hat. Oh look, there is the first thing,
Malone's hat. I see no other clothes. Perhaps Molloy is

not here at all. Could he be, without my knowledge?
The place is no doubt vast. Dim intermittent lights
suggest a kind of distance. To tell the truth I believe
they are all here, at least from Murphy on, I believe
we are all here, but so far I have only seen Malone.
Another hypothesis, they were here, but are here no
longer. I shall examine it after my fashion. Are there
other pits, deeper down? To which one accedes by
mine? Stupid obsession with depth. Are there other
places set aside for us and this one where I am, with
Malone, merely their narthex? I thought I had done
with preliminaries. No no, we have all been here forever, we shall all be here forever, I know it.

No more questions. Is not this rather the place where
one finishes vanishing? Will the day come when Malone
will pass before me no more? Will the day come when
Malone will pass before the spot where I was? Will
the day come when another will pass before me, before
the spot where I was? I have no opinion, on these
matters.

Were I not devoid of feeling his beard would fill me
with pity. It hangs down, on either side of his chin, in
two twists of unequal length. Was there a time when
I too revolved thus? No, I have always been sitting
here, at this selfsame spot, my hands on my knees,
gazing before me like a great horn-owl in an aviary.
The tears stream down my cheeks from my unblinking
eyes. What makes me weep so? From time to time.
There is nothing saddening here. Perhaps it is liquefied
brain. Past happiness in any case has clean gone from

my memory, assuming it was ever there. If I accomplish other natural functions it is unawares. Nothing ever troubles me. And yet I am troubled. Nothing has ever changed since I have been here. But I dare not infer from this that nothing ever will change. Let us try and see where these considerations lead. I have been here, ever since I began to be, my appearances elsewhere having been put in by other parties. All has proceeded, all this time, in the utmost calm, the most perfect order, apart from one or two manifestations the meaning of which escapes me. No, it is not that their meaning escapes me, my own escapes me just as much. Here all things, no, I shall not say it, being unable to. I owe my existence to no one, these faint fires are not of those that illuminate or burn. Going nowhere, coming from nowhere, Malone passes. These notions of forbears, of houses where lamps are lit at night, and other such, where do they come to me from? And all these questions I ask myself. It is not in a spirit of curiosity. I cannot be silent. About myself I need know nothing. Here all is clear. No, all is not clear. But the discourse must go on. So one invents obscurities. Rhetoric. These lights for instance, which I do not require to mean anything, what is there so strange about them, so wrong? Is it their irregularity, their instability, their shining strong one minute and weak the next, but never beyond the power of one or two candles? Malone appears and disappears with the punctuality of clockwork, always at the same remove, the same velocity, in the same direction, the same attitude. But the play of the lights is truly unpredictable. It is only fair to say that to eyes less knowing than mine

they would probably pass unseen. But even to mine do
they not sometimes do so? They are perhaps unwavering and fixed and my fitful perceiving the cause of
their inconstancy. I hope I may have occasion to revert
to this question. But I shall remark without further
delay, in order to be sure of doing so, that I am relying
on these lights, as indeed on all other similar sources
of credible perplexity, to help me continue and perhaps
even conclude. I resume, having no alternative. Where
was I? Ah yes, from the unexceptionable order which
has prevailed here up to date may I infer that such
will always be the case? I may of course. But the mere
fact of asking myself such a question gives me to reflect.
It is in vain I tell myself that its only purpose is to
stimulate the lagging discourse, this excellent explanation does not satisfy me. Can it be I am the prey of a
genuine preoccupation, of a need to know as one might
say? I don't know. I'll try it another way. If one day
a change were to take place, resulting from a principle
of disorder already present, or on its way, what then?
That would seem to depend on the nature of the
change. No, here all change would be fatal and land
me back, there and then, in all the fun of the fair. I'll
try it another way. Has nothing really changed since
I have been here? No, frankly, hand on heart, wait a
second, no, nothing, to my knowledge. But, as I have
said, the place may well be vast, as it may well measure
twelve feet in diameter. It comes to the same thing, as
far as discerning its limits is concerned. I like to think
I occupy the centre, but nothing is less certain. In a
sense I would be better off at the circumference, since
my eyes are always fixed in the same direction. But I

am certainly not at the circumference. For if I were it would follow that Malone, wheeling about me as he does, would issue from the enceinte at every revolution, which is manifestly impossible. But does he in fact wheel, does he not perhaps simply pass before me in a straight line? No, he wheels, I feel it, and about me, like a planet about its sun. And if he made a noise, as he goes, I would hear him all the time, on my right hand, behind my back, on my left hand, before seeing him again. But he makes none, for I am not deaf, of that I am convinced, that is to say half-convinced. From centre to circumference in any case it is a far cry and I may well be situated somewhere between the two. It is equally possible, I do not deny it, that I too am in perpetual motion, accompanied by Malone, as the earth by its moon. In which case there would be no further grounds for my complaining about the disorder of the lights, this being due simply to my insistence on regarding them as always the same lights and viewed always from the same point. All is possible, or almost. But the best is to think of myself as fixed and at the centre of this place, whatever its shape and extent may be. This is also probably the most pleasing to me. In a word, no change apparently since I have been here, disorder of the lights perhaps an illusion, all change to be feared, incomprehensible uneasiness.

That I am not stone deaf is shown by the sounds that reach me. For though the silence here is almost unbroken, it is not completely so. I remember the first sound heard in this place, I have often heard it since. For I am obliged to assign a beginning to my residence

here, if only for the sake of clarity. Hell itself, although
eternal, dates from the revolt of Lucifer. It is therefore
permissible, in the light of this distant analogy, to
think of myself as being here forever, but not as having
been here forever. This will greatly help me in my
relation. Memory notably, which I did not think myself
entitled to draw upon, will have its word to say, if
necessary. This represents at least a thousand words I
was not counting on. I may well be glad of them. So
after a long period of immaculate silence a feeble cry
was heard, by me. I do not know if Malone heard it
too. I was surprised, the word is not too strong. After
so long a silence a little cry, stifled outright. What
kind of creature uttered it and, if it is the same, still
does, from time to time? Impossible to say. Not a
human one in any case, there are no human creatures
here, or if there are they have done with crying. Is
Malone the culprit? Am I? Is it not perhaps a simple
little fart, they can be rending? Deplorable mania,
when something happens, to inquire what. If only I
were not obliged to manifest. And why speak of a cry?
Perhaps it is something breaking, some two things col-
liding. There are sounds here, from time to time, let
that suffice. This cry to begin with, since it was the
first. And others, rather different. I am getting to know
them. I do not know them all. A man may die at the
age of seventy without ever having had the possibility
of seeing Halley's comet.

It would help me, since to me too I must attribute
a beginning, if I could relate it to that of my abode.
Did I wait somewhere for this place to be ready to

receive me? Or did it wait for me to come and people
it? By far the better of these hypotheses, from the
point of view of usefulness, is the former, and I shall
often have occasion to fall back on it. But both are
distasteful. I shall say therefore that our beginnings
coincide, that this place was made for me, and I for it,
at the same instant. And the sounds I do not yet know
have not yet made themselves heard. But they will
change nothing. The cry changed nothing, even the
first time. And my surprise? I must have been expecting
it.

It is no doubt time I gave a companion to Malone.
But first I shall tell of an incident that has only occurred
once, so far. I await its recurrence without impatience.
Two shapes then, oblong like man, entered into collision
before me. They fell and I saw them no more. I naturally thought of the pseudocouple Mercier-Camier. The
next time they enter the field, moving slowly towards
each other, I shall know they are going to collide, fall
and disappear, and this will perhaps enable me to
observe them better. Wrong. I continue to see Malone
as darkly as the first time. My eyes being fixed always
in the same direction I can only see, I shall not say
clearly, but as clearly as the visibility permits, that
which takes place immediately in front of me, that is
to say, in the case before us, the collision, followed by
the fall and disappearance. Of their approach I shall
never obtain other than a confused glimpse, out of the
corner of the eye, and what an eye. For their path too
must be a curve, two curves, and meeting I need not
say close beside me. For the visibility, unless it be the

state of my eyesight, only permits me to see what is close beside me. I may add that my seat would appear to be somewhat elevated, in relation to the surrounding ground, if ground is what it is. Perhaps it is water or some other liquid. With the result that, in order to obtain the optimum view of what takes place in front of me, I should have to lower my eyes a little. But I lower my eyes no more. In a word, I only see what appears immediately in front of me, I only see what appears close beside me, what I best see I see ill.

Why did I have myself represented in the midst of men, the light of day? It seems to me it was none of my doing. We won't go into that now. I can see them still, my delegates. The things they have told me! About men, the light of day. I refused to believe them. But some of it has stuck. But when, through what channels, did I communicate with these gentlemen? Did they intrude on me here? No, no one has ever intruded on me here. Elsewhere then. But I have never been elsewhere. But it can only have been from them I learnt what I know about men and the ways they have of putting up with it. It does not amount to much. I could have dispensed with it. I don't say it was all to no purpose. I'll make use of it, if I'm driven to it. It won't be the first time. What puzzles me is the thought of being indebted for this information to persons with whom I can never have been in contact. Can it be innate knowledge? Like that of good and evil. This seems improbable to me. Innate knowledge of my mother, for example, is that conceivable? Not for me. She was one of their favourite subjects, of conversation.

They also gave me the low-down on God. They told me
I depended on him, in the last analysis. They had it
on the reliable authority of his agents at Bally I forget
what, this being the place, according to them, where
the inestimable gift of life had been rammed down my
gullet. But what they were most determined for me to
swallow was my fellow-creatures. In this they were
without mercy. I remember little or nothing of these
lectures. I cannot have understood a great deal. But I
seem to have retained certain descriptions, in spite of
myself. They gave me courses on love, on intelligence,
most precious, most precious. They also taught me to
count, and even to reason. Some of this rubbish has
come in handy on occasions, I don't deny it, on occasions which would never have arisen if they had left
me in peace. I use it still, to scratch my arse with. Low
types they must have been, their pockets full of poison
and antidote. Perhaps all this instruction was by correspondence. And yet I seem to know their faces. From
photographs perhaps. When did all this nonsense stop?
And has it stopped? A few last questions. Is it merely a
lull? There were four or five of them at me, they called
that presenting their report. One in particular, Basil
I think he was called, filled me with hatred. Without
opening his mouth, fastening on me his eyes like cinders
with all their seeing, he changed me a little more each
time into what he wanted me to be. Is he still glaring
at me, from the shadows? Is he still usurping my name,
the one they foisted on me, up there in their world,
patiently, from season to season? No no, here I am in
safety, amusing myself wondering who can have dealt
me these insignificant wounds.

The other advances full upon me. He emerges as
from heavy hangings, advances a few steps, looks at
me, then backs away. He is stooping and seems to be
dragging invisible burdens. What I see best is his hat.
The crown is all worn through, like the sole of an old
boot, giving vent to a straggle of grey hairs. He raises
his eyes and I feel the long imploring gaze, as if I could
do something for him. Another impression, no doubt
equally false, he brings me presents and dare not give
them. He takes them away again, or he lets them fall,
and they vanish. He does not come often, I cannot be
more precise, but regularly assuredly. His visit has
never coincided, up to now, with the transit of Malone.
But perhaps some day it will. That would not necessarily be a violation of the order prevailing here. For
if I can work out to within a few inches the orbit of
Malone, assuming perhaps erroneously that he passes
before me at a distance of say three feet, with regard
to the other's career I must remain in the dark. For I
am incapable not only of measuring time, which in
itself is sufficient to vitiate all calculation in this connexion, but also of comparing their respective velocities.
So I cannot tell if I shall ever have the good fortune to
see the two of them at once. But I am inclined to think
I shall. For if I were never to see the two of them at
once, then it would follow, or should follow, that between their respective appearances the interval never
varies. No, wrong. For the interval may vary considerably, and indeed it seems to me it does, without ever
being abolished. Nevertheless I am inclined to think,

because of this erratic interval, that my two visitors
may some day meet before my eyes, collide and perhaps
even knock each other down. I have said that all things
here recur sooner or later, no, I was going to say it,
then thought better of it. But is it not possible that
this does not apply to encounters? The only encounter
I ever witnessed, a long time ago now, has never yet
been re-enacted. It was perhaps the end of something.
And I shall perhaps be delivered of Malone and the
other, not that they disturb me, the day I see the two
of them at one and the same time, that is to say in
collision. Unfortunately they are not the only disturbers
of my peace. Others come towards me, pass before me,
wheel about me. And no doubt others still, invisible so
far. I repeat they do not disturb me. But in the long
run it might become wearisome. I don't see how. But
the possibility must be taken into account. One starts
things moving without a thought of how to stop them.
In order to speak. One starts speaking as if it were
possible to stop at will. It is better so. The search for
the means to put an end to things, an end to speech,
is what enables the discourse to continue. No, I must
not try to think, simply utter. Method or no method I
shall have to banish them in the end, the beings, things,
shapes, sounds and lights with which my haste to speak
has encumbered this place. In the frenzy of utterance
the concern with truth. Hence the interest of a possible
deliverance by means of encounter. But not so fast.
First dirty, then make clean.

Perhaps it is time I paid a little attention to myself,
for a change. I shall be reduced to it sooner or later.

At first sight it seems impossible. Me, utter me, in the
same foul breath as my creatures? Say of me that I
see this, feel that, fear, hope, know and do not know?
Yes, I will say it, and of me alone. Impassive, still and
mute, Malone revolves, a stranger forever to my infirmities, one who is not as I can never not be. I am
motionless in vain, he is the god. And the other? I have
assigned him eyes that implore me, offerings for me,
need of succour. He does not look at me, docs not know
of me, wants for nothing. I alone am man and all the
rest divine.

Air, the air, is there anything to be squeezed from
that old chestnut? Close to me it is grey, dimly transparent, and beyond that charmed circle deepens and
spreads its fine impenetrable veils. Is it I who cast the
faint light that enables me to see what goes on under
my nose? There is nothing to be gained, for the moment, by supposing so. There is no night so deep, so
I have heard tell, that it may not be pierced in the
end, with the help of no other light than that of the
blackened sky, or of the earth itself. Nothing nocturnal
here. This grey, first murky, then frankly opaque, is
luminous none the less. But may not this screen which
my eyes probe in vain, and see as denser air, in reality
be the enclosure wall, as compact as lead? To elucidate
this point I would need a stick or pole, and the means
of plying it, the former being of little avail without
the latter, and vice versa. I could also do, incidentally,
with future and conditional participles. Then I would
dart it, like a javelin, straight before me and know, by

the sound made, whether that which hems me round, and blots out my world, is the old void, or a plenum. Or else, without letting it go, I would wield it like a sword and thrust it through empty air, or against the barrier. But the days of sticks are over, here I can count on my body alone, my body incapable of the smallest movement and whose very eyes can no longer close as they once could, according to Basil and his crew, to rest me from seeing, to rest me from waking, to darken me to sleep, and no longer look away, or down, or up open to heaven, but must remain forever fixed and staring on the narrow space before them where there is nothing to be seen, 99% of the time. They must be as red as live coals. I sometimes wonder if the two retinae are not facing each other. And come to think of it this grey is shot with rose, like the plumage of certain birds, among which I seem to remember the cockatoo.

Whether all grow black, or all grow bright, or all remain grey, it is grey we need, to begin with, because of what it is, and of what it can do, made of bright and black, able to shed the former, or the latter, and be the latter or the former alone. But perhaps I am the prey, on the subject of grey, in the grey, to delusions.

How, in such conditions, can I write, to consider only the manual aspect of that bitter folly? I don't know. I could know. But I shall not know. Not this time. It is I who write, who cannot raise my hand from my knee. It is I who think, just enough to write, whose

head is far. I am Matthew and I am the angel, I who
came before the cross, before the sinning, came into
the world, came here.

I add this, to be on the safe side. These things I say,
and shall say, if I can, are no longer, or are not yet, or
never were, or never will be, or if they were, if they
are, if they will be, were not here, are not here, will not
be here, but elsewhere. But I am here. So I am obliged
to add this. I who am here, who cannot speak, cannot
think, and who must speak, and therefore perhaps
think a little, cannot in relation only to me who am
here, to here where I am, but can a little, sufficiently,
I don't know how, unimportant, in relation to me who
was elsewhere, who shall be elsewhere, and to those
places where I was, where I shall be. But I have never
been elsewhere, however uncertain the future. And
the simplest therefore is to say that what I say, what
I shall say, if I can, relates to the place where I am, to
me who am there, in spite of my inability to think of
these, or to speak of them, because of the compulsion
I am under to speak of them, and therefore perhaps
think of them a little. Another thing. What I say, what
I may say, on this subject, the subject of me and my
abode, has already been said since, having always been
here, I am here still. At last a piece of reasoning that
pleases me, and worthy of my situation. So I have no
cause for anxiety. And yet I am anxious. So I am not
heading for disaster, I am not heading anywhere, my
adventures are over, my say said, I call that my adventures. And yet I feel not. And indeed I greatly fear,
since my speech can only be of me and here, that I

am once more engaged in putting an end to both.
Which would not matter, far from it, but for the obligation, once rid of them, to begin again, to start again
from nowhere, from no one and from nothing and win
to me again, to me here again, by fresh ways to be sure,
or by the ancient ways, unrecognizable at each fresh
faring. Whence a certain confusion in the exordia, long
enough to situate the condemned and prepare him for
execution. And yet I do not despair of one day sparing
me, without going silent. And that day, I don't know
why, I shall be able to go silent, and make an end, I
know it. Yes, the hope is there, once again, of not
making me, not losing me, of staying here, where I
said I have always been, but I had to say something
quick, of ending here, it would be wonderful. But is
it to be wished? Yes, it is to be wished, to end would
be wonderful, no matter who I am, no matter where
I am.

I hope this preamble will soon come to an end and
the statement begin that will dispose of me. Unfortunately I am afraid, as always, of going on. For to go
on means going from here, means finding me, losing
me, vanishing and beginning again, a stranger first,
then little by little the same as always, in another place,
where I shall say I have always been, of which I shall
know nothing, being incapable of seeing, moving, thinking, speaking, but of which little by little, in spite of
these handicaps, I shall begin to know something, just
enough for it to turn out to be the same place as always,
the same which seems made for me and does not want
me, which I seem to want and do not want, take your

choice, which spews me out or swallows me up, I'll
never know, which is perhaps merely the inside of my
distant skull where once I wandered, now am fixed,
lost for tininess, or straining against the walls, with my
head, my hands, my feet, my back, and ever murmur-
ing my old stories, my old story, as if it were the first
time. So there is nothing to be afraid of. And yet I am
afraid, afraid of what my words will do to me, to my
refuge, yet again. Is there really nothing new to try? I
mentioned my hope, but it is not serious. If I could
speak and yet say nothing, really nothing? Then I
might escape being gnawed to death as by an old
satiated rat, and my little tester-bed along with me, a
cradle, or be gnawed to death not so fast, in my old
cradle, and the torn flesh have time to knit, as in the
Caucasus, before being torn again. But it seems impossible to speak and yet say nothing, you think you
have succeeded, but you always overlook something,
a little yes, a little no, enough to exterminate a regi-
ment of dragoons. And yet I do not despair, this time,
while saying who I am, where I am, of not losing me,
of not going from here, of ending here. What prevents
the miracle is the spirit of method to which I have
perhaps been a little too addicted. The fact that Pro-
metheus was delivered twenty-nine thousand nine hundred and seventy years after having purged his offence
leaves me naturally as cold as camphor. For between
me and that miscreant who mocked the gods, invented
fire, denatured clay and domesticated the horse, in a
word obliged humanity, I trust there is nothing in
common. But the thing is worth mentioning. In a word,
shall I be able to speak of me and of this place without

putting an end to us, shall I ever be able to go silent, is there any connexion between these two questions? Nothing like issues. There are a few to be going on with, perhaps one only.

All these Murphys, Molloys and Malones do not fool me. They have made me waste my time, suffer for nothing, speak of them when, in order to stop speaking, I should have spoken of me and of me alone. But I just said I have spoken of me, am speaking of me. I don't care a curse what I just said. It is now I shall speak of me, for the first time. I thought I was right in enlisting these sufferers of my pains. I was wrong. They never suffered my pains, their pains are nothing, compared to mine, a mere tittle of mine, the tittle I thought I could put from me, in order to witness it. Let them be gone now, them and all the others, those I have used and those I have not used, give me back the pains I lent them and vanish, from my life, my memory, my terrors and shames. There, now there is no one here but me, no one wheels about me, no one comes towards me, no one has ever met anyone before my eyes, these creatures have never been, only I and this black void have ever been. And the sounds? No, all is silent. And the lights, on which I had set such store, must they too go out? Yes, out with them, there is no light here. No grey either, black is what I should have said. Nothing then but me, of which I know nothing, except that I have never uttered, and this black, of which I know nothing either, except that it is black, and empty. That then is what, since I have to speak, I shall speak of, until I need speak no more. And

Basil and his gang? Inexistent, invented to explain I forget what. Ah yes, all lies, God and man, nature and the light of day, the heart's outpourings and the means of understanding, all invented, basely, by me alone, with the help of no one, since there is no one, to put off the hour when I must speak of me. There will be no more about them.

Texts for Nothing 11,13

The thirteen short pieces, ranging from roughly seven hundred to seventeen hundred words in length, that comprise *Texts for Nothing*, take up, in form and substance, approximately where *The Unnamable* left off.

But whereas *The Unnamable* ended on that resignedly positive note which has echoed throughout Beckett's work at least since *Godot*—that is, the impossibility of going on voiced in close conjunction with the necessity to go on— here the negative dominates:

> Suddenly, no, at last, long last, I couldn't any more, I couldn't go on . . . . How can I go on, I shouldn't have begun, no . . . .

It is this "no" that recurs as the leitmotif of these texts. And as the images repeated are those of tears and ashes, so the color is that of evening, "this evening now that never ends, in whose shadows I'm alone," spiraling down toward darkness:

> And were there one day to be here, where there are no days, which is no place, born of the impossible voice the unmakable being, and a gleam of light, still all would be silent and empty and dark, as now, as soon now, when all will be ended, all said, it says, it murmurs.

The obsessive voice which has prevailed despite all obstacles, which has refused to be stilled despite the constant temptation to silence, seems at this point no more than a murmur. And the prose, which till now—with the possible exception of *The Unnamable*—has not only maintained a fair semblance of syntactical order but often brought language to heights rarely before attained, has been reduced to shorter and shorter phrases, gasps of meaning in the encompassing void, brief stabs of light in the encroaching darkness.

Beckett has been quoted as saying that he considers the *Texts for Nothing* a failure, in that they did not "get him out of the attitude of disintegration" he felt himself to be in. Indeed, the very title of the pieces suggests failure, implies that the battle of the soliloquy has been abandoned, or lost, for in addition to the "for nothing" of the English translation, *pour rien* connotes as well "pointless," "meaningless," "of no consequence."

It would doubtless be more accurate, however, to say that by 1955 Beckett had gone as far as he could, at least for the moment. He had carried his unique experiments in fiction to the utter limits of the possible; there, in the penumbra and near silence, he perhaps had to pause and rest. Whether he would be able to carry it any further, only time would tell.

11

When I think, no, that won't work, when come those who knew me, perhaps even know me still, by sight of course, or by smell, it's as though, it's as if, come on, I don't know, I shouldn't have begun. If I began again, setting my mind to it, that sometimes gives good results, it's worth trying, I'll try it, one of these days, one of these evenings, or this evening, why not this evening, before I disappear, from up there, from down here, scattered by the everlasting words. What am I saying, scattered, isn't that just what I'm not, just what I'm not, I was wandering, my mind was wandering, just the very thing I'm not. And it's still the same old road I'm trudging, up yes and down no, towards one yet to be named, so that he may leave me in peace, be in peace, be no more, have never been. Name, no, nothing is namable, tell, no, nothing can be told, what then, I don't know, I shouldn't have begun. Add him to the repertory, there we have it, and execute him, as I execute me, one dead bar after another, evening after evening, and night after night, and all through the days, but it's always evening, why is that, why is it always evening, I'll say why, so as to have said it, have it behind me, an instant. It's time that can't go on at the hour of the serenade, unless it's dawn, no, I'm not in the open, I'm under the ground, or in my body somewhere, or in another body, and time devours on, but not me, there we have it,

that's why it's always evening, to let me have the best
to look forward to, the long black night to sleep in,
there, I've answered, I've answered something. Or it's
in the head, like a minute time switch, a second time
switch, or it's like a patch of sea, under the passing
lighthouse beam, a passing patch of sea under the passing beam. Vile words to make me believe I'm here, and
that I have a head, and a voice, a head believing this,
then that, then nothing more, neither in itself, nor in
anything else, but a head with a voice belonging to it,
or to others, other heads, as if there were two heads, as
if there were one head, or headless, a headless voice,
but a voice. But I'm not deceived, for the moment I'm
not deceived, for the moment I'm not there, nor anywhere else what is more, neither as head, nor as voice,
nor as testicle, what a shame, what a shame I'm not
appearing anywhere as testicle, or as cunt, those areas,
a female pubic hair, it sees great sights, peeping down,
well, there it is, can't be helped, that's how it is. And I
let them say their say, my words not said by me, me
that word, that word they say, but say in vain. We're
getting on, getting on, and when come those who knew
me, quick quick, it's as though, no, premature. But
peekaboo here I come again, just when most needed,
like the square root of minus one, having terminated my
humanities, this should be worth seeing, the livid face
stained with ink and jam, caput mortuum of a studious
youth, ears akimbo, eyes back to front, the odd stray
hair, foaming at the mouth, and chewing, what is it
chewing, a gob, a prayer, a lesson, a little of each, a
prayer got by rote in case of emergency before the soul
resigns and bubbling up all arsy-varsy in the old mouth
bereft of words, in the old head done with listening,

there I am old, it doesn't take long, a snotty old nipper, having terminated his humanities, in the two-stander urinal on the corner of the Rue d'Assas was it, with the leak making the same gurgle as sixty years ago, my favourite because of the encouragement like mother hissing to baby on pot, my brow glued to the partition among the graffiti, straining against the prostate, belching up Hail Marys, buttoned as to the fly, I invent nothing, through absent-mindedness, or exhaustion, or insouciance, or on purpose, to promote priming, I know what I mean, or one-armed better still, no arms, no hands, better by far, as old as the world and no less hideous, amputated on all sides, erect on my trusty stumps, bursting with old piss, old prayers, old lessons, soul, mind and carcass finishing neck and neck, not to mention the gobchucks, too painful to mention, sobs made mucus, hawked up from the heart, now I have a heart, now I'm complete, apart from a few extremities, having terminated their humanities, then their career, and with that not in the least pretentious, making no demands, rent with ejaculations, Jesus, Jesus. Evenings, evenings, what evenings they were then, made of what, and when was that, I don't know, made of friendly shadows, friendly skies, of time cloyed, resting from devouring, until its midnight meats, I don't know, any more than then, when I used to say, from within, or from without, from the coming night or from under the ground, Where am I, to mention only space, and in what semblance, and since when, to mention also time, and till when, and who is this clot who doesn't know where to go, who can't stop, who takes himself for me and for whom I take myself, anything at all, the old jangle. Those evenings then, but what is this evening made of,

this evening now that never ends, in whose shadows
I'm alone, that's where I am, where I was then, where
I've always been, it's from them I spoke to myself,
spoke to him, where has he vanished, the one I saw
then, is he still in the street, it's probable, it's possible,
with no voice speaking to him, I don't speak to him any
more, I don't speak to me any more, I have no one left
to speak to, and I speak, a voice speaks that can be
none but mine, since there is none but me. Yes, I have
lost him and he has lost me, lost from view, lost from
hearing, that's what I wanted, is it possible, that I
wanted that, wanted this, and he, what did he want,
he wanted to stop, perhaps he has stopped, I have
stopped, but I never stirred, perhaps he is dead, I am
dead, but I never lived. But he moved, proof of animation, through those evenings, moving too, evenings with
an end, evenings with a night, never saying a word, unable to say a word, not knowing where to go, unable to
stop, listening to my cries, hearing a voice crying that
it was no kind of life, as if he didn't know, as if the al-
lusion was to his, which was a kind of one, there's the
difference, those were the days, I didn't know where I
was, nor in what semblance, nor since when, nor till
when, whereas now, there's the difference, now I know,
it's not true, but I say it just the same, there's the difference, I'm saying it now, I'll say it soon, I'll say it in the
end, then end, I'll be free to end, I won't be any more,
it won't be worth it any more, it won't be necessary any
more, it won't be possible any more, but it's not worth
it now, it's not necessary now, it's not possible now,
that's how the reasoning runs. No, something better
must be found, a better reason, for this to stop, another
word, a better idea, to put in the negative, a new no,

to cancel all the others, all the old noes that buried me down here, deep in this place which is not one, which is merely a moment for the time being eternal, which is called here, and in this being which is called me and is not one, and in this impossible voice, all the old noes dangling in the dark and swaying like a ladder of smoke, yes, a new no, that none says twice, whose drop will fall and let me down, shadow and babble, to an absence less vain than inexistence. Oh I know it won't happen like that, I know that nothing will happen, that nothing has happened and that I'm still, and particularly since the day I could no longer believe it, what is called flesh and blood somewhere above in their gonorrhoeal light, cursing myself heartily. And that is why, when comes the hour of those who knew me, this time it's going to work, when comes the hour of those who knew me, it's as though I were among them, that is what I had to say, among them watching me approach, then watching me recede, shaking my head and saying, Is it really he, can it possibly be he, then moving on in their company along a road that is not mine and with every step takes me further from that other not mine either, or remaining alone where I am, between two parting dreams, knowing none, known of none, that finally is what I had to say, that is all I can have had to say, this evening.

13

Weaker still the weak old voice that tried in vain to make me, dying away as much as to say it's going from here to try elsewhere, or dying down, there's no telling, as much as to say it's going to cease, give up trying. No voice ever but it in my life, it says, if speaking of me one can speak of life, and it can, it still can, or if not of life, there it dies, if this, if that, if speaking of me, there it dies, but who can the greater can the less, once you've spoken of me you can speak of anything, up to the point where, up to the time when, there it dies, it can't go on, it's been its death, speaking of me, here or elsewhere, it says, it murmurs. Whose voice, no one's, there is no one, there's a voice without a mouth, and somewhere a kind of hearing, something compelled to hear, and somewhere a hand, it calls that a hand, it wants to make a hand, or if not a hand something some-where that can leave a trace, of what is made, of what is said, you can't do with less, no, that's romancing, more romancing, there is nothing but a voice murmur-ing a trace. A trace, it wants to leave a trace, yes, like air leaves among the leaves, among the grass, among the sand, it's with that it would make a life, but soon it will be the end, it won't be long now, there won't be any life, there won't have been any life, there will be silence, the air quite still that trembled once an instant, the tiny flurry of dust quite settled. Air, dust, there is no air here, nor anything to make dust, and to speak of instants, to speak of once, is to speak of nothing, but there it is, those are the expressions it employs. It has always spoken, it will always speak, of things that don't exist, or only exist elsewhere, if you like, if you must, if that may be called existing. Unfortunately it is not a question of elsewhere, but of here, ah there are the words out at last, out again, that was the only chance, get out of here and go elsewhere, go where time passes and atoms assemble an instant, where the voice belongs perhaps, where it sometimes says it must have belonged, to be able to speak of such figments. Yes, out of here, but how when here is empty, not a speck of dust, not a breath, the voice's breath alone, it breathes in vain, nothing is made. If I were here, if it could have made me, how I would pity it, for having spoken so long in vain, no, that won't do, it wouldn't have spoken in vain if I were here, and I wouldn't pity it if it had made me, I'd curse it, or bless it, it would be in my mouth, cursing, blessing, whom, what, it wouldn't be able to say, in my mouth it wouldn't have much to say, that had so much to say in vain. But this pity, all the same, it wonders, this pity that is in the air, though no air here for pity, but it's the expression, it wonders should it stop and wonder what pity is doing here and if it's not hope gleaming, another expression, evilly among the imaginary ashes, the faint hope of a faint being after all, human in kind, tears in its eyes before they've had time to open, no, no more stopping and wondering, about that or anything else, nothing will stop it any more, in its fall, or in its rise, perhaps it will end on a castrato scream. True there was never much talk of the heart, literal or figurative, but that's no reason for hoping, what, that one day there will be one, to send up above to break in the galanty show, pity. But what more is it waiting for now, when there's no doubt left, no choice left, to stick a sock in its death-rattle, yet another locution. To have rounded off its cock-and-bullshit in a coda worthy of the rest? Last everlasting questions, infant languors in the end sheets, last images, end of dream, of being past, passing and to be, end of lie. Is it possible, is that the possible thing at last, the extinction of this black nothing and its impossible shades, the end of the farce of making and the silencing of silence, it wonders, that voice which is silence, or it's me, there's no telling, it's all the same dream, the same silence, it and me, it and him, him and me, and all our train, and all theirs, and all theirs, but whose, whose dream, whose silence, old questions, last questions, ours who are dream and silence, but it's ended, we're ended who never were, soon there will be nothing where there was never anything, last images. And whose the shame, at every mute micromillisyllable, and unslakable infinity of remorse delving ever deeper in its bite, at having to hear, having to say, fainter than the faintest murmur, so many lies, so many times the same lie lyingly denied, whose the screaming silence of no's knife in yes's wound, it wonders. And wonders what has become of the wish to know, it is gone, the heart is gone, the head is gone, no one feels anything, asks anything, seeks anything, says anything, hears anything, there is only silence. It's not true, yes, it's true, it's true and it's not true, there is silence and there is not silence, there is no one and there is someone, nothing prevents anything. And were the voice to cease quite at last, the old ceasing voice, it would not be true, as it is not true that it speaks, it can't speak, it can't cease. And were there one day to be here, where there are no days, which is no place, born of the impossible voice the unmakable being, and a gleam of light, still all would be silent and empty and dark, as now, as soon now, when all will be ended, all said, it says, it murmurs.

Dramatic Works

Waiting for Godot

So much has been written about this play over the past quarter-century that one is tempted to add no further to the elucidation, or confusion. There are almost as many interpretations, both specific and general, as there are critics and commentators, but my advice is simply to sit forward and enjoy.

As for the facts: *Waiting for Godot* was written in 1948, directly in French. In date of composition, it falls between *Malone Dies* and *The Unnamable*. Beckett turned to drama to "get away from the awful prose I was writing at the time," as he confessed.

Though Beckett's first professionally produced play, *Godot* was far from his first foray into the realm of drama. In 1931 he had written a parody of Corneille's *Le Cid* entitled *Le Kid*; a few years later he labored over a dramatic work based on the life of Dr. Samuel Johnson, which he abandoned when he decided that he couldn't get the right voice. In 1946 he wrote *Mercier and Camier*, which, though a novel, embodied much of the situation and dramatic wordplay later to manifest itself in *Godot*. The following year he composed another play, this one three hours in length, entitled *Eleuthéria*, the Greek word for "freedom," which Beckett has carefully kept from being either performed or published. The point is, by the time he wrote *Godot*, he had already had considerable experience with the dramatic form.

Waiting for Godot had its world première on January 5, 1953, in the tiny Left Bank Théâtre de Babylone in Paris, in Roger Blin's direction. Because it seems so seminal a work of the contemporary theater, one often assumes that it was an immediate success. Having been at one of the early performances, I can vouch for the fact that, however it might have moved me, it did not exactly take Paris by storm. The night I went, perhaps two or three weeks after the opening, the house was barely half full. The laughter was hesitant, the applause more polite than heartfelt. But by slow degrees that ultimate critic, word-of-mouth, went to work, and before very long *Godot* had become the talk of Paris. As productions spread across the globe, reactions were varied, but the very controversy generated by the play tended to assure its "success." Detractors called it everything from "boring" to "Communist" to "existential" (the ultimate insult). Its partisans needed no epithets or labels; they sensed they had been privileged to witness a work of greatness. Rarely has a play labeled "avant-garde" become so quickly a "classic"; and yet, like all true "classics," *Godot* can still today provoke controversy.

Whether it is Beckett's greatest work of drama remains for history to determine. Unquestionably, however, it was a work which captured the imagination of the time—and perhaps all time. Though the battle of interpretation still rages around it today, *Waiting for Godot* has already become part of theater history.

Waiting for Godot

A tragicomedy in 2 acts

WAITING FOR GODOT was first presented (as *En Attendant Godot*) at the Théâtre de Babylone, 38 Boulevard Raspail, Paris, France, during the season of 1952-3. The play was directed by Roger Blin, with décor by Sergio Gerstein. The cast was as follows:

ESTRAGON *Pierre Latour*

VLADIMIR *Lucien Raimbourg*

POZZO *Roger Blin*

LUCKY *Jean Martin*

A BOY *Serge Lecointe*

Act I

A country road. A tree.

Evening.

Estragon, sitting on a low mound, is trying to take
off his boot. He pulls at it with both hands,
panting. He gives up, exhausted, rests, tries again.
As before.
Enter Vladimir.

ESTRAGON: (*giving up again*). Nothing to be done.

VLADIMIR: (*advancing with short, stiff strides, legs wide apart*).
I'm beginning to come round to that opinion. All
my life I've tried to put it from me, saying,
Vladimir, be reasonable, you haven't yet tried
everything. And I resumed the struggle. (*He*
broods, musing on the struggle. Turning to
Estragon.) So there you are again.

ESTRAGON: Am I?

VLADIMIR: I'm glad to see you back. I thought you were gone
for ever.

ESTRAGON: Me too.

VLADIMIR: Together again at last! We'll have to celebrate
this. But how? (*He reflects.*) Get up till I embrace
you.

ESTRAGON: (*irritably*). Not now, not now.

VLADIMIR: (*hurt, coldly*). May one inquire where His
Highness spent the night?

ESTRAGON: In a ditch.

VLADIMIR: (*admiringly*). A ditch! Where?

ESTRAGON: (*without gesture*). Over there.

VLADIMIR: And they didn't beat you?

ESTRAGON: Beat me? Certainly they beat me.

VLADIMIR: The same lot as usual?

ESTRAGON: The same? I don't know.

VLADIMIR: When I think of it . . . all these years . . . but for me . . . where would you be . . . (*Decisively.*) You'd be nothing more than a little heap of bones at the present minute, no doubt about it.

ESTRAGON: And what of it?

VLADIMIR: (*gloomily*). It's too much for one man. (*Pause. Cheerfully.*) On the other hand what's the good of losing heart now, that's what I say. We should have thought of it a million years ago, in the nineties.

ESTRAGON: Ah stop blathering and help me off with this bloody thing.

VLADIMIR: Hand in hand from the top of the Eiffel Tower, among the first. We were respectable in those days. Now it's too late. They wouldn't even let us up. (*Estragon tears at his boot.*) What are you doing?

ESTRAGON: Taking off my boot. Did that never happen to you?

VLADIMIR: Boots must be taken off every day, I'm tired telling you that. Why don't you listen to me?

ESTRAGON: (*feebly*). Help me!

VLADIMIR: It hurts?

ESTRAGON: (*angrily*). Hurts! He wants to know if it hurts!

VLADIMIR: (*angrily*). No one ever suffers but you. I don't count. I'd like to hear what you'd say if you had what I have.

ESTRAGON: It hurts?

VLADIMIR: (*angrily*). Hurts! He wants to know if it hurts!

ESTRAGON: (*pointing*). You might button it all the same.

VLADIMIR: (*stooping*). True. (*He buttons his fly.*) Never
            neglect the little things of life.

ESTRAGON: What do you expect, you always wait till the last
            moment.

VLADIMIR: (*musingly*). The last moment . . . (*He meditates.*)
            Hope deferred maketh the something sick, who
            said that?

ESTRAGON: Why don't you help me?

VLADIMIR: Sometimes I feel it coming all the same. Then I go
            all queer. (*He takes off his hat, peers inside it,
            feels about inside it, shakes it, puts it on again.*)
            How shall I say? Relieved and at the same time
            . . . (*he searches for the word*) . . . appalled.
            (*With emphasis.*) AP-PALLED. (*He takes
            off his hat again, peers inside it.*) Funny. (*He
            knocks on the crown as though to dislodge a
            foreign body, peers into it again, puts it on again.*)
            Nothing to be done. (*Estragon with a supreme
            effort succeeds in pulling off his boot. He peers
            inside it, feels about inside it, turns it upside
            down, shakes it, looks on the ground to see if
            anything has fallen out, finds nothing, feels inside
            it again, staring sightlessly before him.*) Well?

ESTRAGON: Nothing.

VLADIMIR: Show.

ESTRAGON: There's nothing to show.

VLADIMIR: Try and put it on again.

ESTRAGON: (*examining his foot*). I'll air it for a bit.

VLADIMIR: There's man all over for you, blaming on his boots
            the faults of his feet. (*He takes off his hat again,*

peers inside it, feels about inside it, knocks on the crown, blows into it, puts it on again.) This is getting alarming. (*Silence. Vladimir deep in thought, Estragon pulling at his toes.*) One of the thieves was saved. (*Pause.*) It's a reasonable percentage. (*Pause.*) Gogo.

ESTRAGON: What?

VLADIMIR: Suppose we repented.

ESTRAGON: Repented what?

VLADIMIR: Oh . . . (*He reflects.*) We wouldn't have to go into the details.

ESTRAGON: Our being born?

Vladimir breaks into a hearty laugh which he immediately stifles, his hand pressed to his pubis, his face contorted.

VLADIMIR: One daren't even laugh any more.

ESTRAGON: Dreadful privation.

VLADIMIR: Merely smile. (*He smiles suddenly from ear to ear, keeps smiling, ceases as suddenly.*) It's not the same thing. Nothing to be done. (*Pause.*) Gogo.

ESTRAGON: (*irritably*). What is it?

VLADIMIR: Did you ever read the Bible?

ESTRAGON: The Bible . . . (*He reflects.*) I must have taken a look at it.

VLADIMIR: Do you remember the Gospels?

ESTRAGON: I remember the maps of the Holy Land. Coloured they were. Very pretty. The Dead Sea was pale blue. The very look of it made me thirsty. That's where we'll go, I used to say, that's where we'll go for our honeymoon. We'll swim. We'll be happy.

VLADIMIR: You should have been a poet.

ESTRAGON: I was. (*Gesture towards his rags.*) Isn't that obvious?

Silence.

VLADIMIR: Where was I . . . How's your foot?

ESTRAGON: Swelling visibly.

VLADIMIR: Ah yes, the two thieves. Do you remember the story?

ESTRAGON: No.

VLADIMIR: Shall I tell it to you?

ESTRAGON: No.

VLADIMIR: It'll pass the time. (*Pause.*) Two thieves, crucified at the same time as our Saviour. One—

ESTRAGON: Our what?

VLADIMIR: Our Saviour. Two thieves. One is supposed to have been saved and the other . . . (*he searches for the contrary of saved*) . . . damned.

ESTRAGON: Saved from what?

VLADIMIR: Hell.

ESTRAGON: I'm going.

He does not move.

VLADIMIR: And yet . . . (*pause*) . . . how is it—this is not boring you I hope—how is it that of the four Evangelists only one speaks of a thief being saved. The four of them were there—or thereabouts—and only one speaks of a thief being saved. (*Pause.*) Come on, Gogo, return the ball, can't you, once in a way?

ESTRAGON: (*with exaggerated enthusiasm*). I find this really most extraordinarily interesting.

VLADIMIR: One out of four. Of the other three two don't mention any thieves at all and the third says that both of them abused him.

ESTRAGON: Who?

VLADIMIR: What?

ESTRAGON: What's all this about? Abused who?

VLADIMIR: The Saviour.

ESTRAGON: Why?

VLADIMIR: Because he wouldn't save them.

ESTRAGON: From hell?

VLADIMIR: Imbecile! From death.

ESTRAGON: I thought you said hell.

VLADIMIR: From death, from death.

ESTRAGON: Well what of it?

VLADIMIR: Then the two of them must have been damned.

ESTRAGON: And why not?

VLADIMIR: But one of the four says that one of the two was saved.

ESTRAGON: Well? They don't agree and that's all there is to it.

VLADIMIR: But all four were there. And only one speaks of a thief being saved. Why believe him rather than the others?

ESTRAGON: Who believes him?

VLADIMIR: Everybody. It's the only version they know.

ESTRAGON: People are bloody ignorant apes.
He rises painfully, goes limping to extreme left, halts, gazes into distance off with his hand screening his eyes, turns, goes to extreme right, gazes into distance. Vladimir watches him, then

goes and picks up the boot, peers into it, drops it
hastily.

VLADIMIR: Pah!

He spits. Estragon moves to center, halts with his
back to auditorium.

ESTRAGON: Charming spot. (*He turns, advances to front, halts*
facing auditorium.) Inspiring prospects. (*He turns*
to Vladimir.) Let's go.

VLADIMIR: We can't.

ESTRAGON: Why not?

VLADIMIR: We're waiting for Godot.

ESTRAGON: (*despairingly*). Ah! (*Pause.*) You're sure it was
here?

VLADIMIR: What?

ESTRAGON: That we were to wait.

VLADIMIR: He said by the tree. (*They look at the tree.*) Do
you see any others.

ESTRAGON: What is it?

VLADIMIR: I don't know. A willow.

ESTRAGON: Where are the leaves?

VLADIMIR: It must be dead.

ESTRAGON: No more weeping.

VLADIMIR: Or perhaps it's not the season.

ESTRAGON: Looks to me more like a bush.

VLADIMIR: A shrub.

ESTRAGON: A bush.

VLADIMIR: A—. What are you insinuating? That we've come
to the wrong place?

ESTRAGON: He should be here.

VLADIMIR: He didn't say for sure he'd come.

ESTRAGON: And if he doesn't come?

VLADIMIR: We'll come back to-morrow.

ESTRAGON: And then the day after to-morrow.

VLADIMIR: Possibly.

ESTRAGON: And so on.

VLADIMIR: The point is—

ESTRAGON: Until he comes.

VLADIMIR: You're merciless.

ESTRAGON: We came here yesterday.

VLADIMIR: Ah no, there you're mistaken.

ESTRAGON: What did we do yesterday?

VLADIMIR: What did we do yesterday?

ESTRAGON: Yes.

VLADIMIR: Why . . . (*Angrily.*) Nothing is certain when
you're about.

ESTRAGON: In my opinion we were here.

VLADIMIR: (*looking round*). You recognize the place?

ESTRAGON: I didn't say that.

VLADIMIR: Well?

ESTRAGON: That makes no difference.

VLADIMIR: All the same . . . that tree . . . (*turning towards
auditorium*) that bog . . .

ESTRAGON: You're sure it was this evening?

VLADIMIR: What?

ESTRAGON: That we were to wait.

VLADIMIR: He said Saturday. (*Pause.*) I think.

ESTRAGON: You think.

VLADIMIR: I must have made a note of it. (*He fumbles in his
pockets, bursting with miscellaneous rubbish.*)

ESTRAGON: *(very insidious)*. But what Saturday? And is it
Saturday? Is it not rather Sunday? *(Pause.)* Or
Monday? *(Pause.)* Or Friday?

VLADIMIR: *(looking wildly about him, as though the date was
inscribed in the landscape)*. It's not possible!

ESTRAGON: Or Thursday?

VLADIMIR: What'll we do?

ESTRAGON: If he came yesterday and we weren't here you
may be sure he won't come again to-day.

VLADIMIR: But you say we were here yesterday.

ESTRAGON: I may be mistaken. *(Pause.)* Let's stop talking for
a minute, do you mind?

VLADIMIR: *(feebly)*. All right. *(Estragon sits down on the
mound. Vladimir paces agitatedly to and fro,
halting from time to time to gaze into distance off.
Estragon falls asleep. Vladimir halts finally before
Estragon.)* Gogo! . . . Gogo! . . . GOGO!
Estragon wakes with a start.

ESTRAGON: *(restored to the horror of his situation)*. I was
asleep! *(Despairingly.)* Why will you never let me
sleep?

VLADIMIR: I felt lonely.

ESTRAGON: I had a dream.

VLADIMIR: Don't tell me!

ESTRAGON: I dreamt that—

VLADIMIR: DON'T TELL ME!

ESTRAGON: *(gesture towards the universe)*. This one is enough
for you? *(Silence.)* It's not nice of you, Didi. Who
am I to tell my private nightmares to if I can't tell
them to you?

VLADIMIR: Let them remain private. You know I can't bear that.

ESTRAGON: (*coldly*). There are times when I wonder if it wouldn't be better for us to part.

VLADIMIR: You wouldn't go far.

ESTRAGON: That would be too bad, really too bad. (*Pause.*) Wouldn't it, Didi, be really too bad? (*Pause.*) When you think of the beauty of the way. (*Pause.*) And the goodness of the wayfarers. (*Pause. Wheedling.*) Wouldn't it, Didi?

VLADIMIR: Calm yourself.

ESTRAGON: (*voluptuously*). Calm . . . calm . . . The English say cawm. (*Pause.*) You know the story of the Englishman in the brothel?

VLADIMIR: Yes.

ESTRAGON: Tell it to me.

VLADIMIR: Ah stop it!

ESTRAGON: An Englishman having drunk a little more than usual proceeds to a brothel. The bawd asks him if he wants a fair one, a dark one or a red-haired one. Go on.

VLADIMIR: STOP IT!

Exit Vladimir hurriedly. Estragon gets up and follows him as far as the limit of the stage. Gestures of Estragon like those of a spectator encouraging a pugilist. Enter Vladimir. He brushes past Estragon, crosses the stage with bowed head. Estragon takes a step towards him, halts.

ESTRAGON: (*gently*). You wanted to speak to me? (*Silence. Estragon takes a step forward.*) You had something to say to me? (*Silence. Another step forward.*) Didi . . .

VLADIMIR: (*without turning*). I've nothing to say to you.

ESTRAGON: (*step forward*). You're angry? (*Silence. Step forward.*) Forgive me. (*Silence. Step forward. Estragon lays his hand on Vladimir's shoulder.*) Come, Didi. (*Silence.*) Give me your hand. (*Vladimir half turns.*) Embrace me! (*Vladimir stiffens.*) Don't be stubborn! (*Vladimir softens. They embrace. Estragon recoils.*) You stink of garlic!

VLADIMIR: It's for the kidneys. (*Silence. Estragon looks attentively at the tree.*) What do we do now?

ESTRAGON: Wait.

VLADIMIR: Yes, but while waiting.

ESTRAGON: What about hanging ourselves?

VLADIMIR: Hmm. It'd give us an erection.

ESTRAGON: (*highly excited*). An erection!

VLADIMIR: With all that follows. Where it falls mandrakes grow. That's why they shriek when you pull them up. Did you not know that?

ESTRAGON: Let's hang ourselves immediately!

VLADIMIR: From a bough? (*They go towards the tree.*) I wouldn't trust it.

ESTRAGON: We can always try.

VLADIMIR: Go ahead.

ESTRAGON: After you.

VLADIMIR: No no, you first.

ESTRAGON: Why me?

VLADIMIR: You're lighter than I am.

ESTRAGON: Just so!

VLADIMIR: I don't understand.

ESTRAGON: Use your intelligence, can't you?
Vladimir uses his intelligence.

VLADIMIR: (*finally*). I remain in the dark.

ESTRAGON: This is how it is. (*He reflects.*) The bough . . .
the bough . . . (*Angrily.*) Use your head, can't
you?

VLADIMIR: You're my only hope.

ESTRAGON: (*with effort*). Gogo light—bough not break—Gogo
dead. Didi heavy—bough break—Didi alone.
Whereas—

VLADIMIR: I hadn't thought of that.

ESTRAGON: If it hangs you it'll hang anything.

VLADIMIR: But am I heavier than you?

ESTRAGON: So you tell me. I don't know. There's an even
chance. Or nearly.

VLADIMIR: Well? What do we do?

ESTRAGON: Don't let's do anything. It's safer.

VLADIMIR: Let's wait and see what he says.

ESTRAGON: Who?

VLADIMIR: Godot.

ESTRAGON: Good idea.

VLADIMIR: Let's wait till we know exactly how we stand.

ESTRAGON: On the other hand it might be better to strike the
iron before it freezes.

VLADIMIR: I'm curious to hear what he has to offer. Then
we'll take it or leave it.

ESTRAGON: What exactly did we ask him for?

VLADIMIR: Were you not there?

ESTRAGON: I can't have been listening.

VLADIMIR: Oh . . . Nothing very definite.

ESTRAGON: A kind of prayer.

VLADIMIR: Precisely.

ESTRAGON: A vague supplication.

VLADIMIR: Exactly.

ESTRAGON: And what did he reply?

VLADIMIR: That he'd see.

ESTRAGON: That he couldn't promise anything.

VLADIMIR: That he'd have to think it over.

ESTRAGON: In the quiet of his home.

VLADIMIR: Consult his family.

ESTRAGON: His friends.

VLADIMIR: His agents.

ESTRAGON: His correspondents.

VLADIMIR: His books.

ESTRAGON: His bank account.

VLADIMIR: Before taking a decision.

ESTRAGON: It's the normal thing.

VLADIMIR: Is it not?

ESTRAGON: I think it is.

VLADIMIR: I think so too.

Silence.

ESTRAGON: (*anxious*). And we?

VLADIMIR: I beg your pardon?

ESTRAGON: I said, And we?

VLADIMIR: I don't understand.

ESTRAGON: Where do we come in?

VLADIMIR: Come in?

ESTRAGON: Take your time.

VLADIMIR: Come in? On our hands and knees.

ESTRAGON: As bad as that?

VLADIMIR: Your Worship wishes to assert his prerogatives?

ESTRAGON: We've no rights any more?

Laugh of Vladimir, stifled as before, less the smile.

VLADIMIR: You'd make me laugh if it wasn't prohibited.

ESTRAGON: We've lost our rights?

VLADIMIR: (*distinctly*). We got rid of them.

Silence. They remain motionless, arms dangling, heads sunk, sagging at the knees.

ESTRAGON: (*feebly*). We're not tied? (*Pause.*) We're not—

VLADIMIR: Listen!

They listen, grotesquely rigid.

ESTRAGON: I hear nothing.

VLADIMIR: Hsst! (*They listen. Estragon loses his balance, almost falls. He clutches the arm of Vladimir who totters. They listen, huddled together.*) Nor I.

Sighs of relief. They relax and separate.

ESTRAGON: You gave me a fright.

VLADIMIR: I thought it was he.

ESTRAGON: Who?

VLADIMIR: Godot.

ESTRAGON: Pah! The wind in the reeds.

VLADIMIR: I could have sworn I heard shouts.

ESTRAGON: And why would he shout?

VLADIMIR: At his horse.

Silence.

ESTRAGON: (*violently*). I'm hungry!

VLADIMIR: Do you want a carrot?

ESTRAGON: Is that all there is?

VLADIMIR: I might have some turnips.

ESTRAGON: Give me a carrot. (*Vladimir rummages in his
            pockets, takes out a turnip and gives it to
            Estragon who takes a bite out of it. Angrily.*)
            It's a turnip!

VLADIMIR: Oh pardon! I could have sworn it was a carrot.
            (*He rummages again in his pockets, finds nothing
            but turnips.*) All that's turnips. (*He rummages.*)
            You must have eaten the last. (*He rummages.*)
            Wait, I have it. (*He brings out a carrot and gives
            it to Estragon.*) There, dear fellow. (*Estragon
            wipes the carrot on his sleeve and begins to eat it.*)
            Make it last, that's the end of them.

ESTRAGON: (*chewing*). I asked you a question.

VLADIMIR: Ah.

ESTRAGON: Did you reply?

VLADIMIR: How's the carrot?

ESTRAGON: It's a carrot.

VLADIMIR: So much the better, so much the better. (*Pause.*)
            What was it you wanted to know?

ESTRAGON: I've forgotten. (*Chews.*) That's what annoys me.
            (*He looks at the carrot appreciatively, dangles it
            between finger and thumb.*) I'll never forget this
            carrot. (*He sucks the end of it meditatively.*) Ah
            yes, now I remember.

VLADIMIR: Well?

ESTRAGON: (*his mouth full, vacuously*). We're not tied?

VLADIMIR: I don't hear a word you're saying.

ESTRAGON: (*chews, swallows*). I'm asking you if we're tied.

VLADIMIR: Tied?

ESTRAGON: Ti-ed.

VLADIMIR: How do you mean tied?

ESTRAGON: Down.

VLADIMIR: But to whom? By whom?

ESTRAGON: To your man.

VLADIMIR: To Godot? Tied to Godot! What an idea! No
question of it. (*Pause.*) For the moment.

ESTRAGON: His name is Godot?

VLADIMIR: I think so.

ESTRAGON: Fancy that. (*He raises what remains of the carrot
by the stub of leaf, twirls it before his eyes.*)
Funny, the more you eat the worse it gets.

VLADIMIR: With me it's just the opposite.

ESTRAGON: In other words?

VLADIMIR: I get used to the muck as I go along.

ESTRAGON: (*after prolonged reflection*). Is that the opposite?

VLADIMIR: Question of temperament.

ESTRAGON: Of character.

VLADIMIR: Nothing you can do about it.

ESTRAGON: No use struggling.

VLADIMIR: One is what one is.

ESTRAGON: No use wriggling.

VLADIMIR: The essential doesn't change.

ESTRAGON: Nothing to be done. (*He proffers the remains of
the carrot to Vladimir.*) Like to finish it?
*A terrible cry, close at hand. Estragon drops the
carrot. They remain motionless, then together
make a sudden rush towards the wings. Estragon*

*stops halfway, runs back, picks up the carrot,
stuffs it in his pocket, runs to rejoin Vladimir who
is waiting for him, stops again, runs back, picks up
his boot, runs to rejoin Vladimir. Huddled
together, shoulders hunched, cringing away from
the menace, they wait.*
*Enter Pozzo and Lucky. Pozzo drives Lucky by
means of a rope passed round his neck, so that
Lucky is the first to enter, followed by the rope
which is long enough to let him reach the middle
of the stage before Pozzo appears. Lucky carries
a heavy bag, a folding stool, a picnic basket and a
greatcoat, Pozzo a whip.*

POZZO: (*off*). On! (*Crack of whip. Pozzo appears. They
cross the stage. Lucky passes before Vladimir and
Estragon and exit. Pozzo at the sight of Vladimir
and Estragon stops short. The rope tautens. Pozzo
jerks at it violently.*) Back!
*Noise of Lucky falling with all his baggage.
Vladimir and Estragon turn towards him, half
wishing half fearing to go to his assistance.
Vladimir takes a step towards Lucky, Estragon
holds him back by the sleeve.*

VLADIMIR: Let me go!

ESTRAGON: Stay where you are!

POZZO: Be careful! He's wicked. (*Vladimir and Estragon
turn towards Pozzo.*) With strangers.

ESTRAGON: (*undertone*). Is that him?

VLADIMIR: Who?

ESTRAGON: (*trying to remember the name*). Er . . .

VLADIMIR: Godot?

ESTRAGON: Yes.

POZZO: I present myself: Pozzo.

VLADIMIR: (*to Estragon*). Not at all!

ESTRAGON: He said Godot.

VLADIMIR: Not at all!

ESTRAGON: (*timidly, to Pozzo*). You're not Mr. Godot, Sir?

POZZO: (*terrifying voice*). I am Pozzo! (*Silence.*) Pozzo!
(*Silence.*) Does that name mean nothing to you?
(*Silence.*) I say does that name mean nothing to
you?
*Vladimir and Estragon look at each other
questioningly.*

ESTRAGON: (*pretending to search*). Bozzo . . . Bozzo . . .

VLADIMIR: (*ditto*). Pozzo . . . Pozzo . . .

POZZO: PPPOZZZO!

ESTRAGON: Ah! Pozzo . . . let me see . . . Pozzo . . .

VLADIMIR: Is it Pozzo or Bozzo?

ESTRAGON: Pozzo . . . no . . . I'm afraid I . . . no . . . I
don't seem to . . .
Pozzo advances threateningly.

VLADIMIR: (*conciliating*). I once knew a family called Gozzo.
The mother had the clap.

ESTRAGON: (*hastily*). We're not from these parts, Sir.

POZZO: (*halting*). You are human beings none the less.
(*He puts on his glasses.*) As far as one can see. (*He
takes off his glasses.*) Of the same species as
myself. (*He bursts into an enormous laugh.*) Of the
same species as Pozzo! Made in God's image!

VLADIMIR: Well you see—

POZZO: *(peremptory)*. Who is Godot?

ESTRAGON: Godot?

POZZO: You took me for Godot.

VLADIMIR: Oh no, Sir, not for an instant, Sir.

POZZO: Who is he?

VLADIMIR: Oh he's a . . . he's a kind of acquaintance.

ESTRAGON: Nothing of the kind, we hardly know him.

VLADIMIR: True . . . we don't know him very well . . . but all the same . . .

ESTRAGON: Personally I wouldn't even know him if I saw him.

POZZO: You took me for him.

ESTRAGON: *(recoiling before Pozzo)*. That's to say . . . you understand . . . the dusk . . . the strain . . . waiting . . . I confess . . . I imagined . . . for a second . . .

POZZO: Waiting? So you were waiting for him?

VLADIMIR: Well you see—

POZZO: Here? On my land?

VLADIMIR: We didn't intend any harm.

ESTRAGON: We meant well.

POZZO: The road is free to all.

VLADIMIR: That's how we looked at it.

POZZO: It's a disgrace. But there you are.

ESTRAGON: Nothing we can do about it.

POZZO: *(with magnanimous gesture)*. Let's say no more about it. *(He jerks the rope.)* Up pig! *(Pause.)* Every time he drops he falls asleep. *(Jerks the rope.)* Up hog! *(Noise of Lucky getting up and picking up his baggage. Pozzo jerks the rope.)* Back! *(Enter Lucky backwards.)* Stop! *(Lucky*

stops.) Turn! (*Lucky turns. To Vladimir and
Estragon, affably.*) Gentlemen, I am happy to have
met you. (*Before their incredulous expression.*) Yes
yes, sincerely happy. (*He jerks the rope.*) Closer!
(*Lucky advances.*) Stop! (*Lucky stops.*) Yes, the
road seems long when one journeys all alone for
. . . (*he consults his watch*) . . . yes . . . (*he
calculates*) . . . yes, six hours, that's right, six
hours on end, and never a soul in sight. (*To
Lucky.*) Coat! (*Lucky puts down the bag,
advances, gives the coat, goes back to his place,
takes up the bag.*) Hold that! (*Pozzo holds out the
whip. Lucky advances and, both his hands being
occupied, takes the whip in his mouth, then goes
back to his place. Pozzo begins to put on his coat,
stops.*) Coat! (*Lucky puts down bag, basket and
stool, advances, helps Pozzo on with his coat, goes
back to his place and takes up bag, basket and
stool.*) Touch of autumn in the air this evening.
(*Pozzo finishes buttoning his coat, stoops, inspects
himself, straightens up.*) Whip! (*Lucky advances,
stoops, Pozzo snatches the whip from his mouth,
Lucky goes back to his place.*) Yes, gentlemen, I
cannot go for long without the society of my likes
(*he puts on his glasses and looks at the two likes*)
even when the likeness is an imperfect one. (*He
takes off his glasses.*) Stool! (*Lucky puts down bag
and basket, advances, opens stool, puts it down,
goes back to his place, takes up bag and basket.*)
Closer! (*Lucky puts down bag and basket,*

advances, moves stool, goes back to his place,
takes up bag and basket. Pozzo sits down, places
the butt of his whip against Lucky's chest and
pushes.) Back! *(Lucky takes a step back.)* Further!
(Lucky takes another step back.) Stop! *(Lucky*
stops. To Vladimir and Estragon.) That is why,
with your permission, I propose to dally with you
a moment, before I venture any further. Basket!
(Lucky advances, gives the basket, goes back to
his place.) The fresh air stimulates the jaded
appetite. *(He opens the basket, takes out a piece*
of chicken and a bottle of wine.) Basket! *(Lucky*
advances, picks up the basket and goes back to his
place.) Further! *(Lucky takes a step back.)* He
stinks. Happy days!
He drinks from the bottle, puts it down and
begins to eat. Silence. Vladimir and Estragon,
cautiously at first, then more boldly, begin to
circle about Lucky, inspecting him up and down.
Pozzo eats his chicken voraciously, throwing
away the bones after having sucked them. Lucky
sags slowly, until bag and basket touch the
ground, then straightens up with a start and
begins to sag again. Rhythm of one sleeping on
his feet.

ESTRAGON: What ails him?
VLADIMIR: He looks tired.
ESTRAGON: Why doesn't he put down his bags?
VLADIMIR: How do I know? *(They close in on him.)* Careful!
ESTRAGON: Say something to him.

VLADIMIR: Look!

ESTRAGON: What?

VLADIMIR: (*pointing*). His neck!

ESTRAGON: (*looking at the neck*). I see nothing.

VLADIMIR: Here.

Estragon goes over beside Vladimir.

ESTRAGON: Oh I say!

VLADIMIR: A running sore!

ESTRAGON: It's the rope.

VLADIMIR: It's the rubbing.

ESTRAGON: It's inevitable.

VLADIMIR: It's the knot.

ESTRAGON: It's the chafing.

They resume their inspection, dwell on the face.

VLADIMIR: (*grudgingly*). He's not bad looking.

ESTRAGON: (*shrugging his shoulders, wry face*). Would you say so?

VLADIMIR: A trifle effeminate.

ESTRAGON: Look at the slobber.

VLADIMIR: It's inevitable.

ESTRAGON: Look at the slaver.

VLADIMIR: Perhaps he's a halfwit.

ESTRAGON: A cretin.

VLADIMIR: (*looking closer*). Looks like a goiter.

ESTRAGON: (*ditto*). It's not certain.

VLADIMIR: He's panting.

ESTRAGON: It's inevitable.

VLADIMIR: And his eyes!

ESTRAGON: What about them?

VLADIMIR: Goggling out of his head.

ESTRAGON: Looks at his last gasp to me.

VLADIMIR: It's not certain. (*Pause.*) Ask him a question.

ESTRAGON: Would that be a good thing?

VLADIMIR: What do we risk?

ESTRAGON: (*timidly*). Mister . . .

VLADIMIR: Louder.

ESTRAGON: (*louder*). Mister . . .

POZZO: Leave him in peace! (*They turn towards Pozzo who, having finished eating, wipes his mouth with the back of his hand.*) Can't you see he wants to rest? Basket! (*He strikes a match and begins to light his pipe. Estragon sees the chicken bones on the ground and stares at them greedily. As Lucky does not move Pozzo throws the match angrily away and jerks the rope.*) Basket! (*Lucky starts, almost falls, recovers his senses, advances, puts the bottle in the basket and goes back to his place. Estragon stares at the bones. Pozzo strikes another match and lights his pipe.*) What can you expect, it's not his job. (*He pulls at his pipe, stretches out his legs.*) Ah! That's better.

ESTRAGON: (*timidly*). Please Sir . . .

POZZO: What is it, my good man?

ESTRAGON: Er . . . you've finished with the . . . er . . . you don't need the . . . er . . . bones, Sir?

VLADIMIR: (*scandalized*). You couldn't have waited?

POZZO: No no, he does well to ask. Do I need the bones? (*He turns them over with the end of his whip.*) No, personally I do not need them any more. (*Estragon takes a step towards the bones.*) But

. . . (*Estragon stops short*) . . . but in theory the bones go to the carrier. He is therefore the one to ask. (*Estragon turns towards Lucky, hesitates.*) Go on, go on, don't be afraid, ask him, he'll tell you. *Estragon goes towards Lucky, stops before him.*

ESTRAGON: Mister . . . excuse me, Mister . . .

POZZO: You're being spoken to, pig! Reply! (*To Estragon.*) Try him again.

ESTRAGON: Excuse me, Mister, the bones, you won't be wanting the bones?
Lucky looks long at Estragon.

POZZO: (*in raptures*). Mister! (*Lucky bows his head.*) Reply! Do you want them or don't you? (*Silence of Lucky. To Estragon.*) They're yours. (*Estragon makes a dart at the bones, picks them up and begins to gnaw them.*) I don't like it. I've never known him refuse a bone before. (*He looks anxiously at Lucky.*) Nice business it'd be if he fell sick on me!
He puffs at his pipe.

VLADIMIR: (*exploding*). It's a scandal!
Silence. Flabbergasted, Estragon stops gnawing, looks at Pozzo and Vladimir in turn. Pozzo outwardly calm. Vladimir embarrassed.

POZZO: (*to Vladimir*). Are you alluding to anything in particular?

VLADIMIR: (*stutteringly resolute*). To treat a man . . . (*gesture towards Lucky*) . . . like that . . . I think that . . . no . . . a human being . . . no . . . it's a scandal!

ESTRAGON: *(not to be outdone).* A disgrace!
          He resumes his gnawing.
POZZO: You are severe. *(To Vladimir.)* What age are you,
          if it's not a rude question? *(Silence.)* Sixty?
          Seventy? *(To Estragon.)* What age would you say
          he was?
ESTRAGON: Eleven.
POZZO: I am impertinent. *(He knocks out his pipe against
          the whip, gets up.)* I must be getting on. Thank
          you for your society. *(He reflects.)* Unless I smoke
          another pipe before I go. What do you say? *(They
          say nothing.)* Oh I'm only a small smoker, a very
          small smoker, I'm not in the habit of smoking two
          pipes one on top of the other, it makes *(hand to
          heart, sighing)* my heart go pit-a-pat. *(Silence.)* It's
          the nicotine, one absorbs it in spite of one's
          precautions. *(Sighs.)* You know how it is. *(Silence.)*
          But perhaps you don't smoke? Yes? No? It's of no
          importance. *(Silence.)* But how am I to sit down
          now, without affectation, now that I have risen?
          Without appearing to—how shall I say—without
          appearing to falter. *(To Vladimir.)* I beg your
          pardon? *(Silence.)* Perhaps you didn't speak?
          (Silence.) It's of no importance. Let me see . . .
          He reflects.
ESTRAGON: Ah! That's better.
          He puts the bones in his pocket.
VLADIMIR: Let's go.
ESTRAGON: So soon?

POZZO: One moment! (*He jerks the rope.*) Stool! (*He points with his whip. Lucky moves the stool.*) More! There! (*He sits down. Lucky goes back to his place.*) Done it!
He fills his pipe.

VLADIMIR: (*vehemently*). Let's go!

POZZO: I hope I'm not driving you away. Wait a little longer, you'll never regret it.

ESTRAGON: (*scenting charity*). We're in no hurry.

POZZO: (*having lit his pipe*). The second is never so sweet . . . (*he takes the pipe out of his mouth, contemplates it*) . . . as the first I mean. (*He puts the pipe back in his mouth.*) But it's sweet just the same.

VLADIMIR: I'm going.

POZZO: He can no longer endure my presence. I am perhaps not particularly human, but who cares? (*To Vladimir.*) Think twice before you do anything rash. Suppose you go now while it is still day, for there is no denying it is still day. (*They all look up at the sky.*) Good. (*They stop looking at the sky.*) What happens in that case—(*he takes the pipe out of his mouth, examines it*)—I'm out—(*he relights his pipe*)—in that case—(*puff*)—in that case—(*puff*) —what happens in that case to your appointment with this . . . Godet . . . Godot . . . Godin . . . anyhow you see who I mean, who has your future in his hands . . . (*pause*) . . . at least your immediate future?

VLADIMIR: Who told you?

POZZO: He speaks to me again! If this goes on much
longer we'll soon be old friends.

ESTRAGON: Why doesn't he put down his bags?

POZZO: I too would be happy to meet him. The more
people I meet the happier I become. From the
meanest creature one departs wiser, richer, more
conscious of one's blessings. Even you . . . (*he
looks at them ostentatiously in turn to make it
clear they are both meant*) . . . even you, who
knows, will have added to my store.

ESTRAGON: Why doesn't he put down his bags?

POZZO: But that would surprise me.

VLADIMIR: You're being asked a question.

POZZO: (*delighted*). A question! Who? What? A moment
ago you were calling me Sir, in fear and
trembling. Now you're asking me questions. No
good will come of this!

VLADIMIR: (*to Estragon*). I think he's listening.

ESTRAGON: (*circling about Lucky*). What?

VLADIMIR: You can ask him now. He's on the alert.

ESTRAGON: Ask him what?

VLADIMIR: Why he doesn't put down his bags.

ESTRAGON: I wonder.

VLADIMIR: Ask him, can't you?

POZZO: (*who has followed these exchanges with anxious
attention, fearing lest the question get lost*). You
want to know why he doesn't put down his bags,
as you call them.

VLADIMIR: That's it.

POZZO: *(to Estragon).* You are sure you agree with that?

ESTRAGON: He's puffing like a grampus.

POZZO: The answer is this. *(To Estragon.)* But stay still, I beg of you, you're making me nervous!

VLADIMIR: Here.

ESTRAGON: What is it?

VLADIMIR: He's about to speak.

    Estragon goes over beside Vladimir. Motionless, side by side, they wait.

POZZO: Good. Is everybody ready? Is everybody looking at me? *(He looks at Lucky, jerks the rope. Lucky raises his head.)* Will you look at me, pig! *(Lucky looks at him.)* Good. *(He puts the pipe in his pocket, takes out a little vaporizer and sprays his throat, puts back the vaporizer in his pocket, clears his throat, spits, takes out the vaporizer again, sprays his throat again, puts back the vaporizer in his pocket.)* I am ready. Is everybody listening? Is everybody ready? *(He looks at them all in turn, jerks the rope.)* Hog! *(Lucky raises his head.)* I don't like talking in a vacuum. Good. Let me see.

    He reflects.

ESTRAGON: I'm going.

POZZO: What was it exactly you wanted to know?

VLADIMIR: Why he—

POZZO: *(angrily).* Don't interrupt me! *(Pause. Calmer.)* If we all speak at once we'll never get anywhere. *(Pause.)* What was I saying? *(Pause. Louder.)* What was I saying?

Vladimir mimics one carrying a heavy burden.
Pozzo looks at him, puzzled.

ESTRAGON: *(forcibly).* Bags. *(He points at Lucky.)* Why?
Always hold. *(He sags, panting.)* Never put down.
(He opens his hands, straightens up with relief.)
Why?

POZZO: Ah! Why couldn't you say so before? Why he
doesn't make himself comfortable? Let's try and
get this clear. Has he not the right to? Certainly
he has. It follows that he doesn't want to. There's
reasoning for you. And why doesn't he want to?
(Pause.) Gentlemen, the reason is this.

VLADIMIR: *(to Estragon).* Make a note of this.

POZZO: He wants to impress me, so that I'll keep him.

ESTRAGON: What?

POZZO: Perhaps I haven't got it quite right. He wants to
mollify me, so that I'll give up the idea of parting
with him. No, that's not exactly it either.

VLADIMIR: You want to get rid of him?

POZZO: He wants to cod me, but he won't.

VLADIMIR: You want to get rid of him?

POZZO: He imagines that when I see how well he carries
I'll be tempted to keep him on in that capacity.

ESTRAGON: You've had enough of him?

POZZO: In reality he carries like a pig. It's not his job.

VLADIMIR: You want to get rid of him?

POZZO: He imagines that when I see him indefatigable
I'll regret my decision. Such is his miserable
scheme. As though I were short of slaves! *(All
three look at Lucky.)* Atlas, son of Jupiter!

(*Silence.*) Well, that's that I think. Anything else? *Vaporizer.*

VLADIMIR: You want to get rid of him?

POZZO: Remark that I might just as well have been in his shoes and he in mine. If chance had not willed otherwise. To each one his due.

VLADIMIR: You waagerrim?

POZZO: I beg your pardon?

VLADIMIR: You want to get rid of him?

POZZO: I do. But instead of driving him away as I might have done, I mean instead of simply kicking him out on his arse, in the goodness of my heart I am bringing him to the fair, where I hope to get a good price for him. The truth is you can't drive such creatures away. The best thing would be to kill them.

Lucky weeps.

ESTRAGON: He's crying!

POZZO: Old dogs have more dignity. (*He proffers his handkerchief to Estragon.*) Comfort him, since you pity him. (*Estragon hesitates.*) Come on. (*Estragon takes the handkerchief.*) Wipe away his tears, he'll feel less forsaken.

Estragon hesitates.

VLADIMIR: Here, give it to me, I'll do it.

Estragon refuses to give the handkerchief. Childish gestures.

POZZO: Make haste, before he stops. (*Estragon approaches Lucky and makes to wipe his eyes. Lucky kicks him violently in the shins. Estragon drops the*

handkerchief, recoils, staggers about the stage
howling with pain.) Hanky!
Lucky puts down bag and basket, picks up
handkerchief and gives it to Pozzo, goes back to
his place, picks up bag and basket.

ESTRAGON: Oh the swine! (*He pulls up the leg of his*
trousers.) He's crippled me!

POZZO: I told you he didn't like strangers.

VLADIMIR: (*to Estragon*). Show. (*Estragon shows his leg. To*
Pozzo, angrily.) He's bleeding!

POZZO: It's a good sign.

ESTRAGON: (*on one leg*). I'll never walk again!

VLADIMIR: (*tenderly*). I'll carry you. (*Pause.*) If necessary.

POZZO: He's stopped crying. (*To Estragon.*) You have
replaced him as it were. (*Lyrically.*) The tears of
the world are a constant quantity. For each one
who begins to weep somewhere else another stops.
The same is true of the laugh. (*He laughs.*) Let us
not then speak ill of our generation, it is not any
unhappier than its predecessors. (*Pause.*) Let us
not speak well of it either. (*Pause.*) Let us not
speak of it at all. (*Pause. Judiciously.*) It is true
the population has increased.

VLADIMIR: Try and walk.
Estragon takes a few limping steps, stops before
Lucky and spits on him, then goes and sits down
on the mound.

POZZO: Guess who taught me all these beautiful things.
(*Pause. Pointing to Lucky.*) My Lucky!

VLADIMIR: (*looking at the sky*). Will night never come?

POZZO: But for him all my thoughts, all my feelings, would have been of common things. (*Pause. With extraordinary vehemence.*) Professional worries! (*Calmer.*) Beauty, grace, truth of the first water, I knew they were all beyond me. So I took a knook.

VLADIMIR: (*startled from his inspection of the sky*). A knook?.

POZZO: That was nearly sixty years ago . . . (*he consults his watch*) . . . yes, nearly sixty. (*Drawing himself up proudly.*) You wouldn't think it to look at me, would you? Compared to him I look like a young man, no? (*Pause.*) Hat! (*Lucky puts down the basket and takes off his hat. His long white hair falls about his face. He puts his hat under his arm and picks up the basket.*) Now look. (*Pozzo takes off his hat.* He is completely bald. He puts on his hat again.*) Did you see?

VLADIMIR: And now you turn him away? Such an old and faithful servant!

ESTRAGON: Swine!

Pozzo more and more agitated.   •

VLADIMIR: After having sucked all the good out of him you chuck him away like a . . . like a banana skin. Really . . .

POZZO: (*groaning, clutching his head*). I can't bear it . . . any longer . . . the way he goes on . . . you've no idea . . . it's terrible . . . he must go . . . (*he waves his arms*) . . . I'm going mad . . . (*he*

---

* *All four wear bowlers.*

collapses, his head in his hands) . . . I can't bear
it . . . any longer . . .
Silence. All look at Pozzo.

VLADIMIR: He can't bear it.

ESTRAGON: Any longer.

VLADIMIR: He's going mad.

ESTRAGON: It's terrible.

VLADIMIR: (*to Lucky*). How dare you! It's abominable! Such a
good master! Crucify him like that! After so many
years! Really!

POZZO: (*sobbing*). He used to be so kind . . . so helpful
. . . and entertaining . . . my good angel . . .
and now . . . he's killing me

ESTRAGON: (*to Vladimir*). Does he want to replace him?

VLADIMIR: What?

ESTRAGON: Does he want someone to take his place or not?

VLADIMIR: I don't think so.

ESTRAGON: What?

VLADIMIR: I don't know.

ESTRAGON: Ask him.

POZZO: (*calmer*). Gentlemen, I don't know what came over
me. Forgive me. Forget all I said. (*More and more
his old self.*) I don't remember exactly what it was,
but you may be sure there wasn't a word of truth
in it. (*Drawing himself up, striking his chest.*) Do
I look like a man that can be made to suffer?
Frankly? (*He rummages in his pockets.*) What
have I done with my pipe?

VLADIMIR: Charming evening we're having.

ESTRAGON: Unforgettable.

VLADIMIR: And it's not over.

ESTRAGON: Apparently not.

VLADIMIR: It's only beginning.

ESTRAGON: It's awful.

VLADIMIR: Worse than the pantomime.

ESTRAGON: The circus.

VLADIMIR: The music-hall.

ESTRAGON: The circus.

POZZO: What can I have done with that briar?

ESTRAGON: He's a scream. He's lost his dudeen.
Laughs noisily.

VLADIMIR: I'll be back.
He hastens towards the wings.

ESTRAGON: End of the corridor, on the left.

VLADIMIR: Keep my seat.
Exit Vladimir.

POZZO: (*on the point of tears*). I've lost my Kapp and Peterson!

ESTRAGON: (*convulsed with merriment*). He'll be the death of me!

POZZO: You didn't see by any chance—. (*He misses Vladimir.*) Oh! He's gone! Without saying goodbye! How could he! He might have waited!

ESTRAGON: He would have burst.

POZZO: Oh! (*Pause.*) Oh well then of course in that case . . .

ESTRAGON: Come here.

POZZO: What for?

ESTRAGON: You'll see.

POZZO: You want me to get up?

ESTRAGON: Quick! (*Pozzo gets up and goes over beside*
           Estragon. Estragon points off.) Look!
POZZO: (*having put on his glasses*). Oh I say!
ESTRAGON: It's all over.
           Enter Vladimir, somber. He shoulders Lucky out
           of his way, kicks over the stool, comes and goes
           agitatedly.
POZZO: He's not pleased.
ESTRAGON: (*to Vladimir*). You missed a treat. Pity.
           Vladimir halts, straightens the stool, comes and
           goes, calmer.
POZZO: He subsides. (*Looking round.*) Indeed all subsides.
           A great calm descends. (*Raising his hand.*) Listen!
           Pan sleeps.
VLADIMIR: Will night never come?
           All three look at the sky.
POZZO: You don't feel like going until it does?
ESTRAGON: Well you see—
POZZO: Why it's very natural, very natural. I myself in
           your situation, if I had an appointment with a
           Godin . . . Godet . . . Godot . . . anyhow you
           see who I mean, I'd wait till it was black night
           before I gave up. (*He looks at the stool.*) I'd very
           much like to sit down, but I don't quite know how
           to go about it.
ESTRAGON: Could I be of any help?
POZZO: If you asked me perhaps.
ESTRAGON: What?
POZZO: If you asked me to sit down.
ESTRAGON: Would that be a help?

POZZO: I fancy so.

ESTRAGON: Here we go. Be seated, Sir, I beg of you.

POZZO: No no, I wouldn't think of it! (*Pause. Aside.*) Ask me again.

ESTRAGON: Come come, take a seat I beseech you, you'll get pneumonia.

POZZO: You really think so?

ESTRAGON: Why it's absolutely certain.

POZZO: No doubt you are right. (*He sits down.*) Done it again! (*Pause.*) Thank you, dear fellow. (*He consults his watch.*) But I must really be getting along, if I am to observe my schedule.

VLADIMIR: Time has stopped.

POZZO: (*cuddling his watch to his ear*). Don't you believe it, Sir, don't you believe it. (*He puts his watch back in his pocket.*) Whatever you like, but not that.

ESTRAGON: (*to Pozzo*). Everything seems black to him to-day.

POZZO: Except the firmament. (*He laughs, pleased with this witticism.*) But I see what it is, you are not from these parts, you don't know what our twilights can do. Shall I tell you? (*Silence. Estragon is fiddling with his boot again, Vladimir with his hat.*) I can't refuse you. (*Vaporizer.*) A little attention, if you please. (*Vladimir and Estragon continue their fiddling, Lucky is half asleep. Pozzo cracks his whip feebly.*) What's the matter with this whip? (*He gets up and cracks it more vigorously, finally with success. Lucky jumps. Vladimir's hat, Estragon's boot, Lucky's*

hat, fall to the ground. Pozzo throws down the
whip.) Worn out, this whip. (*He looks at Vladimir*
and Estragon.) What was I saying?

VLADIMIR: Let's go.

ESTRAGON: But take the weight off your feet, I implore you,
you'll catch your death.

POZZO: True. (*He sits down. To Estragon.*) What is your
name?

ESTRAGON: Adam.

POZZO: (*who hasn't listened*). Ah yes! The night. (*He raises*
his head.) But be a little more attentive, for pity's
sake, otherwise we'll never get anywhere. (*He*
looks at the sky.) Look! (*All look at the sky except*
Lucky who is dozing off again. Pozzo jerks the
rope.) Will you look at the sky, pig! (*Lucky looks*
at the sky.) Good, that's enough. (*They stop*
looking at the sky.) What is there so extraordinary
about it? Qua sky. It is pale and luminous like any
sky at this hour of the day. (*Pause.*) In these
latitudes. (*Pause.*) When the weather is fine.
(*Lyrical.*) An hour ago (*he looks at his watch,*
prosaic) roughly (*lyrical*) after having poured
forth even since (*he hesitates, prosaic*) say ten
o'clock in the morning (*lyrical*) tirelessly torrents
of red and white light it begins to lose its
effulgence, to grow pale (*gesture of the two hands*
lapsing by stages) pale, ever a little paler, a little
paler until (*dramatic pause, ample gesture of the*
two hands flung wide apart) pppfff! finished! it
comes to rest. But—(*hand raised in admonition*)—

but behind this veil of gentleness and peace night
is charging (*vibrantly*) and will burst upon us
(*snaps his fingers*) pop! like that! (*his inspiration
leaves him*) just when we least expect it. (*Silence.
Gloomily.*) That's how it is on this bitch of an
earth.

Long silence.

ESTRAGON: So long as one knows.
VLADIMIR: One can bide one's time.
ESTRAGON: One knows what to expect.
VLADIMIR: No further need to worry.
ESTRAGON: Simply wait.
VLADIMIR: We're used to it.

*He picks up his hat, peers inside it, shakes it, puts
it on.*

POZZO: How did you find me? (*Vladimir and Estragon
look at him blankly.*) Good? Fair? Middling?
Poor? Positively bad?
VLADIMIR: (*first to understand*). Oh very good, very very
good.
POZZO: (*to Estragon*). And you, Sir?
ESTRAGON: Oh tray bong, tray tray tray bong.
POZZO: (*fervently*). Bless you, gentlemen, bless you!
(*Pause.*) I have such need of encouragement!
(*Pause.*) I weakened a little towards the end, you
didn't notice?
VLADIMIR: Oh perhaps just a teeny weeny little bit.
ESTRAGON: I thought it was intentional.
POZZO: You see my memory is defective.

Silence.

ESTRAGON: In the meantime nothing happens.

POZZO: You find it tedious?

ESTRAGON: Somewhat.

POZZO: (*to Vladimir*). And you, Sir?

VLADIMIR: I've been better entertained.

Silence. Pozzo struggles inwardly.

POZZO: Gentlemen, you have been . . . civil to me.

ESTRAGON: Not at all!

VLADIMIR: What an idea!

POZZO: Yes yes, you have been correct. So that I ask myself is there anything I can do in my turn for these honest fellows who are having such a dull, dull time.

ESTRAGON: Even ten francs would be a help.

VLADIMIR: We are not beggars!

POZZO: Is there anything I can do, that's what I ask myself, to cheer them up? I have given them bones, I have talked to them about this and that, I have explained the twilight, admittedly. But is it enough, that's what tortures me, is it enough?

ESTRAGON: Even five.

VLADIMIR: (*to Estragon, indignantly*). That's enough!

ESTRAGON: I couldn't accept less.

POZZO: Is it enough? No doubt. But I am liberal. It's my nature. This evening. So much the worse for me. (*He jerks the rope. Lucky looks at him.*) For I shall suffer, no doubt about that. (*He picks up the whip.*) What do you prefer? Shall we have him dance, or sing, or recite, or think, or—

ESTRAGON: Who?

POZZO: Who! You know how to think, you two?

VLADIMIR: He thinks?

POZZO: Certainly. Aloud. He even used to think very prettily once, I could listen to him for hours. Now . . . (*he shudders*). So much the worse for me. Well, would you like him to think something for us?

ESTRAGON: I'd rather he'd dance, it'd be more fun.

POZZO: Not necessarily.

ESTRAGON: Wouldn't it, Didi, be more fun?

VLADIMIR: I'd like well to hear him think.

ESTRAGON: Perhaps he could dance first and think afterwards, if it isn't too much to ask him.

VLADIMIR: (*to Pozzo*). Would that be possible?

POZZO: By all means, nothing simpler. It's the natural order.
He laughs briefly.

VLADIMIR: Then let him dance.
Silence.

POZZO: Do you hear, hog?

ESTRAGON: He never refuses?

POZZO: He refused once. (*Silence.*) Dance, misery!
Lucky puts down bag and basket, advances towards front, turns to Pozzo. Lucky dances. He stops.

ESTRAGON: Is that all?

POZZO: Encore!
Lucky executes the same movements, stops.

ESTRAGON: Pooh! I'd do as well myself. (*He imitates Lucky, almost falls.*) With a little practice.

POZZO: He used to dance the farandole, the fling, the brawl, the jig, the fandango and even the hornpipe. He capered. For joy. Now that's the best he can do. Do you know what he calls it?

ESTRAGON: The Scapegoat's Agony.

VLADIMIR: The Hard Stool.

POZZO: The Net. He thinks he's entangled in a net.

VLADIMIR: (*squirming like an aesthete*). There's something about it . . .

Lucky makes to return to his burdens.

POZZO: Woaa!

Lucky stiffens.

ESTRAGON: Tell us about the time he refused.

POZZO: With pleasure, with pleasure. (*He fumbles in his pockets.*) Wait. (*He fumbles.*) What have I done with my spray? (*He fumbles.*) Well now isn't that . . . (*He looks up, consternation on his features. Faintly.*) I can't find my pulverizer!

ESTRAGON: (*faintly*). My left lung is very weak! (*He coughs feebly. In ringing tones.*) But my right lung is as sound as a bell!

POZZO: (*normal voice*). No matter! What was I saying. (*He ponders.*) Wait. (*Ponders.*) Well now isn't that . . . (*He raises his head.*) Help me!

ESTRAGON: Wait!

VLADIMIR: Wait!

POZZO: Wait!

All three take off their hats simultaneously, press their hands to their foreheads, concentrate.

ESTRAGON: (*triumphantly*). Ah!

VLADIMIR: He has it.

POZZO: *(impatient)*. Well?

ESTRAGON: Why doesn't he put down his bags?

VLADIMIR: Rubbish!

POZZO: Are you sure?

VLADIMIR: Damn it haven't you already told us?

POZZO: I've already told you?

ESTRAGON: He's already told us?

VLADIMIR: Anyway he has put them down.

ESTRAGON: *(glance at Lucky)*. So he has. And what of it?

VLADIMIR: Since he has put down his bags it is impossible we
should have asked why he does not do so.

POZZO: Stoutly reasoned!

ESTRAGON: And why has he put them down?

POZZO: Answer us that.

VLADIMIR: In order to dance.

ESTRAGON: True!

POZZO: True!

Silence. They put on their hats.

ESTRAGON: Nothing happens, nobody comes, nobody goes,
it's awful!

VLADIMIR: *(to Pozzo)*. Tell him to think.

POZZO: Give him his hat.

VLADIMIR: His hat?

POZZO: He can't think without his hat.

VLADIMIR: *(to Estragon)*. Give him his hat.

ESTRAGON: Me! After what he did to me! Never!

VLADIMIR: I'll give it to him.

He does not move.

ESTRAGON: *(to Pozzo)*. Tell him to go and fetch it.

POZZO: It's better to give it to him.

VLADIMIR: I'll give it to him.
          *He picks up the hat and tenders it at arm's length
          to Lucky, who does not move.*

POZZO: You must put it on his head.

ESTRAGON: *(to Pozzo).* Tell him to take it.

POZZO: It's better to put it on his head.

VLADIMIR: I'll put it on his head.
          *He goes round behind Lucky, approaches him
          cautiously, puts the hat on his head and recoils
          smartly. Lucky does not move. Silence.*

ESTRAGON: What's he waiting for?

POZZO: Stand back! *(Vladimir and Estragon move away
          from Lucky. Pozzo jerks the rope. Lucky looks at
          Pozzo.)* Think, pig! *(Pause. Lucky begins to
          dance.)* Stop! *(Lucky stops.)* Forward! *(Lucky
          advances.)* Stop! *(Lucky stops.)* Think!
          Silence.*

LUCKY: On the other hand with regard to—

POZZO: Stop! *(Lucky stops.)* Back! *(Lucky moves back.)*
          Stop! *(Lucky stops.)* Turn! *(Lucky turns towards
          auditorium.)* Think!
          During Lucky's tirade the others react as follows.
          *1) Vladimir and Estragon all attention, Pozzo
          dejected and disgusted.*
          *2) Vladimir and Estragon begin to protest, Pozzo's
          sufferings increase.*
          *3) Vladimir and Estragon attentive again, Pozzo
          more and more agitated and groaning.*
          4) Vladimir and Estragon protest violently. Pozzo

jumps up, pulls on the rope. General outcry.
Lucky pulls on the rope, staggers, shouts his text.
All three throw themselves on Lucky who
struggles and shouts his text.

LUCKY: Given the existence as uttered forth in the public
works of Puncher and Wattmann of a personal
God quaquaquaqua with white beard
quaquaquaqua outside time without extension
who from the heights of divine apathia divine
athambia divine aphasia loves us dearly with
some exceptions for reasons unknown but time
will tell and suffers like the divine Miranda with
those who for reasons unknown but time will tell
are plunged in torment plunged in fire whose fire
flames if that continues and who can doubt it will
fire the firmament that is to say blast hell to
heaven so blue still and calm so calm with a calm
which even though intermittent is better than
nothing but not so fast and considering what is
more that as a result of the labors left unfinished
crowned by the Acacacacademy of
Anthropopopometry of Essy-in-Possy of Testew
and Cunard it is established beyond all doubt all
other doubt than that which clings to the labors
of men that as a result of the labors unfinished of
Testew and Cunard it is established as hereinafter
but not so fast for reasons unknown that as a
result of the public works of Puncher and
Wattmann it is established beyond all doubt that
in view of the labors of Fartov and Belcher left

unfinished for reasons unknown of Testew and
Cunard left unfinished it is established what many
deny that man in Possy of Testew and Cunard
that man in Essy that man in short that man in
brief in spite of the strides of alimentation and
defecation wastes and pines wastes and pines and
concurrently simultaneously what is more for
reasons unknown in spite of the strides of physical
culture the practice of sports such as tennis
football running cycling swimming flying floating
riding gliding conating camogie skating tennis of
all kinds dying flying sports of all sorts autumn
summer winter winter tennis of all kinds hockey of
all sorts penicilline and succedanea in a word I
resume flying gliding golf over nine and eighteen
holes tennis of all sorts in a word for reasons
unknown in Feckham Peckham Fulham Clapham
namely concurrently simultaneously what is more
for reasons unknown but time will tell fades away
I resume Fulham Clapham in a word the dead
loss per head since the death of Bishop Berkeley
being to the tune of one inch four ounce per head
approximately by and large more or less to the
nearest decimal good measure round figures stark
naked in the stockinged feet in Connemara in a
word for reasons unknown no matter what matter
the facts are there and considering what is more
much more grave that in the light of the labors
lost of Steinweg and Peterman it appears what is
more much more grave that in the light the light

the light of the labors lost of Steinweg and
Peterman that in the plains in the mountains by
the seas by the rivers running water running fire
the air is the same and then the earth namely the
air and then the earth in the great cold the great
dark the air and the earth abode of stones in the
great cold alas alas in the year of their Lord six
hundred and something the air the earth the sea
the earth abode of stones in the great deeps the
great cold on sea on land and in the air I resume
for reasons unknown in spite of the tennis the
facts are there but time will tell I resume alas
alas on on in short in fine on on abode of stones
who can doubt it I resume but not so fast I
resume the skull fading fading fading and
concurrently simultaneously what is more for
reasons unknown in spite of the tennis on on the
beard the flames the tears the stones so blue so
calm alas alas on on the skull the skull the skull
the skull in Connemara in spite of the tennis the
labors abandoned left unfinished graver still
abode of stones in a word I resume alas alas
abandoned unfinished the skull the skull in
Connemara in spite of the tennis the skull alas the
stones Cunard (*mêlée, final vociferations*) tennis
. . . the stones . . . so calm . . . Cunard . . .
unfinished . . .

POZZO: His hat!

*Vladimir seizes Lucky's hat. Silence of Lucky. He
falls. Silence. Panting of the victors.*

ESTRAGON: Avenged!
            Vladimir examines the hat, peers inside it.
   POZZO: Give me that! (*He snatches the hat from Vladimir,
            throws it on the ground, tramples on it.*) There's
            an end to his thinking!
VLADIMIR: But will he be able to walk?
   POZZO: Walk or crawl! (*He kicks Lucky.*) Up pig!
ESTRAGON: Perhaps he's dead.
VLADIMIR: You'll kill him.
   POZZO: Up scum! (*He jerks the rope.*) Help me!
VLADIMIR: How?
   POZZO: Raise him up!
            *Vladimir and Estragon hoist Lucky to his feet,
            support him an instant, then let him go. He falls.*
ESTRAGON: He's doing it on purpose!
   POZZO: You must hold him. (*Pause.*) Come on, come on,
            raise him up.
ESTRAGON: To hell with him!
VLADIMIR: Come on, once more.
ESTRAGON: What does he take us for?
            They raise Lucky, hold him up.
   POZZO: Don't let him go! (*Vladimir and Estragon totter.*)
            Don't move! (*Pozzo fetches bag and basket and
            brings them towards Lucky.*) Hold him tight! (*He
            puts the bag in Lucky's hand. Lucky drops it
            immediately.*) Don't let him go! (*He puts back the
            bag in Lucky's hand. Gradually, at the feel of the
            bag, Lucky recovers his senses and his fingers
            finally close round the handle.*) Hold him tight!
            (*As before with basket.*) Now! You can let him go.

*(Vladimir and Estragon move away from Lucky
who totters, reels, sags, but succeeds in
remaining on his feet, bag and basket in his hands.
Pozzo steps back, cracks his whip.)* Forward!
(Lucky totters forward.) Back! *(Lucky totters
back.)* Turn! *(Lucky turns.)* Done it! He can walk.
(Turning to Vladimir and Estragon.) Thank you,
gentlemen, and let me . . . *(he fumbles in his
pockets)* . . . let me wish you . . . *(fumbles)* . . .
wish you . . . *(fumbles)* . . . what have I done
with my watch? *(Fumbles.)* A genuine half-hunter,
gentlemen, with deadbeat escapement! *(Sobbing.)*
Twas my granpa gave it to me! *(He searches on
the ground, Vladimir and Estragon likewise.
Pozzo turns over with his foot the remains of
Lucky's hat.)* Well now isn't that just—

VLADIMIR: Perhaps it's in your fob.

POZZO: Wait! *(He doubles up in an attempt to apply his
ear to his stomach, listens. Silence.)* I hear nothing.
*(He beckons them to approach. Vladimir and
Estragon go over to him, bend over his stomach.)*
Surely one should hear the tick-tick.

VLADIMIR: Silence!

All listen, bent double.

ESTRAGON: I hear something.

POZZO: Where?

VLADIMIR: It's the heart.

POZZO: *(disappointed).* Damnation!

VLADIMIR: Silence!

ESTRAGON: Perhaps it has stopped.
           They straighten up.
POZZO: Which of you smells so bad?
ESTRAGON: He has stinking breath and I have stinking feet.
POZZO: I must go.
ESTRAGON: And your half-hunter?
POZZO: I must have left it at the manor.
           Silence.
ESTRAGON: Then adieu.
POZZO: Adieu.
VLADIMIR: Adieu.
POZZO: Adieu.
           Silence. No one moves.
VLADIMIR: Adieu.
POZZO: Adieu.
ESTRAGON: Adieu.
           Silence.
POZZO: And thank you.
VLADIMIR: Thank *you.*
POZZO: Not at all.
ESTRAGON: Yes yes.
POZZO: No no.
VLADIMIR: Yes yes.
ESTRAGON: No no.
           Silence.
POZZO: I don't seem to be able . . . (*long hesitation*) . . .
           to depart.
ESTRAGON: Such is life.
           *Pozzo turns, moves away from Lucky towards the
           wings, paying out the rope as he goes.*

VLADIMIR: You're going the wrong way.

POZZO: I need a running start. (*Having come to the end of the rope, i.e. off stage, he stops, turns and cries.*) Stand back! (*Vladimir and Estragon stand back, look towards Pozzo. Crack of whip.*) On! On!

ESTRAGON: On!

VLADIMIR: On!

Lucky moves off.

POZZO: Faster! (*He appears, crosses the stage preceded by Lucky. Vladimir and Estragon wave their hats. Exit Lucky.*) On! On! (*On the point of disappearing in his turn he stops and turns. The rope tautens. Noise of Lucky falling off.*) Stool! (*Vladimir fetches stool and gives it to Pozzo who throws it to Lucky.*) Adieu!

VLADIMIR:
             (*waving*). Adieu! Adieu!
ESTRAGON:

POZZO: Up! Pig! (*Noise of Lucky getting up.*) On! (*Exit Pozzo.*) Faster! On! Adieu! Pig! Yip! Adieu!

Long silence.

VLADIMIR: That passed the time.

ESTRAGON: It would have passed in any case.

VLADIMIR: Yes, but not so rapidly.

Pause.

ESTRAGON: What do we do now?

VLADIMIR: I don't know.

ESTRAGON: Let's go.

VLADIMIR: We can't.

ESTRAGON: Why not?

VLADIMIR: We're waiting for Godot.

ESTRAGON: *(despairingly).* Ah!
           Pause.
VLADIMIR: How they've changed!
ESTRAGON: Who?
VLADIMIR: Those two.
ESTRAGON: That's the idea, let's make a little conversation.
VLADIMIR: Haven't they?
ESTRAGON: What?
VLADIMIR: Changed.
ESTRAGON: Very likely. They all change. Only we can't.
VLADIMIR: Likely! It's certain. Didn't you see them?
ESTRAGON: I suppose I did. But I don't know them.
VLADIMIR: Yes you do know them.
ESTRAGON: No I don't know them.
VLADIMIR: We know them, I tell you. You forget everything.
           (Pause. To himself.) Unless they're not the
           same . .
ESTRAGON: Why didn't they recognize us then?
VLADIMIR: That means nothing. I too pretended not to
           recognize them. And then nobody ever recognizes
           us.
ESTRAGON: Forget it. What we need—ow! *(Vladimir does not
           react.)* Ow!
VLADIMIR: *(to himself).* Unless they're not the same . . .
ESTRAGON: Didi! It's the other foot!
           He goes hobbling towards the mound.
VLADIMIR: Unless they're not the same . . .
     BOY: *(off).* Mister!
           Estragon halts. Both look towards the voice.
ESTRAGON: Off we go again.

VLADIMIR: Approach, my child.

Enter Boy, timidly. He halts.

BOY: Mister Albert . . . ?

VLADIMIR: Yes.

ESTRAGON: What do you want?

VLADIMIR: Approach!

The Boy does not move.

ESTRAGON: *(forcibly).* Approach when you're told, can't you?

The Boy advances timidly, halts.

VLADIMIR: What is it?

BOY: Mr. Godot . . .

VLADIMIR: Obviously . . . *(Pause.)* Approach.

ESTRAGON: *(violently).* Will you approach! *(The Boy advances timidly.)* What kept you so late?

VLADIMIR: You have a message from Mr. Godot?

BOY: Yes Sir.

VLADIMIR: Well, what is it?

ESTRAGON: What kept you so late?

The Boy looks at them in turn, not knowing to which he should reply.

VLADIMIR: *(to Estragon).* Let him alone.

ESTRAGON: *(violently).* You let me alone. *(Advancing, to the Boy.)* Do you know what time it is?

BOY: *(recoiling).* It's not my fault, Sir.

ESTRAGON: And whose is it? Mine?

BOY: I was afraid, Sir.

ESTRAGON: Afraid of what? Of us? *(Pause.)* Answer me!

VLADIMIR: I know what it is, he was afraid of the others.

ESTRAGON: How long have you been here?

BOY: A good while, Sir.

VLADIMIR:	You were afraid of the whip?
BOY:	Yes Sir.
VLADIMIR:	The roars?
BOY:	Yes Sir.
VLADIMIR:	The two big men.
BOY:	Yes Sir.
VLADIMIR:	Do you know them?
BOY:	No Sir.
VLADIMIR:	Are you a native of these parts? (*Silence.*) Do you belong to these parts?
BOY:	Yes Sir.
ESTRAGON:	That's all a pack of lies. (*Shaking the Boy by the arm.*) Tell us the truth!
BOY:	(*trembling*). But it is the truth, Sir!
VLADIMIR:	Will you let him alone! What's the matter with you? (*Estragon releases the Boy, moves away, covering his face with his hands. Vladimir and the Boy observe him. Estragon drops his hands. His face is convulsed.*) What's the matter with you?
ESTRAGON:	I'm unhappy.
VLADIMIR:	Not really! Since when?
ESTRAGON:	I'd forgotten.
VLADIMIR:	Extraordinary the tricks that memory plays! (*Estragon tries to speak, renounces, limps to his place, sits down and begins to take off his boots. To Boy.*) Well?
BOY:	Mr. Godot—
VLADIMIR:	I've seen you before, haven't I?
BOY:	I don't know, Sir.
VLADIMIR:	You don't know me?

BOY: No Sir.

VLADIMIR: It wasn't you came yesterday?

BOY: No Sir.

VLADIMIR: This is your first time?

BOY: Yes Sir.

          Silence.

VLADIMIR: Word words. (*Pause.*) Speak.

BOY: (*in a rush*). Mr. Godot told me to tell you he won't
          come this evening but surely to-morrow.

          Silence.

VLADIMIR: Is that all?

BOY: Yes Sir.

          Silence.

VLADIMIR: You work for Mr. Godot?

BOY: Yes Sir.

VLADIMIR: What do you do?

BOY: I mind the goats, Sir.

VLADIMIR: Is he good to you?

BOY: Yes Sir.

VLADIMIR: He doesn't beat you?

BOY: No Sir, not me.

VLADIMIR: Whom does he beat?

BOY: He beats my brother, Sir.

VLADIMIR: Ah, you have a brother?

BOY: Yes Sir.

VLADIMIR: What does he do?

BOY: He minds the sheep, Sir.

VLADIMIR: And why doesn't he beat you?

BOY: I don't know, Sir.

VLADIMIR: He must be fond of you.

BOY: I don't know, Sir.

Silence.

VLADIMIR: Does he give you enough to eat? (*The Boy hesitates.*) Does he feed you well?

BOY: Fairly well, Sir.

VLADIMIR: You're not unhappy? (*The Boy hesitates.*) Do you hear me?

BOY: Yes Sir.

VLADIMIR: Well?

BOY: I don't know, Sir.

VLADIMIR: You don't know if you're unhappy or not?

BOY: No Sir.

VLADIMIR: You're as bad as myself. (*Silence.*) Where do you sleep?

BOY: In the loft, Sir.

VLADIMIR: With your brother?

BOY: Yes Sir.

VLADIMIR: In the hay?

BOY: Yes Sir.

Silence.

VLADIMIR: All right, you may go.

BOY: What am I to tell Mr. Godot, Sir?

VLADIMIR: Tell him . . . (*he hesitates*) . . . tell him you saw us. (*Pause.*) You did see us, didn't you?

BOY: Yes Sir.

He steps back, hesitates, turns and exit running. The light suddenly fails. In a moment it is night. The moon rises at back, mounts in the sky, stands still, shedding a pale light on the scene.

VLADIMIR: At last! (*Estragon gets up and goes towards Vladimir, a boot in each hand. He puts them down at edge of stage, straightens and contemplates the moon.*) What are you doing?

ESTRAGON: Pale for weariness.

VLADIMIR: Eh?

ESTRAGON: Of climbing heaven and gazing on the likes of us.

VLADIMIR: Your boots, what are you doing with your boots?

ESTRAGON: (*turning to look at the boots*). I'm leaving them there. (*Pause.*) Another will come, just as . . . as . . . as me, but with smaller feet, and they'll make him happy.

VLADIMIR: But you can't go barefoot!

ESTRAGON: Christ did.

VLADIMIR: Christ! What has Christ got to do with it? You're not going to compare yourself to Christ!

ESTRAGON: All my life I've compared myself to him.

VLADIMIR: But where he lived it was warm, it was dry!

ESTRAGON: Yes. And they crucified quick.
             Silence.

VLADIMIR: We've nothing more to do here.

ESTRAGON: Nor anywhere else.

VLADIMIR: Ah Gogo, don't go on like that. To-morrow everything will be better.

ESTRAGON: How do you make that out?

VLADIMIR: Did you not hear what the child said?

ESTRAGON: No.

VLADIMIR: He said that Godot was sure to come to-morrow. (*Pause.*) What do you say to that?

ESTRAGON: Then all we have to do is to wait on here.
VLADIMIR: Are you mad? We must take cover. (*He takes
            Estragon by the arm.*) Come on.
            *He draws Estragon after him. Estragon yields,
            then resists. They halt.*
ESTRAGON: (*looking at the tree*). Pity we haven't got a bit of
            rope.
VLADIMIR: Come on. It's cold.
            He draws Estragon after him. As before.
ESTRAGON: Remind me to bring a bit of rope to-morrow.
VLADIMIR: Yes. Come on.
            He draws him after him. As before.
ESTRAGON: How long have we been together all the time
            now?
VLADIMIR: I don't know. Fifty years maybe.
ESTRAGON: Do you remember the day I threw myself into the
            Rhone?
VLADIMIR: We were grape harvesting.
ESTRAGON: You fished me out.
VLADIMIR: That's all dead and buried.
ESTRAGON: My clothes dried in the sun.
VLADIMIR: There's no good harking back on that. Come on.
            He draws him after him. As before.
ESTRAGON: Wait!
VLADIMIR: I'm cold!
ESTRAGON: Wait! (*He moves away from Vladimir.*) I
            sometimes wonder if we wouldn't have been
            better off alone, each one for himself. (*He crosses
            the stage and sits down on the mound.*) We
            weren't made for the same road.

VLADIMIR: (*without anger*). It's not certain.

ESTRAGON: No, nothing is certain.

Vladimir slowly crosses the stage and sits down beside Estragon.

VLADIMIR: We can still part, if you think it would be better.

ESTRAGON: It's not worth while now.

Silence.

VLADIMIR: No, it's not worth while now.

Silence.

ESTRAGON: Well, shall we go?

VLADIMIR: Yes, let's go.

They do not move.

Curtain

Act II

Next day. Same time.

Same place.

Estragon's boots front center, heels together, toes
splayed. Lucky's hat at same place.
The tree has four or five leaves.
Enter Vladimir agitatedly. He halts and looks long
at the tree, then suddenly begins to move
feverishly about the stage. He halts before the
boots, picks one up, examines it, sniffs it, manifests
disgust, puts it back carefully. Comes and goes.
Halts extreme right and gazes into distance off,
shading his eyes with his hand. Comes and goes.
Halts extreme left, as before. Comes and goes.
Halts suddenly and begins to sing loudly.

VLADIMIR: A dog came in—
Having begun too high he stops, clears his throat,
resumes:
                    A dog came in the kitchen
                    And stole a crust of bread.
                    Then cook up with a ladle
                    And beat him till he was dead.

                    Then all the dogs came running
                    And dug the dog a tomb—
He stops, broods, resumes:
                    Then all the dogs came running
                    And dug the dog a tomb
                    And wrote upon the tombstone
                    For the eyes of dogs to come:

                    A dog came in the kitchen
                    And stole a crust of bread.

Then cook up with a ladle
And beat him till he was dead.

Then all the dogs came running
And dug the dog a tomb—
He stops, broods, resumes:
Then all the dogs came running
And dug the dog a tomb—
He stops, broods. Softly.
And dug the dog a tomb . . .
He remains a moment silent and motionless, then begins to move feverishly about the stage. He halts before the tree, comes and goes, before the boots, comes and goes, halts extreme right, gazes into distance, extreme left, gazes into distance. Enter Estragon right, barefoot, head bowed. He slowly crosses the stage. Vladimir turns and sees him.

VLADIMIR: You again! (*Estragon halts but does not raise his head. Vladimir goes towards him.*) Come here till I embrace you.

ESTRAGON: Don't touch me!
Vladimir holds back, pained.

VLADIMIR: Do you want me to go away? (*Pause.*) Gogo! (*Pause. Vladimir observes him attentively.*) Did they beat you? (*Pause.*) Gogo! (*Estragon remains silent, head bowed.*) Where did you spend the night?

ESTRAGON: Don't touch me! Don't question me! Don't speak to me! Stay with me!

VLADIMIR: Did I ever leave you?

ESTRAGON: You let me go.

VLADIMIR: Look at me. (*Estragon does not raise his head. Violently.*) Will you look at me!
Estragon raises his head. They look long at each other, then suddenly embrace, clapping each other on the back. End of the embrace. Estragon, no longer supported, almost falls.

ESTRAGON: What a day!

VLADIMIR: Who beat you? Tell me.

ESTRAGON: Another day done with.

VLADIMIR: Not yet.

ESTRAGON: For me it's over and done with, no matter what happens. (*Silence.*) I heard you singing.

VLADIMIR: That's right, I remember.

ESTRAGON: That finished me. I said to myself, He's all alone, he thinks I'm gone for ever, and he sings.

VLADIMIR: One is not master of one's moods. All day I've felt in great form. (*Pause.*) I didn't get up in the night, not once!

ESTRAGON: (*sadly*). You see, you piss better when I'm not there.

VLADIMIR: I missed you . . . and at the same time I was happy. Isn't that a queer thing?

ESTRAGON: (*shocked*). Happy?

VLADIMIR: Perhaps it's not quite the right word.

ESTRAGON: And now?

VLADIMIR: Now? . . . (*Joyous.*) There you are again . . . (*Indifferent.*) There we are again . . . (*Gloomy.*) There I am again.

ESTRAGON: You see, you feel worse when I'm with you. I feel better alone too.

VLADIMIR: (*vexed*). Then why do you always come crawling back?

ESTRAGON: I don't know

VLADIMIR: No, but I do. It's because you don't know how to defend yourself. I wouldn't have let them beat you.

ESTRAGON: You couldn't have stopped them.

VLADIMIR: Why not?

ESTRAGON: There was ten of them.

VLADIMIR: No, I mean before they beat you. I would have stopped you from doing whatever it was you were doing.

ESTRAGON: I wasn't doing anything.

VLADIMIR: Then why did they beat you?

ESTRAGON: I don't know.

VLADIMIR: Ah no, Gogo, the truth is there are things escape you that don't escape me, you must feel it yourself.

ESTRAGON: I tell you I wasn't doing anything.

VLADIMIR: Perhaps you weren't. But it's the way of doing it that counts, the way of doing it, if you want to go on living.

ESTRAGON: I wasn't doing anything.

VLADIMIR: You must be happy too, deep down, if you only knew it.

ESTRAGON: Happy about what?

VLADIMIR: To be back with me again.

ESTRAGON: Would you say so?

VLADIMIR: Say you are, even if it's not true.

ESTRAGON: What am I to say?

VLADIMIR: Say, I am happy.

ESTRAGON: I am happy.

VLADIMIR: So am I.

ESTRAGON: So am I.

VLADIMIR: We are happy.

ESTRAGON: We are happy. (*Silence.*) What do we do now, now that we are happy?

VLADIMIR: Wait for Godot. (*Estragon groans. Silence.*) Things have changed here since yesterday.

ESTRAGON: And if he doesn't come.

VLADIMIR: (*after a moment of bewilderment*). We'll see when the time comes. (*Pause.*) I was saying that things have changed here since yesterday.

ESTRAGON: Everything oozes.

VLADIMIR: Look at the tree.

ESTRAGON: It's never the same pus from one second to the next.

VLADIMIR: The tree, look at the tree.
Estragon looks at the tree.

ESTRAGON: Was it not there yesterday?

VLADIMIR: Yes of course it was there. Do you not remember? We nearly hanged ourselves from it. But you wouldn't. Do you not remember?

ESTRAGON: You dreamt it.

VLADIMIR: Is it possible you've forgotten already?

ESTRAGON: That's the way I am. Either I forget immediately or I never forget.

VLADIMIR: And Pozzo and Lucky, have you forgotten them
           too?

ESTRAGON: Pozzo and Lucky?

VLADIMIR: He's forgotten everything!

ESTRAGON: I remember a lunatic who kicked the shins off me.
           Then he played the fool.

VLADIMIR: That was Lucky.

ESTRAGON: I remember that. But when was it?

VLADIMIR: And his keeper, do you not remember him?

ESTRAGON: He gave me a bone.

VLADIMIR: That was Pozzo.

ESTRAGON: And all that was yesterday, you say?

VLADIMIR: Yes of course it was yesterday.

ESTRAGON: And here where we are now?

VLADIMIR: Where else do you think? Do you not recognize
           the place?

ESTRAGON: (*suddenly furious*). Recognize! What is there to
           recognize? All my lousy life I've crawled about
           in the mud! And you talk to me about scenery!
           (*Looking wildly about him.*) Look at this
           muckheap! I've never stirred from it!

VLADIMIR: Calm yourself, calm yourself.

ESTRAGON: You and your landscapes! Tell me about the
           worms!

VLADIMIR: All the same, you can't tell me that this (*gesture*)
           bears any resemblance to . . . (*he hesitates*) . . .
           to the Macon country for example. You can't
           deny there's a big difference.

ESTRAGON: The Macon country! Who's talking to you about
           the Macon country?

VLADIMIR: But you were there yourself, in the Macon
country.

ESTRAGON: No I was never in the Macon country! I've puked
my puke of a life away here, I tell you! Here! In
the Cackon country!

VLADIMIR: But we were there together, I could swear to it!
Picking grapes for a man called . . . (*he snaps his
fingers*) . . . can't think of the name of the man,
at a place called . . . (*snaps his fingers*) . . .
can't think of the name of the place, do you not
remember?

ESTRAGON: (*a little calmer*). It's possible. I didn't notice
anything.

VLADIMIR: But down there everything is red!

ESTRAGON: (*exasperated*). I didn't notice anything, I tell you!
Silence. Vladimir sighs deeply.

VLADIMIR: You're a hard man to get on with, Gogo.

ESTRAGON: It'd be better if we parted.

VLADIMIR: You always say that and you always come
crawling back.

ESTRAGON: The best thing would be to kill me, like the other.

VLADIMIR: What other? (*Pause.*) What other?

ESTRAGON: Like billions of others.

VLADIMIR: (*sententious*). To every man his little cross. (*He
sighs.*) Till he dies. (*Afterthought.*) And is
forgotten.

ESTRAGON: In the meantime let us try and converse calmly,
since we are incapable of keeping silent.

VLADIMIR: You're right, we're inexhaustible.

ESTRAGON: It's so we won't think.

VLADIMIR: We have that excuse.

ESTRAGON: It's so we won't hear.

VLADIMIR: We have our reasons.

ESTRAGON: All the dead voices.

VLADIMIR: They make a noise like wings.

ESTRAGON: Like leaves.

VLADIMIR: Like sand.

ESTRAGON: Like leaves.

Silence.

VLADIMIR: They all speak at once.

ESTRAGON: Each one to itself.

Silence.

VLADIMIR: Rather they whisper.

ESTRAGON: They rustle.

VLADIMIR: They murmur.

ESTRAGON: They rustle.

Silence.

VLADIMIR: What do they say?

ESTRAGON: They talk about their lives.

VLADIMIR: To have lived is not enough for them.

ESTRAGON: They have to talk about it.

VLADIMIR: To be dead is not enough for them.

ESTRAGON: It is not sufficient.

Silence.

VLADIMIR: They make a noise like feathers.

ESTRAGON: Like leaves.

VLADIMIR: Like ashes.

ESTRAGON: Like leaves.

Long silence.

VLADIMIR: Say something!

ESTRAGON: I'm trying.
            Long silence.
VLADIMIR: (*in anguish*). Say anything at all!
ESTRAGON: What do we do now?
VLADIMIR: Wait for Godot.
ESTRAGON: Ah!
            Silence.
VLADIMIR: This is awful!
ESTRAGON: Sing something.
VLADIMIR: No no! (*He reflects.*) We could start all over again
            perhaps.
ESTRAGON: That should be easy.
VI ADIMIR: It's the start that's difficult.
ESTRAGON: You can start from anything.
VLADIMIR: Yes, but you have to decide.
ESTRAGON: True.
            Silence.
VLADIMIR: Help me!
ESTRAGON: I'm trying.
            Silence.
VLADIMIR: When you seek you hear.
ESTRAGON: You do.
VLADIMIR: That prevents you from finding.
ESTRAGON: It does.
VLADIMIR: That prevents you from thinking.
ESTRAGON: You think all the same.
VLADIMIR: No no, impossible.
ESTRAGON: That's the idea, let's contradict each other.
VLADIMIR: Impossible.
ESTRAGON: You think so?

VLADIMIR: We're in no danger of ever thinking any more.

ESTRAGON: Then what are we complaining about?

VLADIMIR: Thinking is not the worst.

ESTRAGON: Perhaps not. But at least there's that.

VLADIMIR: That what?

ESTRAGON: That's the idea, let's ask each other questions.

VLADIMIR: What do you mean, at least there's that?

ESTRAGON: That much less misery.

VLADIMIR: True.

ESTRAGON: Well? If we gave thanks for our mercies?

VLADIMIR: What is terrible is to *have* thought.

ESTRAGON: But did that ever happen to us?

VLADIMIR: Where are all these corpses from?

ESTRAGON: These skeletons.

VLADIMIR: Tell me that.

ESTRAGON: True.

VLADIMIR: We must have thought a little.

ESTRAGON: At the very beginning.

VLADIMIR: A charnel-house! A charnel-house!

ESTRAGON: You don't have to look.

VLADIMIR: You can't help looking.

ESTRAGON: True.

VLADIMIR: Try as one may.

ESTRAGON: I beg your pardon?

VLADIMIR: Try as one may.

ESTRAGON: We should turn resolutely towards Nature.

VLADIMIR: We've tried that.

ESTRAGON: True.

VLADIMIR: Oh it's not the worst, I know.

ESTRAGON: What?

VLADIMIR: To have thought.

ESTRAGON: Obviously.

VLADIMIR: But we could have done without it.

ESTRAGON: Que voulez-vous?

VLADIMIR: I beg your pardon?

ESTRAGON: Que voulez-vous.

VLADIMIR: Ah! que voulez-vous. Exactly.
Silence.

ESTRAGON: That wasn't such a bad little canter.

VLADIMIR: Yes, but now we'll have to find something else.

ESTRAGON: Let me see.
He takes off his hat, concentrates.

VLADIMIR: Let me see. (*He takes off his hat, concentrates.
Long silence.*) Ah!
They put on their hats, relax.

ESTRAGON: Well?

VLADIMIR: What was I saying, we could go on from there.

ESTRAGON: What were you saying when?

VLADIMIR: At the very beginning.

ESTRAGON: The very beginning of WHAT?

VLADIMIR: This evening . . . I was saying . . . I was
saying . . .

ESTRAGON: I'm not a historian.

VLADIMIR: Wait . . . we embraced . . . we were happy
. . . happy . . . what do we do now that we're
happy . . . go on waiting . . . waiting . . . let
me think . . . it's coming . . . go on waiting . . .
now that we're happy . . . let me see . . . ah!
The tree!

ESTRAGON: The tree?

VLADIMIR: Do you not remember?

ESTRAGON: I'm tired.

VLADIMIR: Look at it.

They look at the tree.

ESTRAGON: I see nothing.

VLADIMIR: But yesterday evening it was all black and bare.
And now it's covered with leaves.

ESTRAGON: Leaves?

VLADIMIR: In a single night.

ESTRAGON: It must be the Spring.

VLADIMIR: But in a single night!

ESTRAGON: I tell you we weren't here yesterday. Another of
your nightmares.

VLADIMIR: And where were we yesterday evening according
to you?

ESTRAGON: How would I know? In another compartment.
There's no lack of void.

VLADIMIR: (*sure of himself*). Good. We weren't here
yesterday evening. Now what did we do yesterday
evening?

ESTRAGON: Do?

VLADIMIR: Try and remember.

ESTRAGON: Do . . . I suppose we blathered.

VLADIMIR: (*controlling himself*). About what?

ESTRAGON: Oh . . . this and that I suppose, nothing in
particular. (*With assurance.*) Yes, now I remember,
yesterday evening we spent blathering about
nothing in particular. That's been going on now
for half a century.

VLADIMIR: You don't remember any fact, any circumstance?

ESTRAGON: (*weary*). Don't torment me, Didi.

VLADIMIR: The sun. The moon. Do you not remember?

ESTRAGON: They must have been there, as usual.

VLADIMIR: You didn't notice anything out of the ordinary?

ESTRAGON: Alas!

VLADIMIR: And Pozzo? And Lucky?

ESTRAGON: Pozzo?

VLADIMIR: The bones.

ESTRAGON: They were like fishbones.

VLADIMIR: It was Pozzo gave them to you.

ESTRAGON: I don't know.

VLADIMIR: And the kick.

ESTRAGON: That's right, someone gave me a kick.

VLADIMIR: It was Lucky gave it to you.

ESTRAGON: And all that was yesterday?

VLADIMIR: Show your leg.

ESTRAGON: Which?

VLADIMIR: Both. Pull up your trousers. (*Estragon gives a leg
to Vladimir, staggers. Vladimir takes the leg. They
stagger.*) Pull up your trousers.

ESTRAGON: I can't.
*Vladimir pulls up the trousers, looks at the leg,
lets it go. Estragon almost falls.*

VLADIMIR: The other. (*Estragon gives the same leg.*) The
other, pig! (*Estragon gives the other leg.
Triumphantly.*) There's the wound! Beginning to
fester!

ESTRAGON: And what about it?

VLADIMIR: (*letting go the leg*). Where are your boots?

ESTRAGON: I must have thrown them away.

VLADIMIR: When?

ESTRAGON: I don't know.

VLADIMIR: Why?

ESTRAGON: (*exasperated*). I don't know why I don't know!

VLADIMIR: No, I mean why did you throw them away?

ESTRAGON: (*exasperated*). Because they were hurting me!

VLADIMIR: (*triumphantly, pointing to the boots*). There they
            are! (*Estragon looks at the boots.*) At the very spot
            where you left them yesterday!
            *Estragon goes towards the boots, inspects them
            closely.*

ESTRAGON: They're not mine.

VLADIMIR: (*stupefied*). Not yours!

ESTRAGON: Mine were black. These are brown.

VLADIMIR: You're sure yours were black?

ESTRAGON: Well they were a kind of gray.

VLADIMIR: And these are brown. Show.

ESTRAGON: (*picking up a boot*). Well they're a kind of green.

VLADIMIR: Show. (*Estragon hands him the boot. Vladimir
            inspects it, throws it down angrily.*) Well of all
            the—

ESTRAGON: You see, all that's a lot of bloody—

VLADIMIR: Ah! I see what it is. Yes, I see what's happened.

ESTRAGON: All that's a lot of bloody—

VLADIMIR: It's elementary. Someone came and took yours
            and left you his.

ESTRAGON: Why?

VLADIMIR: His were too tight for him, so he took yours.

ESTRAGON: But mine were too tight.

VLADIMIR: For you. Not for him.

ESTRAGON: *(having tried in vain to work it out)*. I'm tired!
(Pause.) Let's go.

VLADIMIR: We can't.

ESTRAGON: Why not?

VLADIMIR: We're waiting for Godot.

ESTRAGON: Ah! *(Pause. Despairing.)* What'll we do, what'll
we do!

VLADIMIR: There's nothing we can do.

ESTRAGON: But I can't go on like this!

VLADIMIR: Would you like a radish?

ESTRAGON: Is that all there is?

VLADIMIR: There are radishes and turnips.

ESTRAGON: Are there no carrots?

VLADIMIR: No. Anyway you overdo it with your carrots.

ESTRAGON: Then give me a radish. *(Vladimir fumbles in his
pockets, finds nothing but turnips, finally brings
out a radish and hands it to Estragon who
examines it, sniffs it.)* It's black!

VLADIMIR: It's a radish.

ESTRAGON: I only like the pink ones, you know that!

VLADIMIR: Then you don't want it?

ESTRAGON: I only like the pink ones!

VLADIMIR: Then give it back to me.
Estragon gives it back.

ESTRAGON: I'll go and get a carrot.
He does not move.

VLADIMIR: This is becoming really insignificant.

ESTRAGON: Not enough.
Silence.

VLADIMIR: What about trying them.

ESTRAGON: I've tried everything.

VLADIMIR: No, I mean the boots.

ESTRAGON: Would that be a good thing?

VLADIMIR: It'd pass the time. (*Estragon hesitates.*) I assure
you, it'd be an occupation.

ESTRAGON: A relaxation.

VLADIMIR: A recreation.

ESTRAGON: A relaxation.

VLADIMIR: Try.

ESTRAGON: You'll help me?

VLADIMIR: I will of course.

ESTRAGON: We don't manage too badly, eh Didi, between the
two of us?

VLADIMIR: Yes yes. Come on, we'll try the left first.

ESTRAGON: We always find something, eh Didi, to give us the
impression we exist?

VLADIMIR: (*impatiently*). Yes yes, we're magicians. But let us
persevere in what we have resolved, before we
forget. (*He picks up a boot.*) Come on, give me
your foot. (*Estragon raises his foot.*) The other,
hog! (*Estragon raises the other foot.*) Higher!
(*Wreathed together they stagger about the stage.
Vladimir succeeds finally in getting on the boot.*)
Try and walk. (*Estragon walks.*) Well?

ESTRAGON: It fits.

VLADIMIR: (*taking string from his pocket*). We'll try and lace
it.

ESTRAGON: (*vehemently*). No no, no laces, no laces!

VLADIMIR: You'll be sorry. Let's try the other. (*As before.*)
Well?

ESTRAGON: (*grudgingly*). It fits too.

VLADIMIR: They don't hurt you?

ESTRAGON: Not yet.

VLADIMIR: Then you can keep them.

ESTRAGON: They're too big.

VLADIMIR: Perhaps you'll have socks some day.

ESTRAGON: True.

VLADIMIR: Then you'll keep them?

ESTRAGON: That's enough about these boots.

VLADIMIR: Yes, but—

ESTRAGON: (*violently*). Enough! (*Silence.*) I suppose I might
as well sit down.
*He looks for a place to sit down, then goes and
sits down on the mound.*

VLADIMIR: That's where you were sitting yesterday evening.

ESTRAGON: If I could only sleep.

VLADIMIR: Yesterday you slept.

ESTRAGON: I'll try.
*He resumes his foetal posture, his head between
his knees.*

VLADIMIR: Wait. (*He goes over and sits down beside
Estragon and begins to sing in a loud voice.*)
        Bye bye bye bye
        Bye bye—

ESTRAGON: (*looking up angrily*). Not so loud!

VLADIMIR: (*softly*).   Bye bye bye bye
        Bye bye bye bye
        Bye bye bye bye
        Bye bye . . .

Estragon sleeps. Vladimir gets up softly, takes off his coat and lays it across Estragon's shoulders, then starts walking up and down, swinging his arms to keep himself warm. Estragon wakes with a start, jumps up, casts about wildly. Vladimir runs to him, puts his arms round him.) There . . . there . . . Didi is there . . . don't be afraid . . .

ESTRAGON: Ah!

VLADIMIR: There . . . there . . . it's all over.

ESTRAGON: I was falling—

VLADIMIR: It's all over, it's all over.

ESTRAGON: I was on top of a—

VLADIMIR: Don't tell me! Come, we'll walk it off.

He takes Estragon by the arm and walks him up and down until Estragon refuses to go any further.

ESTRAGON: That's enough. I'm tired.

VLADIMIR: You'd rather be stuck there doing nothing?

ESTRAGON: Yes.

VLADIMIR: Please yourself.

He releases Estragon, picks up his coat and puts it on.

ESTRAGON: Let's go.

VLADIMIR: We can't.

ESTRAGON: Why not?

VLADIMIR: We're waiting for Godot.

ESTRAGON: Ah! *(Vladimir walks up and down.)* Can you not stay still?

VLADIMIR: I'm cold.

ESTRAGON: We came too soon.

VLADIMIR: It's always at nightfall.

ESTRAGON: But night doesn't fall.

VLADIMIR: It'll fall all of a sudden, like yesterday.

ESTRAGON: Then it'll be night.

VLADIMIR: And we can go.

ESTRAGON: Then it'll be day again. (*Pause. Despairing.*) What'll we do, what'll we do!

VLADIMIR: (*halting, violently*). Will you stop whining! I've had about my bellyful of your lamentations!

ESTRAGON: I'm going.

VLADIMIR: (*seeing Lucky's hat*). Well!

ESTRAGON: Farewell.

VLADIMIR: Lucky's hat. (*He goes towards it.*) I've been here an hour and never saw it. (*Very pleased.*) Fine!

ESTRAGON: You'll never see me again.

VLADIMIR: I knew it was the right place. Now our troubles are over. (*He picks up the hat, contemplates it, straightens it.*) Must have been a very fine hat. (*He puts it on in place of his own which he hands to Estragon.*) Here.

ESTRAGON: What?

VLADIMIR: Hold that.

Estragon takes Vladimir's hat. Vladimir adjusts Lucky's hat on his head. Estragon puts on Vladimir's hat in place of his own which he hands to Vladimir. Vladimir takes Estragon's hat. Estragon adjusts Vladimir's hat on his head. Vladimir puts on Estragon's hat in place of Lucky's which he hands to Estragon. Estragon takes Lucky's hat. Vladimir adjusts Estragon's

hat on his head. Estragon puts on Lucky's hat in place of Vladimir's which he hands to Vladimir. Vladimir takes his hat. Estragon adjusts Lucky's hat on his head. Vladimir puts on his hat in place of Estragon's which he hands to Estragon. Estragon takes his hat. Vladimir adjusts his hat on his head. Estragon puts on his hat in place of Lucky's which he hands to Vladimir. Vladimir takes Lucky's hat. Estragon adjusts his hat on his head. Vladimir puts on Lucky's hat in place of his own which he hands to Estragon. Estragon takes Vladimir's hat. Vladimir adjusts Lucky's hat on his head. Estragon hands Vladimir's hat back to Vladimir who takes it and hands it back to Estragon who takes it and hands it back to Vladimir who takes it and throws it down.
How does it fit me?

ESTRAGON: How would I know?

VLADIMIR: No, but how do I look in it?
He turns his head coquettishly to and fro, minces like a mannequin.

ESTRAGON: Hideous.

VLADIMIR: Yes, but not more so than usual?

ESTRAGON: Neither more nor less.

VLADIMIR: Then I can keep it. Mine irked me. (*Pause.*) How shall I say? (*Pause.*) It itched me.
He takes off Lucky's hat, peers into it, shakes it, knocks on the crown, puts it on again.

ESTRAGON: I'm going.
Silence.

VLADIMIR: Will you not play?

ESTRAGON: Play at what?

VLADIMIR: We could play at Pozzo and Lucky.

ESTRAGON: Never heard of it.

VLADIMIR: I'll do Lucky, you do Pozzo. (*He imitates Lucky sagging under the weight of his baggage. Estragon looks at him with stupefaction.*) Go on.

ESTRAGON: What am I to do?

VLADIMIR: Curse me!

ESTRAGON: (*after reflection*). Naughty!

VLADIMIR: Stronger!

ESTRAGON: Gonococcus! Spirochete!
Vladimir sways back and forth, doubled in two.

VLADIMIR: Tell me to think.

ESTRAGON: What?

VLADIMIR: Say, Think, pig!

ESTRAGON: Think, pig!
Silence.

VLADIMIR: I can't!

ESTRAGON: That's enough of that.

VLADIMIR: Tell me to dance.

ESTRAGON: I'm going.

VLADIMIR: Dance, hog! (*He writhes. Exit Estragon left, precipitately.*) I can't! (*He looks up, misses Estragon.*) Gogo! (*He moves wildly about the stage. Enter Estragon left, panting. He hastens towards Vladimir, falls into his arms.*) There you are again at last!

ESTRAGON: I'm accursed!

VLADIMIR: Where were you? I thought you were gone for
ever.

ESTRAGON: They're coming!

VLADIMIR: Who?

ESTRAGON: I don't know.

VLADIMIR: How many?

ESTRAGON: I don't know.

VLADIMIR: (*triumphantly*). It's Godot! At last! Gogo! It's
Godot! We're saved! Let's go and meet him! (*He
drags Estragon towards the wings. Estragon
resists, pulls himself free, exit right.*) Gogo! Come
back! (*Vladimir runs to extreme left, scans the
horizon. Enter Estragon right, he hastens towards
Vladimir, falls into his arms.*) There you are again
again!

ESTRAGON: I'm in hell!

VLADIMIR: Where were you?

ESTRAGON: They're coming there too!

VLADIMIR: We're surrounded! (*Estragon makes a rush
towards back.*) Imbecile! There's no way out
there. (*He takes Estragon by the arm and drags
him towards front. Gesture towards front.*) There!
Not a soul in sight! Off you go! Quick! (*He pushes
Estragon towards auditorium. Estragon recoils in
horror.*) You won't? (*He contemplates auditorium.*)
Well I can understand that. Wait till I see. (*He
reflects.*) Your only hope left is to disappear.

ESTRAGON: Where?

VLADIMIR: Behind the tree. (*Estragon hesitates.*) Quick!
Behind the tree. (*Estragon goes and crouches*

behind the tree, realizes he is not hidden, comes out from behind the tree.) Decidedly this tree will not have been the slightest use to us.

ESTRAGON: (*calmer*). I lost my head. Forgive me. It won't happen again. Tell me what to do.

VLADIMIR: There's nothing to do.

ESTRAGON: You go and stand there. (*He draws Vladimir to extreme right and places him with his back to the stage.*) There, don't move, and watch out. (*Vladimir scans horizon, screening his eyes with his hand. Estragon runs and takes up same position extreme left. They turn their heads and look at each other.*) Back to back like in the good old days. (*They continue to look at each other for a moment, then resume their watch. Long silence.*) Do you see anything coming?

VLADIMIR: (*turning his head*). What?

ESTRAGON: (*louder*). Do you see anything coming?

VLADIMIR: No.

ESTRAGON: Nor I.

They resume their watch. Silence.

VLADIMIR: You must have had a vision.

ESTRAGON: (*turning his head*). What?

VLADIMIR: (*louder*). You must have had a vision.

ESTRAGON: No need to shout!

They resume their watch. Silence.

VLADIMIR:
ESTRAGON: (*turning simultaneously*). Do you—

VLADIMIR: Oh pardon!

ESTRAGON: Carry on.

VLADIMIR: No no, after you.

ESTRAGON: No no, you first.

VLADIMIR: I interrupted you.

ESTRAGON: On the contrary.

They glare at each other angrily.

VLADIMIR: Ceremonious ape!

ESTRAGON: Punctilious pig!

VLADIMIR: Finish your phrase, I tell you!

ESTRAGON: Finish your own!

Silence. They draw closer, halt.

VLADIMIR: Moron!

ESTRAGON: That's the idea, let's abuse each other.

They turn, move apart, turn again and face each other.

VLADIMIR: Moron!

ESTRAGON: Vermin!

VLADIMIR: Abortion!

ESTRAGON: Morpion!

VLADIMIR: Sewer-rat!

ESTRAGON: Curate!

VLADIMIR: Cretin!

ESTRAGON: *(with finality)*. Crritic!

VLADIMIR: Oh!

He wilts, vanquished, and turns away.

ESTRAGON: Now let's make it up.

VLADIMIR: Gogo!

ESTRAGON: Didi!

VLADIMIR: Your hand!

ESTRAGON: Take it!

VLADIMIR: Come to my arms!

ESTRAGON: Your arms?

VLADIMIR: My breast!

ESTRAGON: Off we go!

They embrace. They separate. Silence.

VLADIMIR: How time flies when one has fun!

Silence.

ESTRAGON: What do we do now?

VLADIMIR: While waiting.

ESTRAGON: While waiting.

Silence.

VLADIMIR: We could do our exercises.

ESTRAGON: Our movements.

VLADIMIR: Our elevations.

ESTRAGON: Our relaxations.

VLADIMIR: Our elongations.

ESTRAGON: Our relaxations.

VLADIMIR: To warm us up.

ESTRAGON: To calm us down.

VLADIMIR: Off we go.

*Vladimir hops from one foot to the other.
Estragon imitates him.*

ESTRAGON: *(stopping).* That's enough. I'm tired.

VLADIMIR: *(stopping).* We're not in form. What about a little
deep breathing?

ESTRAGON: I'm tired breathing.

VLADIMIR: You're right. *(Pause.)* Let's just do the tree, for the
balance.

ESTRAGON: The tree?

*Vladimir does the tree, staggering about on one
leg.*

VLADIMIR: (*stopping*). Your turn.

Estragon does the tree, staggers.

ESTRAGON: Do you think God sees me?

VLADIMIR: You must close your eyes.

Estragon closes his eyes, staggers worse.

ESTRAGON: (*stopping, brandishing his fists, at the top of his voice*). God have pity on me!

VLADIMIR: (*vexed*). And me?

ESTRAGON: On me! On me! Pity! On me!

Enter Pozzo and Lucky. Pozzo is blind. Lucky burdened as before. Rope as before, but much shorter, so that Pozzo may follow more easily. Lucky wearing a different hat. At the sight of Vladimir and Estragon he stops short. Pozzo, continuing on his way, bumps into him.

VLADIMIR: Gogo!

POZZO: (*clutching on to Lucky who staggers*). What is it? Who is it?

Lucky falls, drops everything and brings down Pozzo with him. They lie helpless among the scattered baggage.

ESTRAGON: Is it Godot?

VLADIMIR: At last! (*He goes towards the heap.*) Reinforcements at last!

POZZO: Help!

ESTRAGON: Is it Godot?

VLADIMIR: We were beginning to weaken. Now we're sure to see the evening out.

POZZO: Help!

ESTRAGON: Do you hear him?

VLADIMIR: We are no longer alone, waiting for the night, waiting for Godot, waiting for . . . waiting. All evening we have struggled, unassisted. Now it's over. It's already to-morrow.

POZZO: Help!

VLADIMIR: Time flows again already. The sun will set, the moon rise, and we away . . . from here.

POZZO: Pity!

VLADIMIR: Poor Pozzo!

ESTRAGON: I knew it was him.

VLADIMIR: Who?

ESTRAGON: Godot.

VLADIMIR: But it's not Godot.

ESTRAGON: It's not Godot?

VLADIMIR: It's not Godot.

ESTRAGON: Then who is it?

VLADIMIR: It's Pozzo.

POZZO: Here! Here! Help me up!

VLADIMIR: He can't get up.

ESTRAGON: Let's go.

VLADIMIR: We can't.

ESTRAGON: Why not?

VLADIMIR: We're waiting for Godot.

ESTRAGON: Ah!

VLADIMIR: Perhaps he has another bone for you.

ESTRAGON: Bone?

VLADIMIR: Chicken. Do you not remember?

ESTRAGON: It was him?

VLADIMIR: Yes.

ESTRAGON: Ask him.

VLADIMIR: Perhaps we should help him first.

ESTRAGON: To do what?

VLADIMIR: To get up.

ESTRAGON: He can't get up?

VLADIMIR: He wants to get up.

ESTRAGON: Then let him get up.

VLADIMIR: He can't.

ESTRAGON: Why not?

VLADIMIR: I don't know.
Pozzo writhes, groans, beats the ground with his fists.

ESTRAGON: We should ask him for the bone first. Then if he refuses we'll leave him there.

VLADIMIR: You mean we have him at our mercy?

ESTRAGON: Yes.

VLADIMIR: And that we should subordinate our good offices to certain conditions?

ESTRAGON: What?

VLADIMIR: That seems intelligent all right. But there's one thing I'm afraid of.

POZZO: Help!

ESTRAGON: What?

VLADIMIR: That Lucky might get going all of a sudden. Then we'd be ballocksed.

ESTRAGON: Lucky?

VLADIMIR: The one that went for you yesterday.

ESTRAGON: I tell you there was ten of them.

VLADIMIR: No, before that, the one that kicked you.

ESTRAGON: Is he there?

VLADIMIR: As large as life. (*Gesture towards Lucky.*) For the moment he is inert. But he might run amuck any minute.

POZZO: Help!

ESTRAGON: And suppose we gave him a good beating the two of us?

VLADIMIR: You mean if we fell on him in his sleep?

ESTRAGON: Yes.

VLADIMIR: That seems a good idea all right. But could we do it? Is he really asleep? (*Pause.*) No, the best would be to take advantage of Pozzo's calling for help—

POZZO: Help!

VLADIMIR: To help him—

ESTRAGON: *We* help *him*?

VLADIMIR: In anticipation of some tangible return.

ESTRAGON: And suppose he—

VLADIMIR: Let us not waste our time in idle discourse! (*Pause. Vehemently.*) Let us do something, while we have the chance! It is not every day that we are needed. Not indeed that we personally are needed. Others would meet the case equally well, if not better. To all mankind they were addressed, those cries for help still ringing in our ears! But at this place, at this moment of time, all mankind is us, whether we like it or not. Let us make the most of it, before it is too late! Let us represent worthily for once the foul brood to which a cruel fate consigned us! What do you say? (*Estragon says nothing.*) It is true that when with folded arms we weigh the pros and cons we are no less a

credit to our species. The tiger bounds to the help
of his congeners without the least reflexion, or
else he slinks away into the depths of the thickets.
But that is not the question. What are we doing
here, *that* is the question. And we are blessed in
this, that we happen to know the answer. Yes, in
this immense confusion one thing alone is clear.
We are waiting for Godot to come—

ESTRAGON: Ah!

POZZO: Help!

VLADIMIR: Or for night to fall. (*Pause.*) We have kept our
appointment and that's an end to that. We are not
saints, but we have kept our appointment. How
many people can boast as much?

ESTRAGON: Billions.

VLADIMIR: You think so?

ESTRAGON: I don't know.

VLADIMIR: You may be right.

POZZO: Help!

VLADIMIR: All I know is that the hours are long, under these
conditions, and constrain us to beguile them with
proceedings which—how shall I say—which may at
first sight seem reasonable, until they become a
habit. You may say it is to prevent our reason
from foundering. No doubt. But has it not long
been straying in the night without end of the
abyssal depths? That's what I sometimes wonder.
You follow my reasoning?

ESTRAGON: (*aphoristic for once*). We are all born mad. Some
remain so.

POZZO: Help! I'll pay you!

ESTRAGON: How much?

POZZO: One hundred francs!

ESTRAGON: It's not enough.

VLADIMIR: I wouldn't go so far as that.

ESTRAGON: You think it's enough?

VLADIMIR: No, I mean so far as to assert that I was weak in
             the head when I came into the world. But that is
             not the question.

POZZO: Two hundred!

VLADIMIR: We wait. We are bored. (*He throws up his hand.*)
             No, don't protest, we are bored to death, there's
             no denying it. Good. A diversion comes along and
             what do we do? We let it go to waste. Come, let's
             get to work! (*He advances towards the heap,
             stops in his stride.*) In an instant all will vanish
             and we'll be alone once more, in the midst of
             nothingness!
             He broods.

POZZO: Two hundred!

VLADIMIR: We're coming!
             *He tries to pull Pozzo to his feet, fails, tries again,
             stumbles, falls, tries to get up, fails.*

ESTRAGON: What's the matter with you all?

VLADIMIR: Help!

ESTRAGON: I'm going.

VLADIMIR: Don't leave me! They'll kill me!

POZZO: Where am I?

VLADIMIR: Gogo!

POZZO: Help!

VLADIMIR: Help!

ESTRAGON: I'm going.

VLADIMIR: Help me up first, then we'll go together.

ESTRAGON: You promise?

VLADIMIR: I swear it!

ESTRAGON: And we'll never come back?

VLADIMIR: Never!

ESTRAGON: We'll go to the Pyrenees.

VLADIMIR: Wherever you like.

ESTRAGON: I've always wanted to wander in the Pyrenees.

VLADIMIR: You'll wander in them.

ESTRAGON: (*recoiling*). Who farted?

VLADIMIR: Pozzo.

POZZO: Here! Here! Pity!

ESTRAGON: It's revolting!

VLADIMIR: Quick! Give me your hand!

ESTRAGON: I'm going. (*Pause. Louder.*) I'm going.

VLADIMIR: Well I suppose in the end I'll get up by myself.
(*He tries, fails.*) In the fullness of time.

ESTRAGON: What's the matter with you?

VLADIMIR: Go to hell.

ESTRAGON: Are you staying there?

VLADIMIR: For the time being.

ESTRAGON: Come on, get up, you'll catch a chill.

VLADIMIR: Don't worry about me.

ESTRAGON: Come on, Didi, don't be pig-headed!
*He stretches out his hand which Vladimir makes
haste to seize.*

VLADIMIR: Pull!
Estragon pulls, stumbles, falls. Long silence.

POZZO: Help!

VLADIMIR: We've arrived.

POZZO: Who are you?

VLADIMIR: We are men.

Silence.

ESTRAGON: Sweet mother earth!

VLADIMIR: Can you get up?

ESTRAGON: I don't know.

VLADIMIR: Try.

ESTRAGON: Not now, not now.

Silence.

POZZO: What happened?

VLADIMIR: (*violently*). Will you stop it, you! Pest! He can think of nothing but himself!

ESTRAGON: What about a little snooze?

VLADIMIR: Did you hear him? He wants to know what happened!

ESTRAGON: Don't mind him. Sleep.

Silence.

POZZO: Pity! Pity!

ESTRAGON: (*with a start*). What is it?

VLADIMIR: Were you asleep?

ESTRAGON: I must have been.

VLADIMIR: It's this bastard Pozzo at it again.

ESTRAGON: Make him stop it. Kick him in the crotch.

VLADIMIR: (*striking Pozzo*). Will you stop it! Crablouse! (*Pozzo extricates himself with cries of pain and crawls away. He stops, saws the air blindly, calling for help. Vladimir, propped on his elbow,*

observes his retreat.) He's off! (*Pozzo collapses*.)
He's down!

ESTRAGON: What do we do now?

VLADIMIR: Perhaps I could crawl to him.

ESTRAGON: Don't leave me!

VLADIMIR: Or I could call to him.

ESTRAGON: Yes, call to him.

VLADIMIR: Pozzo! (*Silence*.) Pozzo! (*Silence*.) No reply.

ESTRAGON: Together.

VLADIMIR:
                Pozzo! Pozzo!
ESTRAGON:

VLADIMIR: He moved.

ESTRAGON: Are you sure his name is Pozzo?

VLADIMIR: (*alarmed*). Mr. Pozzo! Come back! We won't hurt
you!
Silence.

ESTRAGON: We might try him with other names.

VLADIMIR: I'm afraid he's dying.

ESTRAGON: It'd be amusing.

VLADIMIR: What'd be amusing?

ESTRAGON: To try him with other names, one after the other.
It'd pass the time. And we'd be bound to hit on
the right one sooner or later.

VLADIMIR: I tell you his name is Pozzo.

ESTRAGON: We'll soon see. (*He reflects*.) Abel! Abel!

POZZO: Help!

ESTRAGON: Got it in one!

VLADIMIR: I begin to weary of this motif.

ESTRAGON: Perhaps the other is called Cain. Cain! Cain!

POZZO: Help!

ESTRAGON: He's all humanity. (*Silence.*) Look at the little cloud.

VLADIMIR: (*raising his eyes*). Where?

ESTRAGON: There. In the zenith.

VLADIMIR: Well? (*Pause.*) What is there so wonderful about it?
Silence.

ESTRAGON: Let's pass on now to something else, do you mind?

VLADIMIR: I was just going to suggest it.

ESTRAGON: But to what?

VLADIMIR: Ah!
Silence.

ESTRAGON: Suppose we got up to begin with?

VLADIMIR: No harm trying.
They get up.

ESTRAGON: Child's play.

VLADIMIR: Simple question of will-power.

ESTRAGON: And now?

POZZO: Help!

ESTRAGON: Let's go.

VLADIMIR: We can't.

ESTRAGON: Why not?

VLADIMIR: We're waiting for Godot.

ESTRAGON: Ah! (*Despairing.*) What'll we do, what'll we do!

POZZO: Help!

VLADIMIR: What about helping him?

ESTRAGON: What does he want?

VLADIMIR: He wants to get up.

ESTRAGON: Then why doesn't he?

VLADIMIR: He wants us to help him to get up.

ESTRAGON: Then why don't we? What are we waiting for?
They help Pozzo to his feet, let him go. He falls.

VLADIMIR: We must hold him. (*They get him up again. Pozzo sags between them, his arms round their necks.*) Feeling better?

POZZO: Who are you?

VLADIMIR: Do you not recognize us?

POZZO: I am blind.
Silence.

ESTRAGON: Perhaps he can see into the future.

VLADIMIR: Since when?

POZZO: I used to have wonderful sight—but are you friends?

ESTRAGON: (*laughing noisily*). He wants to know if we are friends!

VLADIMIR: No, he means friends of his.

ESTRAGON: Well?

VLADIMIR: We've proved we are, by helping him.

ESTRAGON: Exactly. Would we have helped him if we weren't his friends?

VLADIMIR: Possibly.

ESTRAGON: True.

VLADIMIR: Don't let's quibble about that now.

POZZO: You are not highwaymen?

ESTRAGON: Highwaymen! Do we look like highwaymen?

VLADIMIR: Damn it can't you see the man is blind!

ESTRAGON: Damn it so he is. (*Pause.*) So he says.

POZZO: Don't leave me!

VLADIMIR: No question of it.

ESTRAGON: For the moment.

POZZO: What time is it?

VLADIMIR: (*inspecting the sky*). Seven o'clock . . . eight o'clock . . .

ESTRAGON: That depends what time of year it is.

POZZO: Is it evening?

Silence. Vladimir and Estragon scrutinize the sunset.

ESTRAGON: It's rising.

VLADIMIR: Impossible.

ESTRAGON: Perhaps it's the dawn.

VLADIMIR: Don't be a fool. It's the west over there.

ESTRAGON: How do you know?

POZZO: (*anguished*). Is it evening?

VLADIMIR: Anyway it hasn't moved.

ESTRAGON: I tell you it's rising.

POZZO: Why don't you answer me?

ESTRAGON: Give us a chance.

VLADIMIR: (*reassuring*). It's evening, Sir, it's evening, night is drawing nigh. My friend here would have me doubt it and I must confess he shook me for a moment. But it is not for nothing I have lived through this long day and I can assure you it is very near the end of its repertory. (*Pause.*) How do you feel now?

ESTRAGON: How much longer are we to cart him around. (*They half release him, catch him again as he falls.*) We are not caryatids!

VLADIMIR: You were saying your sight used to be good, if I heard you right.

POZZO: Wonderful! Wonderful, wonderful sight!
           Silence.
ESTRAGON: (*irritably*). Expand! Expand!
VLADIMIR: Let him alone. Can't you see he's thinking of the
           days when he was happy. (*Pause.*) *Memoria*
           praeteritorum bonorum—that must be unpleasant.
ESTRAGON: We wouldn't know.
VLADIMIR: And it came on you all of a sudden?
POZZO: Quite wonderful!
VLADIMIR: I'm asking you if it came on you all of a sudden.
POZZO: I woke up one fine day as blind as Fortune.
           (*Pause.*) Sometimes I wonder if I'm not still asleep.
VLADIMIR: And when was that?
POZZO: I don't know.
VLADIMIR: But no later than yesterday—
POZZO: (*violently*). Don't question me! The blind have no
           notion of time. The things of time are hidden from
           them too.
VLADIMIR: Well just fancy that! I could have sworn it was
           just the opposite.
ESTRAGON: I'm going.
POZZO: Where are we?
VLADIMIR: I couldn't tell you.
POZZO: It isn't by any chance the place known as the
           Board?
VLADIMIR: Never heard of it.
POZZO: What is it like?
VLADIMIR: (*looking round*). It's indescribable. It's like
           nothing. There's nothing. There's a tree.
POZZO: Then it's not the Board.

ESTRAGON: (sagging). Some diversion!

POZZO: Where is my menial?

VLADIMIR: He's about somewhere.

POZZO: Why doesn't he answer when I call?

VLADIMIR: I don't know. He seems to be sleeping. Perhaps he's dead.

POZZO: What happened exactly?

ESTRAGON: Exactly!

VLADIMIR: The two of you slipped. (Pause.) And fell.

POZZO: Go and see is he hurt.

VLADIMIR: We can't leave you.

POZZO: You needn't both go.

VLADIMIR: (to Estragon). You go.

ESTRAGON: After what he did to me? Never!

POZZO: Yes yes, let your friend go, he stinks so. (Silence.) What is he waiting for?

VLADIMIR: What you waiting for?

ESTRAGON: I'm waiting for Godot.

Silence.

VLADIMIR: What exactly should he do?

POZZO: Well to begin with he should pull on the rope, as hard as he likes so long as he doesn't strangle him. He usually responds to that. If not he should give him a taste of his boot, in the face and the privates as far as possible.

VLADIMIR: (to Estragon). You see, you've nothing to be afraid of. It's even an opportunity to revenge yourself.

ESTRAGON: And if he defends himself?

POZZO: No no, he never defends himself.

VLADIMIR: I'll come flying to the rescue.

ESTRAGON: Don't take your eyes off me.

He goes towards Lucky.

VLADIMIR: Make sure he's alive before you start. No point in exerting yourself if he's dead.

ESTRAGON: *(bending over Lucky).* He's breathing.

VLADIMIR: Then let him have it.

With sudden fury Estragon starts kicking Lucky, hurling abuse at him as he does so. But he hurts his foot and moves away, limping and groaning. Lucky stirs.

ESTRAGON: Oh the brute!

He sits down on the mound and tries to take off his boot. But he soon desists and disposes himself for sleep, his arms on his knees and his head on his arms.

POZZO: What's gone wrong now?

VLADIMIR: My friend has hurt himself.

POZZO: And Lucky?

VLADIMIR: So it is he?

POZZO: What?

VLADIMIR: It is Lucky?

POZZO: I don't understand.

VLADIMIR: And you are Pozzo?

POZZO: Certainly I am Pozzo.

VLADIMIR: The same as yesterday?

POZZO: Yesterday?

VLADIMIR: We met yesterday. *(Silence.)* Do you not remember?

POZZO: I don't remember having met anyone yesterday. But to-morrow I won't remember having met

anyone to-day. So don't count on me to enlighten
you.

VLADIMIR: But—

POZZO: Enough! Up pig!

VLADIMIR: You were bringing him to the fair to sell him. You
spoke to us. He danced. He thought. You had your
sight.

POZZO: As you please. Let me go! (*Vladimir moves away.*)
Up!
Lucky gets up, gathers up his burdens.

VLADIMIR: Where do you go from here.

POZZO: On. (*Lucky, laden down, takes his place before
Pozzo.*) Whip! (*Lucky puts everything down, looks
for whip, finds it, puts it into Pozzo's hand, takes
up everything again.*) Rope!
*Lucky puts everything down, puts end of rope
into Pozzo's hand, takes up everything again.*

VLADIMIR: What is there in the bag?

POZZO: Sand. (*He jerks the rope.*) On!

VLADIMIR: Don't go yet.

POZZO: I'm going.

VLADIMIR: What do you do when you fall far from help?

POZZO: We wait till we can get up. Then we go on. On!

VLADIMIR: Before you go tell him to sing.

POZZO: Who?

VLADIMIR: Lucky.

POZZO: To sing?

VLADIMIR: Yes. Or to think. Or to recite.

POZZO: But he is dumb.

VLADIMIR: Dumb!

POZZO: Dumb. He can't even groan.

VLADIMIR: Dumb! Since when?

POZZO: (*suddenly furious*). Have you not done tormenting
                me with your accursed time! It's abominable!
                When! When! One day, is that not enough for
                you, one day he went dumb, one day I went blind,
                one day we'll go deaf, one day we were born, one
                day we shall die, the same day, the same second,
                is that not enough for you? (*Calmer.*) They give
                birth astride of a grave, the light gleams an
                instant, then it's night once more. (*He jerks the
                rope.*) On!
                *Exeunt Pozzo and Lucky. Vladimir follows them
                to the edge of the stage, looks after them. The
                noise of falling, reinforced by mimic of Vladimir,
                announces that they are down again. Silence.
                Vladimir goes towards Estragon, contemplates
                him a moment, then shakes him awake.*

ESTRAGON: (*wild gestures, incoherent words. Finally.*) Why
                will you never let me sleep?

VLADIMIR: I felt lonely.

ESTRAGON: I was dreaming I was happy.

VLADIMIR: That passed the time.

ESTRAGON: I was dreaming that—

VLADIMIR: (*violently*). Don't tell me! (*Silence.*) I wonder is he
                really blind.

ESTRAGON: Blind? Who?

VLADIMIR: Pozzo.

ESTRAGON: Blind?

VLADIMIR: He told us he was blind.

ESTRAGON: Well what about it?

VLADIMIR: It seemed to me he saw us.

ESTRAGON: You dreamt it. (*Pause.*) Let's go. We can't. Ah!
(*Pause.*) Are you sure it wasn't him?

VLADIMIR: Who?

ESTRAGON: Godot.

VLADIMIR: But who?

ESTRAGON: Pozzo.

VLADIMIR: Not at all! (*Less sure.*) Not at all! (*Still less sure.*)
Not at all!

ESTRAGON: I suppose I might as well get up. (*He gets up
painfully.*) Ow! Didi!

VLADIMIR: I don't know what to think any more.

ESTRAGON: My feet! (*He sits down again and tries to take off
his boots.*) Help me!

VLADIMIR: Was I sleeping, while the others suffered? Am I
sleeping now? To-morrow, when I wake, or think
I do, what shall I say of to-day? That with
Estragon my friend, at this place, until the fall of
night, I waited for Godot? That Pozzo passed,
with his carrier, and that he spoke to us? Probably.
But in all that what truth will there be?
(*Estragon, having struggled with his boots in vain,
is dozing off again. Vladimir looks at him.*) He'll
know nothing. He'll tell me about the blows he
received and I'll give him a carrot. (*Pause.*)
Astride of a grave and a difficult birth. Down in
the hole, lingeringly, the grave-digger puts on the
forceps. We have time to grow old. The air is full

of our cries. (*He listens.*) But habit is a great
deadener. (*He looks again at Estragon.*) At me too
someone is looking, of me too someone is saying,
He is sleeping, he knows nothing, let him sleep
on. (*Pause.*) I can't go on! (*Pause.*) What have I
said?

*He goes feverishly to and fro, halts finally at
extreme left, broods. Enter Boy right. He halts.
Silence.*

BOY: Mister . . . (*Vladimir turns.*) Mister Albert . . .

VLADIMIR: Off we go again. (*Pause.*) Do you not recognize
me?

BOY: No Sir.

VLADIMIR: It wasn't you came yesterday.

BOY: No Sir.

VLADIMIR: This is your first time.

BOY: Yes Sir.

Silence.

VLADIMIR: You have a message from Mr. Godot.

BOY: Yes Sir.

VLADIMIR: He won't come this evening.

BOY: No Sir.

VLADIMIR: But he'll come to-morrow.

BOY: Yes Sir.

VLADIMIR: Without fail.

BOY: Yes Sir.

Silence.

VLADIMIR: Did you meet anyone?

BOY: No Sir.

VLADIMIR: Two other . . . (*he hesitates*) . . . men?

BOY: I didn't see anyone, Sir.

Silence.

VLADIMIR: What does he do, Mr. Godot? (*Silence.*) Do you hear me?

BOY: Yes Sir.

VLADIMIR: Well?

BOY: He does nothing, Sir.

Silence.

VLADIMIR: How is your brother?

BOY: He's sick, Sir.

VLADIMIR: Perhaps it was he came yesterday.

BOY: I don't know, Sir.

Silence.

VLADIMIR: (*softly*). Has he a beard, Mr. Godot?

BOY: Yes Sir.

VLADIMIR: Fair or . . . (*he hesitates*) . . . or black?

BOY: I think it's white, Sir.

Silence.

VLADIMIR: Christ have mercy on us!

Silence.

BOY: What am I to tell Mr. Godot, Sir?

VLADIMIR: Tell him . . . (*he hesitates*) . . . tell him you saw me and that . . . (*he hesitates*) . . . that you saw me. (*Pause. Vladimir advances, the Boy recoils. Vladimir halts, the Boy halts. With sudden violence.*) You're sure you saw me, you won't come and tell me to-morrow that you never saw me! *Silence. Vladimir makes a sudden spring forward, the Boy avoids him and exit running. Silence. The*

sun sets, the moon rises. As in Act 1. Vladimir
stands motionless and bowed. Estragon wakes,
takes off his boots, gets up with one in each hand
and goes and puts them down center front, then
goes towards Vladimir.

ESTRAGON: What's wrong with you?

VLADIMIR: Nothing.

ESTRAGON: I'm going.

VLADIMIR: So am I.

ESTRAGON: Was I long asleep?

VLADIMIR: I don't know.
        Silence.

ESTRAGON: Where shall we go?

VLADIMIR: Not far.

ESTRAGON: Oh yes, let's go far away from here.

VLADIMIR: We can't.

ESTRAGON: Why not?

VLADIMIR: We have to come back to-morrow.

ESTRAGON: What for?

VLADIMIR: To wait for Godot.

ESTRAGON: Ah! (*Silence.*) He didn't come?

VLADIMIR: No.

ESTRAGON: And now it's too late.

VLADIMIR: Yes, now it's night.

ESTRAGON: And if we dropped him? (*Pause.*) If we dropped
        him?

VLADIMIR: He'd punish us. (*Silence. He looks at the tree.*)
        Everything's dead but the tree.

ESTRAGON: (*looking at the tree*). What is it?

VLADIMIR: It's the tree.

ESTRAGON: Yes, but what kind?

VLADIMIR: I don't know. A willow.

Estragon draws Vladimir towards the tree. They
stand motionless before it. Silence.

ESTRAGON: Why don't we hang ourselves?

VLADIMIR: With what?

ESTRAGON: You haven't got a bit of rope?

VLADIMIR: No.

ESTRAGON: Then we can't.

Silence.

VLADIMIR: Let's go.

ESTRAGON: Wait, there's my belt.

VLADIMIR: It's too short.

ESTRAGON: You could hang on to my legs.

VLADIMIR: And who'd hang on to mine?

ESTRAGON: True.

VLADIMIR: Show all the same. (*Estragon loosens the cord*
that holds up his trousers which, much too big for
him, fall about his ankles. They look at the cord.)
It might do at a pinch. But is it strong enough?

ESTRAGON: We'll soon see. Here.

They each take an end of the cord and pull. It
breaks. They almost fall.

VLADIMIR: Not worth a curse.

Silence.

ESTRAGON: You say we have to come back to-morrow?

VLADIMIR: Yes.

ESTRAGON: Then we can bring a good bit of rope.

VLADIMIR: Yes.

Silence.

ESTRAGON: Didi.
VLADIMIR: Yes.
ESTRAGON: I can't go on like this.
VLADIMIR: That's what you think.
ESTRAGON: If we parted? That might be better for us.
VLADIMIR: We'll hang ourselves to-morrow. (*Pause.*) Unless
          Godot comes.
ESTRAGON: And if he comes?
VLADIMIR: We'll be saved.
          *Vladimir takes off his hat (Lucky's), peers inside
          it, feels about inside it, shakes it, knocks on the
          crown, puts it on again.*
ESTRAGON: Well? Shall we go?
VLADIMIR: Pull on your trousers.
ESTRAGON: What?
VLADIMIR: Pull on your trousers.
ESTRAGON: You want me to pull off my trousers?
VLADIMIR: Pull ON your trousers.
ESTRAGON: (*realizing his trousers are down*). True.
          He pulls up his trousers.
VLADIMIR: Well? Shall we go?
ESTRAGON: Yes, let's go.
          They do not move.

                                              Curtain

Krapp's Last Tape

In many ways, Krapp is a typical Beckett character: part music-hall clown, part bawd; part tender, part cynic. But unlike so many of Beckett's other characters, mythological figures in the projection of his inner landscape, Krapp lives and breathes and has his being in a reasonably recognizable world. If the clown aspect is pointed ("Rusty black narrow trousers . . . . White face. Purple nose."), the setting is Krapp's den, with a table and drawers, locks and keys, ledgers . . . and a tape recorder.

Ever since his early essay on Proust, Beckett was always obsessed with "that double-headed monster of damnation and salvation—Time—and its necessary corollary, Memory." When the tape recorder became an available reality in the 1950s, one has to assume that it intrigued and tempted Beckett—not for its worldly ramifications of business and pleasure, but for the new light it cast on the Proustian equation: henceforth one need not steep a madeleine in an infusion of tea to evoke "time past"; one has at one's elbow the means wherewith to evoke it at the press of a button. Memory, which Beckett termed, in that same monograph, "a clinical laboratory stocked with poison and remedy, stimulant and sedative," can be called forth at will.

Krapp, at age sixty-nine—the scatological impulse in Beckett was, happily, always strong—listens to a tape made thirty years earlier, on his thirty-ninth birthday. In that tape the thirty-nine-year-old Krapp comments on a tape made "ten or twelve years" earlier. Each tape, that is, each age, reveals the person Krapp was; the continuity (addiction to bananas, despite the ensuing constipation; addiction to alcohol; addiction to sex) as well as the disjunction, for here as in the three short stories, as in the *Trilogy*, there are three—the young Krapp, the man of middle years ("Hard to believe I

was ever that young whelp!" intones the latter of the former),
and Krapp present, "a wearish old man."

   Krapp's Last Tape was written in 1958 and, like *All That
Fall*, in English. Its earlier title, probably a working one, was
"The Magee Monologue," for the impulse behind the work
was a radio broadcast Beckett heard of the actor Patrick
Magee reading a selection of his prose works. On October
28 of that year, *Krapp's Last Tape* had its première at the
Royal Court Theatre in London. Directed by Donald McWhin-
nie, it starred, quite fittingly, Patrick Magee.

Krapp's Last Tape

A play in one act

A late evening in the future.

Krapp's den.

Front centre a small table, the two drawers of which open towards audience.

Sitting at the table, facing front, i.e. across from the drawers, a wearish old man: Krapp.

Rusty black narrow trousers too short for him. Rusty black sleeveless waistcoat, four capacious pockets. Heavy silver watch and chain. Grimy white shirt open at neck, no collar. Surprising pair of dirty white boots, size ten at least, very narrow and pointed.

White face. Purple nose. Disordered grey hair. Unshaven.

Very near-sighted (but unspectacled). Hard of hearing.

Cracked voice. Distinctive intonation.

Laborious walk.

*On the table a tape-recorder with
microphone and a number of cardboard
boxes containing reels of recorded tapes.*

*Table and immediately adjacent area in
strong white light. Rest of stage in
darkness.*

*Krapp remains a moment motionless,
heaves a great sigh, looks at his watch,
fumbles in his pockets, takes out an
envelope, puts it back, fumbles, takes out
a small bunch of keys, raises it to his eyes,
chooses a key, gets up and moves to front
of table. He stoops, unlocks first drawer,
peers into it, feels about inside it, takes out
a reel of tape, peers at it, puts it back, locks
drawer, unlocks second drawer, peers into
it, feels about inside it, takes out a large
banana, peers at it, locks drawer, puts keys
back in his pocket. He turns, advances to
edge of stage, halts, strokes banana, peels
it, drops skin at his feet, puts end of banana*

*in his mouth and remains motionless,
staring vacuously before him. Finally he
bites off the end, turns aside and begins
pacing to and fro at edge of stage, in the
light, i.e. not more than four or five paces
either way, meditatively eating banana.
He treads on skin, slips, nearly falls,
recovers himself, stoops and peers at skin
and finally pushes it, still stooping, with his
foot over the edge of stage into pit. He
resumes his pacing, finishes banana,
returns to table, sits down, remains a
moment motionless, heaves a great sigh,
takes keys from his pockets, raises them to
his eyes, chooses key, gets up and moves
to front of table, unlocks second drawer,
takes out a second large banana, peers at
it, locks drawer, puts back keys in his
pocket, turns, advances to edge of stage,
halts, strokes banana, peels it, tosses skin
into pit, puts end of banana in his mouth
and remains motionless, staring vacuously
before him. Finally he has an idea, puts
banana in his waistcoat pocket, the end
emerging, and goes with all the speed he*

*can muster backstage into darkness. Ten
seconds. Loud pop of cork. Fifteen
seconds. He comes back into light carrying
an old ledger and sits down at table. He
lays ledger on table, wipes his mouth,
wipes his hands on the front of his
waistcoat, brings them smartly together
and rubs them.*

KRAPP   (*briskly*). Ah! (*He bends over ledger, turns
the pages, finds the entry he wants, reads.*)
Box . . . thrree . . . spool . . . flve. (*He raises
his head and stares front. With relish.*)
Spool! (*Pause.*) Spooool! (*Happy smile.
Pause. He bends over table, starts peering
and poking at the boxes.*) Box . . . thrree
. . . thrree . . . four . . . two . . . (*with
surprise*) nine! good God! . . . seven . . . ah!
the little rascal! (*He takes up box, peers at
it.*) Box thrree. (*He lays it on table, opens
it and peers at spools inside.*) Spool . . . (*he
peers at ledger*) . . . five . . . (*he peers at
spools*) . . . five . . . five . . . ah! the little
scoundrel! (*He takes out a spool, peers at
it.*) Spool five. (*He lays it on table, closes*

*box three, puts it back with the others,
takes up the spool.*) Box thrree, spool five.
(*He bends over the machine, looks up.
With relish.*) Spooool! (*Happy smile. He
bends, loads spool on machine, rubs his
hands.*) Ah! (*He peers at ledger, reads
entry at foot of page.*) Mother at rest at
last . . . Hm . . . The black ball . . . (*He
raises his head, stares blankly front.
Puzzled.*) Black ball? . . . (*He peers again
at ledger, reads.*) The dark nurse . . . (*He
raises his head, broods, peers again at
ledger, reads.*) Slight improvement in
bowel condition . . . Hm . . . Memorable
. . . what? (*He peers closer.*) Equinox,
memorable equinox. (*He raises his head,
stares blankly front. Puzzled.*) Memorable
equinox? . . . (*Pause. He shrugs his
shoulders, peers again at ledger, reads.*)
Farewell to—(*he turns the page*)—love.

*He raises his head, broods, bends over
machine, switches on and assumes listening
posture, i.e. leaning forward, elbows on
table, hand cupping ear towards machine,
face front.*

TAPE   (*strong voice, rather pompous, clearly
Krapp's at a much earlier time.*) Thirty-
nine today, sound as a—(*Settling himself
more comfortably he knocks one of the
boxes off the table, curses, switches off,
sweeps boxes and ledger violently to the
ground, winds tape back to beginning,
switches on, resumes posture.*) Thirty-
nine today, sound as a bell, apart from my
old weakness, and intellectually I have
now every reason to suspect at the . . .
(*hesitates*) . . . crest of the wave—or
thereabouts. Celebrated the awful
occasion, as in recent years, quietly at the
Winehouse. Not a soul. Sat before the fire
with closed eyes, separating the grain from
the husks. Jotted down a few notes, on the
back of an envelope. Good to be back in
my den, in my old rags. Have just eaten I
regret to say three bananas and only with
difficulty refrained from a fourth. Fatal
things for a man with my condition.
(*Vehemently.*) Cut 'em out! (*Pause.*) The
new light above my table is a great
improvement. With all this darkness round

me I feel less alone. (*Pause.*) In a way.
(*Pause.*) I love to get up and move about
in it, then back here to . . . (*hesitates*) . . .
me. (*Pause.*) Krapp.

Pause.

The grain, now what I wonder do I mean
by that, I mean . . . (*hesitates*) . . . I suppose
I mean those things worth having when all
the dust has—when all *my* dust has settled.
I close my eyes and try and imagine them.

Pause. Krapp closes his eyes briefly.

Extraordinary silence this evening, I strain
my ears and do not hear a sound. Old Miss
McGlome always sings at this hour. But
not tonight. Songs of her girlhood, she says.
Hard to think of her as a girl. Wonderful
woman though. Connaught, I fancy.
(*Pause.*) Shall I sing when I am her age, if
I ever am? No. (*Pause.*) Did I sing as a
boy? No. (*Pause.*) Did I ever sing? No.
Pause.

Just been listening to an old year, passages
at random. I did not check in the book, but

it must be at least ten or twelve years ago.
At that time I think I was still living on
and off with Bianca in Kedar Street. Well
out of that, Jesus yes! Hopeless business.
(*Pause.*) Not much about her, apart from
a tribute to her eyes. Very warm. I
suddenly saw them again. (*Pause.*)
Incomparable! (*Pause.*) Ah well . . .
(*Pause.*) These old P.M.s are gruesome, but
I often find them—(*Krapp switches off,
broods, switches on*)—a help before
embarking on a new . . . (*hesitates*) . . .
retrospect. Hard to believe I was ever that
young whelp. The voice! Jesus! And the
aspirations! (*Brief laugh in which Krapp
joins.*) And the resolutions! (*Brief laugh in
which Krapp joins.*) To drink less, in
particular. (*Brief laugh of Krapp alone.*)
Statistics. Seventeen hundred hours, out of
the preceding eight thousand odd,
consumed on licensed premises alone.
More than 20%, say 40% of his waking
life. (*Pause.*) Plans for a less . . . (*hesitates*)
. . . engrossing sexual life. Last illness of his
father. Flagging pursuit of happiness.

Unattainable laxation. Sneers at what he
calls his youth and thanks to God that it's
over. (*Pause.*) False ring there. (*Pause.*)
Shadows of the opus . . . magnum. Closing
with a—(*brief laugh*)—yelp to Providence.
(*Prolonged laugh in which Krapp joins.*)
What remains of all that misery? A girl in
a shabby green coat, on a railway-station
platform? No?

Pause.

When I look—

*Krapp switches off, broods, looks at his
watch, gets up, goes backstage into
darkness. Ten seconds. Pop of cork. Ten
seconds. Second cork. Ten seconds. Third
cork. Ten seconds. Brief burst of quavering
song.*

KRAPP   (*sings*).   Now the day is over,
                      Night is drawing nigh-igh,
                      Shadows—

*Fit of coughing. He comes back into light,
sits down, wipes his mouth, switches on,
resumes his listening posture.*

TAPE   —back on the year that is gone, with what I hope is perhaps a glint of the old eye to come, there is of course the house on the canal where mother lay a-dying, in the late autumn, after her long viduity (*Krapp gives a start*), and the—(*Krapp switches off, winds back tape a little, bends his ear closer to machine, switches on*)—a-dying, after her long viduity, and the—

Krapp switches off, raises his head, stares blankly before him. His lips move in the syllables of "viduity." No sound. He gets up, goes backstage into darkness, comes back with an enormous dictionary, lays it on table, sits down and looks up the word.

KRAPP   (*reading from dictionary*). State—or condition of being—or remaining—a widow —or widower. (*Looks up. Puzzled.*) Being —or remaining? . . . (*Pause. He peers again at dictionary. Reading.*) "Deep weeds of viduity" . . . Also of an animal, especially a bird . . . the vidua or weaver-bird . . . Black plumage of male . . . (*He looks up. With relish.*) The vidua-bird!

*Pause. He closes dictionary, switches on,
resumes listening posture.*

TAPE   —bench by the weir from where I could
see her window. There I sat, in the biting
wind, wishing she were gone. (*Pause.*)
Hardly a soul, just a few regulars,
nursemaids, infants, old men, dogs. I got
to know them quite well—oh by appearance
of course I mean! One dark young beauty
I recollect particularly, all white and
starch, incomparable bosom, with a big
black hooded perambulator, most funereal
thing. Whenever I looked in her direction
she had her eyes on me. And yet when I
was bold enough to speak to her—not
having been introduced—she threatened to
call a policeman. As if I had designs on her
virtue! (*Laugh. Pause.*) The face she had!
The eyes! Like . . . (*hesitates*) . . .
chrysolite! (*Pause.*) Ah well . . . (*Pause.*) I
was there when—(*Krapp switches off,
broods, switches on again*)— the blind went
down, one of those dirty brown roller
affairs, throwing a ball for a little white

dog, as chance would have it. I happened
to look up and there it was. All over and
done with, at last. I sat on for a few
moments with the ball in my hand and the
dog yelping and pawing at me. (*Pause*.)
Moments. Her moments, my moments.
(*Pause*.) The dog's moments. (*Pause*.)
In the end I held it out to him and he took
it in his mouth, gently, gently. A small, old,
black, hard, solid rubber ball. (*Pause*.) I
shall feel it, in my hand, until my dying
day. (*Pause*.) I might have kept it.
(*Pause*.) But I gave it to the dog.

Pause.

Ah well . . .

Pause.

Spiritually a year of profound gloom and
indigence until that memorable night in
March, at the end of the jetty, in the
howling wind, never to be forgotten, when
suddenly I saw the whole thing. The
vision, at last. This I fancy is what I have
chiefly to record this evening, against the

day when my work will be done and
perhaps no place left in my memory, warm
or cold, for the miracle that . . . (*hesitates*)
. . . for the fire that set it alight. What I
suddenly saw then was this, that the belief
I had been going on all my life, namely—
(*Krapp switches off impatiently, winds
tape forward, switches on again*)—great
granite rocks the foam flying up in the
light of the lighthouse and the wind-gauge
spinning like a propellor, clear to me at last
that the dark I have always struggled to
keep under is in reality my most—(*Krapp
curses, switches off, winds tape forward,
switches on again*)—unshatterable
association until my dissolution of storm
and night with the light of the
understanding and the fire—(*Krapp curses
louder, switches off, winds tape forward,
switches on again*)—my face in her breasts
and my hand on her. We lay there without
moving. But under us all moved, and
moved us, gently, up and down, and from
side to side.

Pause.

Past midnight. Never knew such silence.
The earth might be uninhabited.

Pause.

Here I end—

*Krapp switches off, winds tape back,
switches on again.*

—upper lake, with the punt, bathed off the
bank, then pushed out into the stream and
drifted. She lay stretched out on the
floorboards with her hands under her head
and her eyes closed. Sun blazing down, bit
of a breeze, water nice and lively. I noticed
a scratch on her thigh and asked her how
she came by it. Picking gooseberries, she
said. I said again I thought it was hopeless
and no good going on, and she agreed,
without opening her eyes. (*Pause.*) I
asked her to look at me and after a few
moments—(*pause*)—after a few moments
she did, but the eyes just slits, because of
the glare. I bent over her to get them in the
shadow and they opened. (*Pause. Low.*)
Let me in. (*Pause.*) We drifted in among

the flags and stuck. The way they went
down, sighing, before the stem! (*Pause.*)
I lay down across her with my face in her
breasts and my hand on her. We lay there
without moving. But under us all moved,
and moved us, gently, up and down, and
from side to side.

Pause.

Past midnight. Never knew—

*Krapp switches off, broods. Finally he
fumbles in his pockets, encounters the
banana, takes it out, peers at it, puts it
back, fumbles, brings out the envelope,
fumbles, puts back envelope, looks at his
watch, gets up and goes backstage into
darkness. Ten seconds. Sound of bottle
against glass, then brief siphon. Ten
seconds. Bottle against glass alone. Ten
seconds. He comes back a little unsteadily
into light, goes to front of table, takes out
keys, raises them to his eyes, chooses key,
unlocks first drawer, peers into it, feels
about inside, takes out reel, peers at it,*

locks drawer, puts keys back in his pocket,
goes and sits down, takes reel off machine,
lays it on dictionary, loads virgin reel on
machine, takes envelope from his pocket,
consults back of it, lays it on table, switches
on, clears his throat and begins to record.

KRAPP   Just been listening to that stupid bastard
I took myself for thirty years ago, hard to
believe I was ever as bad as that. Thank
God that's all done with anyway. (*Pause.*)
The eyes she had! (*Broods, realizes he is*
recording silence, switches off, broods.
Finally.) Everything there, everything, all
the—(*Realizes this is not being recorded,*
switches on.) Everything there, everything
on this old muckball, all the light and dark
and famine and feasting of . . . (*hesitates*)
. . . the ages! (*In a shout.*) Yes! (*Pause.*)
Let that go! Jesus! Take his mind off his
homework! Jesus! (*Pause. Weary.*) Ah
well, maybe he was right. (*Pause.*) Maybe
he was right. (*Broods. Realizes. Switches*
off. Consults envelope.) Pah! (*Crumples*
it and throws it away. Broods. Switches

on.) Nothing to say, not a squeak. What's
a year now? The sour cud and the iron
stool. (*Pause.*) Revelled in the word spool.
(*With relish.*) Spooool! Happiest moment
of the past half million. (*Pause.*)
Seventeen copies sold, of which eleven at
trade price to free circulating libraries
beyond the seas. Getting known. (*Pause.*)
One pound six and something, eight I have
little doubt. (*Pause.*) Crawled out once or
twice, before the summer was cold. Sat
shivering in the park, drowned in dreams
and burning to be gone. Not a soul.
(*Pause.*) Last fancies. (*Vehemently.*)
Keep 'em under! (*Pause.*) Scalded the eyes
out of me reading *Effie* again, a page a day,
with tears again. Effie . . . (*Pause.*) Could
have been happy with her, up there on the
Baltic, and the pines, and the dunes.
(*Pause.*) Could I? (*Pause.*) And she?
(*Pause.*) Pah! (*Pause.*) Fanny came in a
couple of times. Bony old ghost of a whore.
Couldn't do much, but I suppose better
than a kick in the crutch. The last time
wasn't so bad. How do you manage it, she

said, at your age? I told her I'd been saving
up for her all my life. (*Pause.*) Went to
Vespers once, like when I was in short
trousers. (*Pause. Sings.*)

> Now the day is over,
> Night is drawing nigh-igh,
> Shadows—(*coughing, then almost
>   inaudible*)—of the evening
> Steal across the sky.

(*Gasping.*) Went to sleep and fell off the
pew. (*Pause.*) Sometimes wondered in
the night if a last effort mightn't—(*Pause.*)
Ah finish your booze now and get to your
bed. Go on with this drivel in the morning.
Or leave it at that. (*Pause.*) Leave it at
that. (*Pause.*) Lie propped up in the dark
—and wander. Be again in the dingle on a
Christmas Eve, gathering holly, the red-
berried. (*Pause.*) Be again on Croghan on
a Sunday morning, in the haze, with the
bitch, stop and listen to the bells. (*Pause.*)
And so on. (*Pause.*) Be again, be again.
(*Pause.*) All that old misery. (*Pause.*)

Once wasn't enough for you. (*Pause.*) Lie
down across her.

*Long pause. He suddenly bends over
machine, switches off, wrenches off tape,
throws it away, puts on the other, winds it
forward to the passage he wants, switches
on, listens staring front.*

TAPE —gooseberries, she said. I said again I
thought it was hopeless and no good going
on, and she agreed, without opening her
eyes. (*Pause.*) I asked her to look at me
and after a few moments—(*pause*)—after a
few moments she did, but the eyes just
slits, because of the glare. I bent over her
to get them in the shadow and they
opened. (*Pause. Low.*) Let me in.
(*Pause.*) We drifted in among the flags
and stuck. The way they went down,
sighing, before the stem! (*Pause.*) I lay
down across her with my face in her
breasts and my hand on her. We lay there
without moving. But under us all moved,
and moved us, gently, up and down, and
from side to side.

Pause. Krapp's lips move. No sound.

Past midnight. Never knew such silence.
The earth might be uninhabited.

Pause.

Here I end this reel. Box—(*pause*)—three,
spool—(*pause*)—five. (*Pause.*) Perhaps my
best years are gone. When there was a
chance of happiness. But I wouldn't want
them back. Not with the fire in me now.
No, I wouldn't want them back.

*Krapp motionless staring before him. The
tape runs on in silence.*

CURTAIN

Part III
Later Works
(1960–1975)

Fiction

How It Is (Part 1)

The young English critic Michael Robinson has called *How It Is* "the strangest novel ever written," and, at least at first glance, it might well appear to be just that.

Originally it had been the author's intent to publish the novel in one unpunctuated block, that is, without paragraphs or punctuation, and, except for the three-part division, without breaks. At some point prior to publication he decided to break the text into blocks, or paragraphs, although within these blocks no punctuation exists—all of which prompted some critics to accuse him of making one last effort to "assassinate the novel." Those who do grossly misjudge Beckett's integrity as an artist. Or, perhaps, they simply forget his early conviction that content and form must be one, a conviction that has never wavered from work to work. If the form of *How It Is* differs markedly from that of earlier prose works, it is because the content demanded it.

As for the difficulty of reading it or sorting out the sense, the reader can, quite easily, accustom him- or herself to the rhythms and find the cesuras. Once that is done, meaning follows. The method here is by fits and starts, little gasps on the part of the narrator, a method completely in keeping with his situation. Thus sense is cumulative rather than linear and, as with so much of Beckett, there is circularity here: the end is the beginning (in French, *comment c'est*—"how it is" —is pronounced like *commencer*—"to begin"—a wordplay necessarily lost in translation) and the plan, like the journey, laid out clearly from the start:

> how it was I quote before Pim with Pim after Pim
> how it is three parts I say it as I hear it

Set in the primeval mud, *How It Is* describes, in a language stripped even cleaner than that of the *Trilogy*—bare,

stark, panting, yet charged in every line with pure poetry—
the narrator's painful, inching journey toward another; his
meeting with the other, Pim, whose torturer he will become,
even as earlier (later?) the narrator was the victim of a tor-
mentor referred to as Bom; and the journey away from Pim
the victim toward him who will become the victim's torturer.
Here is how it is, then, in the primeval mud: three creatures,
four stages, with the distinction between past, present, and
future gone, merged into one indistinguishable, timeless time,
and yet doubtless applicable to "millions millions there are
millions of us and there are three."

how it was I quote before Pim with Pim after Pim how it is
three parts I say it as I hear it

voice once without quaqua on all sides then in me when the
panting stops tell me again finish telling me invocation

past moments old dreams back again or fresh like those that
pass or things things always and memories I say them as I
hear them murmur them in the mud

in me that were without when the panting stops scraps of
an ancient voice in me not mine

my life last state last version ill-said ill-heard ill-recaptured
ill-murmured in the mud brief movements of the lower face
losses everywhere

recorded none the less it's preferable somehow somewhere
as it stands as it comes my life my moments not the millionth
part all lost nearly all someone listening another noting or
the same

here then part one how it was before Pim we follow I quote
the natural order more or less my life last state last version
what remains bits and scraps I hear it my life natural order
more or less I learn it I quote a given moment long past vast
stretch of time on from there that moment and following
not all a selection natural order vast tracts of time

part one before Pim how I got here no question not known
not said and the sack whence the sack and me if it's me no
question impossible too weak no importance

life life the other above in the light said to have been mine
on and off no going back up there no question no one asking
that of me never there a few images on and off in the mud
earth sky a few creatures in the light some still standing

the sack sole good sole possession coal-sack to the feel small
or medium five stone six stone wet jute I clutch it it drips in
the present but long past long gone vast stretch of time the
beginning this life first sign very first of life

then on my elbow I quote I see me prop me up thrust in my
arm in the sack we're talking of the sack thrust it in count
the tins impossible with one hand keep trying one day it
will be possible

empty them out in the mud the tins put them back one by
one in the sack impossible too weak fear of loss

no appetite a crumb of tunny then mouldy eat mouldy no
need to worry I won't die I'll never die of hunger

the tin broached put back in the sack or kept in the hand it's
one or the other I remember when appetite revives or I forget open another it's one or the other something wrong
there it's the beginning of my life present formulation

other certainties the mud the dark I recapitulate the sack
the tins the mud the dark the silence the solitude nothing
else for the moment

I see me on my face close my eyes not the blue the others at
the back and see me on my face the mouth opens the tongue
comes out lolls in the mud and no question of thirst ei-

ther no question of dying of thirst either all this time vast stretch of time

life in the light first image some creature or other I watched him after my fashion from afar through my spy-glass side-long in mirrors through windows at night first image

saying to myself he's better than he was better than yester-day less ugly less stupid less cruel less dirty less old less wretched and you saying to myself and you bad to worse bad to worse steadily

something wrong there

or no worse saying to myself no worse you're no worse and was worse

I pissed and shat another image in my crib never so clean since

I scissored into slender strips the wings of butterflies first one wing then the other sometimes for a change the two abreast never so good since

that's all for the moment there I leave I hear it murmur it to the mud there I leave for the moment life in the light it goes out

on my face in the mud and the dark I see me it's a halt noth-ing more I'm journeying it's a rest nothing more

questions if I were to lose the tin-opener there's another object or when the sack is empty that family

abject abject ages each heroic seen from the next when will
the last come when was my golden every rat has its heyday
I say it as I hear it

knees drawn up back bent in a hoop I clasp the sack to my
belly I see me now on my side I clutch it the sack we're talking of the sack with one hand behind my back I slip it under
my head without letting it go I never let it go

something wrong there

not fear I quote of losing it something else not known not
said when it's empty I'll put my head in it then my shoulders
my crown will touch the bottom

another image so soon again a woman looks up looks at me
the images come at the beginning part one they will cease
I say it as I hear it murmur it in the mud the images part
one how it was before Pim I see them in the mud a light
gocs on they will cease a woman I see her in the mud

she sits aloof ten yards fifteen yards she looks up looks at me
says at last to herself all is well he is working

my head where is my head it rests on the table my hand
trembles on the table she sees I am not sleeping the wind
blows tempestuous the little clouds drive before it the table
glides from light to darkness darkness to light

that's not all she stoops to her work again the needle stops
in midstitch she straightens up and looks at me again she
has only to call me by my name get up come and feel me
but no

I don't move her anxiety grows she suddenly leaves the
house and runs to friends

that's all it wasn't a dream I didn't dream that nor a memory
I haven't been given memories this time it was an image the
kind I see sometimes see in the mud part one sometimes
saw

with the gesture of one dealing cards and also to be observed among certain sowers of seed I throw away the
empty tins they fall without a sound

fall if I may believe those I sometimes find on my way and
then make haste to throw away again

warmth of primeval mud impenetrable dark

suddenly like all that was not then is I go not because of the
shit and vomit something else not known not said whence
preparatives sudden series subject object subject object
quick succession and away

take the cord from the sack there's another object tie the
neck of the sack hang it from my neck knowing I'll need
both hands or else instinct it's one or the other and away
right leg right arm push pull ten yards fifteen yards halt

in the sack then up to now the tins the opener the cord but
the wish for something else no that doesn't seem to have
been given to me this time the image of other things with
me there in the mud the dark in the sack within reach no
that doesn't seem to have been put in my life this time

useful things a cloth to wipe me that family or beautiful to
the feel

which having sought in vain among the tins now one now
another in obedience to the wish the image of the moment
which when weary of seeking thus I could promise myself
to seek again a little later when less weary a little less or try
and banish from my thoughts saying true true think no
more about it

no the wish to be less wretched a little less the wish for a
little beauty no when the panting stops I hear nothing of
the kind that's not how I'm told this time

nor callers in my life this time no wish for callers hastening
from all sides all sorts to talk to me about themselves life
too and death as though nothing had happened me perhaps too in the end to help me last then goodbye till we
meet again each back the way he came

all sorts old men how they had dandled me on their knees
little bundle of swaddle and lace then followed in my
career

others knowing nothing of my beginnings save what they
could glean by hearsay or in public records nothing of my
beginnings in life

others who had always known me here in my last place they
talk to me of themselves of me perhaps too in the end of
fleeting joys and of sorrows of empires that are born and die
as though nothing had happened

others finally who do not know me yet they pass with heavy tread murmuring to themselves they have sought refuge in a desert place to be alone at last and vent their sorrows unheard

if they see me I am a monster of the solitudes he sees man for the first time and does not flee before him explorers bring home his skin among their trophies

suddenly afar the step the voice nothing then suddenly something something then suddenly nothing suddenly afar the silence

life then without callers present formulation no callers this time no stories but mine no silence but the silence I must break when I can bear it no more it's with that I have to last

question if other inhabitants here with me yes or no obviously all-important most important and thereupon long wrangle so minute that moments when yes to be feared till finally conclusion no me sole elect the panting stops and that is all I hear barely hear the question the answer barely audible if other inhabitants besides me here with me for good in the dark the mud long wrangle all lost and finally conclusion no me sole elect

and yet a dream I am given a dream like someone having tasted of love of a little woman within my reach and dreaming too it's in the dream too of a little man within hers I have that in my life this time sometimes part one as I journey

or failing kindred meat a llama emergency dream an alpaca
llama the history I knew my God the natural

she would not come to me I would go to her huddle in her
fleece but they add no a beast here no the soul is de rigueur
the mind too a minimum of each otherwise too great an
honour

I turn to the hand that is free draw it to my face it's a
resource when all fails images dreams sleep food for thought
something wrong there

when the great needs fail the need to move on the need
to shit and vomit and the other great needs all my great
categories of being

then to my hand that is free rather than some other part I
say it as I hear it brief movements of the lower face with
murmur to the mud

it comes close to my eyes I don't see it I close my eyes
something is lacking whereas normally closed or open my
eyes

if that is not enough I flutter it my hand we're talking of my
hand ten seconds fifteen seconds close my eyes a curtain
falls

if that is not enough I lay it on my face it covers it entirely
but I don't like to touch myself they haven't left me that
this time

I call it it doesn't come I can't live without it I call it
with all my strength it's not strong enough I grow mor-

tal again

my memory obviously the panting stops and question of
my memory obviously that too all-important too most important this voice is truly changeable of which so little left
in me bits and scraps barely audible when the panting stops
so little so faint not the millionth part I say it as I hear it
murmur it to the mud every word always

what about it my memory we're talking of my memory not
much that it's getting better that it's getting worse that
things are coming back to me nothing is coming back to me
but to conclude from that

to conclude from that that no one will ever come again
and shine his light on me and nothing ever again of other
days other nights no

next another image yet another so soon again the third perhaps they'll soon cease it's me all of me and my mother's
face I see it from below it's like nothing I ever saw

we are on a veranda smothered in verbena the scented sun
dapples the red tiles yes I assure you

the huge head hatted with birds and flowers is bowed down
over my curls the eyes burn with severe love I offer her
mine pale upcast to the sky whence cometh our help and
which I know perhaps even then with time shall pass
away

in a word bolt upright on a cushion on my knees whelmed
in a nightshirt I pray according to her instructions

that's not all she closes her eyes and drones a snatch of the so-called Apostles' Creed I steal a look at her lips

she stops her eyes burn down on me again I cast up mine in haste and repeat awry

the air thrills with the hum of insects

that's all it goes out like a lamp blown out

the space of a moment the passing moment that's all my past little rat at my heels the rest false

false that old time part one how it was before Pim vast stretch of time when I drag myself and drag myself astonished to be able the cord sawing my neck the sack jolting at my side one hand flung forward towards the wall the ditch that never come something wrong there

and Pim part two what I did to him what he said to me

false like that dead head the hand alive still the little table tossing in the clouds the woman jumping to her feet and rushing out into the wind

no matter I don't say any more I quote on is it me is it me I'm not like that any more they have taken that away from me this time all I say is how last how last

part one before Pim before the discovery of Pim have done with that leaving only part two with Pim how it was then leaving only part three after Pim how it was then how it is vast tracts of time

my sack sole variable my days my nights my seasons and
my feasts it says Lent everlasting then of a sudden Hal-
lowmas no summer that year if it is the same not much
real spring my sack thanks to my sack that I keep dying in
a dying age

my tins all sorts dwindling but not so fast as appetite different shapes no preference but the fingers know no sooner
fastened at random

dwindling in what strange wise but what is strange here un-
diminished for years then of a sudden half as many

these words of those for whom and under whom and all
about the earth turns and all turns these words here again
days nights years seasons that family

the fingers deceived the mouth resigned to an olive and
given a cherry but no preference no searching not even for
a language meet for me meet for here no more searching

the sack when it's empty my sack a possession this word
faintly hissing brief void and finally apposition anomaly
anomaly a sack here my sack when it's empty bah I've lash-
ings of time centuries of time

centuries I can see me quite tiny the same as now more or
less only tinier quite tiny no more objects no more food and
I live the air sustains me the mud I live on

the sack again other connexions I take it in my arms talk
to it put my head in it rub my cheek on it lay my lips on it
turn my back on it turn to it again clasp it to me again say
to it thou thou

say say part one no sound the syllables move my lips and all around all the lower that helps me understand

that's the speech I've been given part one before Pim question do I use it freely it's not said or I don't hear it's one or the other all I hear is that a witness I'd need a witness

he lives bent over me that's the life he has been given all my visible surface bathing in the light of his lamps when I go he follows me bent in two

his aid sits a little aloof he announces brief movements of the lower face the aid enters it in his ledger

my hand won't come words won't come no word not even soundless I'm in need of a word of my hand dire need I can't they won't that too

deterioration of the sense of humour fewer tears too that too they are failing too and there another image yet another a boy sitting on a bed in the dark or a small old man I can't see with his head be it young or be it old his head in his hands I appropriate that heart

question am I happy in the present still such ancient things a little happy on and off part one before Pim brief void and barely audible no no I would feel it and brief apostil barely audible not made not really for happiness unhappiness peace of mind

rats no no rats this time I've sickened them what else at this period part one before Pim vast stretch of time

the hand dips clawing for the take instead of the familiar
slime an arse on his belly he too before that what else that's
enough I'm going

not the shit not the vomit something else I'm going the sack
tied to my neck I'm ready first thing free play for the leg
which leg brief void and barely audible the right it's preferable

I turn on my side which side the left it's preferable throw
the right hand forward bend the right knee these joints are
working the fingers sink the toes sink in the slime these are
my holds too strong slime is too strong holds is too strong I
say it as I hear it

push pull the leg straightens the arm bends all these joints
are working the head arrives alongside the hand flat on the
face and rest

the other side left leg left arm push pull the head and upper
trunk rise clear reducing friction correspondingly fall back
I crawl in an amble ten yards fifteen yards halt

sleep duration of sleep I wake how much nearer the last

a fancy I am given a fancy the panting stops and a breath-
clock breath of life head in the bag oxygen for half an hour
wake when you choke repeat five times six times that's
enough now I know I'm rested my strength restored the day
can begin these scraps barely audible of a fantasy

always sleepy little sleep that's how they're trying to tell
me this time sucked down spewed up yawning yawning al-

ways sleepy little sleep

this voice once quaqua then in me when the panting stops part three after Pim not before not with I have journeyed found Pim lost Pim it is over I am in part three after Pim how it was how it is I say it as I hear it natural order more or less bits and scraps in the mud my life murmur it to the mud

I learn it natural order more or less before Pim with Pim vast tracts of time how it was my vanished life then after then now after Pim how it is my life bits and scraps

I say it my life as it comes natural order my lips move I can feel them it comes out in the mud my life what remains ill-said ill-recaptured when the panting stops ill-murmured to the mud in the present all that things so ancient natural order the journey the couple the abandon all that in the present barely audible bits and scraps

I have journeyed found Pim lost Pim it's over that life those periods of that life first second now third pant pant the panting stops and I hear barely audible how I journey with my sack my tins in the dark the mud crawl in an amble towards Pim unwitting bits and scraps in the present things so ancient hear them murmur them as they come barely audible to the mud

part one before Pim the journey it can't last it lasts I'm calm calmer you think you're calm and you're not in the lowest depths and you're on the edge I say it as I hear it and that death death if it ever comes that's all it dies

it dies and I see a crocus in a pot in an area in a basement
a saffron the sun creeps up the wall a hand keeps it in the
sun this yellow flower with a string I see the hand long
image hours long the sun goes the pot goes down lights on
the ground the hand goes the wall goes

rags of life in the light I hear and don't deny don't believe
don't say any more who is speaking that's not said any more
it must have ceased to be of interest but words like now before Pim no no that's not said only mine my words mine
alone one or two soundless brief movements all the lower
no sound when I can that's the difference great confusion

I see all sizes life included if that's mine the light goes on
in the mud the prayer the head on the table the crocus the
old man in tears the tears behind the hands skies all sorts
different sorts on land and sea blue of a sudden gold and
green of the earth of a sudden in the mud

but words like now words not mine before Pim no no that's
not said that's the difference I hear it between then and now
one of the differences among the similarities

the words of Pim his extorted voice he stops I step in all the
needful he starts again I could listen to him for ever but
mine have done with mine natural order before Pim the
little I say no sound the little I see of a life I don't deny don't
believe but what believe the sack perhaps the dark the mud
death perhaps to wind up with after so much life there are
moments

how I got here if it's me no question too weak no interest but here this place where I begin this time present formulation part one my life clutch the sack it drips first sign this place a few scraps

you are there somewhere alive somewhere vast stretch of time then it's over you are there no more alive no more then again you are there again alive again it wasn't over an error you begin again all over more or less in the same place or in another as when another image above in the light you come to in hospital in the dark

the same as which which place it's not said or I don't hear it's one or the other the same more or less more humid fewer gleams no gleam what does that mean that I was once somewhere where there were gleams I say it as I hear it every word always

more humid fewer gleams no gleam and hushed the dear sounds pretext for speculation I must have slipped you are in the depths it's the end you have ceased you slip you continue

another age yet another familiar in spite of its strangenesses this sack this slime the mild air the black dark the coloured images the power to crawl all these strangenesses

but progress properly so called ruins in prospect as in the dear tenth century the dear twentieth that you might say to yourself to a dream greenhorn ah if you had seen it four hundred years ago what upheavals

ah my young friend this sack if you had seen it I could hardly drag it and now look my vertex touches the bottom

and I not a wrinkle not one

at the end of the myriads of hours an hour mine a quarter of an hour there are moments it's because I have suffered must have suffered morally hoped more than once despaired to match your heart bleeds you lose your heart drop by drop weep even an odd tear inward no sound no more images no more journeys no more hunger or thirst the heart is going you'll soon be there I hear it there are moments they are good moments

paradise before the hoping from sleep I come to sleep return between the two there is all all the doing suffering failing bungling achieving until the mud yawns again that's how they're trying to tell me this time part one before Pim from one sleep to the next

then Pim the lost tins the groping hand the arse the two cries mine mute the birth of hope on with it get it over have it behind me feel the heart going hear it said you're nearly there

be with Pim have been with Pim have him behind me hear it said he'll come back another will come better than Pim he's coming right leg right arm push pull ten yards fifteen yards you stay quiet where you are in the dark the mud and on you suddenly a hand like yours on Pim two cries his mute

you will have a little voice it will be barely audible you will whisper in his ear you will have a little life you will whisper it in his ear it will be different quite different quite a different music you'll see a little like Pim a little life music but in your mouth it will be new to you

then go for good and no goodbyes that age will be over all the ages or merely you no more journeys no more couples no more abandons ever again anywhere hear that

how it was before Pim first say that natural order the same things the same things say them as I hear them murmur them to the mud divide into three a single eternity for the sake of clarity I wake and off I go all life part one before Pim how it was leaving only with Pim how it was leaving only after Pim how it was how it is when the panting stops bits and scraps I wake off I go my day my life part one bits and scraps

asleep I see me asleep on my side or on my face it's one or the other on my side it's preferable which side the right it's preferable the sack under my head or clasped to my belly clasped to my belly the knees drawn up the back bent in a hoop the tiny head near the knees curled round the sack Belacqua fallen over on his side tired of waiting forgotten of the hearts where grace abides asleep

I know not what insect wound round its treasure I come back with empty hands to me to my place what to begin with ask myself that last a moment with that

what to begin my long day my life present formulation last a moment with that coiled round my treasure listening my God to have to murmur that

twenty years a hundred years not a sound and I listen not a gleam and I strain my eyes four hundred times my only season I clasp the sack closer to me a tin clinks first respite very first from the silence of this black sap

something wrong there

the mud never cold never dry it doesn't dry on me the air laden with warm vapour of water or some other liquid I sniff the air smell nothing a hundred years not a smell I sniff the air

nothing dries I clutch the sack first real sign of life it drips a tin clinks my hair never dry no electricity impossible fluff it up I comb it that can happen there's another object straight back there's another of my resources was once not now any more part three there's another difference

the morale at the outset before things got out of hand satisfactory ah the soul I had in those days the equanimity that's why they gave me a companion

it's still my day part one before Pim my life present formulation the very beginning bits and scraps I come back to me to my place in the dark the mud clutch the sack a tin clinks I make ready I'm going end of the journey

to speak of happiness one hesitates those awful syllables first asparagus burst abscess but good moments yes I assure you before Pim with Pim after Pim vast tracts of time good moments say what I may less good too they must be expected I hear it I murmur it no sooner heard dear scraps recorded somewhere it's preferable someone listening another noting or the same never a plaint an odd tear inward no sound a pearl vast tracts of time natural order

suddenly like all that happens to be hanging on by the
finger-nails to one's species that of those who laugh too
soon alpine image or speluncar atrocious moment it's here
words have their utility the mud is mute

here then this ordeal before I go right leg right arm push
pull ten yards fifteen yards towards Pim unwitting before
that a tin clinks I fall last a moment with that

enough indeed nearly enough when you come to think of it
to make you laugh feel yourself falling and hang on with a
squeak brief movements of the lower face no sound if you
could come to think of it of what you nearly lost and then
this splendid mud the panting stops and I hear it barely
audible enough to make you laugh soon and late if you
could come to think of it

escape hiss it's air of the little that's left of the little whereby
man continues standing laughing weeping and speaking
his mind nothing physical the health is not in jeopardy a
word from me and I am again I strain with open mouth so as
not to lose a second a fart fraught with meaning issuing
through the mouth no sound in the mud

it comes the word we're talking of words I have some still
it would seem at my disposal at this period one is enough
aha signifying mamma impossible with open mouth it
comes I let it at once or in extremis or between the two
there is room to spare aha signifying mamma or some other
thing some other sound barely audible signifying some
other thing no matter the first to come and restore me to
my dignity

passing time is told to me and time past vast tracts of time
the panting stops and scraps of an enormous tale as heard
so murmured to this mud which is told to me natural order
part three it's there I have my life

my life natural order more or less in the present more or less
part one before Pim how it was things so ancient the journey
last stage I come back to me to my place clutch the sack it
drips a tin clinks loss of species one word no sound it's the
beginning of my life present formulation I can go pursue
my life it will still be a man

what to begin with drink to begin with I turn over on my
face that lasts a good moment I last with that a moment in
the end the mouth opens the tongue comes out lolls in the
mud that lasts a good moment they are good moments perhaps the best difficult to choose the face in the mud the
mouth open the mud in the mouth thirst abating humanity
regained

sometimes in this position a fine image fine I mean in movement and colour blue and white of clouds in the wind sometimes some days this time as it happens this day in the mud
a fine image I'll describe it it will be described then go right
leg right arm push pull towards Pim he does not exist

sometimes in this position I fall asleep again the tongue goes
in the mouth closes the mud opens it's I who fall asleep
again stop drinking and sleep again or the tongue out and
drink all night all the time I sleep that's my night present
formulation I have no other I wake from sleep how much
nearer to the last that of men of beasts too I wake ask my-

self how much nearer I quote on last a moment with that
it's another of my resources

the tongue gets clogged with mud that can happen too only
one remedy then pull it in and suck it swallow the mud or
spit it out it's one or the other and question is it nourishing
and vistas last a moment with that

I fill my mouth with it that can happen too it's another of
my resources last a moment with that and question if swallowed would it nourish and opening up of vistas they are
good moments

rosy in the mud the tongue lolls out again what are the
hands at all this time one must always try and see what the
hands are up to well the left as we have seen still clutches
the sack and the right

the right I close my eyes not the blue the others at the
back and finally make it out way off on the right at the end
of its arm full stretch in the axis of the clavicle I say it as I
hear it opening and closing in the mud opening and closing
it's another of my resources it helps me

it can't be far a bare yard it feels far it will go some day on
its four fingers having lost its thumb something wrong there
it will leave me I can see it close my eyes the others and see
it how it throws its four fingers forward like grapnels the
ends sink pull and so with little horizontal hoists it moves
away it's a help to go like that piecemeal it helps me

and the legs and the eyes the blue closed no doubt no since
suddenly another image the last there in the mud I say it as
I hear it I see me

I look to me about sixteen and to crown all glorious weather egg-blue sky and scamper of little clouds I have my back turned to me and the girl too whom I hold who holds me by the hand the arse I have

we are if I may believe the colours that deck the emerald grass if I may believe them we are old dream of flowers and seasons we are in April or in May and certain accessories if I may believe them white rails a grandstand colour of old rose we are on a racecourse in April or in May

heads high we gaze I imagine we have I imagine our eyes open and gaze before us still as statues save only the swinging arms those with hands clasped what else

in my free hand or left an undefinable object and consequently in her right the extremity of a short leash connecting her to an ash-grey dog of fair size askew on its hunkers its head sunk stillness of those hands

question why a leash in this immensity of verdure and emergence little by little of grey and white spots lambs little by little among their dams what else the bluey bulk closing the scene three miles four miles of a mountain of modest elevation our heads overtop the crest

we let go our hands and turn about I dextrogyre she sinistro she transfers the leash to her left hand and I the same instant to my right the object now a little pale grey brick the empty hands mingle the arms swing the dog has not moved I have the impression we are looking at me I pull in my tongue close my mouth and smile

seen full face the girl is less hideous it's not with her I am con-

cerned me pale staring hair red pudding face with pim-
ples protruding belly gaping fly spindle legs sagging knocking at the knees wide astraddle for greater stability feet
splayed one hundred and thirty degrees fatuous half-smile
to posterior horizon figuring the morn of life green tweeds
yellow boots all those colours cowslip or suchlike in the
buttonhole

again about turn introrse at ninety degrees fleeting face
to face transfer of things mingling of hands swinging of
arms stillness of dog the rump I have

suddenly yip left right off we go chins up arms swinging
the dog follows head sunk tail on balls no reference to us
it had the same notion at the same instant Malebranche less
the rosy hue the humanities I had if it stops to piss it will piss
without stopping I shout no sound plant her there and run
cut your throat

brief black and there we are again on the summit the dog
askew on its hunkers in the heather it lowers its snout to
its black and pink penis too tired to lick it we on the contrary again about turn introrse fleeting face to face transfer
of things swinging of arms silent relishing of sea and isles
heads pivoting as one to the city fumes silent location of
steeples and towers heads back front as though on an
axle

suddenly we are eating sandwiches alternate bites I mine
she hers and exchanging endearments my sweet girl I bite
she swallows my sweet boy she bites I swallow we don't
yet coo with our bills full

my darling girl I bite she swallows my darling boy she bites
I swallow brief black and there we are again dwindling
again across the pastures hand in hand arms swinging heads
high towards the heights smaller and smaller out of sight
first the dog then us the scene is shut of us

some animals still the sheep like granite outcrops a horse
I hadn't seen standing motionless back bent head sunk animals know

blue and white of sky a moment still April morning in the
mud it's over it's done I've had the image the scene is empty
a few animals still then goes out no more blue I stay
there

way off on the right in the mud the hand opens and closes
that helps me it's going let it go I realize I'm still smiling
there's no sense in that now been none for a long time
now

my tongue comes out again lolls in the mud I stay there no
more thirst the tongue goes in the mouth closes it must be a
straight line now it's over it's done I've had the image

that must have lasted a good moment with that I have lasted
a moment they must have been good moments soon it will
be Pim I can't know the words can't come solitude soon over
soon lost those words

I have had company mine because it amuses me I say it as
I hear it and a little girl friend's under the sky of April or of
May we are gone I stay there

way off on the right the tugging hand the mouth shut grim the staring eyes glued to the mud perhaps we shall come back it will be dusk the earth of childhood glimmering again streaks of dying amber in a murk of ashes the earth must have been on fire when I see us we are already at hand

it is dusk we are going tired home I see only the naked parts the solidary faces raised to the east the pale swaying of the mingled hands tired and slow we toil up towards me and vanish

the arms in the middle go through me and part of the bodies shades through a shade the scene is empty in the mud the sky goes out the ashes darken no world left for me now but mine very pretty only not like that it doesn't happen like that

I wait for us perhaps to come back and we don't come back for the evening perhaps to whisper to me what the morning had sung and that day to that morning no evening

find something else to last a little more questions who were they what beings what point of the earth that family whence this dumb show better nothing eat something

that must have lasted a moment there must be worse moments hope blighted is not the worst the day is well advanced eat something that will last a moment they will be good moments

then if necessary my pain which of my many the deep beyond reach it's preferable the problem of my pains the solu-

tion last a moment with that then go not because of the shit
and vomit something else it's not known not said end of the
journey

right leg right arm push pull ten yards fifteen yards arrival
new place readaptation prayer to sleep pending which questions if necessary who they were what beings what point
of the earth

they will be good moments then less good that too must be
expected it will be night present formulation I can sleep
and if ever I wake

and if ever mute laugh I wake forthwith catastrophe Pim
and end of part one leaving only part two leaving only part
three and last

the panting stops I am on my side which side the right it's
preferable I part the mouth of the sack and questions what
my God can I desire what hunger to eat what was my last
meal that family time passes I remain

it's the scene of the sack the two hands part its mouth what
can one still desire the left darts in the left hand in the sack
it's the scene of the sack and the arm after up to the armpit
and then

it strays among the tins without meddling with how many
announces a round dozen fastens who knows on the last
prawns these details for the sake of something

it brings out the little oval tin transfers it to the other hand
goes back to look for the opener finds it at last brings
it out the opener we're talking of the opener with its spin-

dle bone handle to the feel rest

the hands what are the hands at when at rest difficult to see with thumb and index respectively pad of tip and outer face of second joint something wrong there nip the sack and with remaining fingers clamp the objects against the palms the tin the opener these details in preference to nothing

a mistake rest we're talking of rest how often suddenly at this stage I say it as I hear it in this position the hands suddenly empty still nipping the sack never let go the sack otherwise suddenly empty

grope in a panic in the mud for the opener that is my life but of what cannot as much be said could not as much be always said my little lost always vast stretch of time

rest then my mistakes are my life the knees draw up the back bends the head comes to rest on the sack between the hands my sack my body all mine all these parts every part

mine say mine to say something to say what I hear in Erebus in the end I'd succeed in seeing my navel the breath is there it wouldn't stir a mayfly's wing I feel the mouth opening

on the muddy belly I saw one blessed day saving the grace of Heraclitus the Obscure at the pitch of heaven's azure towering between its great black still spread wings the snowy body of I know not what frigate-bird the screaming albatross of the southern seas the history I knew my God the natural the good moments I had

but last day of the journey it's a good day no surprises good
or bad as I went to rest so back I came my hands as I left
them I shall lose nothing more see nothing more

the sack my life that I never let go here I let it go needing
both hands as when I journey that hangs together ah these
sudden blazes in the head as empty and dark as the heart
can desire then suddenly like a handful of shavings aflame
the spectacle then

need journey when shall I say weak enough later later some
day weak as me a voice of my own

with both hands therefore as when I journey or in them take
my head took my head above in the light I let go the sack
therefore but just a moment it's my life I lie across it therefore that hangs together still

through the jute the edges of the last tins rowel my ribs
perished jute upper ribs right side just above where one
holds them holds one's sides held one's sides my life that
day will not escape me that life not yet

if I was born it was not left-handed the right hand transfers
the tin to the other and this to that the same instant the
tool pretty movement little swirl of fingers and palms
little miracle thanks to which little miracle among so many
thanks to which I live on lived on

nothing now but to eat ten twelve episodes open the tin put
away the tool raise the tin slowly to the nose irreproachable
freshness distant perfume of laurel felicity then dream or not
empty the tin or not throw it away or not all that it's not said
I can't see no great importance wipe my mouth that with-

out fail so on and at last

take the sack in my arms strain it so light to me lay my
cheek on it it's the big scene of the sack it's done I have it
behind me the day is well advanced close the eyes at last
and wait for my pain that with it I may last a little more and
while waiting

prayer in vain to sleep I have no right to it yet I haven't yet
deserved it prayer for prayer's sake when all fails when
I think of the souls in torment true torment true souls who
have no right to it no right ever to sleep we're talking of
sleep I prayed for them once if I may believe an old view
it has faded

me again always everywhere in the light age unknown seen
from behind on my knees arse bare on the summit of a
muckheap clad in a sack bottom burst to let the head
through holding in my mouth the horizontal staff of a vast
banner on which I read

in thy clemency now and then let the great damned sleep
here something illegible in the folds then dream perhaps
of the good time their naughtiness procured them what
time the demons may rest ten seconds fifteen seconds

sleep sole good brief movements of the lower face no sound
sole good come quench these two old coals that have
nothing more to see and this old kiln destroyed by fire and
in all this tenement

all this tenement of naught from top to bottom from hair to
toe and finger-nails what little sensation it still has of what
it still is in all its parts and dream

dream come of a sky an earth an under-earth where I am inconceivable aah no sound in the rectum a redhot spike that day we prayed no further

how often kneeling how often from behind kneeling from every angle from behind in every posture if he wasn't me he was always the same cold comfort

one buttock twice too big the other twice too small unless an optical illusion here when you shit it's the mud that wipes I haven't touched them for an eternity in other words the ratio four to one I always loved arithmetic it has paid me back in full

Pim's though undersized were iso he could have done with a third I fleshed them indistinctly something wrong there but first have done with my travelling days part one before Pim how it was leaving only part two leaving only part three and last

in the days when I still hugged the walls in the midst of my brotherly likes I hear it and murmur that then above in the light at every bodily pain the moral leaving me as ice I screamed for help with once in a hundred some measure of success

as when exceptionally the worse for drink at the small hour of the garbage-man in my determination to leave the elevator I caught my foot twixt cage and landing and two hours later to the tick someone came running having summoned it in vain

old dream I'm not deceived or I am it all depends on what is not said on the day it all depends on the day farewell rats the ship is sunk a little less is all one begs

a little less of no matter what no matter how no matter when
a little less of to be present past future and conditional of
to be and not to be come come enough of that on and end
part one before Pim

fire in the rectum how surmounted reflections on the passion of pain irresistible departure with preparatives apper-
taining uneventful journey sudden arrival lights low lights
out bye-bye is it a dream

a dream what a hope death of sack arse of Pim end of part
one leaving only part two leaving only part three and last
Thalia for pity's sake a leaf of thine ivy

quick the head in the sack where saving your reverence I
have all the suffering of all the ages I don't give a curse for
it and howls of laughter in every cell the tins rattle like
castanets and under me convulsed the mud goes guggle-
guggle I fart and piss in the same breath

blessed day last of the journey all goes without a hitch the
joke ·dies too old the convulsions die I come back to the
open air to serious things had I only the little finger to raise
to be wafted straight to Abraham's bosom I'd tell him to
stick it up

some reflections none the less while waiting for things to improve on the fragility of euphoria among the different orders
of the animal kingdom beginning with the sponges when
suddenly I can't stay a second longer this episode is therefore lost

the dejections no they are me but I love them the old half-
emptied tins let limply fall no something else the mud en-
gulfs all me alone it carries my four stone five stone it yields
a little under that then no more I don't flee I am banished

stay for ever in the same place never had any other ambi-
tion with my little dead weight in the warm mire scoop my
wallow and stir from it no more that old dream back again
I live it now at this creeping hour know what it's worth was
worth

a great gulp of black air and have done at last with my
travelling days before Pim part one how it was before the
others the sedentary with Pim after Pim how it was how
it is vast tracts of time when I see nothing more hear his
voice then this other come from afar on the thirty-two winds
from the zenith and depths then in me when the panting
stops bits and scraps I murmur them

done with these fidgets that will not brook one second
longer here at my ease too weak to raise the little finger and
were it the signal for the mud to open under me and then
close again

question old question if yes or no this upheaval daily if daily
ah to have to hear that word to have to murmur it this upheaval yes or no if daily it so heaves me up and out of my
swill

and the day so near its end at last if it is not compact of a
thousand days good old question terrible always for the
head and universally apropos which is a great beauty

to have Pim's timepiece something wrong there and nothing to time I don't eat any more then no I don't drink any more and I don't eat any more don't move any more and don't sleep any more don't see anything any more and don't do anything any more it will come back perhaps all come back or a part I hear yes then no

the voice time the voice it is not mine the silence time the silence that might help me I'll see do something something good God

curse God no sound make mental note of the hour and wait midday midnight curse God or bless him and wait watch in hand but the dark but the days that word again what about them with no memory tear a shred from the sack make knots or the cord too weak

but first have done with my travelling days part one before Pim unspeakable flurry in the mud it's me I say it as I hear it rummaging in the sack taking out the cord tying the neck of the sack tying it to my neck turning over on my face taking leave and away

ten yards fifteen yards semi-side left right leg right arm push pull flat on face imprecations no sound semi-side right left leg left arm push pull flat on face imprecations no sound not an iota to be changed in this description

here confused reckonings to the effect I can't have deviated more than a second or so from the direction imparted to me one day one night at the inconceivable outset by chance by necessity by a little of each it's one of the three from west strong feeling from west to east and so in the mud the dark on the belly in a straight line as near as no matter four hundred miles in other words in eight thousand years if I had not stopped the girdle of the earth meaning the equivalent

it's not said where on earth I can have received my education acquired my notions of mathematics astronomy and even physics they have marked me that's the main thing

intent on these horizons I do not feel my fatigue it is manifest none the less passage more laborious from one side to the other one semi-side prolongation of intermediate procumbency multiplication of mute imprecations

sudden quasi-certitude that another inch and I fall headlong into a ravine or dash myself against a wall though nothing I know only too well to be hoped for in that quarter this tears me from my reverie I've arrived

the people above whining about not living strange at such a time such a bubble in the head all dead now others for whom it is not a life and what follows very strange namely that I understand them

always understood everything except for example history and geography understood everything and forgave nothing never could never disapproved anything really not even cruelty to animals never loved anything

such a bubble at such a time it bursts the day can't do much more to me

you mustn't too weak agreed if you want weaker no you
must as weak as possible then weaker still I say it as I hear
it every word always

my day my day my life so they come back the old words
always no not much more only reacclimatize myself then
last till sleep not fall asleep mad no sense in that

mad or worse transformed à la Haeckel born in Potsdam
where Klopstock too among others lived a space and
laboured though buried in Altona the shadow he casts

at evening with his face to the huge sun or his back I forget
it's not said the great shadow he casts towards his native
east the humanities I had my God and with that flashes of
geography

not much more but in the tail the venom I've lost my latin
one must be vigilant so a good moment in a daze on my belly
then begin I can't believe it to listen

to listen as though having set out the previous evening from
Nova Zembla I had just come back to my senses in a sub-
trophical subprefecture that's how I was had become or
always was it's one or the other the geography I had

question if always good old question if always like that since
the world world for me from the murmurs of my mother
shat into the incredible tohu-bohu

like that unable to take a step particularly at night without
stopping dead on one leg eyes closed breath caught ears
cocked for pursuers and rescuers

I close my eyes the same old two and see me head up rick
in the neck hands tense in the mud something wrong there
breath caught it lasts I last like that a moment until the
quiver of the lower face signifying I am saying have succeeded in saying something to myself

what can one say to oneself possibly say at such a time a
little pearl of forlorn solace so much the better so much the
worse that style only not so cold cheers alas that style only
not so warm joy and sorrow those two their sum divided
by two and luke like in outer hell

it's soon said once found soon said the lips stiffen and all
the adjacent flesh the hands open the head drops I sink a
little further then no further it's the same kingdom as before
a moment before the same it always was I have never left
it it is boundless

I'm often happy God knows but never more than at this
instant never so oh I know happiness unhappiness I know
I know but there's no harm mentioning it

above if I were above the stars already and from the bel-
freys the brief hour there's not much more left to endure
I'd gladly stay as I am for ever but that won't do

uncord sack and neck I do it I must do it it's the way one
is regulated my fingers do it I feel them

in the mud the dark the face in the mud the hands anyhow
something wrong there the cord in my hand the whole body
anyhow and soon it is as if there at that place and no other
I had lived yes lived always

God sometimes somewhere at this moment but I have
chanced on a good day I would gladly eat something but
I won't eat anything the mouth opens the tongue doesn't
come out the mouth soon closes again

it's on the left the sack attends me I turn on my right side
and take it so light in my arms the knees draw up the back
bends the head comes to rest on the sack we must have had
these movements before would they were the last

now yes or no a fold of the sack between the lips that can
happen not in the mouth between the lips in the vestibule

in spite of the life I've been given I've kept my plump lips
two big scarlet blubbers to the feel made for kisses I
imagine they pout out a little more part and fasten on a
ruck of the sack very horsy

yes or no it's not said I can't see other possibilities pray my
prayer to sleep again wait for it to descend open under me
calm water at last and in peril more than ever since all
parries spent that hangs together still

find more words and they all spent more brief movements
of the lower face he would need good eyes the witness if
there were a witness good eyes a good lamp he would have
them the witness the good eyes the good lamp

to the scribe sitting aloof he'd announce midnight no two
in the morning three in the morning Ballast Office brief
movements of the lower face no sound it's my words cause
them it's they cause my words it's one or the other I'll fall a-

sleep within humanity again just barely

the dust there was then the mingled lime and granite stones piled up to make a wall further on the thorn in flower green and white quickset mingled privet and thorn

the depth of dust there was then the little feet big for their age bare in the dust

the satchel under the arse the back against the wall raise the eyes to the blue wake up in a sweat the white there was then the little clouds you could see the blue through the hot stones through the jersey striped horizontally blue and white

raise the eyes look for faces in the sky animals in the sky fall asleep and there a beautiful youth meet a beautiful youth with golden goatee clad in an alb wake up in a sweat and have met Jesus in a dream

that kind an image not for the eyes made of words not for the ears the day is ended I'm safe till tomorrow the mud opens I depart till tomorrow the head in the sack the arms round it the rest anyhow

brief black long black no knowing and there I am again on my way again something missing here only two or three yards more and then the precipice only two or three last scraps and then the end end of part one leaving only part two leaving only part three and last something missing here things one knows already or will never know it's one or the other

I arrive and fall as the slug falls take the sack in my arms it weighs nothing any more nothing any more to pillow my head I press a rag I shall not say to my heart

no emotion all is lost the bottom burst the wet the dragging the rubbing the hugging the ages old coal-sack five stone six stone that hangs together all gone the tins the opener an opener and no tins I'm spared that this time tins and no opener I won't have had that in my life this time

so many other things too so often imagined never named never could useful necessary beautiful to the feel all I was given present formulation such ancient things all gone but the cord a burst sack a cord I say it as I hear it murmur it to the mud old sack old cord you remain

a little more to last a little more untwine the rope make two ropes tie the bottom of the sack fill it with mud tie the top it will make a good pillow it will be soft in my arms brief movements of the lower face would they were the last

when the last meal the last journey what have I done where been that kind mute screams abandon hope gleam of hope frantic departure the cord round my neck the sack in my mouth a dog

abandoned here effect of hope that hangs together still the eternal straight line effect of the pious wish not to die before my time in the dark the mud not to mention other causes

only one thing to do go back or at least only other thrash round where I lie and I go on zigzag give me my due conformably to my complexion present formulation seeking that which I have lost there where I have never been

dear figures when all fails a few figures to wind up with part one before Pim the golden age the good moments the losses of the species I was young I clung on to the species we're talking of the species the human saying to myself brief movements no sound two and two twice two and so on

sudden swerve therefore left it's preferable forty-five degrees and two yards straight line such is the force of habit then right right angle and straight ahead four yards dear figures then left right angle and beeline four yards then right right angle so on till Pim

thus north and south of the abandoned arrow effect of hope series of sawteeth or chevrons sides two yards base three a little less this the base we're talking of the base in the old line of march which I thus revisit an instant between two vertices one yard and a half a little less dear figures golden age so it ends part one before Pim my travelling days vast stretch of time I was young all that all those words chevrons golden vertices every word always as I hear it in me that was without quaqua on all sides and murmur to the mud when the panting stops barely audible bits and scraps

semi-side left right leg right arm push pull flat on face curse God bless him beseech him no sound with feet and hands scrabble in the mud what do I hope a tin lost where I have never been a tin half-emptied thrown away ahead that's all I hope where I have never been but others perhaps long before not long before it's one or the other or it's both a procession what comfort in adversity others what comfort

those dragging on in front those dragging on behind whose lot has been whose lot will be what your lot is endless cortège of sacks burst in the interests of all

or a celestial tin miraculous sardines sent down by God at the news of my mishap wherewith to spew him out another week

semi-side right left leg left arm push pull flat on the face mute imprecations scrabble in the mud every half-yard eight times per chevron or three yards of headway clear a little less the hand dips clawing for the take instead of the familiar slime an arse two cries one mute end of part one before Pim that's how it was before Pim

Imagination Dead Imagine

The ten-year hiatus between the two major prose works *The Unnamable* and *How It Is* suggests the difficulty Beckett was doubtless having in pursuing his experiments further. From 1960 onward—the date of *How It Is*—the problem grew ever more acute. I know, from having been in constant touch with him during these years, that he was always at work, but all that resulted—or rather survived—were short pieces, either fragments of longer works abandoned or brief entities whose denseness and concision made them seem far longer than they really were.

In the two-year period 1965–66 Beckett wrote three short prose works, all in French, in the following order: *Imagination Dead Imagine, Enough,* and *Ping.** Of the three, *Enough,* though second in order of composition, relates in style and subject more to the earlier stories than to *Imagination Dead Imagine* or *Ping*. Although A. Alvarez dismisses it as "another of those pointless pilgrimages," in reality its eight pages encompass a lifetime, and the narrator evokes a long, essentially idyllic relationship, one of mentor to pupil.

The other two, however, are closely related both in subject and style, though in *Imagination Dead Imagine* sentence structure is essentially intact. "No trace anywhere of life," it begins, as the nameless narrator surveys the scene. Then, from the white void, barely visible, appears a white rotunda in which two white bodies, "each in a semicircle," are lying. If life is color and movement, then eternity, one suspects, is white and motionless. The creatures of this extraordinary piece, like the rotunda in which they lie, still breathing,

---

* Some critics date a fourth from this period, *Le Depeupleur*, which Beckett translated as *The Lost Ones*. Actually, though it was begun in 1966, it was not completed until 1970.

though barely ("Hold a mirror to their lips, it mists"), are far
closer to the latter than to the former.

No trace anywhere of life, you say, pah, no difficulty there, imagination not dead yet, yes, dead, good, imagination dead imagine. Islands, waters, azure, verdure, one glimpse and vanished, endlessly, omit. Till all white in the whiteness the rotunda. No way in, go in, measure. Diameter three feet, three feet from ground to summit of the vault. Two diameters at right angles AB CD divide the white ground into two semicircles ACB BDA. Lying on the ground two white bodies, each in its semicircle. White too the vault and the round wall eighteen inches high from which it springs. Go back out, a plain rotunda, all white in the whiteness, go back in, rap, solid throughout, a ring as in the imagination the ring of bone. The light that makes all so white no visible source, all shines with the same white shine, ground, wall, vault, bodies, no shadow. Strong heat, surfaces hot but not burning to the touch, bodies sweating. Go back out, move back, the little fabric vanishes, ascend, it vanishes, all white in the whiteness, descend, go back in. Emptiness, silence, heat, whiteness, wait, the light goes down, all grows dark together, ground, wall, vault, bodies, say twenty seconds, all the greys, the light goes out, all vanishes. At the same time the temperature goes down, to reach its minimum, say freezing-point, at the same instant that the black is reached, which may seem strange. Wait, more or less long, light and heat come back, all grows white and hot together, ground, wall, vault, bodies, say twenty seconds, all the greys, till the initial level is reached whence the fall began. More or less long, for there may intervene, experience shows, between end of fall and beginning of rise, pauses of varying length, from the fraction of the second to what would have seemed, in other times, other places, an eternity. Same remark for the other pause, between end of rise and beginning of fall. The extremes, as long as they last, are perfectly stable, which in the case of the temperature may seem strange, in the beginning. It is possible too, experience shows, for rise and fall to stop short at any point and mark a pause, more or less long, before resuming, or reversing, the rise now fall, the fall rise, these in their turn to be completed, or to stop short and mark a pause, more or less long, before resuming, or again reversing, and so on, till finally one or the other extreme is reached. Such variations of rise and fall, combining in countless rhythms, commonly attend the passage from white and heat to black and cold, and vice versa. The extremes alone are stable as is stressed by the vibration to be observed when a pause occurs at some intermediate stage, no matter what its level and duration. Then all vibrates, ground, wall, vault, bodies, ashen or leaden or between the two, as may be. But on the whole, experience shows, such uncertain passage is not common. And most often, when the light begins to fail, and along with it the heat, the movement continues unbroken until, in the space of some twenty seconds, pitch black is reached and at the same instant say freezing-point. Same remark for the reverse movement, towards heat and whiteness. Next most frequent is the fall or rise with pauses of varying length in these feverish greys, without at any moment reversal of the movement. But whatever its uncertainties the return sooner or later to a temporary calm seems assured, for the moment, in the black dark or the great whiteness, with attendant temperature, world still proof against enduring tumult. Rediscovered miraculously after what absence in perfect voids it is no longer quite the same, from this point of view, but there is no other. Externally all is as before and the sighting of the little fabric quite as much a matter of chance, its whiteness merging in the surrounding whiteness. But go in and now briefer lulls and never twice the same storm. Light and heat remain linked as though supplied by the same source of which still no trace. Still on the ground, bent in three, the head against the wall at B, the arse against the wall at A, the knees against the wall between B and C, the feet against the wall between C and A, that is to say inscribed in the semicircle ACB, merging in the white ground were it not for the long hair of strangely imperfect whiteness, the white body of a woman finally. Similarly inscribed in the other semicircle, against the wall his head at A, his arse at B, his knees between A and D, his feet between D and B, the partner. On their right sides therefore both and back to back head to arse. Hold a mirror to their lips, it mists. With their left hands they hold their left legs a little below the knee, with their right hands their left arms a little above the elbow. In this agitated light, its great white calm now so rare and brief, inspection is not easy. Sweat and mirror notwithstanding they might well pass for inanimate but for the left eyes which at incalculable intervals suddenly open wide and gaze in unblinking exposure long beyond what is humanly possible. Piercing pale blue the effect is striking, in the beginning. Never the two gazes together except once, when the beginning of one overlapped the end of the other, for about ten seconds. Neither fat nor thin, big nor small, the bodies seem whole and in fairly good condition, to judge by the surfaces exposed to view. The faces too, assuming the two sides of a piece, seem to want nothing essential. Between their absolute stillness and the convulsive light the contrast is striking, in the beginning, for one who still remembers having been struck by the contrary. It is clear however, from a thousand little signs too long to imagine, that they are not sleeping. Only murmur ah, no more, in this silence, and at the same instant for the eye of prey the infinitesimal shudder instantaneously suppressed. Leave them there, sweating and icy, there is better elsewhere. No, life ends and no, there is nothing elsewhere, and no question now of ever finding again that white speck lost in whiteness, to see if they still lie still in the stress of that storm, or of a worse storm, or in the black dark for good, or the great whiteness unchanging, and if not what they are doing.

Lessness

Sans, as this work was called in its original French, is another of those brief "fragments" culled from the void that marks Beckett's prose efforts in the years following *How It Is*. ("Fragment" of course is the wrong term, for it implies a piece broken from a larger whole, and here the work, though brief, is complete in itself.)

Having read the original when it was written in 1969, I was somewhat surprised, when Beckett sent his translation the following year, to find that he had chosen as title *Lessness*. And yet the nuance is important for a number of reasons: first, it is more poetic than the more literal "without"; second, it is less final; and third, though *sans* occurs sixty times in the original, Beckett's title enabled him to use throughout the English text various words ending in "-less," notably "endlessness," which slows the movement and gives a whole new cadence to the English version.

Lessness was written immediately following *Ping* (when speaking of Beckett's work, one must always qualify; the "immediately" refers to "directly"; in time-terms, it followed *Ping* by three years). In many ways it resembles that 1966 work, but there are significant differences. Like *Ping*, the units of "thought" are the short phrases, the gasps of meaning (or nonmeaning), repeated and combined in new ways throughout. (The parallels with musical composition increase from work to work.) Here Beckett uses paragraph and sentence, but he uses them for good reason. *Lessness* is composed of twenty-four paragraphs, varying in length (that is, number of words) but each of seven sentences. As far as numbers are concerned, we are in the realm of human time.

As far as light, gray; setting, "ruins," which also appear to be "refuge"; as for characters, one, also gray. Upright.

Music has been evoked: this is one of the most musical

of Beckett's works, and much of its power derives from its musicality, its permutations and variations on the same theme. Like music, the work produces a dual effect, that is, both instantaneous and cumulative, as the echoes of the earlier variations reverberate in the mind as one reads the later.

The work cries to be read aloud; in fact, it has close and obvious parallels with some of Beckett's stage and radio plays. At one point the author apparently decided that it should be spoken, and it was performed on radio several times. But Beckett is said not to have been happy with the results, for the six different voices called for were too different: this is a piece for a single voice.

Ruins true refuge long last towards which so many false time out of mind. All sides endlessness earth sky as one no sound no stir. Grey face two pale blue little body heart beating only upright. Blacked out fallen open four walls over backwards true refuge issueless.

Scattered ruins same grey as the sand ash grey true refuge. Four square all light sheer white blank planes all gone from mind. Never was but grey air timeless no sound figment the passing light. No sound no stir ash grey sky mirrored earth mirrored sky. Never but this changelessness dream the passing hour.

He will curse God again as in the blessed days face to the open sky the passing deluge. Little body grey face features slit and little holes two pale blue. Blank planes sheer white eye calm long last all gone from mind.

Figment light never was but grey air timeless no sound. Blank planes touch close sheer white all gone from mind. Little body ash grey locked rigid heart beating face to endlessness. On him will rain again as in the blessed days of blue the passing cloud. Four square true refuge long last four walls over backwards no sound.

Grey sky no cloud no sound no stir earth ash grey sand. Little body same grey as the earth sky ruins only upright. Ash grey all sides earth sky as one all sides endlessness.

He will stir in the sand there will be stir in the sky the the air the sand. Never but in dream the happy dream only one time to serve. Little body little block heart beating ash grey only upright. Earth sky as one all sides endlessness little body only upright. In the sand no hold one

step more in the endlessness he will make it. No sound
not a breath same grey all sides earth sky body ruins.

Slow black with ruin true refuge four walls over backwards no sound. Legs a single block arms fast to sides
little body face to endlessness. Never but in vanished
dream the passing hour long short. Only upright little
body grey smooth no relief a few holes. One step in the
ruins in the sand on his back in the endlessness he will
make it. Never but dream the days and nights made of
dreams of other nights better days. He will live again
the space of a step it will be day and night again over him
the endlessness.

In four split asunder over backwards true refuge issueless scattered ruins. Little body little block genitals overrun arse a single block grey crack overrun. True refuge
long last issueless scattered down four walls over backwards no sound. All sides endlessness earth sky as one no
stir not a breath. Blank planes sheer white calm eye light
of reason all gone from mind. Scattered ruins ash grey all
sides true refuge long last issueless.

Ash grey little body only upright heart beating face to
endlessness. Old love new love as in the blessed days unhappiness will reign again. Earth sand same grey as the
air sky ruins body fine ash grey sand. Light refuge sheer
white blank planes all gone from mind. Flatness endless
little body only upright same grey all sides earth sky body
ruins. Face to white calm touch close eye calm long last all
gone from mind. One step more one alone all alone in the
sand no hold he will make it.

Blacked out fallen open true refuge issueless towards
which so many false time out of mind. Never but silence
such that in imagination this wild laughter these cries.
Head through calm eye all light white calm all gone from

mind. Figment dawn dispeller of figments and the other called dusk.

He will go on his back face to the sky open again over him the ruins the sand the endlessness. Grey air timeless earth sky as one same grey as the ruins flatness endless. It will be day and night again over him the endlessness the air heart will beat again. True refuge long last scattered ruins same grey as the sand.

Face to calm eye touch close all calm all white all gone from mind. Never but imagined the blue in a wild imagining the blue celeste of poesy. Little void mighty light four square all white blank planes all gone from mind. Never was but grey air timeless no stir not a breath. Heart beating little body only upright grey face features overrun two pale blue. Light white touch close head through calm eye light of reason all gone from mind.

Little body same grey as the earth sky ruins only upright. No sound not a breath same grey all sides earth sky body ruins. Blacked out fallen open four walls over backwards true refuge issueless.

No sound no stir ash grey sky mirrored earth mirrored sky. Grey air timeless earth sky as one same grey as the ruins flatness endless. In the sand no hold one step more in the endlessness he will make it. It will be day and night again over him the endlessness the air heart will beat again.

Figment light never was but grey air timeless no sound. All sides endlessness earth sky as one no stir not a breath. On him will rain again as in the blessed days of blue the passing cloud. Grey sky no cloud no sound no stir earth ash grey sand.

Little void mighty light four square all white blank planes all gone from mind. Flatness endless little body only upright same grey all sides earth sky body ruins. Scattered ruins same grey as the sand ash grey true refuge. Four square true refuge long last four walls over backwards no sound. Never but this changelessness dream the passing hour. Never was but grey air timeless no sound figment the passing light.

In four split asunder over backwards true refuge issueless scattered ruins. He will live again the space of a step it will be day and night again over him the endlessness. Face to white calm touch close eye calm long last all gone from mind. Grey face two pale blue little body heart beating only upright. He will go on his back face to the sky open again over him the ruins the sand the endlessness. Earth sand same grey as the air sky ruins body fine ash grey sand. Blank planes touch close sheer white all gone from mind.

Heart beating little body only upright grey face features overrun two pale blue. Only upright little body grey smooth no relief a few holes. Never but dream the days and nights made of dreams of other nights better days. He will stir in the sand there will be stir in the sky the air the sand. One step in the ruins in the sand on his back in the endlessness he will make it. Never but silence such that in imagination this wild laughter these cries.

True refuge long last scattered ruins same grey as the sands. Never was but grey air timeless no stir not a breath. Blank planes sheer white calm eye light of reason all gone from mind. Never but in vanished dream the passing hour long short. Four square all light sheer white blank planes all gone from mind.

Blacked out fallen open true refuge issueless towards which so many false time out of mind. Head through calm eye all light white calm all gone from mind. Old love new love as in the blessed days unhappiness will reign again.

Ash grey all sides earth sky as one all sides endlessness. Scattered ruins ash grey all sides true refuge long last issueless. Never but in dream the happy dream only one time to serve. Little body grey face features slit and little holes two pale blue.

Ruins true refuge long last towards which so many false time out of mind. Never but imagined the blue in a wild imagining the blue celeste of poesy. Light white touch close head through calm eye light of reason all gone from mind.

Slow black with ruin true refuge four walls over backwards no sound. Earth sky as one all sides endlessness little body only upright. One step more one alone all alone in the sand no hold he will make it. Ash grey little body only upright heart beating face to endlessness. Light refuge sheer white blank planes all gone from mind. All sides endlessness earth sky as one no sound no stir.

Legs a single block arms fast to sides little body face to endlessness. True refuge long last issueless scattered down four walls over backwards no sound. Blank planes sheer white eye calm long last all gone from mind. He will curse God again as in the blessed days face to the open sky the passing deluge. Face to calm eye touch close all calm all white all gone from mind.

Little body little block heart beating ash grey only upright. Little body ash grey locked rigid heart beating face to endlessness. Little body little block genitals overrun arse a single block grey crack overrun. Figment dawn dispeller of figments and the other called dusk.

Dramatic Works

Cascando

It is impossible to emphasize too strongly the importance of music in all Beckett's work. More than any other contemporary writer, he has used the techniques of music and musical composition in structuring his works. In some instances he used music as a character, so to speak, and combined music and words into a dramatic whole. In 1961 Beckett wrote, in English, a radio play entitled *Words and Music* in which the Master of Ceremonies, Croak, tries to control the other two "characters."

The following year he wrote another radio play, this one in French, entitled *Cascando*, also a three-"character" work. Here the Master of Ceremonies, Opener, tries to control even as he limits his role to that which is meant to be his. But things get out of hand, and before long not only is Voice telling its story, of one Woburn—wanting to tell it only to finish, that sleep may follow—but Opener too slips into the storyteller's role.

Words and music have always been part and parcel of drama, used usually in time-worn ways. Beckett has seen fit not merely to use them, but to propel them onto the stage itself and make them the very characters of his drama.

Cascando

A radio play
Music by Marcel Mihalovici

OPENER (*dry as dust*): It is the month of May . . . for me.

Pause.

Yes, that's right.

Pause.

I open.

VOICE (*low, panting*):—story . . . if you could finish it . . .
you could rest . . . you could sleep . . . not before . . .
oh I know . . . the ones I've finished . . . thousands and
one . . . all I ever did . . . in my life . . . with my life
. . . saying to myself . . . finish this one . . . it's the
right one . . . then rest . . . then sleep . . . no more
stories . . . no more words . . . and finished it . . . and
not the right one . . . couldn't rest . . . straight away another . . . to begin . . . to finish . . . saying to myself
. . . finish this one . . . then rest . . . this time it's the
right one . . . this time you have it . . . and finished it
. . . and not the right one . . . couldn't rest . . . straight
away another . . . but this one . . . it's different . . . I'll
finish it . . . then rest . . . it's the right one . . . this
time I have it . . . I've got it . . . Woburn . . . I resume
. . . a long life . . . already . . . say what you like . . . a
few misfortunes . . . that's enough . . . five years later
. . . ten years . . . I don't know . . . Woburn . . . he's
changed . . . not enough . . . recognizable . . . in the
shed . . . yet another . . . waiting for night . . . night
to fall . . . to go out . . . go on . . . elsewhere . . . sleep
elsewhere . . . it's slow . . . he lifts his head . . . now
and then . . . his eyes . . . to the window . . . it's darkening . . . the earth is darkening . . . it's night . . . he gets
up . . . knees first . . . then up . . . on his feet . . . slips

out . . . Woburn . . . same old coat . . . right the sea
. . . left the hills . . . he has the choice . . . he has
only—

OPENER (*with* VOICE): And I close.

Silence.

I open the other.

MUSIC: . . . .

OPENER (*with* MUSIC): And I close.

Silence.

I open both.

VOICE ⎫ (*together*):   —on . . . it's getting on . . . finish it
MUSIC ⎭   . . . .
. . . don't give up . . . then rest . . . sleep . . . not before
. . . .
. . . finish it . . . it's the right one . . . this time you have
. . . .
it . . . you've got it . . . it's there . . . somewhere . . .
. . . .
you've got him . . . follow him . . . don't lose him . . .
. . . .
Woburn story . . . getting on . . . finish it . . . then
. . . .
sleep . . . no more stories . . . no more words . . .
. . . .
come on . . . next thing . . . he—
. . . .

OPENER (*with* VOICE *and* MUSIC): And I close.

Silence.

I start again.

VOICE:—down . . . gentle slope . . . boreen . . . giant aspens . . . wind in the boughs . . . faint sea . . . Woburn . . . same old coat . . . he goes on . . . stops . . . not a soul . . . not yet . . . night too bright . . . say what you like . . . the bank . . . he hugs the bank . . . same old stick . . . he goes down . . . falls . . . on purpose or not . . . can't see . . . he's down . . . that's what counts . . . face in the mud . . . arms spread . . . that's the idea . . . already . . . we're there already . . . no not yet . . . he gets up . . . knees first . . . hands flat . . . in the mud . . . head sunk . . . then up . . . on his feet . . . huge bulk . . . come on . . . he goes on . . . he goes down . . . come on . . . in his head . . . what's in his head . . . a hole . . . a shelter . . . a hollow . . . in the dunes . . . a cave . . . vague memory . . . in his head . . . of a cave . . . he goes down . . . no more trees . . . no more bank . . . he's changed . . . not enough . . . night too bright . . . soon the dunes . . . no more cover . . . he stops . . . not a soul . . . not—

Silence.

MUSIC: . . . .

Silence.

VOICE ⎫
MUSIC ⎭(*together*): —rest . . . sleep . . . no more stories
. . . .
. . . no more words . . . don't give up . . . it's the right
. . . .
one . . . we're there . . . nearly . . . I'm there . . .
. . . .
somewhere . . . Woburn . . . I've got him . . . don't
. . . .
lose him . . . follow him . . . to the end . . . come on
. . . .

. . . this time . . . it's the right one . . . finish . . . sleep

. . . .

. . . Woburn . . . come on—

. . . .

Silence.

OPENER: So, at will.
They say, It's in his head.
It's not. I open.

VOICE:—falls . . . again . . . on purpose or not . . . can't see
. . . he's down . . . that's what matters . . . face in the
sand . . . arms spread . . . bare dunes . . . not a scrub
. . . same old coat . . . night too bright . . . say what
you like . . . sea louder . . . like thunder . . . manes of
foam . . . Woburn . . . his head . . . what's in his head
. . . peace . . . peace again . . . in his head . . . no
further . . . to go . . . to seek . . . sleep . . . no . . .
not yet . . . he gets up . . . knees first . . . hands flat . . .
in the sand . . . head sunk . . . then up . . . on his feet
. . . huge bulk . . . same old broad-brim . . . jammed
down . . . come on . . . he's off again . . . ton weight
. . . in the sand . . . knee-deep . . . he goes down . . .
sea—

OPENER (*with* VOICE): And I close.

Silence.

I open the other.

MUSIC: . . . .
OPENER (*with* MUSIC): And I close.

Silence.

So, at will.
It's my life, I live on that.

Pause.

Yes, that's right.

Pause.

What do I open?
They say, He opens nothing, he has nothing to open,
it's in his head.
They don't see me, they don't see what I do, they
don't see what I have, and they say, He opens nothing,
he has nothing to open, it's in his head.
I don't protest any more, I don't say any more, There
is nothing in my head.
I don't answer any more.
I open and close.

VOICE:—lights . . . of the land . . . the island . . . the sky
. . . he need only . . . lift his head . . . his eyes . . . he'd
see them . . . shine on him . . . but no . . . he—

Silence.

MUSIC (*brief*): ....
Silence.

OPENER: They say, That is not his life, he does not live on
that. They don't see me, they don't see what my life is,
they don't see what I live on, and they say, That is not
his life, he does not live on that.

Pause.

I have lived on it . . . pretty long.
Long enough.
Listen.

VOICE (*weakening*):—this time . . . I'm there . . . Woburn
. . . it's him . . . I've seen him . . . I've got him . . .

come on . . . same old coat . . . he goes down . . . falls
. . . falls again . . . on purpose or not . . . can't see . . .
he's down . . . that's what counts . . . come on—

OPENER (*with* VOICE): Full strength.

VOICE:—face . . . in the stones . . . no more sand . . . all
stones . . . that's the idea . . . we're there . . . this time
. . . no . . . not yet . . . he gets up . . . knees first . . .
hands flat . . . in the stones . . . head sunk . . . then up
. . . on his feet . . . huge bulk . . . Woburn . . . faster . . .
off again . . . he goes down . . . he—

Silence.

MUSIC (*weakening*): . . . .

OPENER (*with* MUSIC): Full strength.

MUSIC: . . . .

Silence.

OPENER: That's not all.
I open both.
Listen.

VOICE ⎫
⎬ (*together*):   —sleep . . . no more searching . . . to
MUSIC ⎭ . . . .
find him . . . in the dark . . . to see him . . . to say him
. . . .
. . . for whom . . . that's it . . . no matter . . . never
. . . .
him . . . never right . . . start again . . . in the dark . . .
. . . .
done with that . . . this time . . . it's right . . . we're
. . . .
there . . . nearly . . . finish—
. . . .

Silence.

OPENER: From one world to another, it's as though they drew together.

We have not much further to go.

Good.

VOICE } (*together*): —nearly . . . I've got him . . . I've
MUSIC   . . . .
seen him . . . I've said him . . . we're there . . . nearly
. . . .
. . . no more stories . . . all false . . . this time . . . it's
. . . .
the right one . . . I have it . . . finish it . . . sleep . . .
. . . .
Woburn . . . it's him . . . I've got him . . . follow him
. . . .
. . . to—
. . . .

Silence.

OPENER: Good.

Pause.

Yes, that's right, the month of May.
You know, the reawakening.

Pause.

I open.

VOICE:—no tiller . . . no thwarts . . . no oars . . . afloat . . . sucked out . . . then back . . . aground . . . drags free . . . out . . . Woburn . . . he fills it . . . flat out . . . face in the bilge . . . arms spread . . . same old coat . . . hands clutching . . . the gunnels . . . no . . . I don't know . . . I see him . . . he clings on . . . out to sea . . . heading nowhere . . . for the island . . . then no more . . . else—

Silence.

MUSIC: ....

Silence.

OPENER: They said, It's his, it's his voice, it's in his head.

Pause.

VOICE:—faster . . . scudding . . . rearing . . . plunging . . .
heading nowhere . . . for the island . . . then no more
. . . elsewhere . . . anywhere . . . heading anywhere . . .
lights—

Silence.

OPENER: No resemblance.
I answered, And that . . .

MUSIC (*brief*): ....

Silence.

OPENER: . . . is that mine too?
But I don't answer any more.
And they don't say anything any more.
They have quit.
Good.

Pause.

Yes, the month of May, that's right, the end of May.
The long days.

Pause.

I open.

Pause.

I'm afraid to open.

But I must open.
So I open.

VOICE:—come on . . . Woburn . . . arms spread . . . same old
coat . . . face in the bilge . . . he clings on . . . island
astern . . . far astern . . . heading out . . . vast deep . . .
no more land . . . his head . . . what's in his head . . .
Woburn—

OPENER (*with* VOICE): Come on! Come on!

VOICE:—at last . . . no more coming . . . no more going . . .
seeking elsewhere . . . always elsewhere . . . we're there
. . . nearly . . . Woburn . . . hang on . . . don't let go
. . . lights gone . . . of the land . . . all gone . . . nearly
all . . . too far . . . too late . . . of the sky . . . those . . .
if you like . . . he need only . . . turn over . . . he'd see
them . . . shine on him . . . but no . . . he clings on . . .
Woburn . . . he's changed . . . nearly enough—

Silence.

MUSIC: . . . .

OPENER (*with* MUSIC): Good God.

MUSIC: . . . .

Silence.

OPENER: Good God good God.

Pause.

There was a time I asked myself, What is it?
There were times I answered, It's the outing.
Two outings.
Then the return.
Where?
To the village.

To the inn.

Two outings, then at last the return, to the village, to the inn, by the only road that leads there.

An image, like any other.

But I don't answer any more.

I open.

VOICE ⎫
MUSIC ⎭ (*together*): —don't let go . . . finish . . . it's the
. . . .
right one . . . I have it . . . this time . . . we're there . . .
. . . .
Woburn . . . nearly—
. . . .

OPENER (*with* VOICE *and* MUSIC): As though they had joined arms.

VOICE ⎫
MUSIC ⎭ (*together*): —sleep . . . no more stories . . . come
. . . .
on . . . Woburn . . . it's him . . . see him . . . say him
. . . .
. . . to the end . . . don't let go—
. . . .

OPENER (*with* VOICE *and* MUSIC): Good.

VOICE ⎫
MUSIC ⎭ (*together*): —nearly . . . just a few more . . . a
. . . .
few more . . . I'm there . . . nearly . . . Woburn . . .
. . . .
it's him . . . it was him . . . I've got him . . . nearly—
. . . .

OPENER (*with* VOICE *and* MUSIC, *fervently*): Good!

VOICE ⎫
MUSIC ⎭ (*together*): —this time . . . it's right . . . finish . . .
. . . .

no more stories . . . sleep . . . we're there . . . nearly . . .

. . . .

just a few more . . . don't let go . . . Woburn . . . he

. . . .

clings on . . . come on . . . come on—

. . . .

Silence.

Eh Joe

Film, Beckett's sole attempt to write for the cinema, made use of the camera as a character: E, the perceiving eye. In this play, written for television three years after *Film*, Beckett again utilizes the camera as more than a simple recording instrument: it is an active force, in tension with the protagonist, Joe, moving in on him each time the Voice pauses.

In this two-character play—three if one includes the camera—the physical Joe, like the O of *Film*, makes every effort to isolate himself from the outside world and perception. And like O, he will fail, for after all outside perception has been suppressed, self-perception remains. Here the self-perception is a voice, a woman's voice but emanating no doubt from within, who relates her own relationship with Joe, and then, in the same "low, distinct, remote" voice, that of a rival, another mistress whom Joe has loved and cast away, and who in despair has killed herself over him.

First produced by the BBC on July 4, 1966, and later by NET in the United States, *Eh Joe* once again demonstrates eloquently Beckett's extraordinary ability to use each medium to maximum advantage, and while reducing the dramatic elements to a bare minimum to evoke a whole life—or lives—in the space of a few unforgettable pages.

Eh Joe

A television play

Joe, late fifties, grey hair, old dressing-gown, carpet slippers, in his room.

1. Joe seen from behind sitting on edge of bed, intent pose, getting up, going to window, opening window, looking out, closing window, drawing curtain, standing intent.

2. Joe do. (=from behind) going from window to door, opening door, looking out, closing door, locking door, drawing hanging before door, standing intent.

3. Joe do. going from door to cupboard, opening cupboard, looking in, closing cupboard, locking cupboard, drawing hanging before cupboard, standing intent.

4. Joe do. going from cupboard to bed, kneeling down, looking under bed, getting up, sitting down on edge of bed as when discovered, beginning to relax.

5. Joe seen from front sitting on edge of bed, relaxed, eyes closed. Hold, then dolly slowly in to closeup of face. First word of text stops this movement.

Camera

Joe's opening movements followed by camera at constant remove, Joe full length in frame throughout. No need to record room as whole. After this opening pursuit, between first and final close-up of face, camera has nine slight moves in towards face, say four inches each time. Each move is stopped by voice resuming, never camera move and voice together. This would give position of camera when dolly stopped by first word of text as one yard from maximum close-up of face. Camera does not move between paragraphs till clear that pause (say three seconds) longer than between phrases. Then four inches in say four seconds when movement stopped by voice resuming.

Voice

Low, distinct, remote, little colour, absolutely steady rhythm, slightly slower than normal. Between phrases a beat of one second at least. Between paragraphs about seven, i.e., three before camera starts to advance and four for advance before it is stopped by voice resuming.

Face

Practically motionless throughout, eyes unblinking during paragraphs, impassive except in so far as it reflects mounting tension of listening. Brief zones of relaxation between paragraphs when perhaps voice has relented for the evening and intentness may relax variously till restored by voice resuming.

WOMAN'S VOICE:

Joe . . .

(*Eyes open, resumption of intentness.*)

Joe . . .

(*Full intentness.*)

Thought of everything? . . . Forgotten nothing? . . . You're all right now, eh? . . . No one can see you now . . . No one can get at you now . . . Why don't you put out that light? . . . There might be a louse watching you . . . Why don't you go to bed? . . . What's wrong with that bed, Joe? . . . You changed it, didn't you? . . . Made no difference? . . . Or is the heart already? . . . Crumbles when you lie down in the dark . . . Dry rotten at last . . . Eh Joe?

Camera move 1

The best's to come, you said, that last time . . . Hurrying me into my coat . . . Last I was favoured with from

you . . . Say it you now, Joe, no one'll hear you . . .
Come on, Joe, no one can say it like you, say it again
now and listen to yourself . . . The best's to come . . .
You were right for once . . . In the end.

Camera move 2

You know that penny farthing hell you call your mind
. . . That's where you think this is coming from, don't
you? . . . That's where you heard your father . . . Isn't
that what you told me? . . . Started in on you one
June night and went on for years . . . On and off . . .
Behind the eyes . . . That's how you were able to
throttle him in the end . . . Mental thuggee you called
it . . . One of your happiest fancies . . . Mental thuggee
. . . Otherwise he'd be plaguing you yet . . . Then your
mother when her hour came . . . "Look up, Joe, look
up, we're watching you" . . . Weaker and weaker till
you laid her too . . . Others . . . All the others . . . Such
love he got . . . God knows why . . . Pitying love . . .
None to touch it . . . And look at him now . . . Throt-
tling the dead in his head.

Camera move 3

Anyone living love you now, Joe? . . . Anyone living
sorry for you now? . . . That slut that comes on Saturday, you pay her, don't you? . . . Penny a hoist tup-
pence as long as you like . . . Watch yourself you
don't run short, Joe . . . Ever think of that? . . . Eh
Joe? . . . What it'd be if you ran out of us . . . Not
another soul to still . . . Sit there in his stinking old
wrapper hearing himself . . . That lifelong adorer . . .
Weaker and weaker till not a gasp left there either . . .

Is it that you want? . . . Well preserved for his age and
the silence of the grave . . . That old paradise you were
always harping on . . . No Joe . . . Not for the likes of
you.

Camera move 4

I was strong myself when I started . . . In on you . . .
Wasn't I, Joe? . . . Normal strength . . . Like those
summer evenings in the Green . . . In the early days
. . . Of our idyll . . . When we sat watching the ducks
. . . Holding hands exchanging vows . . . How you
admired my elocution! . . . Among other charms . . .
Voice like flint glass . . . To borrow your expression
. . . Powerful grasp of language you had . . . Flint glass
. . . You could have listened to it for ever . . . And now
this . . . Squeezed down to this . . . How much longer
would you say? . . . Till the whisper . . . You know
. . . When you can't hear the words . . . Just the odd
one here and there . . . That's the worst . . . Isn't it,
Joe? . . . Isn't that what you told me . . . Before we
expire . . . The odd word . . . Straining to hear . . .
Why is that, Joe? . . . Why must you do that? . . .
When you're nearly home . . . What matter then . . .
What we mean . . . It should be the best . . . Nearly
home again . . . Another stilled . . . And it's the worst
. . . Isn't that what you said? . . . The whisper . . . The
odd word . . . Straining to hear . . . Brain tired squeez-
ing . . . It stops in the end . . . You stop it in the end
. . . Imagine if you couldn't . . . . Ever think of that?
. . . If it went on . . . The whisper in your head . . . Me
whispering at you in your head . . . Things you can't
catch . . . On and off . . . Till you join us . . . Eh Joe?

Camera move 5

How's your Lord these days? . . . Still worth having?
. . . Still lapping it up? . . . The passion of our Joe . . .
Wait till He starts talking to you . . . When you're
done with yourself . . . All your dead dead . . . Sitting
there in your foul old wrapper . . . Very fair health for
a man of your years . . . Just that lump in your bubo
. . . Silence of the grave without the maggots . . . To
crown your labours . . . Till one night . . . "Thou fool
thy soul" . . . Put your thugs on that . . . Eh Joe? . . .
Ever think of that? . . . When He starts in on you . . .
When you're done with yourself . . . If you ever are.

Camera move 6

Yes, great love God knows why . . . Even me . . . But
I found a better . . . As I hope you heard . . . Preferable
in all respects . . . Kinder . . . Stronger . . . More intelligent . . . Better looking . . . Cleaner . . . Truthful
. . . Faithful . . . Sane . . . Yes . . . I did all right.

Camera move 7

But there was one didn't . . . You know the one I
mean, Joe . . . The green one . . . The narrow one . . .
Always pale . . . The pale eyes . . . Spirit made light
. . . To borrow your expression . . . The way they
opened after . . . Unique . . . Are you with me now?
. . . Eh Joe? . . . There was love for you . . . The best's
to come, you said . . . Bundling her into her Avoca
sack . . . Her fingers fumbling with the big horn buttons . . . Ticket in your pocket for the first morning
flight . . . You've had her, haven't you? . . . You've
laid her? . . . Of course he has . . . She went young
. . . No more old lip from her.

Camera move 8

Ever know what happened? . . . She didn't say? . . .
Just the announcement in the *Independent* . . . "On
Mary's beads we plead her needs and in the Holy
Mass" . . . Will I tell you? . . . Not interested? . . .
Well I will just the same . . . I think you should know
. . . That's right, Joe, squeeze away . . . Don't lose
heart now . . . When you're nearly home . . . I'll
soon be gone . . . The last of them . . . Unless that
poor slut loves you . . . Then yourself . . . That old
bonfire . . . Years of that stink . . . Then the silence
. . . A dollop of that . . . To crown all . . . Till His Nibs
. . . One dirty winter night . . . "Mud thou art."

Camera move 9

All right . . . Warm summer night . . . All sleeping . . .
Sitting on the edge of her bed in her lavender slip . . .
You know the one . . . Ah she knew you, heavenly
powers! . . . Faint lap of sea through open window . . .
Gets up in the end and slips out as she is . . . Moon . . .
Stock . . . Down the garden and under the viaduct . . .
Sees from the seaweed the tide is flowing . . . Goes on
down to the edge and lies down with her face in the
wash . . . Cut a long story short doesn't work . . . Gets
up in the end sopping wet and back up to the house
. . . Gets out the Gillette . . . The make you recommended for her body hair . . . Back down the garden
and under the viaduct . . . Takes the blade from the
holder and lies down at the edge on her side . . . Cut
another long story short doesn't work either . . . You
know how she always dreaded pain . . . Tears a strip
from the slip and ties it round the scratch . . . Gets up
in the end and back up to the house . . . Slip clinging

the way wet silk will . ... This all new to you, Joe? . . .
Eh Joe? . . . Gets the tablets and back down the
garden and under the viaduct . . . Takes a few on the
way . . . Unconscionable hour by now . . . Moon going
off the shore behind the hill . . . Stands a bit looking
at the beaten silver . . . Then starts along the edge to
a place further down near the Rock . . . Imagine what
in her mind to make her do that . . . Imagine . . .
Trailing her feet in the water like a child . . . Takes a
few more on the way . . . Will I go on, Joe? . . . Eh
Joe? . . . Lies down in the end with her face a few feet
from the tide . . . Clawing at the shingle now . . . Has
it all worked out this time . . . Finishes the tube . . .
There's love for you . . . Eh Joe? . . . Scoops a little
cup for her face in the stones . . . The green one . . .
The narrow one . . . Always pale . . . The pale eyes . . .
The look they shed before . . . The way they opened
after . . . Spirit made light . . . Wasn't that your description, Joe? . . . (*Voice drops to whisper, almost in-
audible except words in italics.*) All right . . . You've
had the best . . . Now *imagine* . . . Before she goes . . .
Face in the cup . . . Lips on a *stone* . . . Taking Joe
with her . . . Light gone . . . *"Joe Joe"* . . . No sound
. . . To the *stones* . . . Say it now, no one'll hear
you . . . Say "Joe" it parts the *lips* . . . *Imagine* the
hands . . . The *solitaire* . . . Against a *stone* . . . Imagine
the *eyes* . . . Spiritlight . . . Month of June . . . What
year of your Lord? . . . *Breasts* in the stones . . . And
the *hands* . . . Before they go . . . *Imagine* the hands
. . . What are they at? . . . In the *stones* . . .(*Image
fades, voice as before.*) What are they fondling? . . .
Till they go . . . *There's love for you* . . . Isn't it, Joe?
. . . Wasn't it, Joe? . . . *Eh Joe?* . . . Wouldn't you say?
. . . Compared to us . . . Compared to Him . . . *Eh
Joe?* (*Voice and image out.*)

Not I

Beckett's effort as a writer has constantly been to refine, to eliminate all extraneous material. From the desolate landscape with its lone tree in *Godot*, the elements of setting and character have steadily dwindled until, in the later works, we often have only portions of people, as in *Play*, where only heads protrude from the urns. In *Not I* body is further reduced:

> *Stage in darkness but for* MOUTH . . . *faintly lit from close-up and below, rest of face in shadow* . . . .

Anyone who has seen this play cannot help but be struck by the extraordinary quality of this disembodied Mouth, which looks like a gaping wound from which emerges a flow not of blood but of wounded words.

Before the curtain rises we hear unintelligible murmurs, and once the play has begun the staccato flow—intended for a shrouded figure perched on a four-foot podium downstage right, whose only movements are four gestures of hopeless compassion, each shrug less pronounced than the one before —moves so quickly it often defies the most acute ear. Yet the music and meaning are unmistakable, and the play a searing experience, as though the voyeur-public had, for a brief moment, been allowed to witness an exchange somewhere in Dante's hell.

Not I was performed for the first time on December 7, 1972, at the Repertory Theater of Lincoln Center in New York City. It was directed by Alan Schneider, with Jessica Tandy as the Mouth and Henderson Forsythe as the Auditor. The settings were by Douglas W. Schmidt.

Not I

Stage in darkness but for MOUTH, *upstage audience right, about 8′ above stage level, faintly lit from close-up and below, rest of face in shadow. Invisible microphone.* AUDITOR, *downstage audience left, tall standing figure, sex undeterminable, enveloped from head to foot in loose black djellaba, with hood, fully faintly lit, standing on invisible podium about 4′ high, shown by attitude alone to be facing diagonally across stage intent on* MOUTH, *dead still throughout but for four brief movements where indicated. See Note.*

As house lights down MOUTH's *voice unintelligible behind curtain. House lights out. Voice continues unintelligible behind curtain, 10 seconds. With rise of curtain ad-libbing from text as required leading when curtain fully up and attention sufficient into:*

MOUTH . . . out . . . into this world . . . this world . . . tiny little thing . . . before its time . . . in a godfor- . . . what? . . . girl? . . . yes . . . tiny little girl . . . into this . . . out into this . . . before her time . . . godforsaken hole called . . . called . . . no matter . . . parents unknown . . . unheard of . . . he having vanished . . . thin air . . . no sooner buttoned up his breeches . . . she similarly . . . eight months later . . . almost to the tick . . . so no love . . . spared that . . . no love such as normally vented on the . . . speechless infant . . . in the home . . . no . . . nor indeed for that matter any of any kind . . . no love of any kind . . . at any subsequent stage . . . so typical affair . . . nothing of any note till coming up to sixty when— . . . what? . . . seventy? . . . good God! . . . coming up to seventy . . . wandering in a field . . . looking aimlessly for cowslips . . . to make a ball . . . a few steps then stop . . . stare into space . . . then on . . . a few more . . . stop and stare again . . . so on . . . drifting around . . . when suddenly . . . gradually . . . all went out . . . all that early April morning light . . . and she found herself in the

— . . . what? . . . who? . . . no! . . . she! . . .
(*pause and movement 1*) . . . found herself in the
dark . . . and if not exactly . . . insentient . . .
insentient . . . for she could still hear the buzzing
. . . so-called . . . in the ears . . . and a ray of
light came and went . . . came and went . . . such
as the moon might cast . . . drifting . . . in and out
of cloud . . . but so dulled . . . feeling . . . feeling so dulled . . . she did not know . . . what position she was in . . . imagine! . . . what position she
was in! . . . whether standing . . . or sitting . . .
but the brain— . . . what? . . . kneeling? . . .
yes . . . whether standing . . . or sitting . . . or
kneeling . . . but the brain— . . . what? . . . lying? . . . yes . . . whether standing . . . or sitting
. . . or kneeling . . . or lying . . . but the brain
still . . . in a way . . . for her first thought was
. . . oh long after . . . sudden flash . . . brought
up as she had been to believe . . . with the other
waifs . . . in a merciful . . . (*brief laugh*) . . .
God . . . (*good laugh*) . . . first thought was . . .
oh long after . . . sudden flash . . . she was being
punished . . . for her sins . . . a number of which
then . . . further proof if proof were needed . . .
flashed through her mind . . . one after another . . .
then dismissed as foolish . . . oh long after . . . this
thought dismissed . . . as she suddenly realized . . .
gradually realized . . . she was not suffering . . .
imagine! . . . not suffering! . . . indeed could not

remember . . . off-hand . . . when she had suffered
less . . . unless of course she was . . . *meant* to be
suffering . . . ha! . . . *thought* to be suffering . . .
just as the odd time . . . in her life . . . when
clearly intended to be having pleasure . . . she was in
fact . . . having none . . . not the slightest . . . in
which case of course . . . that notion of punishment
. . . for some sin or other . . . or for the lot . . .
or no particular reason . . . for its own sake . . .
thing she understood perfectly . . . that notion of
punishment . . . which had first occurred to her . . .
brought up as she had been to believe . . . with the
other waifs . . . in a merciful . . . (*brief laugh*)
. . . God . . . (*good laugh*) . . . first occurred to
her . . . then dismissed . . . as foolish . . . was
perhaps not so foolish . . . after all . . . so on . . .
all that . . . vain reasonings . . . till another
thought . . . oh long after . . . sudden flash . . .
very foolish really but— . . . what? . . . the buzzing? . . . yes . . . all the time the buzzing . . . so-
called . . . in the ears . . . though of course actually . . . not in the ears at all . . . in the skull . . .
dull roar in the skull . . . and all the time this ray or
beam . . . like moonbeam . . . but probably not
. . . certainly not . . . always the same spot . . .
now bright . . . now shrouded . . . but always the
same spot . . . as no moon could . . . no . . . no
moon . . . just all part of the same wish to . . . torment . . . though actually in point of fact . . . not

in the least . . . not a twinge . . . so far . . . ha!
. . . so far . . . this other thought then . . . oh
long after . . . sudden flash . . . very foolish really
but so like her . . . in a way . . . that she might do
well to . . . groan . . . on and off . . . writhe she
could not . . . as if in actual . . . agony . . . but
could not . . . could not bring herself . . . some
flaw in her make-up. . . incapable of deceit . . . or
the machine . . . more likely the machine . . . so
disconnected . . . never got the message . . . or
powerless to respond . . . like numbed . . .
couldn't make the sound . . . not any sound . . . no
sound of any kind . . . no screaming for help for example . . . should she feel so inclined . . . scream
. . . (*screams*) . . . then   listen . . . (*silence*)
. . . scream again . . . (*screams again*) . . . then
listen   again . . . (*silence*) . . . no . . . spared
that . . . all silent as the grave . . . no part— . . .
what? . . . the buzzing? . . . yes . . . all silent
but for the buzzing . . . so-called . . . no part of
her moving . . . that she could feel . . . just the
eyelids . . . presumably . . . on and off . . . shut
out the light . . . reflex they call it . . . no feeling
of any kind . . . but the lids . . . even best of times
. . . who feels them? . . . opening . . . shutting
. . . all that moisture . . . but the brain still . . .
still sufficiently . . . oh very much so! . . . at this
stage . . . in control . . . under control . . . to
question even this . . . for on that April morning

. . . so it reasoned . . . that April morning . . .
she fixing with her eye . . . a distant bell . . . as she
hastened towards it . . . fixing it with her eye . . .
lest it elude her . . . had not all gone out . . . all
that light . . . of itself . . . without any . . . any
. . . on her part . . . so on . . . so on it reasoned
. . . vain questionings . . . and all dead still . . .
sweet silent as the grave . . . when suddenly . . .
gradually . . . she realiz— . . . what? . . . the
buzzing? . . . yes . . . all dead still but for the buzzing . . . when suddenly she realized . . . words
were— . . . what? . . . who? . . . no! . . . she!
. . . (*pause and movement 2*) . . . realized . . .
words were coming . . . imagine! . . . words were
coming . . . a voice she did not recognize . . . at
first . . . so long since it had sounded . . . then
finally had to admit . . . could be none other . . .
than her own . . . certain vowel sounds . . . she
had never heard . . . elsewhere . . . so that people
would stare . . . the rare occasions . . . once or
twice a year . . . always winter some strange reason
. . . stare at her uncomprehending . . . and now
this stream . . . steady stream . . . she who had
never . . . on the contrary . . . practically speechless . . . all her days . . . how she survived! . . .
even shopping . . . out shopping . . . busy shopping centre . . . supermart . . . just hand in the list
. . . with the bag . . . old black shopping bag . . .
then stand there waiting . . . any length of time . . .

middle of the throng . . . motionless . . . staring
into space . . . mouth half open as usual . . . till it
was back in her hand . . . the bag back in her hand
. . . then pay and go . . . not as much as goodbye
. . . how she survived! . . . and now this stream
. . . not catching the half of it . . . not the quarter
. . . no idea . . . what she was saying . . . imagine! . . . no idea what she was saying! . . . till she
began trying to . . . delude herself . . . it was not
hers at all . . . not her voice at all . . . and no
doubt would have . . . vital she should . . . was on
the point . . . after long efforts . . . when suddenly
she felt . . . gradually she felt . . . her lips moving
. . . imagine! . . . her lips moving! . . . as of
course till then she had not . . . and not alone the
lips . . . the cheeks . . . the jaws . . . the whole
face . . . all those— . . . what? . . . the tongue?
. . . yes . . . the tongue in the mouth . . . all those
contortions without which . . . no speech possible
. . . and yet in the ordinary way . . . not felt at all
. . . so intent one is . . . on what one is saying . . .
the whole being . . . hanging on its words . . . so
that not only she had . . . had she . . . not only
had she . . . to give up . . . admit hers alone . . .
her voice alone . . . but this other awful thought
. . . oh long after . . . sudden flash . . . even
more awful if possible . . . that feeling was coming
back . . . imagine! . . . feeling coming back! . . .
starting at the top . . . then working down . . . the

whole machine . . . but no . . . spared that . . .
the mouth alone . . . so far . . . ha! . . . so far
. . . then thinking . . . oh long after . . . sudden
flash . . . it can't go on . . . all this . . . all that
. . . steady stream . . . straining to hear . . . make
something of it . . . and her own thoughts . . .
make something of them . . . all . . . what? . . .
the buzzing? . . . yes . . . all the time the buzzing
. . . so-called . . . all that together . . . imagine!
. . . whole body like gone . . . just the mouth . . .
lips . . . cheeks . . . jaws . . . never— . . . what?
. . . tongue? . . . yes . . . lips . . . cheeks . . .
jaws . . . tongue . . . never still a second . . .
mouth on fire . . . stream of words . . . in her ear
. . . practically in her ear . . . not catching the half
. . . not the quarter . . . no idea what she's saying
. . . imagine! . . . no idea what she's saying! . . .
and can't stop . . . no stopping it . . . she who but
a moment before . . . but a moment! . . . could not
make a sound . . . no sound of any kind . . . now
can't stop . . . imagine! . . . can't stop the stream
. . . and the whole brain begging . . . something
begging in the brain . . . begging the mouth to stop
. . . pause a moment . . . if only for a moment . . .
and no response . . . as if it hadn't heard . . . or
couldn't . . . couldn't pause a second . . . like
maddened . . . all that together . . . straining to
hear . . . piece it together . . . and the brain . . .
raving away on its own . . . trying to make sense of

it . . . or make it stop . . . or in the past . . .
dragging up the past . . . flashes from all over . . .
walks mostly . . . walking all her days . . . day
after day . . . a few steps then stop . . . stare into
space . . . then on . . . a few more . . . stop and
stare again . . . so on . . . drifting around . . .
day after day . . . or that time she cried . . . the
one time she could remember . . . since she was a
baby . . . must have cried as a baby . . . perhaps
not . . . not essential to life . . . just the birth cry
to get her going . . . breathing . . . then no more
till this . . . old hag already . . . sitting staring at
her hand . . . where was it? . . . Croker's Acres
. . . one evening on the way home . . . home! . . .
a little mound in Croker's Acres . . . dusk . . . sitting staring at her hand . . . there in her lap . . .
palm upward . . . suddenly saw it wet . . . the
palm . . . tears presumably . . . hers presumably
. . . no one else for miles . . . no sound . . . just
the tears . . . sat and watched them dry . . . all
over in a second . . . or grabbing at the straw . . .
the brain . . . flickering away on its own . . . quick
grab and on . . . nothing there . . . . on to the
next . . . bad as the voice . . . worse . . . as little
sense . . . all   that   together . . . can't— . . .
what? . . . the buzzing? . . . yes . . . all the time
the buzzing . . . dull roar like falls . . . and the
beam . . . flickering on and off . . . starting to
move around . . . like moonbeam but not . . . all

part of the same . . . keep an eye on that too . . .
corner of the eye . . . all that together . . . can't
go on . . . God is love . . . she'll be purged . . .
back in the field . . . morning sun . . . April . . .
sink face down in the grass . . . nothing but the larks
. . . so on . . . grabbing at the straw . . . straining to hear . . . the odd word . . . make some sense
of it . . . whole body like gone . . . just the mouth
. . . like maddened . . . and can't stop . . . no
stopping it . . . something she— . . . something
she had to— . . . what? . . . who? . . . no! . . .
she! . . . (*pause and movement 3*) . . . something
she had to— . . . what? . . . the buzzing? . . .
yes . . . all the time the buzzing . . . dull roar . . .
in the skull . . . and the beam . . . ferreting around
. . . painless . . . so far . . . ha! . . . so far . . .
then thinking . . . oh long after . . . sudden flash
. . . perhaps something she had to . . . had to . . .
tell . . . could that be it? . . . something she had to
. . . tell . . . tiny little thing . . . before its time
. . . godforsaken hole . . . no love . . . spared
that . . . speechless all her days . . . practically
speechless . . . how she survived! . . . that time in
court . . . what had she to say for herself . . . guilty
or not guilty . . . stand up woman . . . speak up
woman . . . stood there staring into space . . .
mouth half open as usual . . . waiting to be led away
. . . glad of the hand on her arm . . . now this . . .
something she had to tell . . . could that be it? . . .

something that would tell . . . how it was . . . how
she— . . . what? . . . had   been? . . . yes . . .
something that would tell how it had been . . . how
she had lived . . . lived on and on . . . guilty or not
. . . on and on . . . to be sixty . . . something
she— . . . what? . . . seventy? . . . good   God!
. . . on and on to be seventy . . . something she
didn't know herself . . . wouldn't know if she heard
. . . then forgiven . . . God is love . . . tender
mercies . . . new every morning . . . back in the
field . . . April morning . . . face in the grass . . .
nothing but the larks . . . pick it up there . . . get
on with it from there . . . another few— . . . what?
. . . not that? . . . nothing to do with that? . . .
nothing she could tell? . . . all right . . . nothing
she could tell . . . try something else . . . think of
something else . . . oh long after . . . sudden flash
. . . not that either . . . all right . . . something
else again . . . so on . . . hit on it in the end . . .
think everything keep on long enough . . . then forgiven . . . back in the— . . . what? . . . not that
either? . . . nothing to do with that either? . . .
nothing she could think? . . . all right . . . nothing
she could tell . . . nothing she could think . . .
nothing   she— . . . what? . . . who? . . . no!
. . . she! . . . (*pause and movement 4*) . . . tiny
little thing . . . out before its time . . . godforsaken
hole . . . no love . . . spared that . . . speechless
all her days . . . practically speechless . . . even to

herself . . . never out loud . . . but not completely
. . . sometimes sudden urge . . . once or twice a
year . . . always winter some strange reason . . .
the long evenings . . . hours of darkness . . . sudden urge to . . . tell . . . then rush out stop the first
she saw . . . nearest lavatory . . . start pouring it
out . . . steady stream . . . mad stuff . . . half the
vowels wrong . . . no one could follow . . . till she
saw the stare she was getting . . . then die of shame
. . . crawl back in . . . once or twice a year . . .
always winter some strange reason . . . long hours of
darkness . . . now this . . . this . . . quicker and
quicker . . . the words . . . the brain . . . flickering away like mad . . . quick grab and on . . .
nothing there . . . on somewhere else . . . try somewhere else . . . all the time something begging . . .
something in her begging . . . begging it all to stop
. . . unanswered . . . prayer unanswered . . . or
unheard . . . too faint . . . so on . . . keep on
. . . trying . . . not knowing what . . . what she
was trying . . . what to try . . . whole body like
gone . . . just the mouth . . . like maddened . . .
so on . . . keep— . . . what? . . . the buzzing?
. . . yes . . . all the time the buzzing . . . dull roar
like falls . . . in the skull . . . and the beam . . .
poking around . . . painless . . . so far . . . ha!
. . . so far . . . all that . . . keep on . . . not
knowing what . . . what she was— . . . what?
. . . who? . . . no! . . . she! . . . SHE! . . .

(*pause*) . . . what she was trying . . . what to try
. . . no matter . . . keep on . . . (*curtain starts
down*) . . . hit on it in the end . . . then back . . .
God is love . . . tender mercies . . . new every
morning . . . back in the field . . . April morning
. . . face in the grass . . . nothing but the larks
. . . pick it up—

(*Curtain fully down. House dark. Voice continues behind
curtain, unintelligible, 10 seconds, ceases as house lights up*)

Note

Movement: this consists in simple sideways raising of arms
from sides and their falling back, in a gesture of helpless
compassion. It lessens with each recurrence till scarcely perceptible at third. There is just enough pause to contain it as
MOUTH recovers from vehement refusal to relinquish third
person.

That Time

This is Beckett's most recent play. Written in 1975, it is published here for the first time anywhere in the world.

Dramatically, it bears resemblances to both *Eh Joe* and *Not I*. To the former because, in both this and the earlier television play, the physical protagonist is a silent man hearing, and reacting to, a voice. Joe, in his late fifties, is far younger than the hero of *That Time*, who is described as having an "old white face" and "flaring white hair." And in contrast to Joe, who hears a woman's voice, *That Time's* protagonist hears three voices—A, B, and C—but all his own. As in *Not I*, wherein the darkened stage is interrupted only by the light focused on the Mouth, in this play all is darkness except for the Listener's face.

In language, however, *That Time* harks back to that of some earlier plays, and notably *Krapp's Last Tape*, for the three Voices—one coming from stage left, another from stage right, and the third from above—are in turn nostalgic and scolding, tender and exasperated, as in the space of a few stage-minutes they evoke a whole lifetime. References here are more specific and more of this world than we have become used to in Beckett's more recent works—references to trams and ferry, rain and cold, stone and wood, leaves and dust.

That Time is one of the most poetic and musical of all of Beckett's plays, one in which he returns from the edge of the void, with its half-formed thoughts and broken phrases, to a more human world where memories rise and, mistlike, echo hauntingly down the frail corridors of time.

That Time

Curtain. Stage in darkness. Fade up to Listener's face about ten feet above stage level midstage off centre.

Old white face, long flaring white hair as if seen from above outspread.

Voices A B C are his own coming to him from both sides and above. They modulate back and forth without any break in general flow except where silence indicated. See note below.

Silence 7". Listener's eyes are open. His breath audible, slow and regular.

A: that time you went back that last time to look was the ruin still there where you hid as a child when was that (*eyes close*) grey day took the eleven to the end of the line and on from there no no trams then all gone long ago that time you went back to look was the ruin still there where you hid as a child that last time not a tram left in the place only the old rails when was that

C: when you went in out of the rain always winter then always raining that time in the Portrait Gallery in off the street out of the cold and rain slipped in when no one was looking and through the rooms shivering and dripping till you found a seat marble slab and sat down to rest and dry off and on to hell out of there when was that

B: on the stone together in the sun on the stone at the edge of the little wood and as far as eye could see the wheat turning yellow vowing every now and then you loved each other just a murmur not touching or anything of that nature you one end of the stone she the other long low stone like millstone no looks just there together on the stone in the sun with the little wood behind gazing at the wheat or eyes closed all still no sign of life not a soul abroad no sound

A: straight off the ferry sat up with the nightbag to the high street neither right nor left not a curse for the old scenes the old names straight up the rise from the wharf to the high street and there not a wire to be seen only the old rails all rust when was that was your mother ah for God's sake all gone long ago that time you went back that last time to look was the ruin still there where you hid as a child someone's folly

C: was your mother ah for God's sake all gone long ago all dust the lot you the last huddled up on the slab in the old green greatcoat with your arms round you whose else hugging you for a bit of warmth to dry off and on to hell out of there and on to the next not a living soul in the place only yourself and the odd attendant drowsing around in his felt shufflers not a sound to be heard only every now and then a shuffle of felt drawing near then dying away

B: all still just the leaves and ears and you too still on the stone in a daze no sound not a word only every now and then to vow you loved each other just a murmur one thing could ever bring tears till they dried up altogether that thought when it came up among the others floated up that scene

A: Foley was it Foley's Folly bit of a tower still standing all the rest rubble and nettles where did you sleep no friend all the homes gone was it that kip on the front where you no she was with you then still with you then just the one night in any case off the ferry one morning and back on her the next to look was the ruin still

there where none ever came where you hid as a child
slip off when no one was looking and hide there all day
long on a stone among the nettles with your picture-
book

C: till you hoisted your head and there before your eyes
when they opened a vast oil black with age and dirt
someone famous in his time some famous man or woman
or even child such as a young prince or princess some
young prince or princess of the blood black with age
behind the glass where gradually as you peered trying
to make it out gradually of all things a face appeared
had you swivel on the slab to see who it was there at
your elbow

B: on the stone in the sun gazing at the wheat or the sky
or the eyes closed nothing to be seen but the wheat
turning yellow and the blue sky vowing every now and
then you loved each other just a murmur tears without
fail till they dried up altogether suddenly there in whatever thoughts you might be having whatever scenes
perhaps way back in childhood or the womb worst of
all or that old Chinaman long before Christ born with
long white hair

C: never the same after that never quite the same but that
was nothing new if it wasn't this it was that common
occurrence something you could never be the same after
crawling about year after year sunk in your lifelong
mess muttering to yourself who else you'll never be the
same after this you were never the same after that

A: or talking to yourself who else out loud imaginary
conversations there was childhood for you ten or eleven
on a stone among the giant nettles making it up now
one voice now another till you were hoarse and they
all sounded the same well on into the night some moods

in the black dark or moonlight and they all out on the
roads looking for you

B: or by the window in the dark harking to the owl not a
thought in your head till hard to believe harder and
harder to believe you ever told anyone you loved them
or anyone you till just one of those things you kept
making up to keep the void out just another of those old
tales to keep the void from pouring in on top of you
the shroud

Silence 10". Breath audible. After 3" eyes open.

C: never the same but the same as what for God's sake
did you ever say I to yourself in your life come on now
(*eyes close*) could you ever say I to yourself in your life
turning-point that was a great word with you before
they dried up altogether always having turning points
and never but the one the first and last that time curled
up worm in slime when they lugged you out and wiped
you off and straightened you up never another after that
never looked back after that was that the time or was
that another time

B: muttering that time together on the stone in the sun or
that time together on the towpath or that time together
in the sand that time that time making it up from there
as best you could always together somewhere in the sun
on the towpath facing downstream into the sun sinking
and the bits of flotsam coming from behind and drifting
on or caught in the reeds the dead rat it looked like
came on you from behind and went drifting on till you
could see it no more

A: that time you went back to look was the ruin still there
where you hid as a child that last time straight off the

ferry and up the rise to the high street to catch the
eleven neither right nor left only one thought in your
head not a curse for the old scenes the old names just
head down press on up the rise to the top and there
stood waiting with the nightbag till the truth began
to dawn

C: when you started not knowing who you were from
Adam trying how that would work for a change not
knowing who you were from Adam no notion who it
was saying what you were saying whose skull you were
clapped up in whose moan had you the way you were
was that the time or was that another time there alone
with the portraits of the dead black with dirt and
antiquity and the dates on the frames in case you might
get the century wrong not believing it could be you
till they put you out in the rain at closing-time

B: no sight of the face or any other part never turned
to her nor she to you always parallel like on an axle-tree
never turned to each other just blurs on the fringes of
the field no touching or anything of that nature always
space between if only an inch no pawing in the manner
of flesh and blood no better than shades no worse if it
wasn't for the vows

A: no getting out to it that way so what next no question
of asking not another word to the living as long as you
lived so foot it up in the end to the station bowed half
double get out to it that way all closed down and
boarded up Doric terminus of the Great Southern and
Eastern all closed down and the colonnade crumbling
away so what next

C: the rain and the old rounds trying making it up that
way as you went along how it would work that way for
a change never having been how never having been
would work the old rounds trying to wangle you into

it tottering and muttering all over the parish till the
words dried up and the head dried up and the legs dried
up whosever they were or it gave up whoever it was

B: stock still always stock still like that time on the stone
or that time in the sand stretched out parallel in the
sand in the sun gazing up at the blue or eyes closed
blue dark blue dark stock still side by side scene float
up and there you were wherever it might be

A: gave it up gave up and sat down on the steps in the
pale morning sun no those steps got no sun somewhere
else then gave up and off somewhere else and down on
a step in the pale sun a doorstep say someone's doorstep for it to be time to get on the night ferry and out
to hell out of there no need sleep anywhere not a curse
for the old scenes the old names the passers pausing
to gape at you quick gape then pass pass on pass by
on the other side

B: stock still side by side in the sun then sink and vanish
without your having stirred any more than the two
knobs on a dumbbell except the lids and every now
and then the lips to vow and all around too all still all
sides wherever it might be no stir or sound only faintly
the leaves in the little wood behind or the ears or the
bent or the reeds as the case might be of man no sight
of man or beast no sight or sound

C: always winter then always raining always slipping in
somewhere when no one would be looking in off the
street out of the cold and rain in the old green hole-
proof coat your father left you places you hadn't to pay
to get in like the Public Library that was another great
thing free culture far from home or the Post Office that
was another another place another time

A: huddled on the doorstep in the old green greatcoat in
the pale sun with the nightbag needless on your knees

not knowing where you were little by little not knowing where you were or when you were or what for place
might have been uninhabited for all you knew like that
time on the stone the child on the stone where none
ever came

Silence 10". Breath audible. After 3" eyes open.

B: or alone in the same the same scenes making it up
that way to keep it going keep it out on the stone (*eyes
close*) alone on the end of the stone with the wheat and
blue or the towpath alone on the towpath with the
ghosts of the mules the drowned rat or bird or whatever
it was floating off into the sunset till you could see it no
more nothing stirring only the water and the sun going
down till it went down and you vanished all vanished

A: none ever came but the child on the stone among the
giant nettles with the light coming in where the wall
had crumbled away poring on his book well on into the
night some moods the moonlight and they all out on the
roads looking for him or making up talk breaking up
two or more talking to himself being together that way
where none ever came

C: always winter then endless winter year after year as
if it couldn't end the old year never end like time could
go no further that time in the Post Office all bustle
Christmas bustle in off the street when no one was looking out of the cold and rain pushed open the door like
anyone else and straight for the table neither right nor
left with all the forms and the pens on their chains sat
down first vacant seat and were taking a look round
for a change before drowsing away

B: or that time alone on your back in the sand and no
vows to break the peace when was that an earlier time
a later time before she came after she went or both

before she came after she was gone and you back in
the old scene wherever it might be might have been
the same old scene before as then then as after with the
rat or the wheat the yellowing ears or that time in the
sand the glider passing over that time you went back
soon after long after

A: eleven or twelve in the ruin on the flat stone among
the nettles in the dark or moonlight muttering away
now one voice now another there was childhood for you
till there on the step in the pale sun you heard yourself
at it again not a curse for the passers pausing to gape
at the scandal huddled there in the sun where it had
no warrant clutching the nightbag drooling away out
loud eyes closed and the white hair pouring out down
from under the hat and so sat on in that pale sun forgetting it all

C: perhaps fear of ejection having clearly no warrant in
the place to say nothing of the loathsome appearance
so this look round for once at your fellow bastards
thanking God for once bad and all as you were you
were not as they till it dawned that for all the loathing
you were getting you might as well not have been
there at all the eyes passing over you and through you
like so much thin air was that the time or was that
another time another place another time

B: the glider passing over never any change same blue
skies nothing ever changed but she with you there or
not on your right hand always the right hand on the
fringe of the field and every now and then in the great
peace like a whisper so faint she loved you hard to
believe you even you made up that bit till the time
came in the end

A: making it all up on the doorstep as you went along
making yourself all up again for the millionth time for-

getting it all where you were and what for Foley's Folly
and the lot the child's ruin you came to look was it still
there to hide in again till it was night and time to go
till that time came

C: the Library that was another another place another
time that time you slipped in off the street out of the
cold and rain when no one was looking what was it
then you were never the same after never again after
something to do with dust something the dust said
sitting at the big round table with a bevy of old ones
poring on the page and not a sound

B: that time in the end when you tried and couldn't by
the window in the dark and the owl flown to hoot at
someone else or back with a shrew to its hollow tree
and not another sound hour after hour hour after hour
not a sound when you tried and tried and couldn't any
more no words left to keep it out so gave it up gave up
there by the window in the dark or moonlight gave up
for good and let it in and nothing the worse a great
shroud billowing in all over you on top of you and little
or nothing the worse little or nothing

A: back down to the wharf with the nightbag and the
old green greatcoat your father left you trailing the
ground and the white hair pouring out down from
under the hat till that time came on down neither right
nor left not a curse for the old scenes the old names not
a thought in your head only get back on board and
away to hell out of it and never come back or was that
another time all that another time was there ever any
other time but that time away to hell out of it all and
never come back

C: not a sound only the old breath and the leaves turning
and then suddenly this dust whole place suddenly full
of dust when you opened your eyes from floor to ceiling

nothing only dust and not a sound only what was it it said come and gone was that it something like that come and gone come and gone no one come and gone in no time gone in no time

Silence 10″. Breath audible. After 3″ eyes open. After 5″ smile, toothless for preference. Hold 5″ till fade out and curtain.

NOTE

Moments of one and the same voice A B C relay one another without solution of continuity—apart from the two 10″ breaks. Yet the switch from one to another must be clearly faintly perceptible. If threefold source and context prove insufficient to produce this effect it should be assisted mechanically (e.g. threefold pitch).

Selected Bibliography

Since Beckett wrote in English, French, and German—and to further complicate matters translated much of his own work back from one language into another—any bibliographical effort must necessarily take this into account. Thus, in the list which follows, we differentiate those works composed originally in English from those written originally in French and German. Where possible, in instances where Beckett has translated or co-translated, that information is indicated: the initials "S.B." indicate "Samuel Beckett."

For published works, order of publisher follows date of publication. For dramatic works, dates of premieres are given in parentheses.

Works Written Originally in English

Poetry

Whoroscope. Paris: The Hours Press, 1930. In *Poems in English*, London: Calder & Boyars, 1961; New York: Grove Press, 1962.

Echo's Bones and Other Precipitates. Paris: Europa Press, 1935. In *Poems in English* and in *Gedichte*; see also: *Dublin Magazine*, Vol. VI, No. 4, Oct.–Dec. 1931; *transition*, No. 24, June 1936; *Evergreen Review*, New York, Vol. 1, No. 1, 1957.

Collected Poems in English and French (1930–1976). London: John Calder, 1977; New York: Grove Press, 1977.

Collected Poems 1930–1976. London: John Calder, 1984.

Fiction

"Assumption." *transition*, Nos. 16–17, June 1929, pp. 268–71. In *transition Workshop*, New York, 1949, pp. 41–43.

"Serendo et Quiescendo." *transition*, No. 21, March 1932, pp. 13–20. (Extract from the still unpublished novel *Dream of Fair to Middling Women.*)

More Pricks Than Kicks. London: Chatto & Windus, 1934; New York: Grove Press, 1970. Two stories from this collection were printed separately: 1. "Dante and the Lobster" in *This Quarter*, Paris, Dec. 1932, pp. 222–36 and in *Evergreen Review*, New York, Vol. 1, No. 1, 1957, pp. 24–36; 2. "Yellow" in *New World Writing*, New York, No. 10, Nov. 1956, pp. 108–19.

"A Case in a Thousand." *The Bookman*, Vol. LXXXVI, No. 515, Aug. 1934, pp. 241–42.

Murphy. London: Routledge, 1938; New York: Grove Press, 1957; London: Calder, 1963. French tr. by S.B. and Alfred Péron, Paris: Bordas, 1947; Paris: Editions de Minuit, 1953.

Watt. Paris: Merlin/Olympia, 1953; New York: Grove Press, 1959; London: Calder & Boyars, 1961. Variant extracts in: *Envoy*, Dublin, Vol. I, No. 2, Jan. 1950, pp. 11–19; *Irish Writing*, Cork, No. 17, Dec. 1951, pp. 11–16 and No. 22, March 1953, pp. 16–24; *Merlin*, Paris, Vol. I, No. 3, Winter 1952–53, pp. 118–26.

From an Abandoned Work. (B.B.C. Third Programme, Dec. 14, 1957.) *Evergreen Review*, New York, Vol. 1, No. 3, 1957, pp. 83–91; London: Faber & Faber, 1958; in *First Love and Other Shorts*, New York: Grove Press, 1974.

Fizzles. New York: Grove Press, 1976.

For To End Yet Again. London: John Calder, 1976.

Company. New York: Grove Press, 1980.

Worstward Ho. New York: Grove Press, 1983.

Collected Shorter Prose 1945–1980. London: John Calder, 1984.

Stirrings Still. London: John Calder, 1988.
As the Story Was Told. New York: Riverrun Press, 1990.

Plays for Stage, Film, Radio, and Television

All That Fall. (B.B.C. Third Programme, Jan. 13, 1957.) London: Faber & Faber, 1957; New York: Grove Press, 1960. French tr. by S.B. and Robert Pinget as *Tous ceux qui tombent* in *Les Lettres Nouvelles*, No. 47, March 1957; Paris: Editions de Minuit, 1957.

Krapp's Last Tape. (Royal Court Theatre, Oct. 28, 1958.) *Evergreen Review*, New York, Vol. 2, No. 5, 1958, pp. 13–24; London: Faber & Faber, 1959; New York: Grove Press, 1960. French tr. by S.B. and Pierre Leyris as *La dernière bande*, Paris: Editions de Minuit, 1959. Operatic version, *Krapp ou la dernière bande*, music by Marcel Mihalovici, *Théâtre des Nations*, Feb 13, 1961.

Embers. (B.B.C. Third Programme, June 24, 1959.) London: Faber & Faber, 1959; *Evergreen Review*, New York, Vol. III, No. 10, Nov.–Dec. 1959, pp. 28–41; in *Krapp's Last Tape and Other Dramatic Pieces*, New York: Grove Press, 1960.

Happy Days. (Cherry Lane Theater, New York, Sept. 17, 1961.) New York: Grove Press, 1961; London: Faber & Faber, 1962. French tr. by S.B. as *Oh les beaux jours*, Paris: Editions de Minuit, 1963.

Words and Music. (B.B.C. Third Programme, Nov. 13, 1962, music by John Beckett.) *Evergreen Review*, New York, Vol. 6, No. 27, Nov.–Dec. 1962, pp. 34–43. In *Play and Two Short Pieces for Radio*, London: Faber & Faber, 1964; in *Cascando and Other Short Dramatic Pieces*, New York: Grove Press, 1969. French tr. by S.B. as *Paroles et Musique*, in *Comédie et Actes divers*, Paris: Editions de Minuit, 1966.

Play. (First performed in German, Ulmer-Theater, Ulm, Jan. 14, 1963: *Spiel* tr. by Elmer Tophoven.) London: Faber & Faber, 1964; in *Cascando and Other Short Dramatic Pieces*, New York: Grove Press, 1967.

Film. Made in New York, 1964, directed by Alan Schneider, with Buster Keaton. (Venice Film Festival, Sept. 4, 1965; New York Film Festival, Sept. 15, 1965.) In *Cascando and Other Short Dramatic Pieces*, New York: Grove Press, 1967; in *Eh Joe*, London: Faber & Faber, 1967.

Eh Joe. (B.B.C. Television, July 4, 1966.) In *Cascando and Other Short Dramatic Pieces*, New York: Grove Press, 1967; London: Faber & Faber, 1967. French tr. by S.B. as *Dis Joe*, in *Comédie et Actes divers*, Paris: Editions de Minuit, 1966.

Come and Go. (First performed in German, Schiller Theater, Berlin, 1966.) In *Cascando and Other Short Dramatic Pieces*, New York: Grove Press, 1967; London: Calder & Boyars, 1967. French tr. by S.B. as *Va et vient*, in *Comédie et Actes divers*, Paris: Editions de Minuit, 1966.

Not I. (Repertory Theater of Lincoln Center in New York City, Dec. 7, 1972.) London: Faber & Faber, 1973. In *First Love and Other Shorts*, New York: Grove Press, 1974.

Ends and Odds. Contains *That Time, Not I, Footfalls, Radio I, Radio II, Theatre I, Theatre II* and *Tryst*. New York: Grove Press, 1976.

That Time. (Royal Court Theatre, London, May 20, 1976.) New York: Grove Press, 1976.

Footfalls. (Royal Court Theatre, London, May 20, 1976.) New York: Grove Press, 1976.

Ghost Trio: A Play for Television. (B.B.C. Television, April 17, 1977.) New York: Grove Press, 1976.

. . . but the clouds . . . : A Play for Television. (B.B.C. Television, April 17, 1977.) London: Faber & Faber, 1977.

A Piece of Monologue. (Written for actor David Warrilow in 1979 and performed by him in New York in 1980.) *Kenyon Review*, 1979.

Rockaby. (First performed in Buffalo, New York, in 1981.) New York: Grove Press, 1981.

Ohio Impromptu. (Stadium 2 Theatre, Ohio State University, May 9, 1981.) New York: Grove Press, 1981.

What Where. (Harold Clurman Theatre, New York, June 15, 1983.) London: Faber &
Faber, 1984; *Evergreen Review,* New York, 1984.
Three Plays: Ohio Impromptu, Catastrophe, What Where. New York: Grove Press,
1984.
The Collected Shorter Plays of Samuel Beckett. New York: Grove Press, 1984.
The Complete Dramatic Works. London: Faber & Faber, 1986.

Criticism

Disjecta: Miscellaneous Writings and a Dramatic Fragment. Edited by Ruby Cohn.
New York: Grove Press, 1984.

Works Written Originally in French

Poetry

"Poèmes 38–39." In *Les Temps Modernes,* No. 14, Nov. 1946, pp. 288–93.
"Trois Poèmes." In *transition* No. 48 (bilingual text), pp. 96–97. Reprinted in *Poems in
English.*
"Trois Poèmes." In *Cahiers des saisons,* No. 2, Oct. 1955, pp. 115–16.

Fiction

"Suite." In *Les Temps Modernes,* No. 10, July 1946, pp. 107–19. (This is first portion of
story later published in its entirety as "La Fin.") Tr. by S.B. and Richard Seaver as
"The End" in *Merlin,* Vol. II, No. 3, 1954, pp. 144–58. In *Evergreen Review,* New
York, Vol. 4, No. 15, Nov.–Dec. 1960, pp. 22–41.
"L'Expulsé." In *Fontaine,* No. 57, Dec. 1946–Jan. 1947, pp. 685–708. Tr. by S.B. and
Richard Seaver as "The Expelled" in *Evergreen Review,* New York, Vol. 6, No. 22,
Jan.–Feb. 1962, pp. 8–20.
Molloy. Paris: Editions de Minuit, 1951. English tr. by S.B. and Patrick Bowles, Paris:
Merlin/Olympia, 1954; New York: Grove Press, 1955. In *Three Novels,* London:
Calder & Boyars, 1959; New York: Grove Press, 1965.
Malone meurt. Paris: Editions de Minuit, 1951. English tr. by S.B. as *Malone Dies,* New
York: Grove Press, 1956; London: Calder & Boyars, 1958.
L'Innommable. Paris: Editions de Minuit, 1953. English tr. by S.B. as *The Unnamable,*
New York: Grove Press, 1958. In *Three Novels,* London: Calder & Boyars, 1959;
New York: Grove Press, 1960.
Nouvelles et Textes pour Rien. Paris: Editions de Minuit, 1955. Contains: "La Fin";
"L'Expulsé"; "Le Calmant"; and a series of "Texts for Nothing." English tr. by S.B.
as *Stories and Texts for Nothing,* New York: Grove Press, 1967. Collected edition
under the title *No's Knife,* London: Calder & Boyars, 1966.
Comment C'est. Paris: Editions de Minuit, 1961. English tr. by S.B. as *How It Is,* New
York: Grove Press, 1964; London: Calder & Boyars, 1966.
Imagination morte imaginez. Paris: Editions de Minuit, 1965. In *Têtes-Mortes,* Paris:
Editions de Minuit, 1967, pp. 49–57. English tr. by S.B. as *Imagination Dead
Imagine* in *Evergreen Review,* New York, Vol. 10, No. 39, 1966. London: Calder &
Boyars, 1966. In *First Love and Other Shorts,* New York: Grove Press, 1974.
Bing. Paris: Editions de Minuit, 1966. In *Têtes-Mortes,* Paris: Editions de Minuit, 1967,
pp. 59–66. English tr. by S.B. as *Ping,* London: Calder & Boyars, 1967; in *First
Love and Other Shorts,* New York: Grove Press, 1974.
Assez. Paris: Editions de Minuit, 1967, in *Têtes-Mortes,* pp. 31–48. English tr. by S.B. as
Enough. In *First Love and Other Shorts,* New York: Grove Press, 1974.
Mercier et Camier. Paris: Editions de Minuit, 1970. English tr. by S.B. as *Mercier and
Camier,* New York: Grove Press, 1974; London: Calder & Boyars, 1974.
Premier Amour. Paris: Editions de Minuit, 1970. English tr. by S.B. as "First Love." In
First Love and Other Shorts, New York: Grove Press, 1974.

Le Depeupleur. Paris: Editions de Minuit, 1971. English tr. by S.B. as *The Lost Ones,* New York: Grove Press, 1972; London: Calder & Boyars, 1972.

Mal Vu Mal Dit. Paris: Les Editions de Minuit, 1981. English tr. by S.B. as *Ill Seen Ill Said,* New York: Grove Press, 1981.

Plays for Stage, Radio, and Television

Eleuthéria. Three acts. Unpublished and unperformed.

En Attendant Godot. (Théâtre de Babylone, Jan. 5, 1953.) Paris: Editions de Minuit, 1952. English tr. by S.B. as *Waiting for Godot,* New York: Grove Press, 1954; London: Faber & Faber, 1956.

Fin de Partie. (Royal Court Theatre, April 3, 1957, in French.) Paris: Editions de Minuit, 1957. English tr. by S.B. as *Endgame,* New York: Grove Press, 1958; London: Faber & Faber, 1958.

Acte sans Paroles I. (Mime; music by John Beckett. Royal Court Theatre, April 3, 1957.) Paris: Editions de Minuit, 1957 (together with *Fin de Partie*). English tr. by S.B. as *Act Without Words I,* London: Faber & Faber, 1958 (together with *Endgame*). In *Krapp's Last Tape and Other Dramatic Pieces,* New York: Grove Press, 1960.

Acte sans Paroles II. (Mime; Institute of Contemporary Arts, London, Jan. 1960.) Paris: Editions de Minuit, 1966, in *Comédie et Actes divers.* English tr. by S.B. as *Act Without Words II,* in *New Departures,* No. 1, Summer 1959, pp. 88–90. In *Krapp's Last Tape and Other Dramatic Pieces,* New York: Grove Press, 1960; in *Eh Joe and Other Writings,* London: Faber & Faber, 1967.

Cascando. (Radio play, first performed on French National Radio, Oct. 13, 1963. Music by Marcel Mihalovici.) Paris: Editions de Minuit, 1966, in *Comédie et Actes divers.* English tr. by S.B. as *Cascando,* in *Evergreen Review,* New York, Vol. 7, No. 30, May–June 1963, pp. 47–57; in *Cascando and Other Short Dramatic Pieces,* New York: Grove Press, 1969; in *Play and Two Short Pieces for Radio,* London: Faber & Faber, 1964.

The Collected Works of Samuel Beckett (19 Volumes). New York: Grove Press, 1970.

Rough for Theatre I. English tr. by S.B., in *Ends and Odds,* New York: Grove Press, 1976.

Rough for Theatre II. English tr. by S.B., in *Ends and Odds,* New York: Grove Press, 1976.

Rough for Radio I. First published in English as *Sketch for Radio Play,* in *Stereo Headphones,* No. 7 (Spring 1976).

Rough for Radio II. (First broadcast as *Rough for Radio,* on B.B.C. Radio 3, April 13, 1976.) In *Ends and Odds,* New York: Grove Press, 1976.

Catastrophe. (Avignon Festival, Avignon, France, July 21, 1982; Harold Clurman Theatre, New York, June 15, 1983.) London: Faber & Faber, 1984; *Evergreen Review,* New York, 1984.

Works Written Originally in German

Quad. (First broadcast as *Quadrat 1+2,* by Süddeutscher Rundfunk, 1982; B.B.C. Radio 2, Dec. 16, 1982.) London: Faber & Faber, 1984; in *Collected Shorter Plays,* New York: Grove Press, 1984.

Nacht und Träume. (Süddeutscher Rundfunk, May 19, 1983.) London: Faber & Faber, 1984; in *Collected Shorter Plays,* New York: Grove Press, 1984.